Lecture Notes of the Institute
for Computer Sciences, Social Informatics
and Telecommunications Engineering 162

Stephan Sigg · Petteri Nurmi
Flora Salim (Eds.)

Mobile Computing, Applications, and Services

7th International Conference, MobiCASE 2015
Berlin, Germany, November 12–13, 2015
Revised Selected Papers

 Springer

Editors
Stephan Sigg
Georg-August-Universität Göttingen
Göttingen
Germany

Flora Salim
RMIT University
Melbourne, VIC
Australia

Petteri Nurmi
University of Helsinki
Helsinki
Finland

ISSN 1867-8211   ISSN 1867-822X   (electronic)
Lecture Notes of the Institute for Computer Sciences, Social Informatics
and Telecommunications Engineering
ISBN 978-3-319-29002-7   ISBN 978-3-319-29003-4   (eBook)
DOI 10.1007/978-3-319-29003-4

Library of Congress Control Number: 2015960216

Printed on acid-free paper

This Springer imprint is published by SpringerNature
The registered company is Springer International Publishing AG Switzerland

Preface

On behalf of the Organizing Committee, it is my great pleasure to welcome you to the proceedings of the 7th International Conference on Mobile Computing, Applications and Services (MobiCASE 2015) held in Berlin, Germany. This was the first time that the MobiCASE conference came to Germany and the second time that it was hosted in Europe (after Paris, France, in 2013). MobiCASE is a leading venue for publication and presentation of research results on issues in the area of mobile computing, mobile applications, and mobile services. This year's program featured 16 exciting papers embracing a number of perspectives including activity recognition, crowdsourcing, energy, localization, middleware, mobile frameworks, and intelligent caching. In addition to the regular full paper sessions, this year's program was supplemented by a poster and demo session. The conference was accompanied by the First Workshop on Situation Recognition by Mining Temporal Information (SIREMTI 2015). Last but not least, MobiCASE 2015 hosted an exciting keynote speaker: Gabi Zodik, IBM Mobile First Research Global Leader, provided a stimulating view on the challenges and opportunities of contextual enterprise mobile computing.

Putting together MobiCASE 2015 has been a huge team effort. I would like to thank many people for their tireless work, including the local arrangements chair Olga Streibel, Web chair Shuyu Shi, publicity and social media chair Felix Buesching, industry track chair Victor Munts-Mulero, sponsorship chair Kai Kunze, and EAI conference organizers Barbara Fertalova, Ivana Allen, Lucia Kisova, and Sinziana Vieriu. A special thank you goes to Izumi Takeyama, who provided us with professional images taken in Berlin. I would like to acknowledge the tremendous efforts of the Technical Program Committee, including the chair, Petteri Nurmi, in particular, for putting together an outstanding technical program. In addition, I would like to thank poster, demo, and PhD track chair Mayutan Arumaithurai and workshop chair Till Riedel. Our deepest thanks to our publication chairs Flora Salim and Jonathan Liono for managing and compiling all the details of the proceedings. Finally, I would like to express my gratitude to the sponsors of MobiCASE 2015.

Regarding the submission and review process for MobiCASE 2015, 43 papers were submitted for review. Each paper was reviewed by at least three Technical Program Committee (TPC) members, and reviewers contributed additional discussion together with the technical program chair to reach a consensus on the papers. This year, 16 papers were finally selected for presentation at the conference. The topics of the papers reflect the wide-spectrum research around mobile computing, services, and applications, ranging from system-oriented challenges to novel applications and algorithms. The technical program of MobiCASE included six technical sessions centered on the themes of intelligent caching, activity recognition and crowdsourcing, mobile frameworks, middleware, interactive applications, and mobility. There were three best paper candidates.

We hope that the readers will find these proceedings interesting and thought-pro-
voking and hope that the conference provided participants with a valuable opportunity
to share ideas with other researchers and practitioners from institutions around the
world.

November 2015   Petteri Nurmi
                                                                Stephan Sigg

Organization

Steering Committee

Steering Committee Chair

Imrich Chlamtac   Create-Net, Italy

Steering Committee Member

Ulf Blanke	ETH Zurich, Switzerland
Martin Griss	Carnegie Mellon University, USA
Thomas Phan	Samsung R&D, USA
Petros Zerfos	IBM Research, USA

Organizing Committee

General Chair

Stephan Sigg   Aalto University, Finland

Program Chair

Petteri Nurmi   University of Helsiki, Finland

Local Chair

Olga Streibel   FU Berlin, Germany

Workshops

Till Riedel   Karlsruhe Institute of Technology, Germany

Publicity and Social Media

Felix Buesching   TU-Braunschweig, Germany

Publications Chair

Flora Salim	RMIT University, Australia
Jonathan Liono	RMIT University, Australia

Demos, Posters, and PhD

Mayutan Arumaithurai   Georg-August-University Göttingen, Germany

Web Chair

Shuyu Shi   National Institute of Informatics, Japan

Industry Track Chair

Victor Munts-Mulero   CA Technologies, Spain

Sponsorship Chair

Kai Kunze   Keio University, Japan

EAI Conference Coordinator

Barbara Fertalova   EAI, Slovakia

Photography Berlin Impressions

Izumi Takeyama   Tokyo, Japan

Technical Program Committee

Claudio Bettini	University of Milan, Italy
Sourav Bhattacharya	Bell-Laboratories, Ireland
Henrik Blunck	Aarhus University, Denmark
Eduardo Cuervo	Microsoft Research, USA
Klaus David	University of Kassel, Germany
Denzil Ferreira	University of Oulu, Finland
Kaori Fujinami	Tokyo University of Agriculture and Technology, Japan
Hamed Haddadi	Qatar Computing Research Institute/QMU London, UK
Tristan Henderson	University of St. Andrews, UK
Mikkel Baun Kjaergaard	University of Southern Denmark
Shin'ichi Konomi	University of Tokyo, Japan
Fahim Kawsar	Bell-Laboratories, Ireland
Gerd Kortuem	The Open University, UK
Nic Lane	Bell-Laboratories, Ireland
Robert LiKamWa	Rice University, USA
Eemil Lagerspetz	University of Helsinki, Finland
Mirco Musolesi	University College London, UK
Santi Phithakkitnukoon	Chiang Mai University, Thailand
Daniele Puccinelli	University of Applied Sciences of Southern Switzerland
Thomas Strang	German Aerospace Center (DLR), Germany
Kiran Rachuri	Samsung Research America, USA
Yoshito Tobe	Aoyama Gakuin University, Japan
Moustafa Youssef	Egypt-Japan University of Science and Technology, Egypt

Additional Reviewers

Aidan Boran	Bell-Laboratories, Ireland
Farbod Faghihi	University of Helsinki, Finland
Jorge Goncalves	University of Oulu, Finland
Samuli Hemminki	University of Helsinki, Finland
Enamul Hoque	University of Virginia, USA
Jakob Langdal	Aarhus University, Denmark
Markus Löchtefeld	German Research Centre for Artificial Intelligence (DFKI), Germany
Akhil Mathur	Bell-Laboratories, Ireland
Abhinav Mehrotra	University of Birmingham, UK
Abhishek Mukherji	Samsung Research America, USA
Ella Peltonen	University of Helsinki, Finland
Thor Prentow	Aarhus University, Denmark
Teemu Pulkkinen	Ekahau Oy, Finland
Shuyu Shi	National Institute of Informatics, Tokyo, Japan
Allan Stisen	Aarhus University, Denmark
Theofania Tsapeli	University of Birmingham, UK
Matthew Williams	University of Birmingham, UK
Juan Ye	University of St. Andrews, UK
Siwei Zhang	German Aerospace Center (DLR), Germany
Yuchen Zhao	University of St. Andrews, UK

SIREMTI 2015 Organizing Committee

Organizer

Olga Streibel	FU Berlin, Germany
Kia Teymourian	Rice University, USA

SIREMTI 2015 Technical Program Committee

Jean-Paul Calbimonte	Ecole Polytechnique Federale de Lausanne, Switzerland
Oscar Corcho	Universidad Politecnica de Madrid, Spain
Alessandra Mileo	NUI Galway, Ireland
Adrian Paschke	FU Berlin, Germany
Stephan Sigg	Aalto University, Finland
Olga Streibel	National Institute of Informatics, Tokyo, Japan
Roland Sthmer	FZI Karlsruhe, Germany
Atsuhiro Takasu	National Institute of Informatics, Tokyo, Japan
Kia Teymourian	Rice University Houston, Texas, USA
Robert Tolksdorf	FU Berlin, Germany
Alexandru Todor	FU Berlin, Germany

Contents

Intelligent Caching

Network Data Buffering for Availability Improvement of Mobile Web Applications

Tomoharu Imai[✉], Kouichi Yamasaki, Masahiro Matsuda, and Kazuki Matsui

Network Systems Laboratory, Fujitsu Laboratories Ltd., 4-1-1 Kamikodanaka, Nakahara-Ku, Kawasaki, Kanagawa 211-8588, Japan
{imai.tomoharu, yamasaki.koichi, matsuda, kmatsui}@jp.fujitsu.com

Abstract. In recent years, we have seen an explosion in the use of smart devices. With several different competing OS platforms on these smart devices, developers have turned to web applications as an effective way to provide cross-platform services. However, because many web applications are designed to handle UI interactions locally on a user's device and to process data remotely in the cloud, it is difficult for them to continue running while offline. In this paper, we propose a data synchronization technology that buffers and minimize network communications to address problems associated with dropped network connections as well as low bandwidth and/or high latency environments. To test the technology's effectiveness, we applied it to some typical web applications and compared their performance in environments with dropped connections.

Keywords: Mobile web applications · Data buffering · Synchronization technology

1 Background

In recent years, we have seen an explosion in the use of smartphones, tablets, and other smart devices. These smart devices run a variety of operating systems, including Android, iOS, and Windows Phone. Applications depend on proprietary APIs and SDKs for each mobile operating system, all of which are incompatible with each other. The need to build a separate application for each operating system thus drives up development costs. On the other hand, each operating system also has a browser engine capable of rendering HTML5 content, allowing a single HTML5 web application to be run on a variety of different devices. For this reason, web application development for smart devices has become more popular in recent years.

As shown in Fig. 1, web applications save a variety of data on mobile devices; this includes audio/video data taken with a device's built-in cameras and microphones as well as business data downloaded from the cloud. Consequently, web application security is sometimes lacking. To address this, systems with stringent security requirements—such as those in enterprise businesses—have begun to adopt thin client systems that run applications in the cloud. However, thin client systems can send and receive a large volume of commands and screen data that may noticeably reduce an application's responsiveness on slower network connections (as shown in Fig. 2).

© Institute for Computer Sciences, Social Informatics and Telecommunications Engineering 2015
S. Sigg et al. (Eds.): MobiCASE 2015, LNICST 162, pp. 3–11, 2015.
DOI: 10.1007/978-3-319-29003-4_1

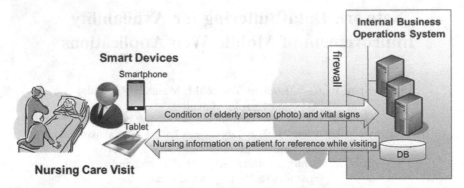

Fig. 1. Web application usage

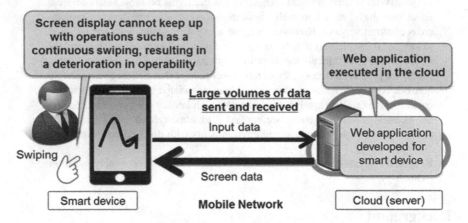

Fig. 2. Reduced responsiveness

We have a developed a virtualization technology for mobile web applications ("VMA") that automatically splits a web application into two parts—UI processing and data processing—in the cloud. VMA maintains security by processing and storing data remotely in the cloud; at the same time, it also makes applications highly responsive by handling UI interactions locally on each device. This technology allows service providers to offer existing line-of-business web applications that are highly responsive and secure at a low cost.

2 Issues and Existing Technology

VMA distributes and executes stand-alone web application for smart devices. This technology distributes a web application's logic so that smart devices handle UI interactions locally and servers in the cloud process data remotely. The UI and data processing parts of the application assume they always have a network connection through which to communicate with each other. Because, the UI and data processing parts usually executed on same device. However, it's easy for smart devices, which often use mobile networks, to get disconnected frequently. If a web application is run with distributed UI and data processing in this kind of environment, dropped network connections can cause data loss, unexpected application behavior associated with failed requests, and reduced responsiveness associated with high network latency.

To address these issues, existing technologies have cached data in local storage for offline use [2] and also gracefully degraded to limited feature sets while offline [3].

Before an application can use internal storage or graceful degradation, however, every part of it that sends or receives data over the network needs to be updated accordingly. Furthermore, every new feature that uses a network connection would also need to deal with being offline. This additional processing has entailed increased costs.

3 Data Synchronization with VMA

In response to these issues, we developed a data synchronization technology with VMA that does its best to compensate for dropped network connections. This technology buffers network traffic and does not require developers to edit existing web applications' source code directly. Figure 3 illustrates the data synchronization technology in more detail while providing an overview of its architecture.

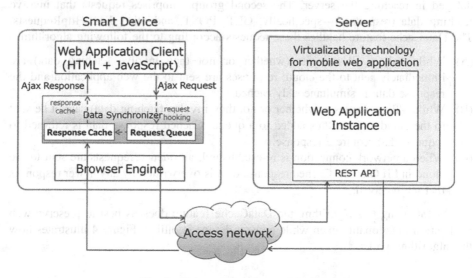

Fig. 3. Data synchronizer architecture

3.1 Overview

The data synchronization technology has a DataCache feature that hooks into the XMLHttpRequest API through which web applications send data to and receive data from the cloud. This feature allows requests to be sent from cached data even while offline. The data synchronization technology also has a DataShrink feature that detects duplicate data to minimize network traffic. The data synchronization technology use transparent proxy technique for unmodified embedding into web application. These features reduce the amount of data that needs to be sent and received and make applications pleasantly responsive.

3.2   DataCache

The DataCache feature hooks into the XMLHttpRequest API to cache all upstream and downstream data.

The DataCache feature replaces the XMLHttpRequest browser API used by web applications with its own Hooking API. Because the Hooking API presents the same interface as the XMLHttpRequest API provided by browser engines, web applications do not need to be modified to use it. A transparent proxy adds the necessary code to load the Hooking API when a web application is transferred, thus replacing the XMLHttpRequest API and enabling the DataCache feature without burdening the web application developers.

The DataCache feature caches data that can largely be classified into two groups. The first group comprises requests that do not involve fetching data—specifically, GET (for posting parameters), SET, PUT, and other XMLHttpRequests. These requests are not considered to affect a web application over short periods of time, even if they are delayed in reaching the server. The second group comprises requests that involve fetching data (responses)—specifically, GET, POST, and other XMLHttpRequests. The DataCache feature handles these requests according to the following algorithm.

(A)   While online, all requests (whether or not they involve fetching data) are immediately sent to the cloud; responses are sent to the web application and the response data is simultaneously cached.
(B)   While offline, requests (whether or not they involve fetching data) cannot be sent to the cloud and are thus added to a queue. Cached response data is returned to requests that require a response.
(C)   When a network connection is re-established, all queued requests are sent to the cloud in FIFO order. Cached response data is overwritten by any newer responses that are received.

By following this algorithm, the DataCache feature does its best to preserve web application functionality even while a client device is offline. Figure 4 illustrates how this algorithm works.

3.3   DataShrink

The DataShrink feature minimizes the amount of data that needs to be sent by checking both the content of requests when they are queued by the DataCache feature and the content of cached response data when it is sent or updated by the DataCache feature.

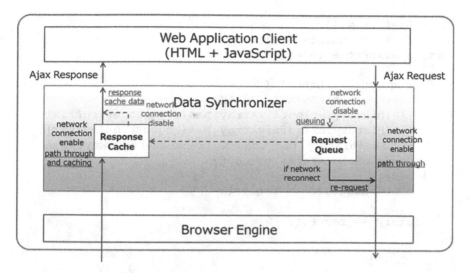

Fig. 4. Data synchronizer DataCache algorithm

The DataCache feature queues request data and pre-caches response data as a precaution against dropped connections. Though the DataCache feature queues and caches all request and response data, the uniqueness of that data does not necessarily need to be preserved. For example, a series of periodic requests to get all the latest data can be saved as a single request (along with its response) without any adverse effects on a web application's data integrity. On the other hand, periodic requests to get the latest data via a series of deltas and requests that contain data must all be run individually and their responses must be preserved. The DataCache feature sends its queued requests out to the cloud in FIFO order when a network connection is re-established, but as explained above the uniqueness of all that request and response data does not need to be preserved. Sending data without uniqueness constraints thus leads to unnecessary network traffic, wasted bandwidth, and slower response times.

By automatically identifying and eliminating superfluous requests and responses when unique copies do not need to be preserved, the DataShrink feature can avoid wasting network bandwidth and prevent decreased responsiveness. The DataShrink feature uses the following algorithm to determine which of a web application's requests and responses must remain unique.

(A) If a request has one or more mutable parameters, a unique copy of its data must be preserved.
(B) If a request does not have any mutable parameters, a unique copy of its data does not need to be preserved.

The following pseudocode shows how a request is checked for mutable parameters.

```
var history = [];
var dynamicRequests = [];
var staticRequests = [];

if (request == 'http') {
  if (request.hasOnTail(/?||&/)
      || !history.urlsuffixArray.has(request.urlsuffix)
      || (history.urlsuffixArray.has(request.urlsuffix)
          && !history.body.hasKey(request.body.key))) {
    dynamicRequests += request;
  } else {
    staticRequests += request;
  }
  history += request;
}
```

The DataShrink feature considers it necessary to preserve the uniqueness of a request when it has parameters; when it is the first request sent to a particular endpoint (URI); or when it contains the same data as some other past request (i.e. "A" above). Uniqueness is not considered a requirement for any other requests (i.e. "B" above).

The following pseudocode shows how the DataShrink feature removes redundant requests and responses that it has determined it does not need to uniquely preserve.

```
var mergeRequests = []
for (var i = 0; i < staticRequests.length; i++) {
  if (!mergeRequests.has(staticRequests[i].url) {
    mergeRequests += staticRequests[i];
  } else if (mergeRequests.has(staticRequests[i]) {
    var oldentry = mergeRequests.has(staticRequests[i]);
    if (staticRequests[i].requestDate >
oldentry.requestDate) {
    mergeRequests[staticRequests[i].key] =
staticRequests[i].value;
    }
}
```

This code extracts requests with unique URIs from the set of requests identified in step "B" of the algorithm above (staticRequests). If more than one request has the same URI, only the most recent one is selected.

Using these algorithms and procedures, the DataShrink feature minimizes the amount of data that is sent and received.

4   Results

To evaluate our data synchronization technology, we measured the following three metrics associated with web applications on a mobile data network: data retention rates, responsiveness, and bandwidth usage.

Specifically, we compared the performance of three different types of web applications with versions of those applications that dynamically loaded our data synchronization technology. The architecture of a web application that VMA has split into UI and data processing components is similar to the architecture of a web application that developers have split into server and client components; as a result, we can compare performance by applying (or not applying) our data synchronization technology to an entire web application.

We chose the following three web applications.

- A to-do application.
- A text chat application.
- A video chat application.

We arranged to test these three types of applications because they cover a spectrum of real-time demands on processing that needs to communicate with the cloud. The to-do application does not have real-time constraints because it can take a long time to update a to-do list on a server without any adverse effects. The text chat application has real-time constraints of several seconds or less because user input intervals are generally several seconds or more. The video chat application has real-time constraints of one second or less because on-screen video is updated by at least one frame per second.

We prepared a mobile network environment under simulated conditions in which devices would be randomly disconnected for 9 s at a time. We assumed that devices could spend 9 s offline before reconnecting because it takes devices up to about 9 s to reconnect after entering Sleep Mode and losing their network connection [4].

Figure 5 shows a comparison of the data retention rates measured when network connections were dropped for both unmodified web applications and web applications that loaded our data synchronization technology.

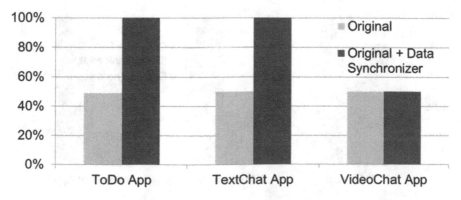

Fig. 5. Data retention rates (Color figure online)

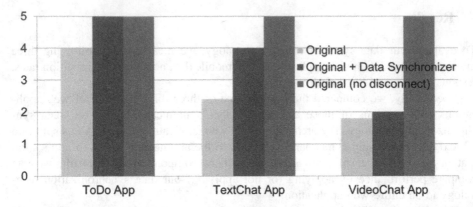

Fig. 6. Responsiveness survey results (Color figure online)

The results show that the to-do and text chat applications achieved 100 % deliverability rates without any data loss when they loaded our data synchronization technology, regardless of their connection patterns.

We also evaluated the web applications' responsiveness and bandwidth usage when they lost and subsequently re-established a network connection. To compare responsiveness, we had multiple test subjects try to use each of the three web applications with a randomly selected set of conditions from the following list. The test subjects then rated each application's ease of use on a 5-point scale.

- The original web application on a network connection that would be randomly dropped for 9 s at a time.
- The original web application with data synchronization on a network connection that would be randomly dropped for 9 s at a time.
- The original web application on a network connection that was never dropped.

To evaluate bandwidth usage when losing and re-establishing a network connection, we measured the amount of traffic generated by the three web applications both with and without dropped connections; we then made a relative comparison of the results.

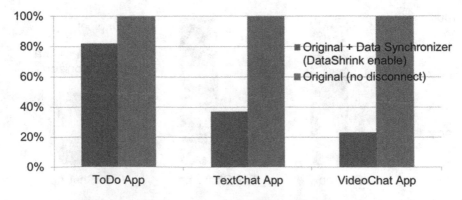

Fig. 7. Bandwidth usage (Color figure online)

Figure 6 shows a comparison of UI responsiveness and Fig. 7 shows a comparison of bandwidth usage.

The results show that our data synchronization technology was able to reduce the perceived loss of responsiveness accompanying dropped network connections for both the to-do application, which has no real-time constraints, and the text chat application, which has real-time constraints on the order of several seconds. On the other hand, the results also show that our data synchronization technology was not able to reduce the perceived loss of responsiveness for the video chat application.

Our evaluation of bandwidth usage revealed savings of approximately 20 % for the to-do application and 60 % for the text chat application when our data synchronization technology was loaded.

5 Conclusion, Discussion, and Future Work

The DataCache and DataShrink features of VMA's data synchronization technology buffer web applications' network communications to compensate for frequently dropped connections on mobile networks. Our experimental results show that web applications with real-time constraints of several seconds or less remain just as usable and responsive when they are temporarily offline. On the other hand, we also found that our data synchronization technology could not compensate for dropped network connections in web applications with real-time constraints of one second or less.

Furthermore, our DataShrink feature was able to reduce bandwidth usage and improve responsiveness by eliminating redundant web application requests and responses.

In addition to the data synchronization technology introduced in this paper, VMA also has the ability to dynamically adjust UI and data processing in accordance with user input. Together, these features allow VMA to make web applications safer and more responsive.

We plan to apply our data synchronization technology to an even wider range of web and native applications for further evaluation.

References

1. Fujitsu Laboratories Ltd.: Fujitsu Laboratories Develops Virtualization Technology that Brings Security and Operability to Web Applications, 29 May 2015. http://www.fujitsu.com/global/about/resources/news/press-releases/2015/0529-01.html
2. Ijtihadie, R.M., Chisaki, Y., Usagawa, T., Cahyo, H.B., Affandi, A.: Offline web application and quiz synchronization for e-learning activity for mobile browser. In: 2010 IEEE Region 10 Conference, TENCON 2010, 21–24 November 2010, pp. 2402–2405 (2010)
3. Goncalves, E., Leitao, A.M.: Offline execution in workflow-enabled Web applications. In: 6th International Conference on the Quality of Information and Communications Technology, QUATIC 2007, 12–14 September 2007, pp. 204–207 (2007)
4. Chen, W.-P., Licking, S., Ohno, T., Okuyama, S., Hamada, T.: Performance measurement, evaluation and analysis of Push-to-Talk in 3G networks. In: IEEE International Conference on Communications, ICC 2007, 24–28 June 2007, pp. 1893–1898 (2007)

Upgrading Wireless Home Routers for Enabling Large-Scale Deployment of Cloudlets

Christian Meurisch[1](✉), Alexander Seeliger[1], Benedikt Schmidt[1],
Immanuel Schweizer[1], Fabian Kaup[2], and Max Mühlhäuser[1]

[1] Telecooperation Lab, Technische Universität Darmstadt, Darmstadt, Germany
{meurisch,seeliger,schmidt,schweizer,max}@tk.tu-darmstadt.de
[2] Peer-to-Peer Systems Engineering Lab, Technische Universität Darmstadt,
Darmstadt, Germany
fkaup@ps.tu-darmstadt.de

Abstract. Smartphones become more and more popular over recent years due to their small form factors. However, such mobile systems are resource-constrained in view of computational power, storage and battery life. Offloading resource-intensive tasks (aka *mobile cloud computing*) to distant (e.g., *cloud computing*) or closely located data centers (e.g., *cloudlet*) overcomes these issues. Especially, cloudlets provide computational power with low latency for responsive applications due to their proximity to mobile users. However, a large-scale deployment of range-restricted cloudlets is still an open challenge. In this paper, we propose a novel concept for a large-scale deployment of cloudlets by upgrading wireless home routers. Beside router's native purpose of routing data packets through the network, it can now offer computing resources with low latency and high bandwidth without additional hardware. Proving our concept, we conducted comprehensive benchmark tests against existing concepts. As result, the feasibility of this concept is shown and provide a promising way to large-scale deploy cloudlets in existing infrastructures.

Keywords: Wireless home router · Mobile cloud computing · Cloudlet · Smartphones · Offloading · Edge computing

1 Introduction

Many mobile services require complex computations, e.g., voice processing for a dialogue system or image processing for an augmenting application. Such services need to address the performance requirements while considering the short battery life of mobile devices [22]. To address this challenge most service providers rely on *mobile cloud computing* [10,12]: resource-intensive tasks are offloaded to distant servers [18]. However, latency and network traffic are one of the downsides of this approach. Therefore, mobile cloud computing is best suited for applications with need of high availability and global view like social networks. Applications with high computing requirements and the need for responsiveness are not perfectly suited for the cloud computing approach.

© Institute for Computer Sciences, Social Informatics and Telecommunications Engineering 2015
S. Sigg et al. (Eds.): MobiCASE 2015, LNICST 162, pp. 12–29, 2015.
DOI: 10.1007/978-3-319-29003-4_2

An alternative to mobile cloud computing is the use of *cloudlets* [24]. Cloudlets are small-scale servers which are distributed over the environment. Mobile devices connect to nearby cloudlets to distribute computation tasks and benefit from a one-hop latency over wireless communication technologies [24]. Thus, cloudlets offer a promising tradeoff between performance gain, low network traffic and especially low latency. This makes cloudlets especially relevant for applications with high computation and responsiveness requirements like face or object recognition with the fast processing of big sensor data [17].

A combination of cloud computing and an extensive dissemination of cloudlets would address the requirements of various types of mobile services. While mobile cloud computing is well-established, there is no extensive dissemination of cloudlets, yet. Two different approaches for the realization of cloudlets have been proposed. First, a grassroots perspective, focusing on the deployment by local businesses (e.g., cafes or shopping malls) which step-by-step evolves to a large-scale infrastructure offered and maintained by the businesses [24]. The second perspective is the integration of cloudlets into Internet's routing infrastructure at the gateways of ISPs [6] or by combining cloudlets and wireless mesh networks, deployed in hotspots [16]. However, each concept requires the deployment of additional computing hardware by different entities resulting in deployment and operation costs. Therefore, the realization of a dense and economic cloudlet infrastructure is still an open challenge.

In this paper, we propose a router-based cloudlet concept to realize an extensive dissemination of cloudlets based on existing infrastructure. Our concept promises a dense distribution of cloudlets in many countries while avoiding unpredictable economic risks for the involved parties. On average, 73.0 % of EU households [27] and 75.6 % of US households [13] have access to the Internet in 2011, many of them using wireless routers to connect to the Internet. Hence, in our view, wireless home routers are well-suited for a large-scale, dense and economic infrastructure [19] to offload computational tasks from mobile systems.

Beside router's native purpose of routing data packets through the network, our concept offers its computing resources to mobile devices without deploying additional hardware. In other words, we treat a wireless home router as cloudlet with both networking and computing capabilities. Mobile devices connecting to such nearby located router via wireless technologies (i.e., WLAN) benefit from offloading capabilities with low latency and high bandwidth. We imagine two use cases; *on the one hand*, responsive applications (e.g., face recognition), that require low latency and fast responses, can be directly served by the router maintaining a soft state (i.e., temporary cache). *On the other hand*, contextual applications, that require historical data in some circumstances, can leverage the router as intermediate layer to the cloud which preprocesses data and, thus, reduces network traffic for connections with high latency.

The concept needs to be assessed with respect to two main aspects: (1) feasibility – what is necessary to use current state of the art routers as cloudlet (2) performance – do the limited computational capabilities of routers justify the effort compared to other techniques. In this paper, we report the concept, assess the feasibility and conduct performance benchmark tests covering energy consumption, resource usage, network traffic, latency and processing time for the following approaches: (1) local mobile processing, (2) cloudlet processing, and (3) cloud computing.

In summary, the contributions of this paper are twofold:

Concept for Router-based Cloudlets. We propose a novel concept for solving large-scale, dense and economic deployment issues of range-restricted cloudlets utilizing existing wireless home routers for mobile cloud computing. In detail, a nearby located wireless home router can now offer computing resources to mobile devices without deploying additional hardware, beside router's native purpose of routing data packets through the network.

Performance Benchmarks. Proving our concept we conducted comprehensive benchmark tests against existing concepts like cloud or common cloudlets. These tests cover measurements of energy consumption, resource usage, network traffic, latency, and processing time from the viewpoint of a mobile device.

The remainder of this paper is organized as follows. First, we give an overview of related work and work out open issues. Second, we report the concept of upgrading wireless home routers as cloudlet for enabling large-scale deployment on existing infrastructure. After reporting, the experimental setup and methodology is described. The paper closes with benchmark report, discussion of the benchmark results, and conclusion.

2   Related Work

The need for offloading computational tasks and storage from resource-constrained mobile systems (e.g., smartphones, Internet-of-things devices) introduced *mobile cloud computing* [1,12,15,21] or *cyber foraging* [3,23] about fifteen years ago. Since then, various offloading approaches regarding networked computing infrastructures (e.g., *cloud computing* [18], *cloudlets* [24,25,30], *fog computing* [4,28]) and offloading strategies (e.g., MAUI [9], CloneCloud [7]) were proposed to find a tradeoff between performance, latency and network traffic.

In the following we revisit different strategies to realize computation tasks with mobile devices [10]:

Mobile Computing. Mobile devices are able to process data locally without latency issues. However, due to their small form factor and high mobility mobile devices have limited resources, e.g., battery life, storage and computational power [22].

Cloud Computing. Resource-intensive tasks are offloaded via the internet from mobile devices to centralized resourceful data centers, the *cloud*. The cloud is a highly scalable computing and storage infrastructure hosted by cloud providers (e.g., Google, Amazon, and Salesforce) [18]. A cloud serves and stores personal data of hundreds or thousand users at a time. Security, privacy and trust are highly critical points. However, clouds are distant to

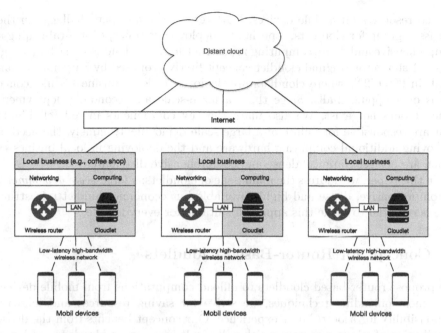

Fig. 1. Original *cloudlet* concept firstly proposed by [24] and deployment challenges for a comprehensive computing network infrastructure are marked in red (Color figure online).

mobile users and have too long WAN latency for responsive applications. But they are well-suited for applications requiring a global view or historical data. Moreover, only few data centers are deployed in the world with high building and operational costs.

Cloudlet. Resource-intensive tasks can also be offloaded from mobile devices via wireless technologies (e.g., WLAN) to a *cloudlet* (cf. Fig. 1), a proximate decentralized computing infrastructure hosted by a local business (e.g., coffee shop) [24] or ISPs [6]. It provides low latency due to its proximity to mobile users and high bandwidth. Thus, cloudlets are well-suited for real-time responsive applications like face, gesture or object recognition that only need temporary caches [20]. Cloudlets only need to serve few users at a time. However, a large-scale deployment of current approaches is difficult due to their range restrictions and their high costs.

In summary, we identified three issue groups that need to be considered in terms of mobile cloud computing: limited mobile resources (e.g., battery life, storage, computational power), communication issues (e.g., latency, bandwidth, network traffic) and remote processing issues (e.g., security, privacy, ownership, scalability, deployment and operational costs). Focussing on *cloudlets*, the first two issue groups are overcome by that approach [24], i.e., cloudlets offer offloading resource-intensive tasks with low latency and high bandwidth to overcome limited resources on mobile devices. However, we see an open challenge in the last issue group for cloudlets, especially a deployment concept for establishing a comprehensive and dense computing infrastructure with cloudlets is still missing. Figure 1 shows the original cloudlet concept firstly proposed by Satyanarayanan et al. in 2009 [24], where cloudlets are deployed in local businesses like coffee shops or shopping malls. Since then, a large-scale and economic deployment concept does not exist. We also mark the key components in red (cf. Fig. 1) that are responsible for failure of a large-scale deployment, namely, the need of deploying additional computing hardware and the deploying in local businesses which are not geographical dense and comprehensive distributed.

In this paper, we address the main issue of cloudlets: a *large-scale deployment*. A comprehensive, dense and highly available but economic cloudlet infrastructure is essential to make this approach suitable for everyday life.

3   Concept for Router-Based Cloudlets

We propose router-based cloudlets to offload computations from mobile device. Like most offloading techniques, we strive for saving resources and increase responsibility for a better user experience. Our concept benefits from the dense distribution of wireless routers which will result in a large-scale, dense and economic cloudlet infrastructure without the need for new infrastructure invests. This approach can complement existing cloudlet deployment concepts (e.g. , local business, ISP gateway). A router-based cloudlet infrastructure will increase the overall awareness of cloudlets and their benefits. This might also facilitate the existing deployment concepts with more computational power. In the following, we specify our concept for router-based cloudlets. *First*, we investigate the feasibility on device level: can routers be used as cloudlets? *Second*, we investigate the creation of an infrastructure based on cloudlets of routers to be used by mobile devices. *Third*, we consider the community environment of the concept and address legal and social challenges of the process.

3.1   Device (Router)

Inspired by active network research [14,29], our goal is to leverage computational power from wireless home routers. While these routers are currently only used as network devices, we also want to use them as cloudlets, i.e., providing computational power in the network (cf. Fig. 2). To add this functionality, a basic software update or firmware customization is sufficient for many routers (see the evaluation section of this paper for details). This process can open a socket for computational task requests. In the future the cloudlet functionality could be integrated from manufactures or ISPs that provide routers to customers.

Mobile devices can simply connect to wireless routers and benefit either from high-bandwidth to the cloud for contextual applications that need global or historical view (Internet latency) or from computational power of routers for

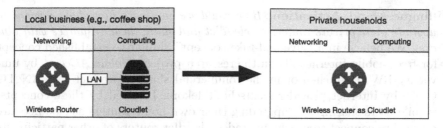

Fig. 2. Original *cloudlet* concept firstly proposed by [24] (*left*) and our approach for enabling a large-scale deployment of cloudlets by upgrading wireless home routers (*right*).

responsive applications (LAN latency). Depending on the need of mobile applications, requests are sent to different endpoints: benefiting from cloud, requests are addressed to cloud's IP address or hostname. These requests are automatically forwarded by routers (*sharing of high-bandwidth Internet connection*).

A specific benefit of routers for the intended purpose is that they are always online (Internet, power grid), have a low latency (near located), and a high bandwidth (WLAN). Drawbacks of routers are their low range and low computational power. It is necessary to address the low range with respective infrastructure protocol (see next paragraph). For the low computational power, a further investigation of the performance of modern routers considering the benefit of low latency is required (see evaluation section).

3.2 Infrastructure

The router-based cloudlets need to be accessible as an infrastructure to be used by mobile devices. As already mentioned, we assume that the router-based cloudlet infrastructure will be complemented by dedicated cloudlets. All cloudlet types need to be integrated on one infrastructure.

The most important challenge is how to access the devices and structure the use. Next to the discovery, challenges with respect to congestion handling, failure handling and handover need to be addressed. For most problems, similar challenges have already been addressed for cellular networks, therefore we plan to transfer existing solutions to the cloudlet domain. To realize discovery, we plan to build a router guest network with all routers using a similar SSID. If computations are not finalized before a device leaves the range, handover mechanisms are required. Additionally, failure handling mechanisms, which also take account of the cloud as a fallback solution, will be considered.

3.3 Community

The real world deployment of routers as cloudlets has to address different social and legal challenges. In the following, we consider three important aspects:

Willingness and Activation. *How could we motivate household owners to upgrade their private routers as cloudlet and share these resources with others?* We believe in a "give-and-take concept" similar to established concept for free mobile Internet like in the research project *Mobile ACcess*[1] by university RWTH Aachen or in the commercial sharing product "WLAN TO GO"[2] by Internet provider Deutsche Telekom. Inspired by these concepts, mobile users sharing and upgrading their own home routers as cloudlets are allowed to connect to nearby upgraded cloudlet routers of other participants and benefit from these offloading resources. Activation or upgrading router to a cloudlet could be simply software-based done by either a firmware update through owners or already customized firmware of manufactures or Internet providers.

Security and Privacy. *How could both the home network and its resources be secured? How could we protect the privacy of members of the households and participating mobile users?* Modern customary routers provide the possibility to setup a home network and an isolated guest network (including our test router Asus RT-AC87U[3]). We could utilize such software-based separation of two networks to isolate home network and the public accessible network providing cloudlet functionalities. In future, manufacturers can think about hardware-based separation of both networks and provide dedicated cloudlet functionalities inherently.

Legal Issues and Digital ID. *How is the legal position in crime situation by sharing resources? How could we identify and authorize users to allow them access to routers' resources?* The legal position in crime situation is still an open question in our concept or in common cloudlet deployment (e.g., in a coffee shop) and depends from country to country. However, we propose an authorization and an authentication mechanisms to get access to other routers. First, a household owner upgrades and shares his wireless home router to other participants. As consequence, he gets the right to access other routers of participants (*authorization*). Second, his upgraded router and his mobile devices exchange device IDs and a digital ID similar to an authentication token that is unique for each household. Connecting to other routers this token is sent for checking participating users (*authentication*). A centralized instance (e.g., Internet provider) need to maintain digital IDs and access rights. In this way, every usage of other routers are personalized and the use can be traced back to specific household and natural person for law cases.

Nevertheless, to show the feasibility and the high potentials of our concept to build a dense, comprehensive and economic computing infrastructure that is highly available, we conducted benchmark tests against current cloudlet concepts

---

[1] http://mobile-access.org (accessed 2015-08-10).

[2] http://www.telekom.de/privatkunden/zuhause/zubuchoptionen/internet-optionen/hotspot/wlan-to-go (accessed 2015-08-10).

[3] http://www.asus.com/Networking/RTAC87U/specifications (accessed 2015-08-10).

and clouds. The tests should show that routers suffice the performance requirements; in other words, it is first necessary to show that the comparatively weak computational power of a home router is of no consequence in processing time of offloading tasks because of benefiting from the low latency due to the proximity and high bandwidth over wireless LAN technologies. In the next section we describe the experimental setup, before we report and discuss the results of conducted benchmark tests.

4   Experimental Setup

In this section the experimental setup, i.e. hardware components and measurement methodology is described. Our experimental setup consists of a mobile device and different offloading systems (i.e., cloud, cloudlet, our router-based cloudlet) for comparing. Our goal is to show that modified wireless routers match performance requirements of a cloudlet. For that, we measure energy consumption and resource usage on mobile device as well as task completion time divided into network delay and processing delay when offloading computational tasks to each system.

4.1   Hardware

Mobile Device. We use a LG Nexus 5 smartphone with quad-core ARM processor (Qualcomm Snapdragon 800) which each core running at 2.26 GHz, 2GB memory and 16GB storage (cf. Table 1). The operating system is updated to the recent standard Android 5.1.1 ROM, namely Lollipop. All background services not required for running the operating system are disabled. Nexus 5 is equipped with 2300mAh Lithium polymer (LiPo) battery by default. We chose that smartphone because it includes all electronics required for measuring the battery voltage and the current flowing from battery to the device. Thanks to integrated MAX170485 fuel-gauge chip[4] that provides high-accuracy voltage measurements and battery level estimation. It has a resolution of 1.25 mV with an error of 7.5 mV. Accurate enough for our measurement purpose to detect differences between the single offloading use cases. Nexus 5 is also equipped with an IEEE 802.11 a/b/g/n/ac wireless transmitter and supports all digital cellular networks ranging from 2G (GSM) to 4G (LTE). As result, this smartphone is able to offload tasks over Internet to the cloud as well as over wireless LAN to cloudlets or wireless routers.

Cloud. As cloud backend, we deployed three Amazon Elastic Compute Cloud[5] (EC2) instances, namely *c3.large*, hosted at different countries with different pricing models (cf. Table 2). Each instance provides two compute units, 4GB

---

[4] http://www.maximintegrated.com/en/products/power/battery-management/
MAX17048.html (accessed 2015-08-10).
[5] https://aws.amazon.com/en/ec2 (accessed 2015-08-10).

Table 1. Smartphone specifications

Model	LG Nexus 5
Processor	Quad-core 2.26 GHz Qualcomm Snapdragon 800 (ARM)
Memory	2 GB RAM
Storage	16 GB
OS	Android v5.1.1 (Lollipop)
Power	3.8 V, 2300 mAh LiPo battery (8.74 Wh)
WLAN	IEEE 802.11 a/b/g/n/ac, dual-band (2.4/5 GHz)
Network	GSM (2G)/UMTS (3G)/HSDPA (3.5G)/LTE (4G)

RAM and 32GB SSD storage. For deploying our processing code written in JavaScript, we utilize Amazon Elastic Beanstalk[6] to automatically setup an appropriate runtime environment (i.e., Linux, NodeJS).

One focus of our benchmarking is task completion time, not only computational power is relevant, but also network latency. Thus, we test three different located clouds (US West, central Europe, Asia Pacific) with same computational power to get the impact of network latency [8]. In Table 2, linear distances between our measurement conducting location (Darmstadt, Germany) and the cloud data centers are listed. Only considering the distance, clouds are at a disadvantage compared to nearby located cloudlets regarding latency because of physical constraints: information cannot propagate faster than the speed of light ($\sim 3 \cdot 10^8$ m/s) when dealing with long distance. While light is able to use beeline, information travels through deployed glass fiber infrastructure with a slightly longer path (let's assume 20 % longer) and with refractive index of about 1.5. Simple mathematical calculations provide us the result how long light need only to travel via air and via glass fiber to the cloud and back (cf. Table 2, RTT). As result of this simple calculations, we can say latency cannot be ignore when talking about distant clouds. Regarding costs: building and operating a data center is extremely expensive for a cloud provider; that is the reason why only few data centers exist worldwide. As user, the setup of a cloud is free but using resources are expensive, as you see the pricing model (costs per working hour) in Table 2.

Cloudlet. As cloudlet we use a desktop computer with quad-core x64 processor (Intel Core i7) running each core at 3.6 GHz, 16 GB RAM, 1TB HDD storage and linux-based operating system (Table 3). The same processing code as used for the cloud is also used for the cloudlet. The cloudlet is placed in the near of the mobile device as well as has one-hop latency and LAN bandwidth. Deploying such a cloudlet server would cost about 1,000$ acquisition cost and about 11 Cent operational costs per hour. Considering these sums of money and range

---

[6] https://aws.amazon.com/en/elasticbeanstalk (accessed 2015-08-10).

Table 2. Cloud specifications: Amazon EC2 instances (as of 08/2015)

	US West (Oregon)	EU (Frankfurt)	Asia Pacific (Sydney)
Instance	c3.large		
Processor	2 vCPU (Intel Xeon E5-2680 v2 2.8 GHz)		
Memory	4 GB RAM		
Storage	2x 16 GB SSD		
OS	64 bit Amazon Linux 2015.03 v2.0.0		
Distance (beeline) [km]	8,500	30	16,500
RTT (air) [ms]	57	0.2	110
RTT (glass fiber) [ms]	85	0.3	165
Costs (asset/working) [$]	–/0.105	–/0.129	–/0.132

Table 3. Cloudlet specifications

Processor	Quad-core 3.6 GHz Intel Core i7-4790 (x64)
Memory	16 GB RAM
Storage	1 TB HDD
OS	Linux
Power	350 W power adapter
LAN	Realtek PCIe 10/100/1000 Mbps Gigabit Ethernet
Costs (asset/working) [$]	1000/0.11

restrictions, a comprehensive, dense and economic infrastructure of cloudlets using this deployment concept becomes unrealistic.

Wireless Home Router as Cloudlet. We built a proof-of-concept prototype to show the feasibility and explore the performance of our concept. For that, we use a customary wireless home router (Asus RT-AC87U) with a dual-core ARM processor, 256MB memory and OpenWRT[7], an open-source linux-based operating system (cf. Table 4). This operation system provides us SSH access to the router. Taking no account of security and privacy for the first prototype, we installed required softwares directly on the router's system. We chose NodeJS[8] - an open source, lightweight, cross-platform runtime environment - for building our network application. Three main benefits were decisive: *firstly*, the fast and easily developing on high-level programming language (JavaScript). *Secondly*, NodeJS is built on C++-written *Google's V8 JavaScript engine*[9] that is extremely fast, uses minimal resources and compiles JavaScript source code

---

[7] https://openwrt.org (accessed 2015-08-10).
[8] https://nodejs.org (accessed 2015-08-10).
[9] https://code.google.com/p/v8 (accessed 2015-08-10).

Table 4. Wireless Home Router specifications

Model	Asus RT-AC87U
Processor	Dual-core 1 GHz Broadcom BCM4709 (ARM Cortex-A9)
Memory	256 MB RAM
Storage	128 MB
OS	DD-WRT
Power	19 V, 1.75 A
WLAN	IEEE 802.11 a/b/g/n/ac, 4×4 dual-band (2.4/5 GHz)
Costs (asset/working) [\$]	270/0.005

directly to native machine code. *Thirdly*, we can reuse and easily deploy the same code for data processing to the servers (e.g., cloud, cloudlet). Thus, NodeJS matches all requirements to build real-time networking applications. We open a socket for leveraging computational power of router via wireless technologies (802.11) by the mobile device. In our first prototype we used established Internet protocols: TCP as transport protocol and HTTP as application protocol. In this case, we are able to send and compare same requests to wireless router, cloudlet or cloud.

While a deployment of cloudlets required additional computing hardware as proposed by [24] is very expensive, our concept is based on a simple firmware update of already existing infrastructure components (i.e., wireless home router). Household owners do not have additional acquisition costs. Due to the fact that routers as network devices are already continuously online, we recognize minimal high operational costs for utilizing additional computing power. Nevertheless, for that, household owners benefit from offloading possibilities to other routers.

4.2 Measurement Methodology

Application Profiler. Program profiling is an obvious approach for optimization and comparison systems [5,31]. Thus, an implemented lightweight runtime profiler (i.e., an Android app running in the background) measures following metrics for our benchmarks: task completion time, processing time, and network delay time. In addition to them, the profiler permanently monitors and logs resource usages: CPU usage, memory usage, and energy consumption on the mobile device. We chose a sampling rate of 500 ms for CPU and memory monitoring and a sampling rate of 50 ms - a good, empirical determined balance between accuracy and CPU load - for energy measurements.

Dataset and Computational Task. While our main goal is to compare performance locally against offloading concepts, the choice of the dataset and the computational task is secondary and replaceable. We chose a set of sensor data, more precisely raw location values, and evaluate them for place detection utilizing resource-intensive clustering algorithm DBSCAN with an overall average

Table 5. Theoretical and measured network configurations

Network	Theoretical bandwidth	Measured bandwidth (up-/download) [Mbps]
LAN	100 Mbps–1 Gbps	310.80 ± 120.39
WLAN (802.11n/ac)	6.5–300 Mbps (4 × 4, 20 MHz)	160.95 ± 23.12
DSL (6,000)	6,016 kbps	0.63 ± 0.04/5.44 ± 0.77
GSM (2G)	9.6 kbps	0.24 ± 0.06/0.10 ± 0.01
UTMS (3G)	384 kbps	1.90 ± 0.25/5.75 ± 1.00
LTE (4G)	150 Mbps–1 Gbps	2.19 ± 0.28/16.00 ± 1.43

runtime complexity of $\mathcal{O}(n \log n)$ [11]. But other responsive use cases or dataset are imaginable, e.g., speak, activity, face, object or gesture recognition [20]. To ensure repeatability across different benchmark runs, the input data consisting of location values is fixed and equal, i.e., we ignore the tracking of sensor data that is not relevant for this paper, but we reference to our previous work for measuring sensor tracking [26]. For our benchmark purpose, we created six datasets varying in their data size (50 kB, 100 kB, 200 kB, 300 kB, 400 kB, 500 kB) in advance to measure their impact.

Measurements. We tested 15 different scenarios consisting of local and offloading processing: (1) locally on the device, (2) cloudlet over wireless LAN, (3–14) three different located clouds (US West, EU, Asia Pacific) over four different wireless networks (2G, 3G, 4G, wireless LAN/DSL), and (15) our router-based cloudlet concept over wireless LAN. The theoretical and measured network configuration used in our benchmark tests can be found in Table 5. For measuring, we disabled all background services not required for running the operating system. The display was switched off during the measurement runs. We start to monitor and log energy consumption, CPU and memory usage. Each measurement scenario was then measured with our six different datasets as follows: *first*, we run a baseline measurement for 30 s to get the default average resource usage of operating system processes and our profiler tool. *Second*, we executed five times the same task processing with the same dataset - either locally or on a remote system depending on the scenario - and measure for each task processing its completion time consisting of network delay and processing time on the executable system. A task processing run works as follows: the smartphone sends the specific dataset to the offloading system, the offloading system processes these data by executing the DBSCAN algorithm, and sends the resulting clusters as well as the processing time back to the mobile device. *Finally*, the resulting values of these five runs were averaged to reduce measurement errors. From these values (i.e., energy consumption, CPU and memory usage) were subtracted the baseline values to get isolated values only for the offloading tasks. In the next section, we report these benchmark results and discuss implications.

5 Benchmark Results

To prove our novel and economic deployment concept of cloudlets in terms of performance and being suitable for daily use, we conducted benchmark tests against local processing on the mobile device and existing state of the art offloading concepts, i.e., cloud and cloudlets. While all three clouds in our test are equipped with the same resources (cf. Table 2), we only report one of them in our benchmark results for better clarity. For that, we chose the one (US West instance) with the intermediate latency of the three various distant clouds (cf. Fig. 3).

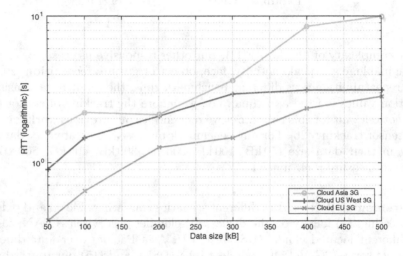

Fig. 3. Comparison of network delays between different located Amazon clouds

Figure 4 shows the entire benchmark results over different computational tasks, where the computational expense and the network traffic depends on the data size. We measured completion times consisting of network transmission delay (except in the case of local processing) and the pure processing time for analyzing the sensor data (cf. Fig. 4(a)–(c)) as well as resource usages on the mobile device, i.e., cpu usage, memory usage, and energy consumption (cf. Fig. 4(d)–(f)).

Considering completion times, cloudlets with additional hardware (comparable to the cloud resources in this benchmark tests) are the best choice in our computational task use case (cf. Fig. 4(a)). Our router-based cloudlet approach, that does not need any additional hardware, even outperforms the clouds with weak Internet access at small data sizes. Local processing on mobile device is sufficient at small data sizes because of enough computational power for that task and no network delay. However, if the complexity of the computational task increases, the need for offloading becomes obvious. In our laboratory test, the offloading systems are only utilized by one client. But, we need to consider

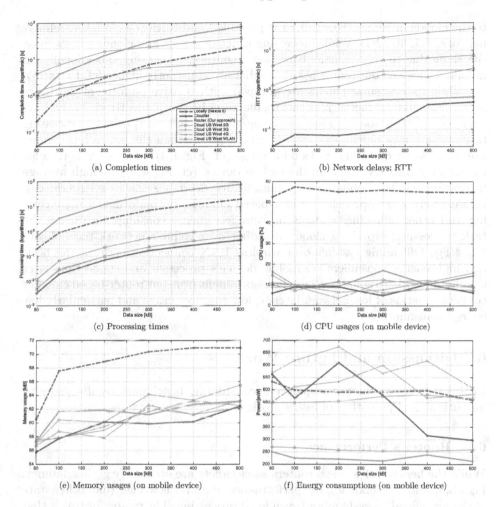

(a) Completion times

(b) Network delays: RTT

(c) Processing times

(d) CPU usages (on mobile device)

(e) Memory usages (on mobile device)

(f) Energy consumptions (on mobile device)

Fig. 4. Benchmark results over different computational tasks (represented by data size); where (a)–(c) are metrics to measure the offloading process while (d)–(f) monitor resources of the mobile device during that process. Our router approach is colored in *green*, cloudlet in *red*, US West cloud with four different network configurations (2G, 3G, 4G, WLAN) is displayed in *blue* and local processing on mobile device in *black* (Color figure online).

performance losses in real world scenario because of having multiple clients connecting to offloading systems and using the shared resources. The count of connecting clients strongly depends on range restrictions: while clouds are accessible from everywhere over Internet, cloudlets and wireless routers are only accessible in their radio range. As expected, cloudlets and our router-based cloudlet approach have lowest network transmission delays over all data sizes due to their nature of nearby located computing capabilities accessible over wireless LAN (cf. Fig. 4(b)). Depending on the used network technologies the network delay to the clouds increases the smaller the possible bandwidth (i.e., WLAN, cellular network: 4G, 3G, 2G). While processing times of clouds and cloudlet are almost the same due to their similar hardware resources, processing times locally on mobile device and our router-based cloudlet are constantly higher (cf. Fig. 4(c)).

While today's smartphones are quipped with relative performant hardware for their small form factor, reasons for offloading becomes directly visible by having a look at the resource usages on the mobile device. Unsurprisingly, processing tasks locally uses much more computational power than the network transmission process for offloading tasks on average (cf. Fig. 4(d)). The same is true for the average memory usage on the mobile device (cf. Fig. 4(e)). A high average utilization on the mobile device dramatically decreases the user experiences. Interestingly, our approach of router-based cloudlet outperforms local processing and other offloading systems in averaged energy consumption during the task processing, especially cloud offloading over cellular network technologies (cf. 4(f)). Offloading systems over wireless LAN connection perform the best, i.e., high energy consumers are mobile device's processor and connections over cellular network. In summary, mobile users benefit from our router-based cloudlet concept in terms of low network latency, low resource usage and particularly low energy consumption.

6   Discussion and Future Work

In this section, we discuss our concept considering benchmark results and give an outlook and potentials of future works.

6.1   Router's Performance

While the benefits of wireless routers as cloudlets are obvious (e.g., low latency, high bandwidth, economic), the performance of router is weaker than other state of the art offloading systems and even local processing. The reason for this is that typical routers are primarily constructed for routing tasks. Nevertheless, latest home routers are already equipped with multi-core and offloading processors for concurrent task processing and will become more and more powerful. We will also connect neighboring wireless routers of various households to a computing mesh network and increase both the computational power as well as the range for connecting to this infrastructure. Such dense and decentralized infrastructure is well suited for distributed computing (inspired by SETI@Home [2]) and is also resilient in disaster scenarios, as proposed and proved in our previous work [19]. Additionally, each router can also use its connected existing intranet resources (e.g., smart tv, laptop) after a software-based upgrade through (wireless) LAN to overcome performance issues. In this scenario, the router acts as master and distributes computational tasks over its dynamically online LAN resources.

6.2   Offloading Strategy

We see our concept of router-based cloudlets as economic complement to existing offloading systems to enable large-scale deployment. In this light, while wireless routers are always connected to Internet, we will research in offloading strategies where the router decide when and where to offload computational task, e.g., to the cloud. It is also imaginable that routers accessible through high-bandwidth WLAN preprocess specific data to reduce network traffic to distant offloading systems.

6.3   Discovery, Handover, and Failure Handling

How can mobile users discover and connect to router-based cloudlets? is still an open and important question to make cloudlets suitable for daily use. Inspired by cellular network technologies that solve some of these issues, e.g., handover of computational tasks, a failure handling strategy for the case if the mobile user gets out of range before the task is finished.

7   Conclusion

In this paper, we proposed a novel concept for enabling a large-scale deployment of cloudlets only using existing infrastructure by software-based upgrading wireless home routers. Beside router's native purpose of routing data packets through the network, it can now offer computing resources with low latency and high bandwidth without additional hardware.

Proving our concept in terms of performance and being suitable for daily use, we conducted benchmark tests against local processing on the mobile device and existing state of the art offloading concepts, i.e., cloud and cloudlets. As result, we cannot show computational performance gain but low network delays and traffic towards existing offloading systems by now. Nevertheless, overcoming computational weaknesses, e.g., through also utilizing connected intranet resources by software-based upgrade or building computing mesh network with neighboring wireless routers, this concept provides enormous potentials for real world usage of in-network computing capabilities.

The feasibility of this concept is already given. Router-based cloudlets provide a promising and complementary way to enable a large-scale deployment of cloudlets in existing infrastructures. This also opens an interesting field for diverse real-time constrained and contextual applications, e.g., assistance systems or face recognition.

Acknowledgments. This work has been co-funded by the LOEWE initiative (Hessen, Germany) within the NICER project and by the German Research Foundation (DFG) as part of project B02 within the Collaborative Research Center (CRC) 1053 – MAKI.

References

1. Aijaz, A., Aghvami, H., Amani, M.: A survey on mobile data offloading: technical and business perspectives. IEEE Wireless Commun. **20**(2), 104–112 (2013)
2. Anderson, D.P., Cobb, J., Korpela, E., Lebofsky, M., Werthimer, D.: SETI@home: an experiment in public-resource computing. Commun. ACM **45**(11), 56–61 (2002)
3. Balan, R., Flinn, J., Satyanarayanan, M., Sinnamohideen, S., Yang, H.-I.: The case for cyber foraging. In: 10th Workshop on ACM SIGOPS European Workshop, pp. 87–92. ACM (2002)
4. Bonomi, F., Milito, R., Zhu, J., Addepalli, S.: Fog computing and its role in the internet of things. In: 1st Workshop on Mobile Cloud Computing (MCC 2012), pp. 13–16. ACM (2012)
5. Carroll, A., Heiser, G.: An analysis of power consumption in a smartphone. In: USENIX Annual Technical Conference, vol. 14 (2010)
6. Chen, Y., Liu, B., Chen, Y., Li, A., Yang, X., Bi, J.: PacketCloud: an open platform for elastic in-network services. In: 8th International Workshop on Mobility in the Evolving Internet Architecture (MobiArch 2013), pp. 17–22. ACM (2013)
7. Chun, B.-G., Ihm, S., Maniatis, P., Naik, M., Patti, A.: CloneCloud: elastic execution between mobile device and cloud. In: 6th Conference on Computer Systems (EuroSys 2011), pp. 301–314. ACM (2011)
8. Clinch, S., Harkes, J., Friday, A., Davies, N., Satyanarayanan, M.: How close is close enough? understanding the role of cloudlets in supporting display appropriation by mobile users. In: 10th International Conference on Pervasive Computing and Communications (PerCom 2012), pp. 122–127. IEEE (2012)
9. Cuervo, E., Balasubramanian, A., Cho, D.-K., Wolman, A., Saroiu, S., Chandra, R., Bahl, P.: MAUI: making smartphones last longer with code offload. In: 8th International Conference on Mobile Systems, Applications, and Services (MobiSys 2010), pp. 49–62. ACM (2010)
10. Dinh, H.T., Lee, C., Niyato, D., Wang, P.: A survey of mobile cloud computing: architecture, applications, and approaches. Wireless communications and mobile computing **13**(18), 1587–1611 (2013)
11. Ester, M., Kriegel, H.-P., Sander, J., Xu, X.: A density-based algorithm for discovering clusters in large spatial databases with noise. In: 2th International Conference on Knowledge, Discovery and Data Mining (KDD 1996), vol. 96, pp. 226–231 (1996)
12. Fernando, N., Loke, S.W., Rahayu, W.: Mobile cloud computing: a survey. Future Gener. Comput. Syst., Elsevier **29**(1), 84–106 (2013)
13. File, T.: Computer and internet use in the United States. Current Population Survey Reports, P20–568. US Census Bureau, Washington, DC (2013)
14. Keller, R., Choi, S., Dasen, M., Decasper, D., Fankhauser, G., Plattner, B.: An active router architecture for multicast video distribution. In: 19th International Conference on Computer Communications, vol. 3, pp. 1137–1146. IEEE (2000)
15. Khan, A.K., Kiah, M.L.M., Khan, S.U., Madani, S.A.: Towards secure mobile cloud computing: a survey. Future Gener. Comput. Syst., Elsevier **29**(5), 1278–1299 (2013)
16. Khan, K.A., Wang, Q., Grecos, C., Luo, C., Wang, X.: MeshCloud: integrated cloudlet and wireless mesh network for real-time applications. In: 20th International Conference on Electronics, Circuits, and Systems (ICECS 2013), pp. 317–320. IEEE (2013)

17. Makris, P., Skoutas, D.N., Skianis, C.: On networking and computing environments' integration: a novel mobile cloud resources provisioning approach. In: International Conference on Telecommunications and Multimedia, pp. 71-76. IEEE (2012)
18. Mell, P., Grance, T.: The NIST Definition of Cloud Computing (2011)
19. Panitzek, K., Schweizer, I., Schulz, A., Bönning, T., Seipel, G., Mühlhäuser, M.: Can we use your router, please?: benefits and implications of an emergency switch for wireless routers. Int. J. Inf. Syst. Crisis Response. Manage. 4(4), 59–70 (2012)
20. Ra, M.-R., Sheth, A., Mummert, L., Pillai, P., Wetherall, D., Govindan, R.: Odessa: enabling interactive perception applications on mobile devices. In: 9th International Conference on Mobile Systems, Applications, and Services (MobiSys 2011), pp. 43–56. ACM (2011)
21. Sanaei, Z., Abolfazli, S., Gani, A., Buyya, R.: Heterogeneity in mobile cloud computing: taxonomy and open challenges. IEEE Commun. Surv. Tutorials 16(1), 369–392 (2014)
22. Satyanarayanan, M.: Fundamental challenges in mobile computing. In: 15th Symposium on Principles of Distributed Computing (PODC 1996), pp. 1–7. ACM (1996)
23. Satyanarayanan, M.: Pervasive computing: vision and challenges. IEEE Pers. Commun. 8(4), 10–17 (2001)
24. Satyanarayanan, M., Bahl, P., Caceres, R., Davies, N.: The case for VM-based cloudlets in mobile computing. IEEE Pervasive Comput. 8(4), 14–23 (2009)
25. Satyanarayanan, M., Lewis, G., Morris, E., Simanta, S., Boleng, J., Ha, K.: The role of cloudlets in hostile environments. IEEE Pervasive Comput. 12(4), 40–49 (2013)
26. Schweizer, I., Bärtl, R., Schmidt, B., Kaup, F., Mühlhäuser, M.: Kraken.me mobile: the energy footprint of mobile tracking. In: 6th International Conference on Mobile Computing, Applications and Services (MobiCase 2014), pp. 82–89. IEEE (2014)
27. Seybert, H.: Internet use in households and by individuals in 2011. Eurostat Stat. Focus 66, 2011 (2011)
28. Stojmenovic, I.: Fog computing: a cloud to the ground support for smart things and machine-to-machine networks. In: Telecommunication Networks and Applications Conference (ATNAC 2014), Australasia, pp. 117–122. IEEE (2014)
29. Tennenhouse, D.L., Smith, J.M., Sincoskie, W.D., Wetherall, D.J., Minden, G.J.: A survey of active network research. Commun. Mag. 35(1), 80–86 (1997)
30. Verbelen, T., Simoens, P., DeTurck, F., Dhoedt, B.: Cloudlets: bringing the cloud to the mobile user. In: 3th Workshop on Mobile Cloud Computing and Services (MCS 2012), pp. 29–36. ACM (2012)
31. Wang, C., Li, Z.: A computation offloading scheme on handheld devices. J. Parallel Distrib. Comput. 64(6), 740–746 (2004)

Activity Recognition and Crowdsourcing

Adaptive Activity and Context Recognition Using Multimodal Sensors in Smart Devices

Sébastien Faye(✉), Raphael Frank, and Thomas Engel

Interdisciplinary Centre for Security, Reliability and Trust,
University of Luxembourg,
4 rue Alphonse Weicker, 2721 Luxembourg, Luxembourg
{sebastien.faye,raphael.frank,thomas.engel}@uni.lu

Abstract. The continuous development of new technologies has led to the creation of a wide range of personal devices embedded with an ever increasing number of miniature sensors. With accelerometers and technologies such as Bluetooth and Wi-Fi, today's smartphones have the potential to monitor and record a complete history of their owners' movements as well as the context in which they occur. In this article, we focus on four complementary aspects related to the understanding of human behaviour. First, the use of smartwatches in combination with smartphones in order to detect different activities and associated physiological patterns. Next, the use of a scalable and energy-efficient data structure that can represent the detected signal shapes. Then, the use of a supervised classifier (i.e. Support Vector Machine) in parallel with a quantitative survey involving a dozen participants to achieve a deeper understanding of the influence of each collected metric and its use in detecting user activities and contexts. Finally, the use of novel representations to visualize the activities and social interactions of all the users, allowing the creation of quick and easy-to-understand comparisons. The tools used in this article are freely available online under a MIT licence.

Keywords: Sensing system · Wearable computing · Activity detection

1 Introduction

In recent years, the growing availability and falling cost of smart devices have opened up a world of opportunities for new applications. Apart from smartphones, these connected objects include a wide range of ultra-portable devices that constantly interact with the users and their environment. Among those *wearables*, the vast majority are smartwatches and activity trackers. These have become very diverse and are equipped with high-performance sensors that allow users to monitor their physical activity in a way never possible before. Their sensors can read metrics from arm or hand movements with an accuracy comparable to specialized experimental devices [1]. These devices include physical sensors that are permanently in contact with the user's wrist, such as motion detectors (e.g. accelerometers) and environmental monitoring sensors (e.g. light sensors, microphone). Their

© Institute for Computer Sciences, Social Informatics and Telecommunications Engineering 2015
S. Sigg et al. (Eds.): MobiCASE 2015, LNICST 162, pp. 33–50, 2015.
DOI: 10.1007/978-3-319-29003-4_3

ability to monitor other physiological metrics, such as heart rate, leads to new areas of research. Further, the recent arrival on the market of major players, like Apple, Google and Microsoft, has facilitated the development and widespread adoption of sensing applications, opening the way to many new areas, including health, sport, and personal monitoring. According to ABI Research, it is estimated that the global market for wearables will reach 170 million in 2017 [2].

At present, whether we are talking about smartphones or wearables, these connected objects are generally used individually and for specific consumer applications (e.g. fitness). In most cases, the classic data fusion from sensors is adapted to be made in real time (e.g. pattern finding). This requires heavy-duty processing algorithms and consumes energy. Moreover, most systems only use smartphones, whereas wearables are more suitable for detecting user activities. Finally, few studies have looked at all types of existing sensors with the intention of arriving at a scalable and easy-to-implement solution.

In this paper, we intend to go one step further by presenting a sensing system that combines the data collected by one smartwatch and one smartphone. The platform that we have developed makes use of commercially-available devices and can be used to analyse the activity of a monitored user in great detail. Possible applications range from sports tracking systems to human behaviour modeling. Our contribution addresses four complementary objectives. (1) The design of an energy-efficient sensing system, using a streamlined fusion of data collected on two devices (a smartphone and a smartwatch). (2) The use of a supervised machine learning model to recognize user activities and their contexts. (3) The combination of multimodal metrics to obtain more advanced feature sets and generalize the recognition process. Finally, (4) the comparison of activities and social interactions of different users using novel 3D visual representations.

In the following section we provide a review of existing literature. Next, in Sect. 3, we present of our sensing system, which is focused on the devices used for data collection and on how they communicate to exchange data. Section 4 describes our experimental campaign and how we used the collected metrics to create the data set used for our analysis. Section 5 focuses on the analysis of the data set and presents some relationships between metrics and a set of predetermined activities using a Support Vector Machine (SVM) model. These relationships form the basis for the recognition of activities and contexts to be inferred. Finally, two profile comparison methods are introduced in Sect. 6, before we conclude in Sect. 7.

2   Related Work

The use of mobile devices as key elements in a sensing system has been discussed for many years, both in industrial and research communities, as an opportunistic [3] or a participative system [4]. The classic architecture for such a sensing system consists of three parts [5,6]. First, individual devices collect the sensor data. Then, information is extracted from the sensor data by applying learning methods, generally on one of the devices or in the cloud, depending on the sensitivity of the data, the sampling strategy or the privacy level applied. Finally, the data can be shared and visualized from the cloud.

Smartwatches have their place in this kind of architecture and can open up new perspectives as they can collect the user's activity and physiological signals [7], while smartphones are reserved for recording the user's context. Smartwatches and smartphones are usually connected via Bluetooth Low Energy [8], a relatively new technology standardized under the Bluetooth 4.0 specification [9]. Compared to smartwatches, smartphones have a better battery capacity and can launch several tasks at the same time. By using a smartphone as a local gateway to access the Internet – via Wi-Fi or Cellular – we can turn this local sensing platform into a connected ecosystem [6].

As the applications need to be running on the devices permanently to collect and send data, there is an important compromise to be found between sample rate, rate of transmission and the consumption of energy [8]. The authors of [10] show, for example, that using all the sensors of a LG Nexus 4 E960 can reduce its battery from 214.3 h (no sensors) to 10.6 h (all sensors). Some systems attempt to circumvent this energy limit by offloading data processing onto servers [11]. Others propose sharing the data among neighboring phones [12]. By these means, cloud computing is widely used with smartphones and allows the creation of elastic models [13], where applications are launched on the mobile phone, and the data is processed in the cloud.

In the surveyed literature, accelerometers are the sensors most commonly used to recognize various physical and upper body activities. Indeed, [1] shows that specific movements of the arms, the hands and the fingers, generate sufficient energy to be distinguished by the accelerometer and the gyroscope in a smartwatch with 98 % precision. By correlating different sources of data, other sensors such as GPS, microphones and Wi-Fi signals can also be used to improve the classification accuracy and estimate, for example, the mode of transport (e.g. bike, car) [14]. By continuously recording sound, it is possible to identify different user contexts, whether having a conversation, sitting in an office, walking out on the street or even making coffee [15,16]. SPARK [17] is a framework that can detect symptoms associated with Parkinson's disease using a smartwatch on the wrist (to detect dyskinesia using motion sensors), and a smartphone in the pocket (gait analysis and sound). Shin et al. [18] study patients with mental disorders and use smartwatches to help quantify the exercise and the amount of sunlight wearers have received, using GPS, accelerometer and the light sensor. Video sensing also permits various activities to be recognized [19]. However, video analysis is both algorithmically and computationally expensive, especially in a resource-constrained environment. Finally, social interactions can be identified using Bluetooth, Wi-Fi, Near-Field Communications (NFC) or cellular [10].

Activity detection involves the recognition of spatio-temporal patterns from sensor data that is usually incomplete and noisy. There is significant number of models that are able to characterize human behaviour from different features (e.g. accelerometer data). The temporal signal shape can be analyzed both in time and frequency domains. Time-domain features include basic waveform characteristics and signal statistics that can be considered to be features of a given signal, e.g. the statistical moments, time between peaks, binned distribution,

Table 1. Specification of the devices used of our studies.

Devices	RAM / Storage	CPU	Battery	Network Interfaces	Collectable Data
Samsung Gear Live	512 MB / 4 GB	Quad-core 1.2 GHz	300 mAh	Bluetooth 4.0	Heart rate, heart rate accuracy, pedometer, linear acceleration, time.
LG Nexus 5	2 GB / 16 GB	Quad-core 2.3 GHz	2,300 mAh	4G/LTE, GPS, 802.11 a/b/g/n/ac dual-band Wi-Fi, NFC, Bluetooth 4.0	Proximity, ambient light, linear acceleration, ambient sound, detected activity, activity confidence, pedometer, mobile network information, detected Bluetooth devices, Wi-Fi networks, GPS (location, altitude, speed, bearing, distance), local weather (from OpenWeatherMap.org), time.

mean value of local maxima [20]. Data set reduction techniques such as Principal Component Analysis and Linear Discriminant Analysis can be used to extract the most significant discriminating features while reducing the dimensionality of the data representation [21]. Combining the feature extraction techniques above, activity recognition can be trained using (semi-)supervised methods in a controlled setting. These methods include Decision Trees, Neural Networks and Support Vector Machines, all of which have been successfully used in human activity recognition [22]. For example, Frame-based Descriptor and multi-class Support Vector Machine [23] is an approach that can classify a large variety of gestures. Unsupervised methods (e.g. k-means clustering [24]) can then be used to find structures in the different activity sequences and durations that were identified to find common properties or behaviours of user groups.

3   Sensing System

In order to carry out our studies and obtain the results presented in this article, we used our own system, SWIPE [7], which is available online[1] under a MIT licence. It is composed of two main parts: an Android application for data collection and a web platform for data processing.

3.1   Hardware

We used two devices running Android 5.1.1. One was a smartwatch (Samsung Galaxy Gear Live) that records the wearer's activity by registering wrist movements and other physiological data (i.e. heart rate). The other, a smartphone (LG Nexus 5), is responsible for collecting contextual data (e.g. with its microphone) as well as some additional activity data (e.g. accelerometer). The decision to run SWIPE on Android makes sense because of its maturity and its leading role in the current generation of smartwatches. Table 1 summarizes the specifications of the two devices, including details of the data that our system is able to collect.

---

[1] https://github.com/sfaye/SWIPE/.

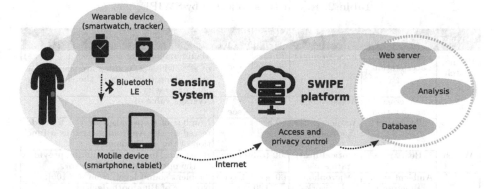

Fig. 1. SWIPE overall architecture.

3.2 Architecture

The architecture of SWIPE is shown in Fig. 1 and consists of two parts. First, the sensing system is composed of a watch (worn on the wrist) and a phone (carried in the pocket) as introduced in Sect. 3.1. The watch periodically sends the data it has collected to the smartphone, which acts as a local collection point and as a gateway to access the SWIPE platform over the Internet (via Wi-Fi or a cellular network). The SWIPE platform is divided into several modules, which (1) receive data following authentication and (2) store, (3) analyse and (4) display the data by means of a web interface. Each user is identified by a unique hash string and his or her data is stored on an internal University of Luxembourg server, which is accessible only on the local network. The link between the server and the sensing system is performed by an intermediate server that acts as a relay.

3.3 Metrics Collected by SWIPE

The main metrics that our system collects are shown in Table 2. The "recording rate" column indicates the frequency at which a metric is saved in a data file, while the "sampling rate" indicates the frequency at which the system acquires raw data from sensors. Since the user is wearing the watch all the time, metrics associated with the watch include the ability to recognize activity. The average speed of movement of the user's arm is recorded every 30 seconds, along with the maximum speed in order to detect sudden, unusual gestures. Metrics collected by the phone include contextual data. This includes accelerometer readings that are complementary to those provided by the watch. We also store microphone readings to register the level of ambient noise, enabling us to distinguish between noisy and a quiet places. Network data also enables us to collect information on both mobility (GPS, Wi-Fi) and interaction with other users (Bluetooth).

Table 2. Key metrics collected by SWIPE.

Devices	Metrics	Sensors	Recording & Sampling rates		
Phone, watch	Maximum acceleration	Accelerometer	30 sec.	< 1 sec.	Maximum value of $\alpha = \sqrt{(x^2 + y^2 + z^2)}$ $m.s^{-2}$, where x, y and z are the acceleration along each axis of the device, excluding gravity.
	Average acceleration	Accelerometer	30 sec.	< 1 sec.	Average value of α.
	Pedometer	Accelerometer, Android API	60 sec.	~	Number of steps taken by the user, detected by the Android system as a function of the accelerometer.
Watch	Heart rate	Optical heart rate sensor	60 to 300 sec.		Heart rate, in beats per minute, provided by the optical heart rate sensor.
Phone	Ambient sound	Microphone	60 sec.	1 sec.	Ambient sound level, from [0 : 100].
	Bluetooth devices	Network	120 sec.		Number of Bluetooth devices.
	Wi-Fi APs	Network	300 sec.		Number of Wi-Fi Access Points.
	Mobile network data state	Network	300 sec.		Value expressing the use of cell phone network. A reading of zero indicates that the phone is connected to a Wi-Fi AP. For our experiments, only the access point of our workplace was configured.
	Speed	GPS	60 sec.		Travel speed, in $km.h^{-1}$.

3.4 Energy Saving Strategy

The provision of a sensing system launched as a background service represents a potential burden on the batteries of the devices used, which (particularly in the case of smartwatches) are not renowned for their longevity. It is therefore critical that we make every effort to save energy. This includes finding the right compromise between energy consumption and data collection. The proposed system aims to run uninterrupted for at least 12 h in order to collect enough data to obtain an overview of daily activities. To achieve this, we implemented the following optimization strategy.

(1) Data transmission consumes a significant amount of energy. We first configure our application so that the watch, if close enough, uploads its data to the smartphone every 20 min rather than continuously. This allows the application to automatically turn off Bluetooth most of the time and makes the watch fully autonomous (i.e. the user can wear the watch without having to carry the phone). Data collected and transmitted by the smartwatch is received and stored locally by the smartphone to be sent once a day to our servers for later analysis. The data is sent at a predefined time (at midnight) or when the battery level of either of the devices drops below a threshold of 5 %.

(2) Another factor that contributes to energy consumption is the frequency at which the sensors record data. The higher the frequency and the longer the transmission time, the more energy is consumed. On the other hand, a lower data acquisition rate will dilute the quality of the resulting data set. Consequently, each metric is configured with the parameters set out in Sect. 3.3. Note that while most of the metrics are configured with a fixed and adequate sampling frequency with respect to the tests carried out, other strategies are set up for specific cases.

Indeed, the acquisition frequency of the heart rate sensor is designed to adapt to the activity of the user. When the user is making little or no movement, the sampling frequency is low, since his heart rate should be stable and the measurements reliable. Conversely, when the user moves, the sensor becomes more sensitive and his heart rate is likely to change. In this case, the data acquisition rate increases in order to take more probes.

(3) Finally, the devices are configured to prevent users from interacting with them. Each is locked with a password and all the unnecessary services managed by Android, such as notifications, are disabled. This allows us to record the data without interruption and under the same conditions for every participant.

This energy saving strategy is evaluated by comparing it with the settings where transmission, harvesting and recording frequencies were high (i.e. all set to 1 second). We find an autonomy gain of about 287 % for the smartwatch (13.5 h vs. 4.7 h) and on the order of 189 % for the smartphone (15.7 h vs. 8.3 h).

4 Building a Data Set

4.1 Scenario

The studies we conducted involved 13 participants working in the same building at the University of Luxembourg. These participants were selected as a representative sample of both genders and of different ages. Each participant was systematically subjected to the same requirements: (1) wear the watch and smartphone for one day, from 10:00 to 23:59; (2) complete a questionnaire[2] asking for an exact description of activities carried out (work, commute and leisure activities); (3) sign an informed consent form to accept the privacy policy of the study.

4.2 Example

Figure 2 shows data from one of the participants over a period of about 14 h. The accelerometer data and the level of ambient noise immediately reveal several distinct situations. Around 19:00, for example, the participant appears to perform much faster movements than usual with both his watch and his phone – indicating that he is carrying both devices. The noise level is also high, indicating either a noisy place or excessive friction (which is common when the phone is carried in a pocket). We can easily deduce that the user was running. This is confirmed by the activity recognition algorithm provided by Android, which is able to detect basic activities. The situation is similar around 18:00. The environmental noise level is high, but both devices detect much less movement and the GPS records more rapid progress from place to place: the user was driving. These initial observations form the basis of our intuitive understanding of the user's activity.

---

[2] Available online: http://swipe.sfaye.com/mobicase15/questionnaire.pdf.

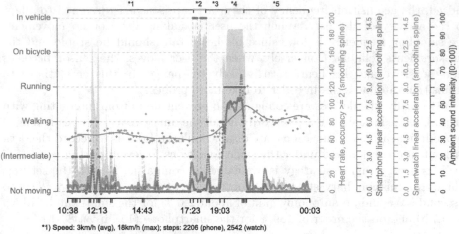

*1) Speed: 3km/h (avg), 18km/h (max); steps: 2206 (phone), 2542 (watch)
*2) Speed: 32km/h (avg), 107km/h (max); steps: 1 (phone), 0 (watch)
*3) Speed: 6km/h (avg), 20km/h (max); steps: 2394 (phone), 2404 (watch)
*4) Speed: 8km/h (avg), 14km/h (max); steps: 9573 (phone), 9574 (watch)
*5) Speed: 1km/h (avg), 5km/h (max); steps: 456 (phone), 623 (watch)

Fig. 2. Example of collected metrics for one participant.

Table 3. Identified activity and context classes with their total durations in our data set, which consists of 157.2 h of recordings.

| Activity | | | | | | | | | Context | | | | | |
| Physical | | | | | In vehicle | | | | | | | | | Total |
Sitting	Standing	Walking	Running	Tennis	Bus	Train	Motorcycle	Car	Working	Meeting	Shopping	Break	At home	
5.2h	11h	3.8h	1.9h	0.8h	1.4h	0.6h	0.3h	7.8h	5.2h	8.1h	3.4h	8.7h	7.3h	**65.4h**

4.3 Activity and Context Classes

In order to build a data set, we used both the information provided by users in the questionnaire and the information from the sensing platform. Each participant told us about the activities he or she had performed. By gathering all the information from the 13 participants, we obtained a total of nine activities (i.e. sitting, standing, walking, running, playing tennis, on a train, on a bus, on a motorcycle, in a car) that can be classified within five different contexts (i.e. working in an office, attending a meeting, in a shopping centre, on a break at work, at home), as represented in Table 3. Since we have the time slots for each activity (e.g. Figure 2), we are able to assign a set of representative values for each activity and context considering multiple inputs.

5 Activity and Context Recognition Using SVM

5.1 Parameters

The problem to be solved is how to identify a class based on a set of metrics. We chose to use SVM (Support Vector Machine) [25], a set of supervised learning techniques to classify data into separate categories. SVMs have the ability to deal with large amounts of data while providing effective results. They can be used to solve problems of discrimination, i.e. deciding which class a sample is in, or regression, i.e. predicting the numerical value of a variable.

For our evaluation we used the SVM classifier provided by the e1071 package for R [26]. The default optimisation method – C-classification – is used, as well as the classic radial kernel. Grid-search with 10-fold cross validation [27] was used to adjust the cost parameter C (within a range of 1 to 100), as well as γ (within a range of 0.00001 to 0.1).

5.2 Feature Set

The numerous measurements that we have in our data set were not all recorded at the same frequency. As shown in Table 2, acceleration was recorded twice as often as GPS speed. To simplify future operations, we chose to refine the data for each metric by sampling the same number of values from each. For each of the known classes selected in Sect. 4.3, we use a sliding window of ten minutes, moving over the data stream every five minutes. With each movement of the window, two representative values of data included in the window – referred to as x – are recorded: their average $\bar{x}$, which gives an overall view of the data over the interval; and their standard deviation $\sigma(x)$, which is fundamental to understanding the variations around the average. Finally, each activity and context class is represented as a set M of m metrics, each of which is represented, for each 10-minute data interval x, as $\bar{x}$ and $\sigma(x)$. The following matrix illustrates the structure of the data set:

$$
\begin{array}{c}
\\
T_1 \\
\vdots \\
T_n
\end{array}
\begin{array}{c}
Class \quad M_1^{avg} \quad M_1^{std} \quad \cdots \quad M_m^{avg} \quad M_m^{std} \\
\left(\begin{array}{cccccc}
class_1 & x_{1,1}^- & \sigma(x_{1,1}) & \cdots & x_{1,m}^- & \sigma(x_{1,m}) \\
\vdots & \vdots & \vdots & \vdots & \vdots & \vdots \\
class_\Delta & x_{n,1}^- & \sigma(x_{n,1}) & \cdots & x_{n,m}^- & \sigma(x_{n,m})
\end{array}\right)
\end{array} \tag{1}
$$

This representation is simple and has the advantage of abstracting from the excessive precision of the data. It also has the advantage of being lighter and less expensive to treat with a classification algorithm. Assuming we have a set of data composed of t seconds of recording, that the length of the sliding window is t_{window} seconds and that it moves every $t_{step} \leq t_{window}$ seconds, we obtain a data matrix whose size is:

$$
columns = (2 \cdot m + 1) \qquad rows = \frac{t - (t_{window} - t_{step})}{t_{step}} \tag{2}
$$

Our activities database contains, for example, a total of 65.4h of recordings and is 19×784 in size.

5.3   Recognition Using Metrics Individually

First of all, we investigate the individual influence that each metric can have on the recognition of an activity and/or context. Figure 3 represents some selected normalized metric averages over all participants and for each class. For reasons of visualization, the vehicle activities are grouped into the "In vehicle" class. The colour transition between each class represents half the distance that separates their average. The findings are logical, but they confirm the individual importance of each metric. For example, on average the GPS speed reading can help to detect whether the user is traveling in a vehicle, running or at rest. Maximum accelerometer readings can help us recognize a sport activity, such as tennis. Noise in a shopping centre seems to be higher than noise during a meeting.

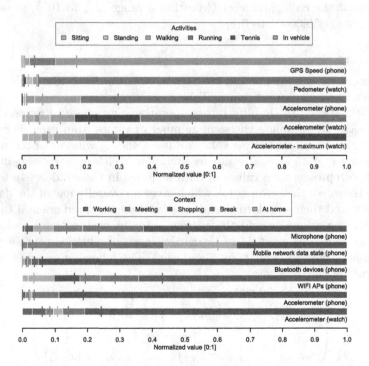

Fig. 3. Selected metric averages for each class.

We want to use streamlined versions of the data set described in Sect. 5.2, with the aim of representing each metric individually to see whether or not it can accurately detect a class. Each data set is evaluated in order to discover how accurately we can predict a class based on a single metric. To do this, each data set is randomly divided into two parts. The first is the training set, comprising 70 % of instances. The second is the test set, comprising the remaining 30 %. The training set is subjected to a grid search to find the cost and γ that minimize the error rate. An SVM model is created from the training set using the best cost and the best γ. The model is then confronted with the test set with the aim of predicting the number of instances in the test set whose class is correctly recognized by the training set. In order to ensure a representative average value for the error rate, this operation is performed 100 times for each combination and calculated for each iteration as $1 - Accuracy$. The results are shown in Table 4 with $Accuracy = \frac{true\ value}{total\ value}$.

We notice a huge disparity between all combinations of metrics and classes. The overall findings were quite polarized: some metrics can identify a class with very high reliability (e.g. the relationship between acceleration and running), while others cannot. Of course, the combinations shown are representative of our data set, where activities were taking place in an urban environment. For example, it is normal to see Wi-Fi sometimes taking particular prominence. This would probably not be the case if environments were more heterogeneous.

5.4 Recognition Using a Combination of Multiple Metrics

It makes sense to use a classifier such as an SVM when combining multiple metrics to deduce an activity, which can be seen as a more advanced feature set. We are interested in minimizing the error rate returned by an SVM model, that takes a set of metrics as its input, i.e. finding a combination that minimizes the error rate for both of the activity category and the context category. To do this, we generate all possible combinations of metrics and create a data set for each combination (e.g. watch acceleration and heart rate, Wi-Fi access points and GPS speed and Bluetooth devices, etc.). In the same manner and with the same parameters as above, for all possible combinations, each data set is randomly divided into a test set and a training set in order to calculate the average error rate provided by the combination, over 100 iterations. The combination retained is the one with the minimum average error rate.

Table 5 represents the best combination of metrics obtained for each class of activity and context and for three cases: combined watch and phone metrics, watch metrics, and phone metrics. For each line, the best combination presented is the one that has the best accuracy. For example, the best combination for recognizing the "standing" class is a combination of metrics on the watch and on the smartphone, giving us a 95.3 % average recognition accuracy. We can also see that, for the "running" and "motorcycle" classes, using the watch alone provides better accuracy than a combination of the watch and phone sensors. However, in most cases, the combined use of both devices offers better results than a phone or a watch alone. On the whole, the conclusions on the dataset are the same as those of Sect. 5.3. However, we can see that activity classes tend to be better served by motion metrics, whereas context classes are based more on Bluetooth, microphone, or network metrics. Finally, the two "Average" lines indicate a common combination in all classes that minimizes the average error rate. For example, the average context category combination is the one with the lowest average error rate for the classes of the category. These two lines are used in the next section to determine users' classes.

Table 4. Influence of each metric on the recognition of classes. The red to yellow gradient indicates high to low prediction accuracy. Grey indicates that no data was available for the performed activity.

Device	Metric	Sitting	Standing	Walking	Running	Tennis	Bus	Train	Motorcycle	Car	Working	Meeting	Shopping	Break	At home
Watch	Max. Acceleration														
	Acceleration														
	Pedometer														
	Heart rate														
Phone	Max. Acceleration														
	Acceleration														
	Pedometer														
	Microphone														
	Bluetooth devices														
	Wi-Fi APs														
	Mobile network data state														
	GPS speed														

Accuracy: 0% ———————————————— 100%

Table 5. Best combinations of metrics for each activity. The "Best accuracy" columns denote the best possible percentage of the test data set which is correctly identified in the training data set. "Average" rows show the best combination for the entire class.

Category	Class	Watch: Max. Acceleration	Watch: Acceleration	Watch: Pedometer	Watch: Heart rate	Phone: Max. Acceleration	Phone: Acceleration	Phone: Pedometer	Phone: Microphone	Phone: Bluetooth devices	Phone: Wi-Fi APs	Phone: Mobile network data state	Phone: GPS speed	Phone & Watch	Phone only	Watch only
Activity	Sitting					■		■					■	**99.5**	99.0	85.6
	Standing			■					■					**95.3**	81.4	68.8
	Walking	■					■	■						**95.8**	87.0	73.2
	Running	■												100	97.4	100
	Tennis													100	-	100
	Bus			■			■			■				**88.9**	69.5	73.1
	Train							■			■			100	96.6	83.9
	Motorcycle	■												100	97.8	100
	Car					■		■			■			**93.2**	90.4	77.0
	Average	■						■					■	**93.2**	88.1	81.5
Context	Working					■		■						**95.3**	95.3	72.3
	Meeting		■				■	■						**94.7**	85.8	73.4
	Shopping	■				■		■						**86.6**	76.7	80.6
	Break								■					**95.5**	84.9	69.4
	At home		■						■					100	99.5	92.4
	Average	■						■					■	**90.4**	86.6	74.7

5.5   Application Example

To illustrate our conclusions on the data set, we have taken as an example the participant shown in Fig. 2. Each activity and context class is identified using the average combinations (Table 5). The recognition method is applied by progressively comparing the individual user's data with the data in our full data set using SVM. Figure 4(a) and (b) illustrate the activity and user context recognition respectively, when the user's data is not included in the full data set.

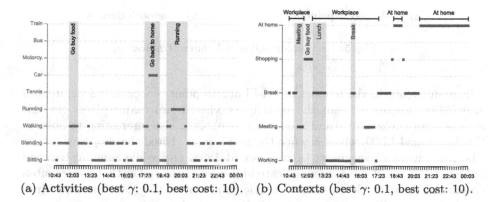

(a) Activities (best γ: 0.1, best cost: 10).   (b) Contexts (best γ: 0.1, best cost: 10).

Fig. 4. Detected classes. Grey bars and black text are the main activities and contexts reported by the user.

The participant's data is divided into ten-minute intervals. For each interval, we calculate the mean and the standard deviation of each metric. The set of values for the participant is small and therefore relatively easy to obtain. Each ten-minute interval consists of 14 values for activity detection and ten values for context recognition. As we can see from the figures and by consulting the participant's questionnaire, we obtain a very realistic result, which is made possible by the collaboration of all participants and the pooling of their data. In Fig. 4(a), for example, we see that at around 18:00 the participant was driving, and at between about 19:00 and 20:00 he was running. He took a lunch break around noon, which required him to move (walk) to buy food, as confirmed in Fig. 4(b). The same figure also indicates that the participant was in his office most of the afternoon. Some errors are noted around 18:00, where it was detected that the participant was in a shopping centre, where in fact he was in his car. Similar findings are noted around 19:00, when the participant was running. The reason for this is the lack of a corresponding context class, and therefore the closest alternative is indicated.

Figure 5(a) and (b) respectively show the changes in the number of Wi-Fi access points and Bluetooth devices that the participant encounters. It is interesting to compare these figures with the previous ones, because they highlight certain geographic and social characteristics. In Fig. 5(a), for example, there is

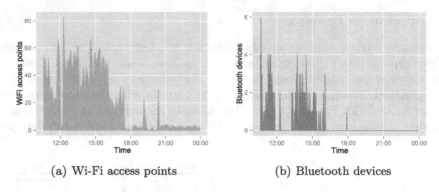

(a) Wi-Fi access points   (b) Bluetooth devices

Fig. 5. Geographic and social characteristics.

a huge difference in the number of Wi-Fi access points encountered before and after 18:00, suggesting that the participant visited two major places (in this case, a work environment and a domestic one). It is also interesting to observe the dip around 12:00, which is when the participant visited the shopping centre. The participant's movement, by car around 18:00 and while running between around 19:00 and 20:00, is also indicated by some slight spikes that we are often associated with travel: the more a participant moves, the more he comes into proximity with different access points. However, these figures do not provide a particularly accurate information base for estimating the participant's social interactions. To do this, in the following section, we compare activities and social interactions among the participants.

6   Comparing Participants

If the recognition of user activity is an essential step that we can approach with great accuracy, another critical step is to compare several participants. In this section, we introduce novel visual representations, allowing comparison of the 13 participants in the study.

Figure 6 is a 3D plot showing the distribution of types of activity following three different axes. The first reflects the proportion of time the participants were inactive (e.g. sitting). Because the measurements were taken during workdays, the proportion is very high and goes from 63 % (P13) to 90 % (P8). The second reflects the proportion of time the participants were active and were performing an activity (e.g. walking, running). This number distinguishes two categories: those with a sporting activity outside of work and those who are required to move (e.g. to meetings). The third axis reflects the proportion of time the participants were aboard a vehicle. This number is the lowest, and corresponds mainly to journeys between work and home. However, participants such as P10 or P11 have work activities involving frequent trips during the day (e.g. to move from one campus to another). Finally, note that the size of a bubble is proportional to the sum of all acceleration recorded by the watch. Thus, a small bubble indicates very little sports activity while a larger bubble indicates more frequent, abrupt movement (e.g. running).

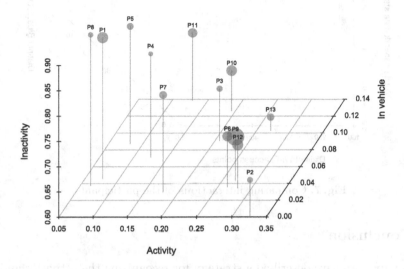

Fig. 6. Comparing activities of the participants.

Figure 7 uses the same principle as the previous figure but is based on three network metrics. First, the average mobile network data state tends to 0 if the mobile phone is connected to a Wi-Fi access point and it tends to 1 if the mobile phone uses cellular data. As the devices are set up only to connect to workplace access points (Table 2), this value is a good indicator of whether the user is more likely to be in the workplace or outside. The number of different access points gives us information about geographic locations visited by the participants. If two people are working in the same place, the participant with the higher value is moving around more and coming into contact with more access points. Finally, the number of distinct devices encountered gives us a measure of the interaction that the participants have. The higher this number, the more devices (a proxy for people) the person has encountered during his or her recording session.

Comparing the two graphs allows us to make some interesting observations. For example, participant P9 seems to perform more physical activity than anyone else, judging from his relatively high activity rate. Moreover, looking at Fig. 7, we find that P9 does not spend much time at the workplace, as he or she encounters the lowest number of access points. Conversely, participant P7 was mainly working during the study and hardly moved at all. Participant P4 is an interesting case, since he or she seems to have been in a vehicle and been in the proximity of a large number of access points. This indicates movement through many public spaces or buildings.

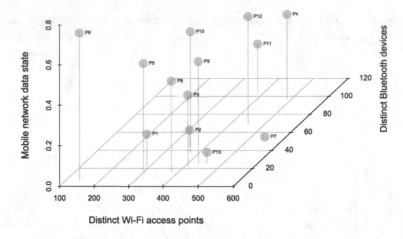

Fig. 7. Comparing interactions of the participants.

7 Conclusion

In this paper, we have described a strategy for recognizing the activities and the contexts within which a user is located. Our results show that using a condensed data set, along with energy-efficient sampling parameters, has the advantage of being easy to use with a classification algorithm such as SVM. Moreover, as such a structure implies lower transmission, harvesting and recording frequencies, it allows energy savings (resulting in an autonomy of about one day using our sensing system). We then showed that using a smartwatch in addition to traditional smartphones leads to better detection accuracy, in particular regarding physical activities such as running (100 % accuracy over our dataset) or walking (95.8 %). In addition, as these wearables are permanently on the user's wrist, they can detect specific activities without the help of any smartphone (e.g. tennis). Overall, the use of multimodal metrics as advanced feature sets for an SVM model allows the recognition of nine user-defined activities and five contexts, with an average accuracy greater than 90 %. Finally, we presented a new approach that graphically compares the activity and social relations of different users, allowing a better understanding of their behaviour.

The relatively small number of participants and their often vague answers to the questionnaire prevented us from expanding our data set. However, the study suggests great potential for the detection of personal activities if carried out on a wider sample group of users. In future work, in addition to using new devices and extending our energy saving strategy, we plan to carry out similar tests on a larger scale, performing new experiments and/or using public data sets. This will not only allow us to use other learner types and refine our classification model (e.g. adding FFT-based features), but also to accumulate a more extensive activity database that can be used as training set. We also plan to extend our study to capture user activities and contexts on a weekly basis, which would further help us to recognize patterns and characteristics specific to each user.

References

1. Xu, C., Pathak, P.H., Mohapatra, P.: Finger-writing with smartwatch: a case for finger and hand gesture recognition using smartwatch. In: Proceedings of the 16th International Workshop on Mobile Computing Systems and Applications, pp. 9–14. ACM (2015)
2. Tilenius, S.: Will An App A Day Keep The Doctor Away? The Coming Health Revolution. Forbes CIO Network (2013)
3. Campbell, A.T., Eisenman, S.B., Lane, N.D., Miluzzo, E., Peterson, R.A.: People-centric urban sensing. In: Proceedings of the 2nd annual international workshop on Wireless internet, p. 18. ACM (2006)
4. Burke, J.A., Estrin, D., Hansen, M., Parker, A., Ramanathan, N., Reddy, S., Srivastava, M.B.: Participatory sensing. In: Center for Embedded Network Sensing (2006)
5. Lane, N.D., Miluzzo, E., Lu, H., Peebles, D., Choudhury, T., Campbell, A.T.: A survey of mobile phone sensing. IEEE Commun. Mag. **48**(9), 140–150 (2010)
6. Yang, F., Wang, S., Li, S., Pan, G., Huang, R.: MagicWatch: interacting & segueing. In: Proceedings of the ACM International Joint Conference on Pervasive and Ubiquitous Computing: Adjunct Publication, pp. 315–318. ACM (2014)
7. Faye, S., Frank, R.: Demo: using wearables to learn from human dynamics. In: Proceedings of the 13th Annual International Conference on Mobile Systems, Applications, and Services, pp. 445–445. ACM (2015)
8. Zheng, X., Ordieres-Meré, J.: Development of a human movement monitoring system based on wearable devices. In: The International Conference on Electronics, Signal Processing and Communication Systems (ESPCO 2014) (2014)
9. Bluetooth, S.: Bluetooth specification version 4.0. In: Bluetooth SIG (2010). http://www.bluetooth.org/en-us/specification/adopted-specifications
10. Rodrigues, J.G., Aguiar, A., Barros, J.: SenseMyCity: Crowdsourcing an Urban Sensor. arXiv preprint arxiv:1412.2070 (2014)
11. Cuervo, E., Balasubramanian, A., Cho, D.-K., Wolman, A., Saroiu, S., Chandra, R., Bahl, P.: MAUI: making smartphones last longer with code offload. In: Proceedings of the 8th International Conference on Mobile Systems, Applications, and Services, pp. 49–62. ACM (2010)
12. Honicky, R., Brewer, E.A., Paulos, E., White, R.: N-smarts: networked suite of mobile atmospheric real-time sensors. In: Proceedings of the Second ACM SIGCOMM Workshop on Networked Systems for Developing Regions, pp. 25–30. ACM (2008)
13. Hussain, S., Bang, J.H., Han, M., Ahmed, M.I., Amin, M.B., Lee, S., Nugent, C., McClean, S., Scotney, B., Parr, G.: Behavior life style analysis for mobile sensory data in cloud computing through MapReduce. Sensors **14**(11), 22001–22020 (2014)
14. Han, M., Lee, Y.-K., Lee, S., et al.: Comprehensive context recognizer based on multimodal sensors in a smartphone. Sensors **12**(9), 12588–12605 (2012)
15. Lu, H., Pan, W., Lane, N.D., Choudhury, T., Campbell, A.T.: Sound- Sense: scalable sound sensing for people-centric applications on mobile phones. In: Proceedings of the 7th International Conference on Mobile systems, Applications, and Services, pp. 165–178. ACM (2009)

16. Ma, L., Smith, D., Milner, B.: Environmental noise classification for context-aware applications. In: Mařík, V., Štěpánková, O., Retschitzegger, W. (eds.) DEXA 2003. LNCS, vol. 2736, pp. 360–370. Springer, Heidelberg (2003)
17. Sharma, V., Mankodiya, K., De La Torre, F., Zhang, A., Ryan, N., Ton, T.G.N., Gandhi, R., Jain, S.: SPARK: personalized parkinson disease interventions through synergy between a smartphone and a smartwatch. In: Marcus, A. (ed.) DUXU 2014, Part III. LNCS, vol. 8519, pp. 103–114. Springer, Heidelberg (2014)
18. Shin, D., Shin, D., Shin, D.: Ubiquitous health management system with watch-type monitoring device for dementia patients. J. Appl. Math. **2014**(2014), Article ID 878741, 8 (2014). http://dx.doi.org/10.1155/2014/878741
19. Porzi, L., Messelodi, S., Modena, C.M., Ricci, E.: A smart watch-based gesture recognition system for assisting people with visual impairments. In: Proceedings of the 3rd ACM International Workshop on Interactive Multimedia on Mobile & Portable Devices, pp. 19–24. ACM (2013)
20. He, Z., Liu, Z., Jin, L., Zhen, L.-X., Huang, J.-C.: Weightlessness feature–a novel feature for single tri-axial accelerometer based activity recognition. In: 19th International Conference on Pattern Recognition, ICPR 2008, pp. 1–4. IEEE (2008)
21. Kao, T.-P., Lin, C.-W., Wang, J.-S.: Development of a portable activity detector for daily activity recognition. In: IEEE International Symposium on Industrial Electronics, ISIE 2009, pp. 115–120 (2009)
22. Qian, H., Mao, Y., Xiang, W., Wang, Z.: Recognition of human activities using SVM multi-class classifier. Pattern Recogn. Lett. **31**(2), 100–111 (2010)
23. Wu, J., Pan, G., Zhang, D., Qi, G., Li, Shijian: Gesture recognition with 3-D accelerometer. In: Zhang, D., Portmann, M., Tan, A.-H., Indulska, J. (eds.) UIC 2009. LNCS, vol. 5585, pp. 25–38. Springer, Heidelberg (2009)
24. Jain, A.K.: Data clustering: 50 years beyond K-means. Pattern Recogn. Lett. **31**(8), 651–666 (2010)
25. Bishop, C.M.: Pattern Recognition and Machine Learning. Springer, New York (2006)
26. Dimitriadou, E., Hornik, K., Leisch, F., Meyer, D., Weingessel, A.: e1071: Misc Functions of the Department of Statistics (e1071), TU Wien (2011). http://CRAN.R-project.org/package=e1071
27. Bergstra, J., Bengio, Y.: Random search for hyper-parameter optimization. J. Mach. Learn. Res. **13**(1), 281–305 (2012)

Characterization of User's Behavior Variations for Design of Replayable Mobile Workloads

Shruti Patil, Yeseong Kim[(✉)], Kunal Korgaonkar, Ibrahim Awwal,
and Tajana S. Rosing

University of California San Diego, San Diego, USA
{patil,yek048,kkorgaon,iawwal,tajana}@ucsd.edu

Abstract. Mobile systems leverage heterogeneous cores to deliver a desired user experience. However, how these cores cooperate in executing interactive mobile applications in the hands of a real user is unclear, preventing more realistic studies on mobile platforms. In this paper, we study how 33 users run applications on modern smartphones over a period of a month. We analyze the usage of CPUs, GPUs and associated memory operations in real user interactions, and develop microbenchmarks on an automated methodology which describes realistic and replayable test runs that statistically mimic user variations. Based on the generated test runs, we further empirically characterize memory bandwidth and power consumption of CPUs and GPUs to show the impact of user variations in the system, and identify user variation-aware optimization opportunities in actual mobile application uses.

Keywords: Mobile device · User variation · Heterogeneous cores · GPU usage

1 Introduction

With growing expectations from mobile platforms, mobile SoCs utilize heterogeneous cores to deliver the desired performance within small power budgets. The compute cores in mobile SoCs comprise of CPUs, GPUs and custom hardware blocks (IP) such as DSPs, Multimedia Accelerators and Audio/Video decoders. Mobile CPU and GPU cores together are the second highest power hungry components after display components [3,17]. Architectural research efforts seek to optimize these cores, thus a way to characterize realistic workloads is needed so as to clarify the possible impacts of optimizations on actual device systems.

However, benchmarking them has been exceedingly challenging since mobile workloads are inherently interactive in nature. Real-world inputs must be user-initiated, therefore are subject to large variations in user behavior. User variations can arise from a number of factors, including differences in content type, speed and frequency of interactions. The subtle differences in these factors can affect the workload to a large extent. For example, in our initial study, Facebook use cases exhibit a 16–93% utilization range in GPU acceleration for different

© Institute for Computer Sciences, Social Informatics and Telecommunications Engineering 2015
S. Sigg et al. (Eds.): MobiCASE 2015, LNICST 162, pp. 51–70, 2015.
DOI: 10.1007/978-3-319-29003-4_4

factor combinations. Thus, to evaluate the effectiveness of an optimization, we should consider the variations in real user behavior. A popular approach is to prototype new ideas and deploy them in a user study. However this approach has several shortcomings. First, a before-and-after comparison is not possible due to replayability issues. Thus, ideas that cannot be easily prototyped (e.g. hardware optimizations) could not be rigorously evaluated. Moreover, it is not always possible to obtain representative samples of users from a user study.

Developing parameterized mobile benchmarks that can encompass a range of user variations is a viable solution to addressing such challenges. Mobile benchmark suites with replayable, interactive applications have been proposed recently [10, 11, 15]. These suites consist of popular mobile applications, and allow a small amount of parameterization to change user behavior. They still lack any model of realistic user behavior or user variation. Tools [9] have been also developed to capture and replay user touch interactions allowing repeatable and interactive runs. However, these alternative cannot reproduce same workload due to other important factors, e.g., time-dependent content changes of webpages.

In this paper, we propose an analytic way to characterize realistic workloads in the wild and generate representative workloads of real mobile applications for replayable evaluation. We first study utilization of compute cores as a way to study the amount of user variations that is experienced by the system during a typical user session. To account for actual user variations, we analyze CPU and GPU usage statistics from 33 real users for seven most frequently used mobile applications over all applications executed in a month-long study. We first study the usage of CPUs, GPUs, and their interactions with main memory to understand how much and when power-intensive compute processors are used in interactive mobile applications.

We also focus on GPU usage to indicate the intensity of user interaction in mobile workloads. The use of GPU acceleration in gaming applications has been well-characterized [13, 14, 16], but GPU usage in general applications on modern mobile platforms is not yet well understood. We show that the GPU is widely used for hardware acceleration for rendering text and images, and for enabling smooth and responsive user interaction (UI). Thus, the amount of GPU acceleration during user sessions can be a good indicator of variations related to both content and interactions. In this study, we find that non-gaming applications such as browser and facebook utilize GPUs average 51 % of the time with a standard deviation of 27.5 during an interactive session. This non-trivial range in GPU acceleration occurs due to user-behavior driven variations.

Using a clustering analysis on our data, we find that the variations can be reduced to relatively few characteristic groups. We use our analysis to develop a framework to generate representative test turns that are parameterized for the intensity of user interactions desired. We complement our automated benchmark generation efforts with more realistic, replayable test runs, that reproduce user interactions to actual mobile devices. These runs statistically cluster with the user runs, maintaining clustering 'goodness' within 0.1–3.3 % of the user clusters.

In order to present the practical value of the replayable test runs, we then show detailed user-accounted analysis on mobile platforms. Through power and memory bandwidth evaluations, we find that user variations have a significant impact on these metrics. This shows that the use of the proposed replayable test runs allows realistic evaluations for debugging and testing of mobile systems, and also gives the guideline for user variation-oriented optimizations, for example, those that judiciously use mobile GPU acceleration and clock frequency adjustment depending on user behavior.

The overall contributions of this paper are as follows:

- We show that the differences in user behaviors result in significant variations in the utilization of the compute cores. This motivates user-based optimizations for interactive mobile workloads. This also shows the need to develop benchmarks that can incorporate and model user variations.
- We formulate an automated methodology to generate representative microbenchmarks, allowing us to study the specific effects of user variations. We also create realistic and replayable test runs that allow us to study the system under realistic usage patterns with user variations.

This paper is organized as follows: Sect. 2 discusses related work. Section 3 describes our experimental setup. Section 4 illustrates analysis from user study and Sect. 5 describes how test runs are created. Section 6 discusses the results from our characterization study. Finally, Sect. 7 concludes with the key take-away from our analysis.

2 Related Work

Numerous user studies have been previously undertaken on mobile systems. Long-term studies [5, 7, 19, 20, 22, 25] highlight the diversity of mobile users in terms of applications, frequency of use, duration, etc. These studies have uncovered traffic patterns, relationships between context and usage, power usage of mobile SoC units, which have aided optimization strategies. Our user study seeks to understand CPU and GPU utilization of mobile applications in short-term user interactive sessions. Previous studies lack information about simultaneous GPU acceleration used, which is the key to modeling our interaction and the focus of our study.

Unlike the workload of general multicore architectures [2], prior researches have shown that mobile systems are likely to be affected by how the user interacts with their devices [11]. Based on the interactive nature of the mobile device usage, architectural studies for mobile-specific workloads have also been recently proposed. Interactive applications covering genres such as browser, game, photo, video and chat have been designed with automatic scrolling or touch events [10,11,15]. Although these are interactive benchmarks, the interactions are not formally related to user behavior and there are no models for user variations. In this paper, we first study how these benchmarks can be adapted to the range of user variations that we have observed. For more accurate representation of user behavior, we create interactions with realistic speeds, which vary based on content, as expected from real users.

Table 1. Mobile Platform Specifications

	MSM8660 (45 nm)	MSM8960 (28 nmLP)
CPU	Up To 1.7 GHz, Dual-core Scorpion	Up To 1.7 GHz Dual-core Krait
3D GPU	Adreno 220	Adreno 225
Memory	Single-channel 500 MHz ISM, 333 MHz LPDDR2	Dual-channel 500 MHz LPDDR2
Android OS	Ice Cream Sandwich	Jelly Bean
Example Devices	HTC Evo 3D, LG Optimus, SS Galaxy Note	SS Galaxy S3, Nokia Lumia 1020, Sony Xperia V

Prior mobile core characterization studies have typically focused on single cores. Publications presented in [10,11,15,24] utilize proposed workloads for detailed CPU characterization with performance counters. One recent effort [8] studies thread-level parallelism in a mobile multi-core environment. Their findings suggest that while two CPU cores are sufficient to parallelize popular use cases in mobile benchmarks, GPU acceleration is limited. However, a single workload is executed for each mobile application to draw conclusions about its nature. In our study, we find that user variation significantly varies the utilization of multiple cores, in particular the GPU hardware acceleration significantly influenced by different factors such as content types and user interactions.

Mobile GPU studies have focused on gaming applications since they are known to be both GPU-intensive and power-intensive. A few publications [13,14,16] show the bottlenecks in GPU pipelines, while [1,4,18] propose power management schemes that trade-off on user experience. Recent efforts have studied general-purpose benchmarks such as image rendering and computer vision algorithms using GPGPUs in mobile systems [12,23]. In contrast, this paper characterizes CPU, GPU and memory interactions focusing on non-gaming applications. We show the large amount of GPU acceleration used, and its impact on power consumption. While power characterization could be performed in a field study, creating replayable test runs tied to user behavior allows comparison of metrics measured separately, as well as for future architectural research.

3   Experimental Setup

Development phones from two state-of-the-art mobile platforms, Qualcomm's MSM8660 and MSM8960 running Android OS (Table 1) were used in our study. These allowed fine-grained power and memory bandwidth measurements within the system, normally unavailable on commercial phones. Both phones support camera, bluetooth and sensors, and have dual-core CPUs, two 2D GPUs for vector graphics and one 3D GPU for 3D graphics. 33 on-campus students[1] used the phones for a month, with full access to Amazon Android App Store. During the user study, the users were asked to use the device for one month without any detailed usage direction, so they could use the device and applications as usual. Sim cards were not used, instead wi-fi network access was available throughout campus. Since the focus was to observe the range of user variations experienced by the cores for mobile applications, lack of cellular usage does not significantly affect the results of compute core usages for the studied applications.

The rooted Android phones were instrumented to record utilization and frequency every 100 ms during short-term interactive sessions, i.e. when a user engages with the phone for a short duration of either seconds or minutes to complete activities using a mobile application. Unlike long-term user studies [20, 22], e.g. targeted to daily application usage patterns, the short-term analysis allows to understand fine-grained system activities such as detailed CPU and GPU usages. The utilization and frequency of the CPUs and GPUs were profiled during these sessions, using information obtained from the /sysfs and /proc file system support. Power saving features were active on the phones, including DVFS (Dynamic Voltage and Frequency Scaling) and *mpdecision* daemon, which power-gates a CPU core when possible. Further detailed characterization was performed on the Qualcomm 8960 phone. Power measurements were obtained using Qualcomm's Trepn tool [21] which collects power consumption of system components such as per-core power using hardware sensors. Finally, memory bus monitoring was carried out using an internal bus monitor tool.

Users ran a total of 125 applications (or 'apps') on their devices during the one month study. Of these, we selected seven highest used applications for detailed analysis so that collected information of the selected apps sufficiently represent device usage of the app for each user. These include the interactive applications: Browser, Facebook and Email, streaming applications: Skype, Camera and Music and Templerun2 game. Browser, Email, Music and Camera represent widely used mobile applications. Similarly, Facebook, Skype and Templerun2 feature in the top 50 Android apps on Google Play.

4   Analysis of User Workloads

To explore the CPU and GPU usage of the applications, we analyze the temporal utilization data from the user study. Different sessions varied in duration, therefore we analyze the relative amount of time the CPUs and GPUs used within each session, and classify the quantified workload of compute cores of each session into different clusters. We first analyze usage into 16 combinations of the two cores (c0,c1), one 2D GPU (g2) and the 3D GPU (g3) for the target platforms described in Table 1 (Second 2D GPU showed negligible utilization and is neglected in the further study). This reduced each session to a 16-valued

---

[1] The study participants include undergraduate and graduate students. Even though we collected the data from the on-campus students, we could find a wide range of variations in mobile usages.

vector, where each value denotes the proportion of session time when a core combination had non-zero utilization. For example, combination (c0,g3) is the proportion of session time with active CPU0 and GPU3D and inactive CPU1 and GPU2D. Using these vectors, characteristic clusters for the sessions can be derived with k-means clustering analysis [6]. Each cluster is a closely-knit group of data points, with high separation from other clusters. This translates into a standard 'goodness' metric for clusters:

$$\text{Goodness} = \frac{\text{Variation between clusters}}{\text{Total Variation in Data}}$$

where the variation is computed as sum-of-square distances between groups of clusters and within each cluster. We select k, which specifies the number of clusters to identify, such that the clustering goodness is at least 80 % in all of our analyzes. Thus, we could capture at least 80 % of the variation by choosing this criterion. The analysis is performed at intra-app and inter-app levels to study the per application user variations, and overall degree of user variations.

4.1   Intra-App

Figure 1 shows examples of two user runs in each cluster generated for Browser. This presents the eleven representative clusters of core combinations in order of the right stacked labels while the other rare combinations are grouped as 'others'. 105 sessions were grouped into 5 clusters with 81 % clustering ratio. Since CPU0 is the master core, it is utilized throughout the active portions of the runs. Browser runs used one or more GPU cores (as 'GPU Used' label denotes) an average 46 % of the session time with a standard deviation of 21. This shows that mobile browser activities are highly using GPU acceleration, which varies dramatically with the variation in user behavior. Figure 2 shows the average proportion of time which the core combinations are utilized in clusters for the other six most used applications. There are up to 36 sessions within a cluster. Facebook, Templerun, Skype and Email use GPUs average 50 % time in sessions. The variance in their use of 3D GPUs show the impact of user behavior on GPU acceleration exercised. Music and Camera, due to their use of DSP and Audio/Video accelerators instead of GPU, appear to be CPU dominant.

Typical core usage of applications illustrates their expected energy draw. Music tends to use a single CPU core (and an accelerator) while Skype or Templerun require 2–4 cores for majority of the time in their respective sessions. Thus, a 30-min Skype or Templerun session draws more battery power than a 30-min Music session. We study the power usage in Sect. 6. The user variation as experienced by the cores is significant. The number of sessions per application ranged from 24 to 105, with the exception of Camera, which had 9. The user sessions are distilled into relatively few clusters representing the dominant variations. We leverage these representative groups to study the applications closely through detailed characterization and to develop our automated generation of replayable test runs.

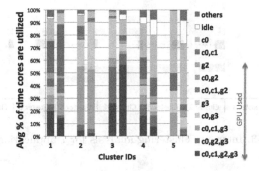

Fig. 1. Browser clusters with two different runs for each cluster

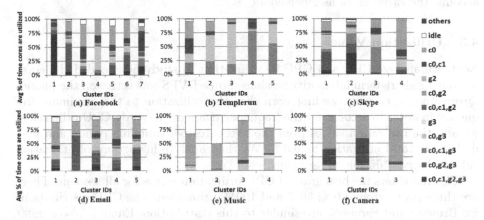

Fig. 2. Clusters for user sessions for 6 most used apps out of 125 total

4.2 Inter-App

We next perform clustering analysis on all user sessions to extract patterns in the resource usage independent of the applications. Goodness ratio of 80 % divides data into seven clusters using k-means analysis. Figure 3 shows the split of the sessions of the seven applications in seven clusters. Sessions from different applications show many similarities with each other. For example, Cluster 1 captures heavily GPU-accelerated sessions (80 % or more GPU usage) from Browser, Templerun and Skype. Cluster 4 has the sessions that used GPU3D for an average 76 % of the time, while Cluster 5 grouped sessions that used GPU2D for an average 52 % of the time. The rest of the clusters represent subtle differences in their proportions of GPU acceleration.

We make two key observations from these results: First, the clusters with gaming sessions also contain sessions from non-gaming applications. This shows that GPU acceleration in non-gaming applications is not negligible. Second, Templerun, Facebook and Browser sessions split into 5–6 of the total 7 clusters showing the prevalence of user variations. Thus, in order to thoroughly evaluate

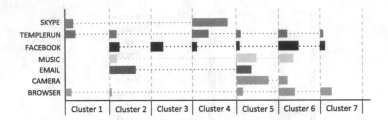

Fig. 3. Inter-app clustering analysis for 7 applications

actual workloads interacted with users, this shows that we must take into explicit account the variation of user behaviors.

4.3   Utilization Values

Next, we analyze CPU and GPU3D utilization to study how loaded the cores are during short-term interactive sessions. Since DVFS was active on the phones during the experiment, we first normalize the utilization to the maximum frequency in order to account for the frequency changes. To study CPU utilization, we add the utilization values from the two cores per sampling period and normalize the total utilization to 100 %. We then analyze histograms of utilization values observed during all user runs.

Figure 4 shows the histogram of CPU utilization values for all sessions. There are three peaks around 0 %, 50 % and 100 % utilization. The CPU distributions for Browser and Facebook are similar to this distribution. Email is also similar in that it shows the three peaks, but has higher idle values than the other peaks. The result presents the interactive nature of mobile workloads. For example, the highest peak for idle periods represent that there were no user interactions to be processed. Thus, this implies that workloads of compute cores are significantly affected by how long users interact with applications, reaffirming the observation that user behaviors highly influence to the system usage.

The GPU distribution of all applications except Templerun are similar to each other, shown by the example of Skype in Fig. 4c. Skype shows a small spike at 100 % utilization, not seen in the other applications. This presents that Skype-like video chat applications use relatively high GPU acceleration compared to other interactive apps, and therefore chat applications similar to Skype should be included in GPU characterization studies along with gaming and graphics applications. Templerun shows a more interesting GPU3D distribution (Fig. 4d). Although it peaks at 0 %, the game exhibits non-significant utilization over the full range of GPU3D utilization.

When all applications are considered together, we observe that GPU3D utilization seldom exceeded 60 % as shown in Fig. 4b. Further, the average GPU utilization across the seven applications was 16 %. The results present that, although our analysis of active cores shows an average 50 % use of GPUs during interactive sessions, the actual load experienced by the GPU3D is low. Thus, in

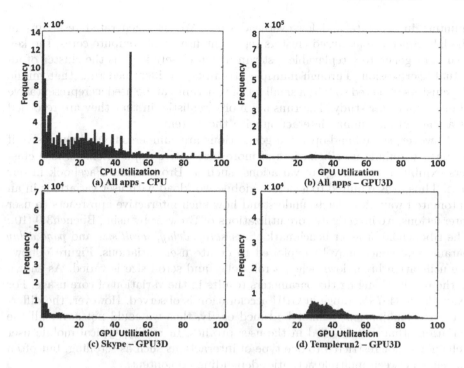

Fig. 4. Histograms of core utilizations for all user sessions

order to save GPU power, more intelligent power gating techniques for GPUs will be effective, such as turning off individual streaming cores and allowing shorter time scale in power gating.

5 Automated Test Run Generation

To reliably analyze the impact of user behavior on heterogeneous processing, we require replayable test runs that are representative of the observed diversity. Previous efforts in mobile benchmarking have proposed workloads with popular applications [10,11,15], but their inputs have not been associated with user behavior. We first explore how these interactive benchmarks can be adapted to exhibit our observed user variations. Then, to simulate more realistic user behavior, we generate new test runs that match the principal characteristics of user clusters with more than 80 % goodness with an aggregate clustering analysis. This provides a real user basis and creates representative variations for more accurate evaluation.

5.1 Automated Generation of Test Runs

The test runs are designed to be replayable using a record- and-replay utility [9]. This allows statistical rigor with multiple runs and collecting data from various counters in separate and low-overhead runs. We first generated test runs in the lab. Since the analyzed clusters represent usages of compute cores, the key goal is to generate a replayable test run which closely matchs the cluster of an actual user session. Through multiple attempts, we identified runs that mimic the clusters observed so that a small set of test runs can be used as representative of our larger user study. The runs are more 'realistic' in that they are recorded as a trace of real human interaction with the system.

However, these hand-operated generations are cumbersome and expensive if we need to mimic user behaviors of more interactive applications, whose clusters exhibit a wide range of variations, such as Browser and Facebook in our case. Thus, it is required to generate mobile workload with user variations in an automated way. In order to understand how such interactive app reacts to user interactions, we investigate core utilizations of Browser by using Bbench3.0 [10]. The Bbench3.0 browser benchmark offers *scroll delay*, *scroll size* and *page delay* parameters, which may be exploited to create user variations. Figure 5 shows the utilization breakdown when scroll delay and scroll size is varied. As shown in the result, changing the parameters results in the variation of core usage. For example, a 34–78 % range in GPU acceleration is observed. However, the different core combinations cannot be tuned easily, thus we could not cover all the variations that we observed in the user profiles. In reality, typical mobile user behavior is not restricted to one type of interactions such as scrolling, but often switches between multiple activities depending on content.

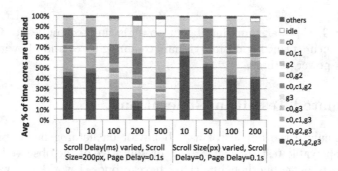

Fig. 5. Core utilization of BBench with different scrolling parameters

Thus, we further profile more detailed characteristics for diverse common interactions in Browser and Facebook by creating different microbenchmarks. We explore the actions of scrolling (down), browsing through photos (scrolling horizontally) and video viewing, and vary the speed of interaction (scrolling delay, scrolling size) and contents being viewed (images, text, images and text). Figure 6 describes the experimental results of clusters for different microbench-marks in the Browser app. The result shows that the speed of interaction (scroll delay) impacted the amount of GPU acceleration most, however core combinations were impacted by the variation in the content. In addition, the profiled

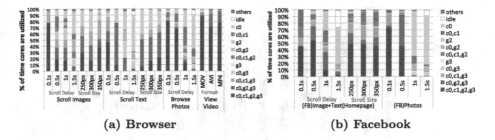

(a) Browser   (b) Facebook

Fig. 6. Clusters for common interactions of two mobile applications

microbenchmarks exhibit a wide range of variations in compute cores. In Fig. 6b, we show the example of Facebook use cases. Although common interactions vary for different applications, we found the similar observation that the speed of user interactions significantly affect GPU usage. We also observed the wide variations, for example, 10–90 % in GPU acceleration.

Using the profiled microbenchmarks which allow creating different workloads, we develop a framework to automatically generate mobile test runs to with user variations. We exploit the CPU-GPU profiles of microbenchmarks as a library of scenarios. The library creation can be repeated for other applications of interest. These are then combined in a calculated mix to generate a desired proportion of CPU-GPU interaction, that represents a target level of user interactions. This can be framed as the following optimization problem (1):

$$\underset{x}{\text{minimize}} \quad \|Ax - b\| + \lambda|x|$$
$$\text{subject to} \quad 1 \geq x_i \geq 0$$
$$\sum_i x_i = 1 \tag{1}$$

where $\mathbf{A}$ is the matrix representing the library of interactions, $\mathbf{b}$ is the desired core utilization profile, and $\mathbf{x}$ is the proportion of the test run that each microbenchmark is used. λ is a regularization constant used to encourage sparsity. In our case, the profiled compute core usage of each microbenchmark, which is a vector for the time percentage of each cluster, is given by a column of the matrix $\mathbf{A}$, while a cluster profile of an actual user workload is set to $\mathbf{b}$. Then, this optimization problem computes a vector $\mathbf{x}$ that contains the proportion of each scenario to be executed.

These proportions form the parameters of a MonkeyRunner script that consists of the automated inputs for each microbenchmark. The resultant script drives the workload on the Android system. Figure 7 shows an example of generated CPU-GPU profiles for a range of desired GPU acceleration. GPU usage observed is within ±3.3 % of the desired usage. High GPU acceleration characterizes high user engagement and vice-versa. Thus, the range of inputs can model the behavior of a vast range of users, from a power user to a light user.

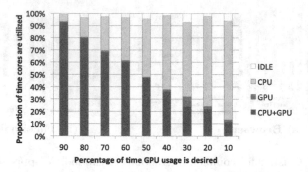

Fig. 7. Generating runs with varying intensity of user interactions

5.2 Comparison with User Workloads

Table 2 lists the interactions that comprise each test. The test runs use a combination of common interactions within a 3–6 min session for the apps. Templerun is not replayable due to the game dynamics, instead the test constitutes a 4-min play. We also include the BBench (BB) benchmark in the characterization, which matches a Browser cluster closely as shown.

Table 2. User Interactions in Test Runs

		Interaction
Browser	$B1$	Search for a Video, Play a Youtube video(A), Scroll while video is playing(B), Scroll while video is stopped(C).
	$B2$	Search for pictures, swipe through full-screen pictures from Google images(A), Scroll through the image results(B).
	BB	Display and scroll through webpages from 11 sites provided in BBench3.0 [3], with 1 s page delay, 0.5s scroll delay, 200px scroll size in 5 iterations.
Facebook	$F1$	View albums and pictures in a profile
	$F2$	View a video that plays within the app(A), view photos(B), view a video that plays on an external website in Browser(C).
Email	$E1,E2$	Quick scrolling through four emails multiple times (two text emails, one email with inline photos and one email with a single link that is viewed but not clicked).
Skype	$S1$	5 min Skype call: 1 min guest video on, 2mins host front camera on, 1 mins host back camera on.
Templerun	$T1$	A 4 min play, with 4–5 instances of lost game lives.
Music	$M1$	Play-Pause-Play music for 2mins each.
Camera	$C1$	3 min video capture with zoom-in/out

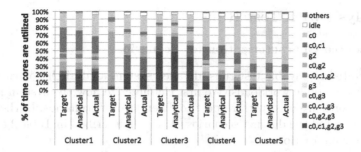

Fig. 8. Comparing automated test run generation for clusters

Figure 8 illustrates the use of the framework to generate the average clusters observed with the Browser app in our user study. The GPU usage in the analytical profile is within $\pm 2\%$ of the desired profile, while that in the observed profile is within $\pm 5\%$ of the desired profile, for all clusters except Cluster-2. In these clusters, the library of microbenchmarks was also able to closely match the various core combinations in the desired profile. In Cluster-2, with our current library profiles, the total GPU usage in the best library combination was 13% lower than the average GPU usage in the cluster. With a richer library, such clusters can be matched better.

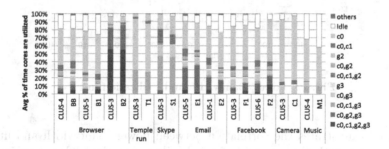

Fig. 9. Replayable test runs for 7 apps and clustered with user runs

We cluster replayable runs of all test apps along with user runs for the same number of clusters as before, ensuring that test runs cluster with user data while maintaining $\geq 80\%$ goodness ratio. Figure 9 shows the replayable test runs that match different clusters as denoted by 'CLUS' in short. Test runs are compared to closest matching data runs according to distance criterion to show similarity with real user runs. For each application, the difference in goodness ratio after test runs were added was $0.1\text{--}3.3\%$, meaning that the replayable test runs can represent the use of compute cores.

6   Analysis with Test Runs

6.1   Resource Characterization for Scenarios

With generated replayable test runs, detailed system analysis becomes possible
under realistic mobile workloads. We first characterize how the system resource
of compute cores are used with respect to different user scenarios. In the experiment, we exploited the distinct scenarios (A, B, C) described in Table 2 to replay
different user interactions.

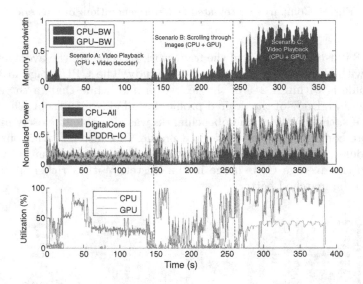

Fig. 10. Power, Bandwidth and Utilization in F2

Figure 10 illustrates the correlation between power, bandwidth and utilization, best seen with the example of $F2$. While video playback occurs in both
scenarios A and C, the system experiences lower core usage in A (in-app playable
video) than C (youtube video playback in browser). This translates into lower
memory bandwidth requirements and power dissipation of the cores. GPU memory bandwidth scales with the GPU utilization. Power measurements include the
power consumption from other digital core components such as video decoder,
but show a similar scaling.

6.2   Memory Bandwidth and User Interaction

We then analyze the memory bandwidth requirements of the applications. Our
systems embed LPDDR memory shared between compute cores, enabling CPU
and GPU interactions. Figure 11 shows the temporal memory bandwidth usage
of test runs measured on LPDDR links with the CPU and GPU. The bandwidth

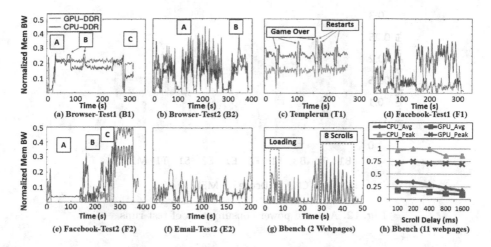

Fig. 11. Memory bandwidth usage by CPU and GPU for six applications and Bbench scrolling

is normalized to the peak total bandwidth experienced by the system across all runs. Specific interaction scenarios described in Table 2 are annotated.

We observe that while Templerun game shows a constant use of GPU acceleration, even the non-gaming applications show frequent memory transfers. This suggests fine-grained interactions with the CPU. To probe deeper, we profile memory bandwidth during slow browser scrolling (delay = 2 s) in Bbench. Figure 11g shows an experiment with two webpages (bbc and slashdot). Each scroll generates a CPU and GPU spike, highlighting its use of GPU acceleration. User 'wait' events in Bbench, $B2$, $E1$ and $E2$ are experienced as bandwidth dips on GPU ports. When scrolling was profiled at varying speeds (Fig. 11h), the GPU peak bandwidth did not change significantly, but average GPU bandwidth experienced by the system decreased by ∼14 % as scroll delays doubled. This suggests that predicting scroll action and its delays could allow for shaving off GPU bandwidth spikes for slow interactions without affecting user experience.

We make several other observations from these results: One, browser session $B1$ and Templerun, $T1$ show comparable memory bandwidth use. $B1$ is actively playing a video, but shows clear peaks in bandwidth when scrolling (events B,C). Similarly, the GPU bandwidth of email $E1$ and $E2$ approach the average bandwidth of $B1$ and $T1$ during routine scrolling events. This indicates that the GPU bandwidth requirements of UI engine are often higher than those needed for the gaming application, which presents an opportunity for optimization. Two, the memory bandwidth of CPU and GPU were quite different during the video and photo viewing actions in Browser and Facebook. F1 used 3x higher CPU than GPU bandwidth for photo viewing, while with B2 they were comparable. This may be imputed to both content and the application differences, however it is dramatic for essentially a similar type of user interaction. The interactive Email application also uses 3D UI to render emails, requiring GPU bandwidth

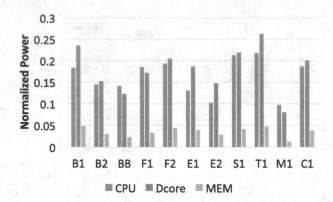

Fig. 12. Average power consumption of test runs

comparable to that of the CPU. Lastly, sudden bandwidth jumps are observed in Templerun at the end of a game, where the GPU bandwidth shoots up for the entire duration of the *'play again'* screen, although it displays static content. This suggests that game computations could be optimized for their use of CPU and GPU during this time. In all, due to the frequent GPU acceleration during the highly interactive applications, any optimization of the CPU-GPU interaction data path would be useful for performance or power improvements.

6.3 Impact on Power and Optimization

Figure 12 shows the relative power expended in the CPUs, GPUs and memory I/O in test runs. GPU power draw is inferred from Digital Core power rail which includes the GPUs, video decoder and modem digital core. Power is normalized to the maximum average battery power observed in all our tests. This occurred during Skype run due to wi-fi for video call. As conjectured in Sect. 4.1, the power consumption of the system depends on the types of cores used by the mobile applications (e.g. Templerun compared to Music) and is impacted by the user variations within an app.

The power consumption trends are well explained from the usage analysis of cores. As shown in Fig. 13a, the CPU and Digital Core (DC) power consumption of test runs is correlated with the proportion of time the CPUs and the 3D GPU are active respectively. By design, test runs from the same application showed distinct CPU-GPU usage based on user variation, and these differences clearly scaled the power consumption. Thus, the large range of GPU utilization observed due to user variation resulted in significantly large range of power consumption in GPU (45–100 % with respect to Templerun power.) This motivates the need to uncover more user behavior based optimizations for better power efficiencies. Applications at same utilization proportion require deeper analysis of the utilization levels to understand power consumption. For example, $B2$, $F1$ and $E2$ each show about 20 % 3D GPU usage, yet they consume varying amounts of power due to inter-app differences.

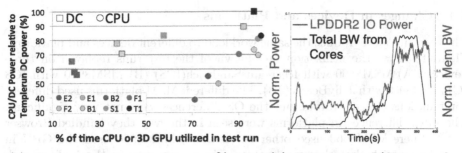

(a) **Power trends correlate to % time** (b) $F2$ **memory I/O power &**
cores are active   **bandwidth**

Fig. 13. Impact of user variation on optimization

Furthermore, the power consumption of memory I/O is also highly affected by user interactions. As shown in Fig. 13b, the LPDDR2 IO power is correlated to the amount of IO accesses. Since memory bandwidth trends are changed by the speed of user interactions as discussed in Sect. 6.2, this suggests that the memory system can utilize the remained bandwidth by considering user interactions.

When normalized to their respective average battery power, CPUs, digital cores and memory consume about 50 % of the average battery power across all test runs. Since these power measurements include the effect of the on-demand Linux governor for DVFS and mpdecision, we further investigate how the user interaction variations affect the optimization policy behavior. Figure 14 shows three example benchmarks with varied user interaction intensity. Using the Opt-OFF case, which the frequencies of two cores are maintained at the maximum level with Performance Governor, as the baseline, we compared to the Opt-ON case that the two cores are controlled by Android Linux default CPU management policy, i.e., Ondemand Governor and Mpdecision daemon. Power measurements on MSM8660 showed 8 − 15 % lower core power due to the effect of DVFS and mpdecision. This is again an example where replayability helped to compare power savings given 'real user-like' interactive sessions.

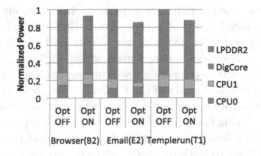

Fig. 14. Comparing savings due to power optimizations

6.4   Changes in Devices and Platforms

The test run can reproduce the same workload to different devices and platforms. Figure 15 shows the utilization breakdown of the test runs replayed on three devices: (A) MSM8660 with Icecream Sandwich(ICS) (B) MSM8960 with ICS (C) MSM8960 with JellyBeans (JB). The different MSM platforms used different combinations of accelerators, but the OS differences were not very significant. The most differences in platforms were seen in the way they handled Browser tests. Where MSM8660 used other accelerators, MSM8960 used the GPU in conjunction with the other accelerators. This is also seen in the MobileBench benchmarks of PhotoView and VideoView. MSM8960 also utilized the GPU cores more efficiently in that it avoided use of 2DGPU in Email and Bbench in contrast to MSM8660. Overall, the experiments show that different devices may use accelerators in different combinations, however, more recent platforms used higher amounts of GPU acceleration in most of the test runs.

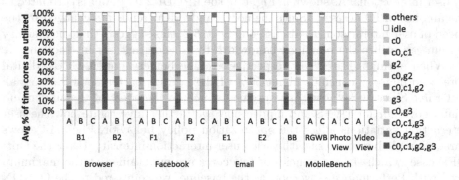

Fig. 15. Utilization breakdown of test runs on three devices

7   Conclusion

Mobile systems must provide rich user experience in extremely low power budgets. The demands placed on these heterogeneous cores in typical user scenarios are unclear, limiting usage behavior driven power and performance optimizations. In this paper, we analyze how real users utilize CPUs and GPUs and show the large amount of GPU acceleration used in non-gaming, interactive mobile applications. With a detailed study of the CPU-GPU-memory interactions under user behavior variation, we developed a framework that automatically generates replayable test runs. Using the replayable test runs which reproduce realistic user behaviors, we show the impact on memory bandwidth and power consumption, which suggests the need to optimize GPU acceleration for common interaction tasks.

Acknowledgments. This work was supported in part by TerraSwarm, one of six centers of STARnet, a Semiconductor Research Corporation program sponsored by MARCO and DARPA, National Science Foundation (NSF) award 1344153 and Qualcomm.

References

1. Arnau, J.-M., et al.: Parallel frame rendering: trading responsiveness for energy on a mobile GPU. In: PACT 2013 (2013)
2. Bogdan, P., Marculescu, R.: Workload characterization and its impact on multicore platform design. In: CODES+ISSS, pp. 231–240. ACM (2010)
3. Carroll, A., Heiser, G.: An analysis of power consumption in a smartphone. In: USENIXATC (2010)
4. Cho, C.-W., et al.: Performance optimization of 3D applications by opengl es library hooking in mobile devices. In: ICIS (2014)
5. Do, T.M.T., et al.: Smartphone usage in the wild: a large-scale analysis of applications and context. In: ICMI (2011)
6. Duda, R.O., Hart, P.E.: Pattern Classification and Scene Analysis. Willey, New York (1973)
7. Falaki, H., et al.: Diversity in smartphone usage. In: MobiSys, pp. 179–194 (2010)
8. Gao, C., et al. A study of mobile device utilization. In: ISPASS, pp. 225–234 (2015)
9. Gomez, L., et al.: RERAN: Timing- and touch-sensitive record and replay for Android. In: ICSE (2013)
10. Gutierrez, A., et al.: Full-system analysis and characterization of interactive smart phone applications. In: IISWC, pp. 81–90 (2011)
11. Huang, Y., et al.: Moby: a mobile benchmark suite for architectural simulators. In: ISPASS (2014)
12. Kim, S., et al.: Computing energy-efficiency in the mobile GPU. In: ISOCC, pp. 219–221 (2013)
13. Ma, X., et al.: Characterizing the performance and power consumption of 3D mobile games. In: Computer (2013)
14. Mochocki, B., et al.: Signature-based workload estimation for mobile 3D graphics. In: DAC (2006)
15. Pandiyan, D., et al.: Performance, energy characterizations and architectural implications of an emerging mobile platform benchmark suite. In: IISWC 2013 (2013)
16. Park, J.-G., et al.: Quality-aware mobile graphics workload characterization for energy-efficient DVFS design. In: ESTIMedia (2014)
17. Pathak, A., et al.: Where is the energy spent inside my app?: fine grained energy-accounting on smartphones with eprof. In: EuroSys, pp. 29–42 (2012)
18. Pathania, A., et al.: Integrated CPU-GPU power management for 3D mobile games. In: DAC (2014)
19. Peters, J.F.: Topology of digital images. In: Peters, J.F. (ed.) ISRL, vol. 63, pp. 1–76. Springer, Heidelberg (2014)
20. Shepard, C., et al.: Livelab: measuring wireless networks and smartphone users in the field. SIGMETRICS Perform. Eval. Rev. **38**(3), 15–20 (2011)
21. Trepn profiler. https://developer.qualcomm.com/mobile-evelopment/increase-app-performance/trepn-profiler
22. Trestian, I., et al.: Measuring serendipity: connecting people, locations and interestsin a mobile 3G network. In: IMC 2009 (2009)

23. Wang, G., et al.: Accelerating computer vision algorithms using opencl framework on the mobile GPU - a case study. In: ICASSP, pp. 2629–2633 (2013)
24. Wang, R., et al.: Architectural characterization and analysis of high-end mobile client workloads. In: ICEAC (2013)
25. Xu, Q., et al.: Identifying diverse usage behaviors of smartphone apps. In: IMC, pp. 329–344 (2011)

Worker Selection for Reliably Crowdsourcing Location-Dependent Tasks

Kevin Emery$^{(\boxtimes)}$, Taylor Sallee, and Qi Han

Department of Electrical Engineering and Computer Science,
Colorado School of Mines, Golden, CO 80401, USA
{kemery,qhan}@mines.edu, taylorsallee@gmail.com

Abstract. Obtaining accurate information about specific locations is of great importance to today's many crowdsourced smartphone applications. To verify information about a location, smartphone users are selected to go to the location and answer a yes/no question about the location. Our research focuses on the location-aware worker selection problem, which is the problem of selecting a group of workers who, together, can give the most accurate answer to the location-based question. We define the location-aware worker selection problem, mathematically formulate it, and then show that an optimal solution is exponential in time complexity. We present our heuristic solutions that take into account both the reliability of the users and the level of convenience for each user to complete the task. We evaluate and compare our approaches to three other heuristic algorithms via simulation.

Keywords: Crowdsourcing · Mobile sensing · Worker selection

1 Introduction

As the number of smartphone users worldwide continues to grow, the use of crowdsourcing applications has become increasingly prevalent. One important problem for many crowdsourcing applications is data verification; that is, when smartphone users provide information to a crowdsourced application, the data is not guaranteed to be accurate. One solution to this problem is to select users that are both willing and reliable enough to provide accurate information.

Many of today's mobile applications rely heavily on accurate location data. Take, for example, a coffee shop locator application that allows users to locate the nearest/cheapest/best coffee shop. In an app such as this, the quality of the user experience depends on the accuracy of location information. Many other applications benefit from knowing exactly where certain restaurants, shops, offices, etc. are located. Our research applies to two classes of location-based problems: one is location verification, where we believe a specific business is at a specific address, but we are not certain about the veracity of the information; and the second is information verification, where we believe a certain event is happening at an address (or a specific person is there, etc.), but we need to confirm the information.

© Institute for Computer Sciences, Social Informatics and Telecommunications Engineering 2015
S. Sigg et al. (Eds.): MobiCASE 2015, LNICST 162, pp. 71–86, 2015.
DOI: 10.1007/978-3-319-29003-4_5

Both of these classes of applications involve simply verifying information (i.e. they can be phrased as a yes/no question). Both classes also require someone to physically go to the address to answer the question. Crowdsourcing can be of great help in these applications. We propose to ask individuals near the address to physically go to the address to answer a question. Our research attempts to solve the "location-aware worker selection problem", which is essentially the question of finding the best individuals to select in the interest of answering a location-dependent question.

Selecting a group of workers to answer a question about a physical location comes with a set of unique challenges. First, to motivate people to respond to location-dependent queries, incentives need to be used. However, in the real world there is always a budget that limits the amount of money available to pay users as an incentive. We must choose a group of workers to pay in order to get the best possible answer to the location-based question, while staying under the budget constraint. Second, users are unlikely to respond to a query unless they are near the location in question. For this reason, we must consider workers' current locations and commute patterns to help us select the best workers. Finally, as with any worker selection problem, we must consider the reliability of our users and their responses and find a way to judge the accuracy of responses.

Problem Definition. We assume each worker is associated with a set of attributes: reliability rating, incentives needed, home location, work location, and current location. The reliability rating is a simple way to determine a worker's past response record. We use the home and work locations to determine a commute route for the worker, and this information is useful in determining how convenient completing the task would be for each worker. Informally, the location-aware worker selection problem can be defined as follows: given a yes or no question about a specific location, a set of workers that are reasonably near the location, and a budget to spend on incentives, find a subset of workers to dispatch to the location such that the answer given by the group as a whole is as accurate as possible.

Existing works have looked at worker selection, but as of yet, none have considered the location-aware worker selection problem, which is distinct because it requires workers to physically go to the location in question to perform a task. In addition, most previous works have only considered worker reliability in their selection process. Because our work is specific to physical locations, we consider a convenience factor for each worker. The addition of convenience to the problem adds additional complexity. This work makes the following contributions:

- We mathematically define the objective function that serves as a metric for evaluating solutions to the location-aware worker selection problem.
- We theoretically analyze the time complexity of an optimal solution for the problem.
- We propose RECON and CORE, two heuristics that seek to choose only workers that are both highly reliable and can respond to queries with a high level of convenience.

– We carry out extensive experiments to evaluate our proposed algorithms, comparing them to two other algorithms and showing that RECON out-performs others.

2 Related Work

Much research has already been done on various versions of the worker selection problem. Some call this problem the task assignment problem. Both of these problems involve distributing a set of tasks among a set of workers, hopefully in a way that gives the tasks to the users best-suited to perform them. Different worker selection algorithms have different goals. Some seek to maximize the reliability of the workers (this concept is explored in-depth in [8]), while others seek to minimize budget as in [5]. Our work is focused on maximizing the accuracy of the answers given by our selected workers. We have no time constraint, but we do have a budget constraint.

Many previous works focused on online crowdsourcing markets, such as Amazon's Mechanical Turk [1]. These online markets allow requesters to post tasks (sometimes called Human Interaction Tasks, or HITs) on the market, and then workers select the tasks they wish to perform. Many previous works focus specifically on efficient task allocation in online markets. For example, [4] attempted to allocate workers to tasks in a way that maximizes the benefit to the requester, and tested their algorithm on Mechanical Turk. In [2], the authors performed an experiment on CrowdFlower to test their CRITICAI algorithm, which determines the best human workers to assign a set of tasks to ensure reliable results while meeting real-time constraints.

Selecting reliable workers to answer a question is one step towards solving the truth estimation problem. The truth estimation problem is simply the problem of estimating the ground truth from a crowd-provided answer. Papers such as [3] discuss the challenges involved with resolving the truth in a crowdsourced application. When estimating the truth, choosing reliable workers will increase the probability of the majority vote being the ground truth. [9] used a streaming approach to solve the truth estimation problem. [7] studies a slightly different version of the truth estimation problem, which they call the "fact-finding problem". Both of these papers assume that workers give answers of unknown reliability, and finding the truth from the many answers may be a little more complex than simply using the majority vote.

Both the worker selection/task assignment problem and the truth estimation/fact-finding problem assume that more reliable workers will provide better responses, and that their responses can be trusted with a high level of confidence. None of the works so far have considered the convenience for the worker to actually perform the task. This paper shows that we can achieve better results when the convenience to the worker is considered in the algorithm.

None of the previous works mentioned have studied the location-based worker selection problem. They assume an online pool of workers that can perform tasks from their computer, without the need to travel and actually observe a physical location. Adding a physical location to the problem introduces additional complexity. Our work is unique in that it considers a worker's location, commute patterns, and historic reliability, and in that it requires workers to actually go to a physical location to perform the assigned task.

3   Our Approaches

To better formulate the location-aware worker selection problem, we describe the models we use to define and solve the problem.

3.1   Definition of Accuracy Metric

Since we rely only on the selected workers to determine the ground truth of our questions, we use a majority voting scheme to determine the "correct" answer to the location-based question. Other methodologies can be used to determine ground truth [3,7,9], but majority voting is the most common. In order to judge the correctness of any solution to this problem, a metric must be used. We propose to use the following scheme: given a set of workers, W, consisting of users who have provided an answer to the location-related question, the metric used to judge correctness is defined as the ratio of the number of users who agree with the majority vote over the total number of users in W. For example, if W contains 100 workers, and 78 of them agree that the answer to the given question is yes, then the metric will have the value .78, or 78 %. This implies that we seek to maximize the number of users who agree, because our goal is to be as sure as possible that the group has provided a correct answer. We call this metric the Majority Agreement Percentage (MAP).

We use pc_i to denote the probability of user i providing a correct answer for a given question. If each worker's pc_i value was the same (pc) the distribution of MAP values for different tasks would be a binomial distribution centered at pc. Because each user may potentially have a different value for their individual pc_i, a binomial distribution cannot be used. However, a binomial distribution is simply a special case of the more generic Poisson binomial distribution [10]. In a Poisson binomial distribution, each event in the model can be considered to have a unique probability, exactly like what we are dealing with when determining $MAP(W)$. Furthermore, because a poisson distribution is a normal distribution, the piece of the distribution that shows the most likely response for a group W is the mean. For a Poisson distribution, the mean value of the distribution is simply the sum of all of the individual probabilities that make up the distribution divided by the total number of probabilities. We now formally define the probabilistic formulation of MAP: $MAP(W) = \sum_{i=1}^{\|W\|} (pc_i)/\|W\|$.

3.2   Formal Problem Statement

Given a location L, a yes or no question Q about the location, a budget B to spend on incentives, a global set of users $U = \{u_1, ..., u_n\}$ where user i needs incentive I_i to go and find out the answer to the question and has a probability pc_i of responding correctly, find a set of workers $W = \{w_1, ..., w_m\}$ that contains at least m workers such that after all users in W have provided their answers to Q, MAP(W) is maximized. This is formulated mathematically as follows:

Maximize MAP(W)
subject to
1. $W \subseteq U$.
2. $\|W\| \geq m$
3. $B \geq \sum_{i=1}^{\|W\|} I_i$.

The first constraint basically requires that W must be a subset of U. This must always be true; we cannot have workers that are not part of the original user set. The second constraint is due to the fact that if the system was deployed in the real world, the person seeking the answer to the question would want to have a certain number of respondents in order to be confident in the response that they get. This constraint ensures that the set W containers at least as many workers as their minimum threshold specifies. The third constraint states that the sum of the incentives I_i paid to each worker in W must not exceed the budget B.

Time complexity analysis of an optimal solution In order to find the optimal solution to this problem, one must look at all possible subsets W where $\|W\| \geq m$. If we simplify that statement to only look at cases where $\|W\| = m$, then we need to look at $\binom{n}{m} = \frac{n!}{m!(n-m)!}$ different subsets. This can be expanded to $\frac{(n)(n-1)(n-2)...(n-m+1)(n-m)!}{m!(n-m)!}$ when $m \leq n/2$, and $\frac{(n)(n-1)(n-2)...(m+1)(m!)}{(n-m)!m!}$ when $m > n/2$, and from there they can simplified to $\frac{(n)(n-1)(n-2)...(n-m+1)}{m!}$ when $m \leq n/2$, and $\frac{(n)(n-1)(n-2)...(m+1)}{(n-m)!}$ when $m > n/2$. The reason for the split on $m = n/2$ is because when $m \leq n/2$ the $(n-m)!$ term is larger than the $m!$ term and therefore it is more efficient to cancel that term, while the opposite is true when $m > n/2$. The case where $m \leq n/2$ has a time complexity of $O(n^m)$ and the case where $m > n/2$ has a time complexity of $O(n^{n-m})$.

In order to look at the time complexity required to consider all possible subsets where $\|W\| \geq m$, it is just the summation of all of the discrete time complexities used for each value of $\|W\|$. The case where this is largest is where $m = n/2$, and this has a time complexity of $O(n^{n/2})$ which simplifies to $O(n^n)$. The optimal solution, therefore, has an exponential time complexity and cannot be solved in a reasonable amount of time. For this reason we propose our own heuristic algorithms.

3.3 Our Algorithms

When considering which users to choose to dispatch to a location, it is useful to know how reliable each user is. In other words, it is helpful to know their previous answer history. For this reason, we assume each user has a reliability rating, r_i. In addition, when considering which users to choose to answer the location-based question, it is prudent to choose workers close to the location in question. We go a step further and consider the overall convenience for the worker to respond, based on their normal movement patterns and current location. This is useful because users are more likely to respond to a task if it is very convenient for them. For each location-dependent task, we calculate a convenience factor, c_i, for each user that captures the convenience of completing the task. Note that while a user's reliability rating is an attribute of the user and independent of any single task, a user's convenience factor must be calculated for each task.

Model of User Reliability. We use the following scheme to track user reliability, r_i. We first assume each user u_i begins with a reliability rating of 0.5. When a task is created, a group of workers W is selected to perform the task. After getting responses from each of the selected workers in W, majority voting determines which workers in W gave the correct answer. Each worker's reliability is then dynamically adjusted as follows:

- If a worker in W gave a correct answer, he is awarded a reliability of 1 for that task.
- If a worker in W gave an incorrect answer, he is awarded a reliability of 0 for that task.
- The worker's new reliability rating is the average of all the reliability ratings for all tasks he has performed.

For example, a new worker who starts with a rating of 0.5 and is chosen to perform one task will have a new rating of 0.75 if he answers the task correctly, and a rating of 0.25 if he answers incorrectly. We can also take into account the case when a user does not respond, which does not fundamentally change our approach. Our reliability model can also be replaced with another such as [9].

Model of User Convenience. We use the following scheme to calculate the convenience factor, c_i, for a given user to perform a given task. This factor will be calculated for each location-based question. We assume each user u_i has a current location, a work location, and a home location. We then calculate the diameter of the city in question (the distance from top left to bottom right corner). The convenience factor c_i is then calculated for each worker as follows:

- Calculate the distance from the user's current location, d_c.
- Calculate the distance from the user's work location, d_w.
- Calculate the distance from the user's home location, d_h.
- Calculate the shortest distance from any point along the user's commute path, d_p.
- Calculate min = MIN(d_c, d_w, d_h, d_p).
- Calculate c_i = 1 - min/diameter

The convenience factor is clearly based on both the user's current location and their normal commute patterns. Note that because the convenience takes into account the diameter of the city in question, convenience values are always between 0 and 1, which normalizes convenience factors across different-sized cities. We acknowledge that this is a simplified model of user convenience. A more realistic model is to incorporate existing work studying people's commute or mobility patterns using either synthetic models or realistic traces, as well as map information.

Model of Incentive Scheme. As mentioned, we pay users an incentive to complete tasks. The sum of the incentives paid for a given task may not exceed the budget for that task. We use a monetary incentive, but this could easily be replaced by another type of incentive.

Choosing which users to pay and how much to pay them should be based on the probability that they will provide a correct response. Therefore, we pay users with a higher reliability rating more than we would a user with lower reliability. However, we must also consider the convenience for the user. If a user is very far away (has low convenience), we want to provide a larger incentive, so they do not feel like responding is a waste of time. We use the following incentive scheme that takes into account both user reliability and convenience: $I_i = k_1 * r_i + \frac{k_2}{c_i}$. This equation increases a user's incentive if they have a high reliability ranking and/or if they have a low convenience factor. This makes sense in a real-world situation because users who are further away (i.e., have low convenience) are less likely to give good answers, and users with higher reliability are more likely to give good answers.

Proposed Heuristics. Considering the NP-completeness of the problem, we propose two heuristics.

- RECON (REliable and CONvenient). For each location-based question, it first creates a group of high-convenience workers, with every worker in the group having a convenience factor no less than a certain threshold α. The value of α controls how selective RECON will be in choosing workers for W. A higher α means RECON chooses workers that are very close to the location in question, which means the incentives paid to those workers will be smaller, allowing the size of W to be larger. The algorithm then sorts the group in order of reliability rating. It then selects users for W in order of highest reliability to lowest, until the sum of the incentives paid to the users is as large as possible without exceeding the budget.

  RECON avoids picking users that have high reliability but low convenience, thereby improving the probability of the users in W providing a quality response. This algorithm chooses the users that are both highly reliable and conveniently located, so we can be confident they will produce an accurate response. Also, this algorithm is able to choose more users for each W, because users with a higher convenience are paid less than those with low convenience, assuming their reliability ratings are equal. Selecting more users for W is good, because it makes MAP(W) more precise. The larger $\|W\|$ is, the more confident we are that MAP(W) is a trustable number.

RECON has a complexity of $O(n + nlog(n))$, where n is the size of the user group U. The $nlog(n)$ piece comes from sorting the workers by reliability rating, and the additional n comes from walking through U and selecting only workers with a convenience greater than α.

– CORE (COnvenient and REliable). This heuristic is based on a similar model as RECON, but instead of focusing on selecting workers for W that have a high reliability rating, CORE instead focuses on using workers for which the location is most convenient. A subset of workers that have a reliability above a certain threshold β are selected, and then from those workers those with highest convenience are selected for W.

Similar to RECON, CORE has a computational complexity of $O(n+nlog(n))$, where n is the size of the user group U, because the users still need to be sorted in $nlog(n)$ by convenience and then in the worst case we need to look at all n workers to fill W.

4   Performance Evaluation

To evaluate our heuristics to the location-aware worker selection problem, we built a simulator in Java. We decided to use a simulator instead of a real-world deployment mainly because of the logistics involved in getting actual workers. We could not use Mechanical Turk or CrowdFlower, because these services are just people sitting at their computer, and the workers are not expected to leave their computer to go visit a location. We envision our algorithms being used for commercial crowdsourcing applications, where the workers would be users with a mobile app installed, and the location-based questions are for verifying that a certain business exists at the location in question, or a certain event is happening there.

4.1   Simulation Setup

The simulator takes a city (consisting of many locations and workers) and an algorithm as input. The simulator runs the given algorithm on every location in the city, pulling workers to populate W from the many workers within the city. Over time, the reliability ratings of the users change, since some users give good answers and some give bad answers.

The constants k_1 and k_2 used in the incentive mechanism are to change the weight of each factor, and we imposed the following limit on k_1 and k_2: $k_1 + k_2 = 10$. After running a few preliminary tests, we settled on the values $k_1 = 7$ and $k_2 = 3$. This means that we gave more weight to reliability in deciding the incentive, but give the convenience term the ability to grow indefinitely as the c_i value gets smaller and smaller. Basically, the smallest incentive a user can get is 3 cents (when $c_i = 1$ and $r_i = 0$, and although the largest incentive is uncapped (because c_i is in the denominator), our algorithms basically never choose a user with really low convenience, because the incentive for that user would be too high.

Our goal is to maximize the average MAP value for each group of selected workers W. In a real-world situation, we would know which workers gave correct responses once they had all responded. In our simulator, we need to model pc_i. In a real-world situation, the value of pc_i for each user would be unknown; however, in our model we assume that both convenience and reliability affect the worker's ability to respond correctly. The probability that each user chooses correctly for a given task is be determined as this: $pc_i = (1 - k_3 * (1 - c_i)) * (r_i)$. This equation primarily uses user reliability to determine pc_i, but it also takes into consideration the possibility that the user's convenience factor is low, which could potentially cause them to go to the wrong location and provide the wrong information. The frequency with which this occurs is accounted for in the constant k_3, and the value of this constant can be adjusted to add more weight to the convenience factor. For our simulations, we settled on a k_3 value of $1/8$. k_3 essentially represents how often the user gets lost, is unable to find the given location, or gets confused as to where they are and gives the wrong answer.

After a few preliminary tests of RECON, we set α to be 0.7, because we noticed that anything below 0.7 allowed too many low-convenience workers into the group. Similarly, after testing CORE the value for β was set to be 0.45. This allows new workers to be included in the chosen group, but if a worker provides more incorrect responses than correct responses then they are excluded from all future selections of W.

We test the performance of five different algorithms with the last three as baseline comparison. Each algorithm uses the aforementioned incentive scheme to determine how much each user will be paid for a specific task. The algorithms are listed below:

- RECON: An algorithm that sorts workers by reliability and then selects workers for W from highest reliability to lowest so long as the worker's convenience is greater than α
- CORE: An algorithm that sorts workers by convenience and then selects workers for W from highest reliability to lowest so long as the worker's convenience is greater than β
- RELIABLE: An algorithm that sorts the users in order of reliability rating, and selects workers for W from highest reliability to lowest, until the maximum number of workers have been selected while still under the budget constraint.
- CONVENIENT: An algorithm that sorts the users in order of convenience factor, and selects workers for W from highest convenience to lowest, until the maximum number of workers have been selected while still under the budget constraint.
- RANDOM: An algorithm that picks users randomly from the group U until the maximum number of workers have been selected while still under the budget constraint.

We assume each city contains a finite number of both locations and workers, with the number of workers being greater than the number of locations.

We wrote a city creator as part of our simulator. The city creator randomly distributes locations throughout a 2-dimensional space, and then randomly distributes workers throughout the same space. Each worker is assigned a permanent home and work location. Figure 1 shows what a small portion of a generated city would look like. Locations are red squares, workers are blue circles, home locations are green pentagons, and work locations are yellow triangles. Note that some workers are at home, some are at work, some are between their home and work locations, and some are just randomly distributed. The probability model we used to decide the workers' current locations is described below.

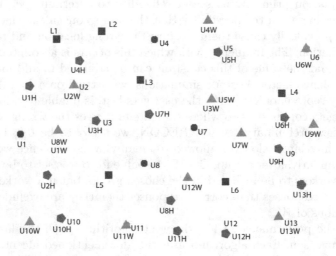

Fig. 1. A small portion of a city, showing 6 locations, 13 workers, and the home and work addresses of each worker (color figure online).

We tested each algorithm on three different cities, each with a different population density. The city width (1077 units), height (1077 units), and number of locations (1000) remained constant, with the worker population varying for each city. We decided to use this approach because the ratio of workers to shops for a given unit area is the most relevant factor for deciding the accuracy of a selection algorithm. For each city, we used three different budgets (100, 200, and 300 cents). We called these budgets low, medium, and high, respectively. The four city populations were 5K, 20K, 40K, and 60K workers. We named these cities sparse density, low density, medium density, and high density, respectively. Therefore, every algorithm was run on 12 different city/budget combinations. For each of the 12 distinct city/budget combinations, we ran 20 trials for each algorithm. Once the four different-density cities were created, we did not change them for the rest of the testing. This ensured that we ran the different algorithms on the same cities every time.

The simulator walks through every location in the city (which are distributed randomly), and for each location, runs the given algorithm on that location. The algorithm selects a group of workers W, and the workers provide a response, which is generated based on their pc_i value. The simulator then calculates MAP(W) for the group, records it, and moves on to the next location. As workers provide responses to the location-based questions, their reliability ratings are updated by the simulator (as previously discussed). Although the problem as defined only considers one task, any good algorithm will take into account the outcome of previous tasks, and seek to improve the MAP value of each task over time.

Simulating Worker Location. Before each location-based question is asked, each user's current location is calculated based on the following probability model:

- 32 % of the time, the worker is at work.
- 9 % of the time, the worker is commuting.
- 22 % of the time, the worker is away from home, but not at work or commuting. This is for leisure/social activities, travel, etc.
- 37 % of the time, the worker is at home.

We obtained these percentages from estimates we made based on the information in [6]. We assumed that the average person spent 60 hours per week sleeping, and so 108 hours in the week were available for them to respond to queries. Of those hours, we estimated 35 hours would be spent at work, 10 hours in commute, 23 hours away from home, and 40 hours at home. To determine the user's current location in our simulator, we generated a random number between 1 and 108, and chose the worker's current location based on the interval into which the random number fell.

4.2 Experimental Results

The following figures highlight the results of our simulations. Figure 2 shows a scatter of MAP values for all five algorithms, as tested on the high density city (60,000 workers) with the low budget (100 cents). Each point represents the average MAP value over 20 trials of the algorithm for one location. As more locations were processed, worker reliabilities were updated. Figure 3 shows best-fit lines for each algorithm using the high density city (60,000 workers) with the low budget (100 cents). Both of these figures show the MAP values for RECON and RELIABLE increasing as more locations are processed. Both stabilize at a very high percentage near the end, but RECON outperforms RELIABLE at almost every location processed. This is because RELIABLE's biggest flaw is that it does not consider convenience. Convenience is important because it affects the worker's likelihood of providing the correct response.

Figures 4 and 5 show similar trends for the medium (200 cents) and high (300 cents) budgets. As we can see, the CONVENIENT and RANDOM heuristics did not perform very well, always selecting a W with a MAP value of around 0.5, and this holds true for every city/budget combination we tested. While CORE performed better than CONVENIENT and RANDOM, it was not significantly

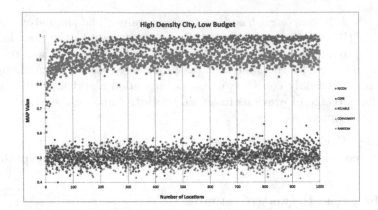

Fig. 2. Scatter plots of MAP values of all five algorithms over time, as the number of locations processed increases. The budget is fixed at $1, and the city population is 60,000.

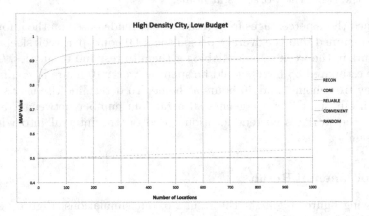

Fig. 3. Best-fit trend lines of MAP values of all five algorithms over time, as the number of locations processed increases. The budget is fixed at $1, and the city population is 60,000.

better than either algorithm. The biggest reason for this was because the threshold β cannot be set any higher than 0.5, otherwise a brand new worker would never be selected. For these reasons, we omit any further results for these three heuristics.

Figure 6 shows the MAP values, with 95 % confidence intervals, for each different budget. We show only the results from the high density city (60,000 workers), and the MAP value reported is the trend line value after processing all 1000 locations in the city. This is the most relevant point to report, because it shows how each algorithm performs after having ample time to update each worker's reliability rating. This plot shows that the confidence intervals for RECON at each tested budget are above those of RELIABLE when the algorithms have

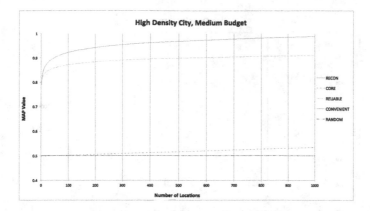

Fig. 4. Best-fit trend lines of MAP values of all five algorithms over time, as the number of locations processed increases. The budget is fixed at \$2, and the city population is 60,000.

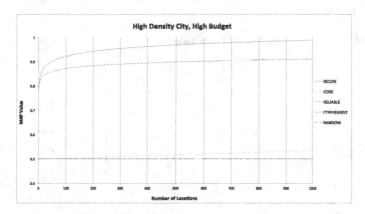

Fig. 5. Best-fit trend lines of MAP values of all five algorithms over time, as the number of locations processed increases. The budget is fixed at \$3, and the city population is 60,000.

processed 1000 locations. This means that we can say, with 95 % confidence, that RECON outperforms RELIABLE at every budget we tested. The results from other cities are similar, with MAP consistently outperforming RELIABLE for every budget/city-density combination.

Figure 7 shows the MAP values, with 95 % confidence intervals, for each of the cities tested. We show only the results for the low budget (100 cents), and again we report the MAP value from the trend line, after processing all 1000 locations in each city. This plot shows that the confidence intervals for RECON at each tested population density are above those of RELIABLE when the algorithms have processed 1000 locations. This means that we can say, with 95 % confidence, that RECON outperforms RELIABLE at every population density

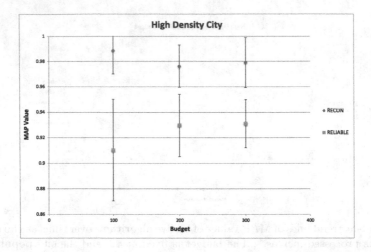

Fig. 6. Impact of budget on MAP value. City population is fixed at 60,000, and number of locations is 1000.

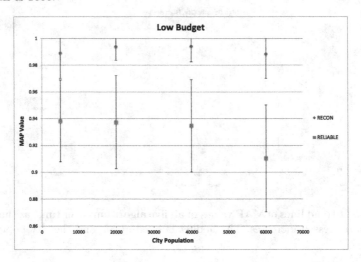

Fig. 7. Impact of population on MAP values. The budget is fixed at $1, and the number of locations is 1000.

we tested. The results from other budgets are similar, with RECON consistently outperforming RELIABLE for every budget/city-density combination.

5   Conclusions

As the number of smartphone users continues to rise, the use of crowdsourcing has become a standard practice for many applications. Getting quality information from the crowd can be a challenge, especially when the ground truth is unknown. Selecting workers that are both reliable and willing to perform tasks is hard enough, but verifying the validity of a crowdsourced answer can be even harder. For all applications that depend on crowdsourcing today, data quality is of paramount importance.

The location-based worker selection problem is a new frontier in crowd-sourced worker selection problems. Requiring users to actually go to a physical location adds a new dimension to the classic task assignment problem. With location-based tasks, incentives vary with each user's distance from the location in question. Consequently, considering a user's reliability is no longer enough when choosing the best workers to respond. We have introduced the location-aware worker selection problem, presented our algorithm, RECON, which considers worker reliability and convenience, and shown that RECON outperforms three heuristic algorithms for all of our test cases. RECON's advantage comes from its consideration of user convenience in addition to reliability, because it only selects workers with a high convenience factor. This allows more workers to be chosen for a given task and budget, thus improving the accuracy of the group's response.

Future Work. The results we have shown here give us confidence that RECON is a strong algorithm. In simulation, it is more effective than the RELIABLE approach for solving the location-based worker selection problem. The natural next step would be to test RECON in a real-world environment. We would like to create a smartphone application that pays users for answers to location-based questions, and deploy the app to as many users as possible in at least one city. However, we would first like to see how RECON performs with some different modeling methods. For example, we want to test using other methods than majority voting to determine the ground truth of worker answers. We would also like to use a more realistic commute pattern model, instead of simply using a straight line from the worker's home location to work location. We would like to test our algorithm on a model of a real city, using maps of roads, homes, and businesses. We would also like to try out different worker reliability models. Our simple model is not bad, but using a more sophisticated model may provide different results. Eventually we would design experiments to test RECON and RELIABLE's performance on real users and locations. Empirically showing that our model and algorithm is applicable to real-world problems would be very useful for many companies, organizations, etc. The end goal is to provide a robust service that allows anyone to pay a small amount of money to get highly reliable answers to location-based questions, without having to go out and verify the answers in person.

In the future (and even now), selecting workers to answer location-based questions will become a standard practice. Smartphone users can make a little money on their way home from work with just a couple taps on their device, and organizations can save huge amounts of money by outsourcing their data gathering to the crowd. Confidence in the collected data will be key, and RECON can be a first step in verifying the correctness of collected data.

References

1. Amazon. https://www.mturk.com/mturk/welcome
2. Boutsis, I., Kalogeraki, V.: On task assignment for real-time reliable crowdsourcing. In: Proceedings of IEEE 34th International Conference on Distributed Computing Systems, June 2014
3. Cox, L.P.: Truth in crowdsourcing. IEEE Secur.Priv. **9**(5), 74–76 (2011)
4. Ho, C., Vaughan, J.W.: Online task assignment in crowdsourcing markets. In: Proceedings of 26th Conference on Artificial Intelligence (2012)
5. Karger, D., Oh, S., Shah, D.: Budget-optimal task allocation for reliable crowdsourcing systems. Oper. Res. **62**(1), 1–24 (2014)
6. Bureau of Labor Statistics. http://www.bls.gov/tus/
7. Tejchman, J., Kozicki, J.: Experimental and Theoretical Investigations of Steel-Fibrous Concrete. SSGG, vol. 3, pp. 3–26. Springer, Heidelberg (2010)
8. Peer, E., Vosgerau, J., Acquisti, A.: Reputation as a sufficient condition for data quality on amazon mechanical turk. Behav. Res. Methods. **46**(4), 1023–1031 (2014)
9. Wang, D., Abdelzaher, T., Kaplan, L., Aggarwal, C.: Recursive fact-finding: a streaming approach to truth estimation in crowdsourcing applications. In: Proceedings of IEEE 33rd International Conference on Distributed Computing Systems, July 2013
10. WolframMathWorld. Poisson distribution. http://mathworld.wolfram.com/Poisson Distribution.html

Mobile Frameworks

AppSachet: Distributed App Delivery from the Edge Cloud

Ketan Bhardwaj$^{(\boxtimes)}$, Pragya Agrawal, Ada Gavrilovska, and Karsten Schwan

Georgia Institute of Technology, Atlanta, GA 303332, USA
{kbhardwaj6,pragya.agarwal,ada,schwan}@gatech.edu

Abstract. With total app installs touching 100 Billion in 2015, the increasing number of active devices that support apps are posed to result in 200 billion downloads by 2017. Data center based App stores offering users convenient app access, however, cause congestion in the last mile of the Internet, despite use of content delivery networks (CDNs) or ISP-based caching. This paper explores the new paradigm of eBoxes, situated in the 'edge cloud' tier beyond the last mile, which can be used to alleviate this congestion. With redesigned app caches – termed AppSachet – such edge cloud based distributed caching can achieve a hit ratio of up to 83 %, demonstrated on real-world Internet traffic. The redesign leverages proposed new caching policies, termed p-LRU and c-LRU, specifically targeted at eBoxes' limited storage and for the traffic caused by app installs and updates. A cost benefit analysis shows that the additional cost required to deploy AppSachet on eBoxes can be recovered within the first three months of operation.

Keywords: App delivery · Internet traffic measurement · Edge cloud · Caching

1 Introduction

The number of active smart phones worldwide is posed to cross 3 billion by 2018, and additional increases in mobile devices stem from wearable and embedded devices, like smart watches and glasses, devices supporting smart vehicles, etc. Coupled with that is a continuing explosion in the number of apps available to end users, with roughly 100 billion app downloads reported in 2015, set to reach a staggering 200 billion by 2017. App installs and more so, app updates, therefore, place measurable pressure on the Internet infrastructure used for their delivery, currently relying on Internet Service Provider (ISP) links to reach remote datacenter-based app stores or the Content Delivery Networks (CDNs) they use[1].

Specifically, the issue is congestion in *the last mile* of the Internet, which is well known to be a bottleneck for delivered service quality [7]. For apps, CDNs cannot mitigate this bottleneck because they operate behind ISPs and cannot consolidate app requests on their behalf. At the same time, ISP-based caching

---

[1] Data Source: http://mobithinking.com/.

© Institute for Computer Sciences, Social Informatics and Telecommunications Engineering 2015
S. Sigg et al. (Eds.): MobiCASE 2015, LNICST 162, pp. 89–106, 2015.
DOI: 10.1007/978-3-319-29003-4_6

is difficult if apps and updates are flagged as non-cachable content due to their pay-per-download nature, issues related to intellectual property protection, etc. Our previous work [11] showed the feasibility of using devices operating at the 'edge cloud' tier beyond the last mile of the Internet, to deliver apps/updates. Examples of such devices – termed eBoxes – include small cells [9,10], WiFi routers [4,5,8], or cloudlet servers [20], shown useful in recent research for supporting new edge services [12,16,18,20]. In that work, we also developed novel app streaming technology, which, without any disruption to how apps are currently developed and used, permits users to install apps or app updates directly from eBoxes with 2× faster speed, while also reducing last mile congestion by up to 70 %. Such work, however, focused on the client-facing eBox capabilities, and its obtained benefits relied on age-based (i.e., LRU-based) eBox-resident resource management mechanisms. However, that approach leads to comparatively inefficient use of limited eBox resources (e.g., storage capacity), limiting eBox benefits. In comparison, this paper seeks to answer the following questions:

- How to best cache apps and/or updates – *AppSachets* – on eBoxes?
- How to efficiently use the eBox's limited resources (i.e., storage capacity) to maximize hit ratio or minimize caching cost for Internet traffic due to apps and their updates?
- How to articulate cost vs. benefit of AppSachet deployment on eBoxes?

This paper presents AppSachets – a system for distributed app delivery from the edge cloud. Based on our analysis of real world Internet traffic due to Android apps and their updates, we highlight the cacheability characteristics of app traffic. Based on those characteristics, we propose two new caching policies implemented as part of AppSachet: (i) p-LRU which takes into account local app popularity and (ii) c-LRU which takes into account the cost of caching apps on eBoxes. We present an end-to-end system design that caters to end client devices using AppSachets and fits in the existing Android app ecosystem, without requiring any changes from app developers or any changes visible to end users. Further, we present a cost model for eBox based AppSachets operation inspired by the pricing model of CDNs. Overall, the technical contributions of this paper can be summarized as follows:

1. **Cacheability of app traffic**: We establish cacheability (Sect. 6.2) in app traffic using real world measurements of Android app install and updates (Sect. 2). We highlight the long tail in app access and updates, which also exhibits the peculiar characteristic that the popular apps in the long tail change on an hourly basis.
2. **Efficient app cache:** We show experimentally that the proposed p-LRU cache and c-LRU cache outperform other popular cache policies in terms of hit ratio (Sect. 6.3). While p-LRU maximizes hit ratio – 83 %, c-LRU minimizes the cost associated with caching apps on eBoxes.
3. **Cost-benefit analysis for AppSachets:** We show that the cost of deploying AppSachets on eBoxes can be fully recovered by app stores within the first 3 months (Sect. 6.5) of its operation. We estimate the additional cost

of deploying AppSachets in terms of the cost of storage required (Sect. 6.4), while benefit is estimated based on the pricing of CDNs.

2   Internet Traffic Due to App Delivery

To assess the impact of app-related traffic on the Internet and assess the improvement opportunities that can be provided via a solution like AppSachet, we collected data about all users at Georgia Institute of Technology over an extensive, representative time period (from May 19, 2014 to Aug 21, 2014). We next describe the methodology of data collection and the findings these measurements that are most relevant to the design of AppSachet.

2.1   Data Collection Methodology

Android app installs or updates are not directly identifiable in the traffic traces available to us. Instead, we observed that whenever a device initiates an install or update of an app from the Google Play store, this leads to a HTTP 301 response code from the store, which points to the location of the app within Google's CDN or server. This 301 response contains a location URL that points to the domain "play.google.com", and contains the URL path element "/market/". The URL also contains in its parameters the name and the version number of the app being installed/updated. The version information is either a single version number if installing a new app or if an app update results in removal of old version and installation of a newer one, or a colon separated list of two version numbers, i.e., the current and new versions. This information is sufficient for determining the overall set of IP addresses for which play.google.com resolves, as many portions of Google's overall infrastructure (including app distribution) are served via their CDNs.

Prior to obtaining the traces, we systematically resolved the IP for play. google.com over a multi-week period and recorded all resolved IP addresses. We configure our collection server with this IP information, to collect all packets that have any of these derived IPs in the source address section of the IP header and that utilize the TCP source port 80 (HTTP). After collecting all such traffic, we then used tshark to perform TCP packet reassembly, filtering out all traffic that does not fit the parameters of Google Play HTTP 301 responses. The resulting set of response codes represent all detectable Google Play app installs and updates for that two week period within our organization's network. While traffic collection is ongoing, we used softflowd to generate netflow information for the network. At the conclusion of the data collection process, we use nfdump to read in, aggregate, and produce total bandwidth utilization for the time period of collection. The resulting measurements report a total of 2 Terabytes of 301 requests pcaps for this period from the Google Play Store. Unfortunately, updates and installs over encrypted connections (e.g., HTTPS) cannot be detected in this fashion and are not included in the data presented because the information to detect an app install or update requires the contents of the HTTP 301 response.

Table 1. Summary of measured traffic due to app intalls and updates.

	Per app		Per day		Per hour		Total
	Max	90%	Max	90%	Max	90%	
Installs	755	10	1377	420	217	11	9536
Updates (raw)	1288	19	4626	1540	443	44	31338
Updates (versioned)	895	20	1377	420	443	44	31338

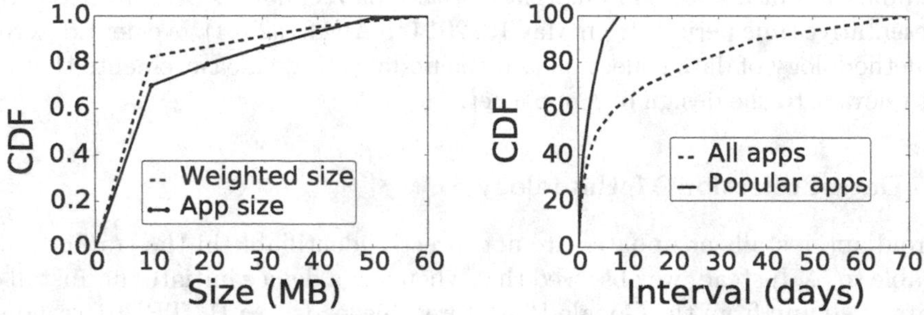

Fig. 1. Showing CDF of the (i) Size of the apps at the time data was collected; (ii) caching benefit i.e., number of days between successive app installs and updates observed in the measurements.

2.2 Observations

Table 1 summarizes our app traffic measurements. The results are further divided to show the number on app installs or updates observed per app, number of installs and updates observed per day, and finally, number of apps and updates seen during a particular hour of a day. Figure 1(i) shows the distribution of app sizes and the distribution of weighted app sizes where weights for an app is derived from its access frequency seen in our measurements. Figure 1(ii) shows the distribution of app access with respect to interval at which apps and/or their updates are accessed shown for all apps and popular apps separately. We derive an app's popularity by ranking apps on their access frequency. It is clear that all popular app updates are finished within 10 days of the first roll out suggesting that the app updates occur in cycle of 10 days. We were not able to find an exact reason for this cycle, but intuitively, it is likely either due to app store's scheduling of app updates or a period arising out of different developers pushing out updates for their apps. In any case, this suggests there is a significant period for eBoxes to absorb updates. Further, the difference in max and 90th%ile shown in Table 1, clearly highlights the bursty nature of app traffic in which app updates outnumber app installs by a factor of 3. The above observations bolsters our hypothesis about the benefits of caching app traffic on eBoxes. However, leveraging this redundancy in app traffic, to reduce congestion in the last mile, requires careful design of the app cache and caching algorithms. Regarding which we derive the following two hypothesis:

1. The gap between popular apps and all apps seen in Fig. 1(ii) leads us to hypothesize that a caching scheme that explicitly considers app popularity in its operation can provide the best cache hit ratio.
2. The difference in weighted app size and app size seen in Fig. 1(i) leads us to hypothesize that a caching scheme based on (a) cost derived from storage and time an app resides on an eBox and (b) benefit derived from reduction in bytes transferred, can provide good hit ratio while limiting caching costs and hence, pave way for a cost model for edge cloud services.

In addition to the above mentioned technical challenges, AppSachet also requires changes in the way android devices handle app updates. We discuss the design of AppSachet system that addresses all those concerns next.

3   App Sachet System Design

AppSachet acts as source of the latest apps and their updates to connected end client devices in similar ways as existing app stores and is placed in the app eco-system as shown in Fig. 2. AppSachet sees all requests made for apps and/or their updates to app-stores. Its goal is to leverage redundancy in app traffic and provide benefits to end-users and reductions in last-mile bandwidth use, while operating efficiently within limited eBox resources. AppSachet operation starts as a simple LRU cache of web responses (from the app stores) which contain the actual binaries of apps and/or updates requested by end clients connected to the AppSachet enabled eBox. If an end user's request cannot be fulfilled by AppSachet i.e., a cache miss is observed then, it proxies the request to remote app stores and saves the response in its local storage. To ensure high hit ratio, AppSachet ranks the seen apps after a pre-definded bootstrapp time, and based on that ranking segments its own cache into two parts. The segment created are either based on app popularity (i.e., in case of p-LRU cache) or cost of caching (in case of c-LRU cache) or simple LRU. AppSachet syncs or pre-fetches popular or cost effective apps and their updates from remote app stores. Thereafter, the popular or most cost effective apps are updated proactively and pre-fetched every hour. When an end client device that supports AppSachet connects to that eBox, the device starts by sharing information about installed apps on-device to which an eBox response in form of apps and/or updates available at the eBox, depending on user-preferences.

For completeness sake, we outline a simpler version of our vision for how AppSachet is integrated in the Android app ecosystem, by focusing only on interactions related to app installs and updates. These mechanisms are useful even in the context of the existing app download/install/upgrade model, but their benefits can be further enhanced through systems support for app-streaming, developed in our previous work [11]. AppSachet achieves its goals via the following four components:

1. **AppSachet Cache:** An eBox resident module that houses a cache containing apps, updates, and anonymized app-profiles on its local storage.

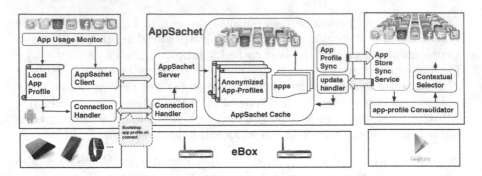

Fig. 2. AppSachet design showing different system components, their interactions and their placement in app ecosystem.

2. **AppSachet Server:** An eBox resident server that services end client devices' request for apps and/or updates, and collects anonymized app-profiles from the connected devices.
3. **AppSachet Sync:** An eBox resident module pro-actively fetching apps, handling update notifications from app stores and notifying app stores about the delivered apps and/or updates.
4. **AppSache Client** is a module embedded in the Android app framework that enables handling of app installs and/or updates from an AppSachet server.

3.1   AppSachet Cache

The AppSachet cache is an eBox-resident module that maintains an indexed repository of app and update binaries fetched from app stores. It houses aggregate app usage information – referred to as *app-profile* – from all connected clients, and a list of delivered apps and/or updates mapped to particular user, used for required app-store notifications. Although the policy used for app cache management can be as simple as an age-based LRU policy, we demonstrate significant gains from targeting the cache management policy to the characteristic of the app traffic. In response, we define two policies – p-LRU and c-LRU – described in greater detail in Sect. 4. The updates of the app cache rely on AppSachet's Sync service.

In addition to apps and their updates, AppSachet also maintains per-app *App Profiles*. An App Profile is simply a relational structure containing the state collected from end user devices on connection. It includes the following user specific persistent information from device: (i) a list of apps, (ii) their versions and (iii) usage patterns of installed on end user device. It also contains session specific device configuration, e.g., current IP address of the device needed to deliver an app or update, and the current App Sachet user preferences indicating how user wants his device to interact with AppSachet enabled eBox. For instance, the preferences can indicate whether a user wants to update all available app updates or to disable updating specific app from eBoxes, of is a user wants to see new contextual apps available for installation from eBox, etc. An app-profile is exchanged during the bootstrapping when a device first connects to an AppSachet-enabled eBox.

App-profiles are also kept on eBoxes in another cache instance. The rationale behind keeping a cache vs. a persistent copy of app profiles is first based on the limited amount of storage on eBoxes, and the fact that app-profiles are synced with app-stores anyway. Second, considering the predictability of human movement, i.e., we often go the same places at particular times, e.g. office, coffee shop, etc., creates opportunities for applying proactive and predictive caching algorithms.

Note, however, that sharing this information about a device poses a potential privacy threat; it is avoided by sharing only anonymized app profiles with eBoxes. The anonymization of app profiles is designed to be carried out on the device, in the App usage monitor, vs. on the eBox, to prevent privacy concerns. Another concerns is mismatch in app version installed on device and the one known by backend app stores due to eBox based updates. For the current prototype, it is a non issue because of the way eBox based AppSachet fetches apps and their updates on behalf of an end user effectively syncing the current version of app on device and known by app stores. But we posit that a delegation of authorization from end user to eBox could be used in real-world deployments.

3.2   AppSachet Server

AppSache server residing on an eBox carries out interaction with a device. It is responsible for bootstrapping device-eBox interaction on connection by presenting a valid certificate which established that eBox as valid provider of apps and updates. Another choice is to have remote app stores involved during the bootstrapping process but that leads to longer bootstrapp process as the device and eBox have to reach out to app stores, which then can issue a common token which can be used to verify identity of an eBox. The server interacts with the cache of apps and shared app profiles, and updates and considers user preferences, e.g., to create a tailored response for the device.

Actual App Delivery. From an eBox is facilitated by Android Debug Bridge (ADB) over Wi-Fi to connect to the device and carry out actual app installs and updates when requested by a device resident AppSachet client, an app at a time. The decision to not batch multiple app updates from eBox to end client device is to ensure correctness of updates on a device, and also not to overwhelm the end user device's network with large number of updates.

3.3   AppSachet Sync

App-Sachet's Sync service is responsible interacting with existing app-stores on behalf of end clients. Its interaction involves (i) fetching apps and/or updates not cached on an eBox and (ii) periodically checking and pre-fetching updates for apps based on p-LRU or c-LRU policy. It supports a pull-based mechanism for update distribution for which AppSachet on eBox registers a push notification handler, i.e., **update handler**, listening to push notifications from the app store for apps present in its app cache. When a notification arrives, the AppSachet sync service fetches the updates.

App stores transmit app as full apks to end clients devices but updates are transmitted either (i) as full apks if there exists is a wide gap in version of app installed on device vs. app version that is currently available app store or (ii) as incremental updates [22] which are binary diff of previously installed app apk and the current version of apk submitted by developer at app store. AppSachet supports incremental updates to end clients and also handles incremental updates for its own cache. To ensure correctness of incremental updates, app cache follows a 2 phase commit approach i.e., it commits an update to the app cache only when there are no current users installing the app or its update to avoid misalignment of app versions, but once committed, the update is immediately available to eBox connected devices.

A push-based approach to app cache updates, allowing app stores to dynamically push apps or their updates to a device, could leverage global context, e.g., trending apps, important updates, etc. However, given that our current implementation is limited by the existing unofficial Google Play API, AppSachets are restricted to a pull-based approach explicitly requesting apps and updates from the store.

The Sync component is also responsible for aggregating and propagating to the app store notifications about delivery of an app or an update. These notifications are sent asynchronously to app stores to avoid causing slowdowns in AppSachet-end user device interaction but still ensuring consistency in the versions of apps installed on end user device and what is known to remote app-stores. The choice of lazy and asynchronous reporting to remote app stores by eBoxes ensures that devices are not burdened to communicate with remote app stores. It also avoids making remote interactions between eBoxes and app stores a bottleneck while eBox updates are ongoing. However, this may be problematic for apps that require payments. We posit that to support paid apps on AppSachets app stores, either this communication would have to be made synchronous or the eBox must be enabled to process payments. We believe there are additional challenges related to authorization and authentication of eBoxes, which we plan to explore in our future work.

AppSachet relies on app store-resident functionality to provide the aforementioned callbacks or eBox-initiated sync operations, and leverages app profiles and other information gleaned from eBox usage patterns to guide the distribution of app updates across eBoxes, or to otherwise allow app stores to benefit from the presence of eBoxes in the end-to-end app ecosystem. Even though this paper has not yet explored challenges concerning the efficient operation of an eBox-App Store interface, we believe that with ~100 apps installed on a average device [2,3] and an update cycle of 10 days, there are significant opportunities to reduce considerable overhead from app stores. By using eBox based app stores, congestion is reduced by (i) providing flexibility in scheduling app store interactions and updates, and (ii) by distributing the app and app update delivery load across a number of eBoxes, which then can handle per device installs/updates.

3.4 AppSachet Client

The AppSachet client resides deep in the Android's app framework on the end user device. It is responsible for starting the bootstrapping process when a device first connects to an AppSachet enabled eBox. Mechanisms like Wi-Fi beacons or a central registry based service discovery etc. can be used to kick-off bootstrapping. However, our current AppSachet client prototype does this by listening to wpa supplicant connection notifications and simply querying a AppSachet server running on pre-defined IP:Port combination. A similar approach is deployed on most Wi-Fi routers that provide the control panel of that router over a predefined address, e.g., 192.168.1.0 etc.

On connection, it establishes an eBox's integrity as a valid supplier of apps and/or updates by requesting a CA issued certificate from eBox. On successful verification, the device resident AppSachet client shares an anonymized app profile with eBox. After successful completion of the bootstrapping, the client component is also responsible for requesting and acknowledging individual apps and/or updates from eBox by choosing from those available in list shared by an eBox as app-profile.

The AppSachet client also includes a **App Usage Monitor** interfaces with Android's package manager to get the list of installed apps and uses native hooks to app usage APIs [1] to create anonymous app profiles, stored in a separate file on the device's file system. It is run lazily in the background when the device is locked by the end user. The decision to invoke the app usage monitor lazily ensures that (i) mining relevant information doesn't impact user experience when the device is being actively used and (ii) utilizes the period between user locking the device and system's decision to put device in a deep sleep state to minimize its impact on device's battery usage. The app-profile is anonymized by passing it through a filter to ensure that information shared with eBox is clear of any personal information. In the current prototype, this simply removes keywords provided by users in their preference, but better anonymization techniques could be deployed for improved privacy guarantees.

4   AppSachet Cache Policy Design

We present the two novel cache policies for managing the cache of apps and app updates on AppSachet eBoxes. Policies are specifically defined based on opportunities observed from the app-traffic characteristics captured in our measurements. The two policies – p-LRU and c-LRU – are described next, and the overall description of the cache management operations with either policy follows the same operating flow illustrated in Fig. 3.

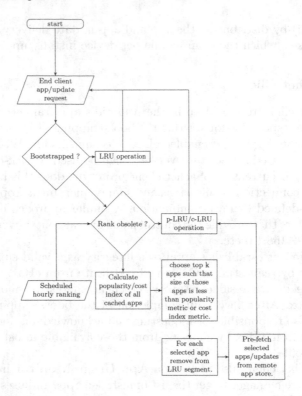

Fig. 3. Showing the operation of AppSachet on eBoxes.

4.1 Popularity-Aware Caching: p-LRU

p-LRU cache is designed to operate based on app popularity, observed as an important characteristics of app traffic. p-LRU divides the available storage space for caching in two parts: (i) LRU based and (ii) popularity based. The size of each segment is decided based on popularity metric which is defined as percent of storage space allocated to popular apps on an eBox. p-LRU cache is similar to a segmented LRU (SLRU) [19] in the way it keeps two separate segments of cache, but differs in the eviction strategies in the LRU-vs. the popularity based segment. The p-LRU cache works as follows:

During p-LRU bootstapp period, e.g., the first 24 hours, p-LRU acts as simple LRU. After that, apps are ranked according to the apps that were accessed in the past 24 hours based on the number of times they were accessed or *popularity metric*. For instance, if we have a cache of size 1 GB, and we see that 40 % of apps are being accessed repeatedly, we set popularity metric at 40 %. This will result in reserving 40 % storage space, i.e., 400 MB, for storing popular apps and 60 %, i.e., 600 MB, for storing recently used apps.

The popular apps and their updates are then pre-fetched until the popular segment is full. If the app is present in both LRU and popular segment, it is kept in the popular segment, so that LRU can accommodate more apps. Note that there are many apps that although not popular, not caching them would result in a considerable reduction in hit ratio, also highlighted by the gap in all apps and popular apps in Fig. 4(ii). Since, there are considerable number of apps that are often not popular but not caching them would result in a considerable reduction in hit ratio also highlighted by the gap in all apps and popular apps in Fig. 4(ii). Once p-LRU is bootstrapped, app ranking is repeated every hour and popular apps are pre-fetched for that hour.

4.2   Cost-Aware Caching: c-LRU

Similar to p-LRU cache, **c-LRU cache** divides the available storage space for caching in two parts: (i) LRU based and (ii) cost of caching based. It uses a cost index to quantify the cost of caching an app on eBox. Intuitively, the cost of caching can be derived from the following metrics: (i) The number of times it is downloaded when compared to all the apps downloaded from that eBox or the *download ratio*; (ii) the time for which a particular app is kept on eBox's storage compared to its first download or *utilization ratio*; (iii) the time an app has already spent in the cache without actually being requested by end users or *recency ratio*; and (iv) the size of the app that needs to be stored. e.g., if any particular app whose size is 50 MB and is accessed 10 times and we have two other apps whose sizes are 20MB and 30MB, and are accessed 5 and 8 times respectively in the same interval, then we should give preference to caching the two smaller apps than one large app. One exception to this rule is that c-LRU must handle updates and installs separately because updates are always smaller than installs and this would lead to installs never being cached on eBox. We started with giving equal weights to each metric, and the value of each is normalized i.e., varies from 0 to 1. The app with the lowest cost caclulated this way is considered the most suitable one for caching at an ebox. After experimenting with different combinations of weights and metrics, we zeroed to the below mentioned definition of cost index of an app stored on eBox:

Cost index $= [DR * (1/Appsize) + UR + RR)]^{-1}$, where,
Download ratio (DR) = number of downloads of that app / total number of downloads

Utilization ratio (UR) = hours spent in cache / hours since first download
Recency ratio (RR) = 1/hours since last download

The lower cost index results in lower cost associated with storing and hence, higher benefit, because the app may be accessed too frequently or uses very little space or a combination of both. The c-LRU cache works as follows: during c-LRU bootstrapp process, i.e., the first 24 hours, c-LRU acts as a simple LRU. After that, apps are ranked according to the cost index of apps accessed in the past 24 hours. The segmentation, pre-fetching and eviction in c-LRU work similarly to p-LRU except the use of cost index vs. popularity.

The cost function described above tries to maximize the utilization of eBox resources. However, the model permits for additional cost functions, including ones that incorporate consideration of different value generated from different apps. The ability to attach a value to an app in case of AppSachet or generally a service running on an eBox can pave the way to creating a quantifiable economic model for the upcoming 'edge cloud' infrastructure, a concern of utmost importance regarding edge cloud deployment, which hasn't been addressed in any of the recent edge cloud research [12,16,18,20].

5   AppSachet Implementation

The implementation of AppSachet uses either available Android platform components or open source technologies. Specifically, (i) the eBox-resident elements are implemented using the node.js and python API on top of an OpenWRT router, (ii) the device-side AppSachet client elements are implemented as a patch for Android, and (iii) the additional elements of the eBox-app store interface are implemented using the unofficial HTTP API of the Google Play Store. With our limitations to evaluate eBox-AppStore interface owing to it requiring changing app-store's internals and its interface, we present detailed evaluations of the other components of AppSachet mechanisms next.

6   Evaluation

6.1   Experimental Testbed

App traffic measurements are obtained from a network tap that has the capability of logging all traffic flowing in and out of our institution. We used offline analysis to filter the data after logging. The AppSachet is deployed on an eBox emulated with a Core2Duo machine housing apps in its local storage and connected to a Linksys wrt 1900ac router via a Gigabit port. We generate a representative app traffic workload for our experiments using captured app traffic. The AppSachet client is prototyped using a Nexus 5 phone running Android (CyanogenMod 11.2 ∼ Android KitKat).

6.2   Cacheability of App Traffic

Figure 4(i) shows the number of times a particular app or its update in accessed from the measured app traffic. The most popular app was accessed 1403 times and then access frequency decreases exponentially. Specifically, the 100th app was accessed only 68 times, showing a clear long-tail distribution of apps and their updates. To gain insights into finer temporal cache characteristics of app traffic, we divided the complete dataset into 6 equal smaller periods – where each line in Fig. 4(ii) d_i corresponds to a different period – and found that the caching characteristics persist for small periods as well as for the overall traffic trace.

Going a step further, we analyse the observed app traffic on a per-hour basis to capture local popularity of apps on an eBox based cache. Figure 4(iii) shows

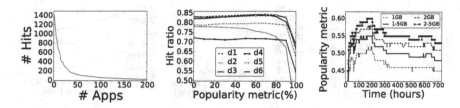

Fig. 4. For the measured app traffic showing (i) the number of times each app is accessed in the complete dataset; (ii) temporal caching characteristics of app traffic workload by dividing observed traffic in 6 small periods; (iii) number of popular apps vs. other apps accessed from the cache per hour;

that for every hour, 40 %–60 % of apps are accessed from what we call the local popular app cache. We notice that every hour, the local popularity of apps on an eBox changes, requiring hourly updates to keep the app cache clear of outdated apps, also seen from the pattern in the Fig. 4(iii). *These results establish that traffic due to apps and their updates is suitable for caching on an hourly basis and provided justification for our rationale behind the design of the p-LRU and c-LRU caching policies.*

6.3   p-LRU and c-LRU Cache Performance

We compared the proposed p-LRU and c-LRU with a number of popular cache policies, i.e., LRU, Random and Belady's optimal eviction policy. The experimental results, summarized in Fig. 5(i) and Table 2 are obtained using eBoxes with up to 2.5GB of cache storage.

Table 2. For the measured app traffic, showing comparisons of cache policies with varying cache sizes.

	Cache Size	1 GB	1.5 GB	2 GB	2.5 GB
Cache Policies	Oracle	0.8386	0.8558	0.8647	0.8688
	p-LRU	0.7837	0.8105	0.8247	0.8352
	c-LRU	0.7782	0.8078	0.824	0.8328
	LRU	0.7665	0.7965	0.8149	0.8274
	Random	0.6266	0.671	0.6994	0.714

It is clear that p-LRU outperforms all other policies and is closest to the optimal cache closely followed by c-LRU policy. Figure 5(ii) shows the overall performance of p-LRU cache for varying sizes of app cache which shows that the best ratio is obtained when the cache size for popularity metric is between 40 %–60 % which drops drastically after 80 %. This also shows why one segment must

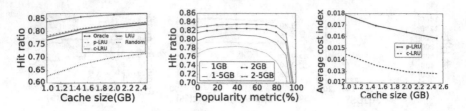

Fig. 5. For the measured app traffic showing (i) the comparison of caching policies; (ii) p-LRU cache performance with different size of eBox based cache; (iii) the average cost index observed (i.e., by all the apps stored on eBox at a time) when using p-LRU and c-LRU caching policy while varying cache size.

be assigned as a LRU cache, i.e., LRU also plays a very important role in maintaining a high cache ratio whereas the popularity metric or cost index ensures that the popular apps or apps with high cost index are always cached, even on their first access. *We conclude that efficient use of the capabilities of upcoming edge cloud platforms (e.g., for caching) would require defining new application specific metrics (e.g., popularity, cost) and/or implement new mechanisms (e.g., p-LRU, c-LRU).*

6.4   Storage Requirements on eBox

Figure 5(ii) shows the variation of cache hit ratio of the p-LRU cache with increasing cache size. Figure 5 shows that using a p-LRU cache on an eBox with a capacity of 2.5 GB results in the highest hit ratio; this is also closest to the optimal Belady's algorithm shown as Oracle. We conclude that with 2.5 GB of additional storage at eBoxes and a p-LRU cache, AppSachet achieves a 83 % hit ratio. Figure 5(iii) shows the average cost index observed, i.e., average of cost indexes of all apps stored on the eBox, updated hourly, while running through the complete workload and using p-LRU and c-LRU. As apparent, c-LRU beats p-LRU consistently in terms of lower cost index and hence, lower cost of caching resulting in higher benefits, while still slightly sacrificing hit ratio as seen from Table 2 This highlight a trade off in cache performance vs. cost particularly for eBoxes with less storage due to cost constraints. *Generally, for edge services (e.g., AppSachet) deployed on edge cloud platforms with resource constraints (e.g., storage capacity), designing mechanisms (e.g., c-LRU policy) must consider other factors (e.g., cost) vs. just performance (e.g., hit ratio).*

6.5   Cost Benefit Analysis of Deploying eBox Based AppSachets

Without real world deployments of eBoxes and in the absence of any real cost models for eBox revenue, we base our cost-benefit analysis on the retail cost of SSD storage and the benefit of the latest pricing information about content delivery networks prices. Simply put, the benefit from an AppSachet on an eBox is directly proportional to the reduction in volume of traffic served by an eBox. Consider the following:

1. There is a wide range on prices offered by CDNs [6], e.g., typically $0.01 per GB to $0.05 per GB depending on the volume of traffic.
2. Additional storage cost of 2.5 GB flash storage varies from $3-$20 based on its quality. Assuming that we also add 2GB DDR3 RAM as well to the eBox, which costs anywhere from $10-$20, this would result in a maximum increase of $40 in eBox cost.
3. Based on the size of app installs/updates in Sect. 2, the total amount of bytes served by an app store are ~2.6TB. With a 83 % hit ratio shown to be achieved by p-LRU cache would serve ~2TB from eBoxes.

Conservatively, using $0.01 per GB, an eBox can save ($0.01 × 2000 = $20) in three months, i.e., an eBox would be able to recover the additional cost of storage within 3 months of its deployment. Even if we consider the additional RAM as a cost increase in eBoxes, it will be recovered in the first 6 months of eBox deployment. *From this, we want to highlight the value proposition of edge cloud based services (e.g., AppSachet) in terms of reduced operational costs for cloud based services.*

7   Discussion and Future Work

This paper leaves a number of open questions on the device side, about eBox deployment models, privacy, and required system software changes. Ones which we plan to undertake in the future are discussed below:

eBox Deployment Model. Given that realworld deployments of eBoxes don't exist as yet, there are open questions about their ownership – individuals, businesses or public infrastructure? Security and Trust aspects of apps from AppSachet on those eBoxes? Another open area is DRM of the app cache on eBox. We posit that authentication and authorization methods can be deployed on eBoxes, theoretically but those authorization and authentication assume a human user which is authenticated or authorizes which is not the case AppSachet operating on eBox. We believe that this is an interesting problem which plan to pursue in future.

Privacy Concerns. Privacy concerns arising out of sharing app profiles and methods to anonymize app profiles leaves out an open question – First, is it possible to fingerprint users based on app users and if so, what obfuscation methods can be applied to avoid those concerns. However, it is important to note that sharing app profiles is not invasive than use current app usage API in Android [1] (which AppSachet also uses) which lets developers to track app usage. However, this aspect certainly needs a detailed evaluation.

System Software on Devices and eBoxes. Without any standard definition of am eBox, their deployment mechanism and consequently new functionalities, e.g., app caching etc., provide an wide open space for research. In our future work, we are exploring additional functionality that can further improve the app ecosystem and their automatic provisioning eBoxes.

Device Side Evaluation. We also carried out experiments to gauge the benefit of AppSachets on end client devices. However, we did not observe any significant benefits or any new finding other than what is already reported in our previous work [11] so we omitted those results from this paper.

8   Related Work

Previous work on characterizing Internet traffic workload has mainly focussed on video e.g., youtube access patterns [13, 14, 17, 21, 23] etc., and web but, there has been no work done in collecting the android app access patterns. Our paper is the first of its kind to capture and analyse the download behaviour of android apps. Using dynamic caching for prefetching content, Gandhi et al. [17] suggested that k-means clustering used more intervals while reducing error rate compared to dynamic programming. However, based on our android app access pattern, k-means clustering gave a cache-hit ratio of 75 %, which is lower than the cache-hit ratio of the proposed p-LRU algorithm. Zink et al. [23] observed a similar pattern for youtube videos and proposed a caching policy based on LRU and popularity of a movie. The results showed an improvement in the cache-hit ratio. However, their algorithm depended on a global list of popular movies. Access to a global list may or may not be there. Also, it might happen that the global popularity list might differ from local lists [23], where they proved that there is no strong correlation is observed between global and local popularity and video clips of local interest have a high local popularity. The p-LRU algorithm addresses these issues, as it generates the popularity list by learning the access patterns locally.

   Prior efforts have considered support app execution via edge-cloud platforms [12, 16, 18, 20] to leverage resource-rich execution environment to partially or fully offload app execution from resource constrained devices. But none of them considered use of edge cloud platforms for app delivery which is the focus of AppSachets approach. Recent work to reduce mobile app update traffic proposes micro app updates [15, 22] which would complement AppSachets.

9   Conclusions

AppSachet is a distributed app delivery system for the Android ecosystem that shows that deploying proposed app caches (p-LRU, c-LRU) on eBoxes in the 'edge cloud' tier can recover the already modest additional costs within 3 months of its deployment. The design of AppSachet is based on extensive experimental measurements of app traffic and keeping in mind practical deployment concerns, i.e., not requiring changes to apps by developers and/or changes in how end users employ these apps. More generally, we conclude that while moving conventional services to the edge cloud can have benefits in terms of latency and bandwidth but designing services for edge cloud platforms requires more than just running existing backend cloud services in the edge cloud. There remains interesting tradeoffs to be explored and new mechanisms to be developed leading to efficient use of future edge clouds providing a fertile ground for systems research.

Acknowledgement. This work was partially supported through research grants from Intel, VMware, and NSF CNS1148600.

References

1. Android app usage api @ https://goo.gl/39dqlu
2. Android apps per device - yahoon avaite @ http://goo.gl/3zb3ob
3. Android apps per device @ http://goo.gl/zkaxsx
4. Att small cell deployment plans. http://goo.gl/XdfkfH
5. Att wifi hotspot locations. http://goo.gl/XdfkfH
6. Cdn pricing 2014. http://goo.gl/717fkd
7. Level 3 cdn reports last mile as new bottleneck @ http://goo.gl/3ir9kg
8. Mobile world congress -small cells. http://goo.gl/cWaARN
9. Qualcomm small cells. http://goo.gl/HEpudP
10. Qualcomm smart gateways. http://goo.gl/BwPc7f
11. Bhardwaj, K., Agarwal, P., Gavrilovska, A., Schwan, K., Allred, A.: Appflux: Taming mobile app delivery via app streaming. In: 2015 Conference on Timely Results in Operating Systems (TRIOS15) Monterey, CA, USA (2015) USENIX Association (2015)
12. Bhardwaj, K., Sreepathy, S., Gavrilovska, A., Schwan, K.: Ecc: Edge cloud composites. In: Proceedings of the 2014 2Nd IEEE International Conference on Mobile Cloud Computing, Services, and Engineering MOBILECLOUD 2014, pp. 38–47. Washington, DC, USA (2014), IEEE Computer Society (2014)
13. Braun, L., Klein, A., Carle, G., Reiser, H., Eisl, J.: Analyzing caching benefits for youtube traffic in edge networks x2014; a measurement-based evaluation. In: Network Operations and Management Symposium (NOMS) 2012, pp. 311–318. IEEE, April 2012
14. Cheng, X.: Understanding the characteristics of internet short video sharing: Youtube as a case study. In: Proceedings of the 7th ACM SIGCOMM Conference on InternetMeasurement, San Diego, CA, USA, vol. 15, p. 28 (2007)
15. Cheung, A., Ravindranath, L., Wu, E., Madden, S., Balakrishnan, H.: Mobile applications need targeted micro-updates. In: APSys 2013 (2013)
16. Dixon, C., Mahajan, R., Agarwal, S., Brush, A., Lee, B., Saroiu, S., Bahl, P.: An operating system for the home. In: USENIX conference on NSDI, April 2012
17. Gandhi, A., Chen, Y., Gmach, D., Arlitt, M., Marwah, M.: Minimizing data center sla violations and power consumption via hybrid resource provisioning. In: Proceedings of the 2011 International Green Computing Conference and Workshops, Washington, DC, USA, 2011, IGCC 2011, pp. 1–8. IEEE Computer Society (2011)
18. Jang, M., Schwan, K., Bhardwaj, K., Gavrilovska, A., Avasthi, A.: Personal clouds: sharing and integrating networked resources toenhance end user experiences. In: INFOCOM, 2014 Proceedings IEEE, April 2014
19. Karedla, R., Love, J.S., Wherry, B.G.: Caching strategies to improve disk system performance. Computer **27**(3), 38–46 (1994)
20. Koukoumidis, E., Lymberopoulos, D., Strauss, K., Liu, J., Burger, D.: Pocket cloudlets. ACM SIGPLAN Notices **47**(4), 171–184 (2012)
21. Krishnappa, D.K., Khemmarat, S., Gao, L., Zink, M.: On the feasibility of prefetching and caching for online tv services: a measurement study on hulu. In: Spring, N., Riley, G.F. (eds.) PAM 2011. LNCS, vol. 6579, pp. 72–80. Springer, Heidelberg (2011)

22. Samteladze, N., Christensen, K.: Delta: Delta encoding for less traffic for apps. In: Proceedings of the 2012 IEEE 37th Conference on Local Computer Networks (LCN 2012), Washington, DC, USA, 2012, LCN 2012, pp. 212–215. IEEE Computer Society (2012)
23. Zink, M., Suh, K., Gu, Y., Kurose, J.: Watch global, cache local: Youtube network traffic at a campus network: measurements and implications. In: Electronic Imaging 2008, p. 681805. International Society for Optics and Photonics (2008)

Typed JS: A Lightweight Typed JavaScript Engine for Mobile Devices

Ryan H. Choi[✉] and Youngil Choi

Software R&D Center, Samsung Electronics, Suwon, South Korea
{ryan.choi,duddlf.choi}@samsung.com

Abstract. Web applications have been gaining huge popularity due to being platform independent and also enabling fast development. Unfortunately, due to insufficient performance of web applications, they are generally limited to non-performance-critical use. The performance of web applications is largely affected by the performance of JavaScript. To address this problem, modern JavaScript engines such as Google's V8 incorporate many state-of-the-art optimization and engineering techniques. In industry, recent approaches are to extend JavaScript to decorate objects with types to better utilize just-in-time (JIT) compilers.

In this paper, we present Typed JS, a subset of JavaScript that utilizes type-decorated syntax. Unlike previous approaches, Typed JS supports most of the JS core operations while utilizing the ahead-of-time (AOT) compilation technique, which was not possible in the existing solution. Typed JS is specifically designed for running Web applications on mobile devices with goals of having smaller memory footprint while achieving high-performance, which is accomplished by utilizing the type information and AOT technique. Experiments show that Typed JS requires significantly much less memory usage while performing better than industry-leading JavaScript engines on a mobile platform.

Keywords: Typed JavaScript · Static type · Mobile

1 Introduction

JavaScript is the standard Web programming language, commonly integrated to web browsers to allow users interact on client-side applications. Also, together with HTML and CSS, it defines the standard Web application framework, which allows developers to create large-scale and complex Web-based applications. Some popular web applications include Gmail, Google Docs, Facebook, etc. In these applications, JavaScript is typically used to execute complex user interaction and business logic. The strength of Web applications is, unlike traditional applications, it does not have platform dependency—any platform including desktop and mobile that includes a modern web browser can execute web applications. Furthermore, Web applications are self-maintainable from user's view in a way that users do not worry about installing and updating web applications.

© Institute for Computer Sciences, Social Informatics and Telecommunications Engineering 2015
S. Sigg et al. (Eds.): MobiCASE 2015, LNICST 162, pp. 107–121, 2015.
DOI: 10.1007/978-3-319-29003-4_7

Due to significant influence of JavaScript in the Web framework, recently, improving the performance of JavaScript has received much attention from both industry and academia. Modern industry-leading JavaScript engines including V8 [9] and JSC [2] have been heavily optimized over the last decade. Some well known optimization techniques include JIT (just-in-time), hidden class and inline cache. These optimization techniques are to address one of the fundamental designs of JavaScript—that is, JavaScript is a dynamic language such that, a JavaScript's object layout is unknown during the JavaScript compilation phase, but gradually known during runtime. For each object, information about the object layout is collected while executing JavaScript, and when the object layout is hardly altered, these optimization techniques start to optimize execution steps by generating machine code for faster execution (i.e., JIT) and caching properties (i.e., inline cache). A key concept of these techniques is that, object layouts do not change much after JavaScript executes for a while. Hence, one drawback is that, when object layout changes frequently, JIT and inline cache are not as effective. Furthermore, techniques such as JIT is a resource-intensive technique, so it may not be suitable for platforms with limited CPU and memory resources such as mobile platforms.

JavaScript, being dynamic by nature, presents many performance and memory optimization challenges. To address these problems, recently, a few variants of JavaScript are proposed, and being actively developed in industry. One common goal among these variants is to restrict JavaScript's dynamicity without much affecting JavaScript's design by adding static types. Objects declared with static types are not allowed to change types during runtime. Hence, by utilizing these extra type information, JIT and inline cache can be more effective, and more aggressive optimization techniques can be applied. TypeScript [14] is one of the first attempt in this direction. It extends JavaScript to accept type-decorated syntax. Flow [8] is a subset of JavaScript that also accepts type-decorated syntax. Unlike TypeScript, Flow is a type-checker such that, it analyzes type-decoration for consistency and correctness, and relies an existing JavaScript engine for code execution. They both attempt to fully utilize current optimization techniques such as JIT already implemented in JavaScript virtual machines (VMs) to maximize the performance on desktop by supplying type information and not modifying object layouts.

Ahead-of-time (AOT) compilation technique, unlike JIT optimization, requires all object types to be known during the code compilation phase. By fully understanding object types and not allowing changing object layouts during runtime, it can aggressively optimize for maximum performance. But due to not knowing object types and dynamicity in objects, AOT is not suitable for JavaScript. However, there is an attempt to integrate the strength of AOT compilation into JavaScript virtual machines. asm.js [15] translates C++ code into non-dynamic JavaScript code to make it execute faster than typical JavaScript code with some forms of dynamicity. Unfortunately, functionality of asm.js is limited in a way that, it cannot represent JavaScript core design such as objects, prototype, etc. Nevertheless, it proves that, eliminating dynamic behaviors can significantly increase the performance.

In this paper, we propose a design of a subset of JavaScript called Typed JavaScript (Typed JS), which utilizes type-decorated syntax, and is compiled by an AOT compiler. Unlike V8 and JSC, Typed JS is specifically designed for running Web applications on mobile devices with goals of having smaller memory footprint and binary size while achieving high-performance when integrated to mobile web applications. Unlike asm.js, which supports only a small set of operators, Typed JS supports most of JavaScript core design such as object model, prototype, functions and closures, and garbage collection. In brief, high performance is achieved by having fixed object layout, which allows us to access objects by using memory offsets. Also, by supporting AOT compilation, JavaScript VM is not required, and thus, the overhead from executing a VM is removed. This also results in having smaller memory footprint and binary size, as typical JavaScript virtual machine is replaced by a much compact native runtime library.

Other than the performance and smaller memory footprint, Typed JS provides additional advantages. Rigorous type checking in Typed JS improves productivity especially when implementing a large application, by early detecting errors and bugs that are caused by type-mismatching in the development phase. Typed JS is also portable such that, applications written in Typed JS runs on any platform without modifying the source code. However, it may need to be recompiled for each target platform. Furthermore, by distributing only binary files, application source code can be effectively hidden to prevent from unauthorized modification, which is often an important requirement in industry.

Finally, Typed JS can become the main language to easily implement efficient mobile applications. A binding mechanism between Typed JS and EFL[1] graphics library on Tizen mobile platform is implemented, and we successfully reimplemented mobile demo applications that came with Tizen SDK 2.3 originally written in C++ in Typed JS.

Organization: Section 2 presents related literature in the area of script languages. Section 3 presents design principles of Typed JS. Section 4 gives design, model, and implementation details of Typed JS. Section 5 shows experiment results. Lastly, we conclude in Sect. 6.

2   Related Work

JIT Compilers: Self [6] and StrongTalk [5] define many core techniques in JIT compilers such as polymorphic inline caches [11] and deoptimization [12]. Recent works on JIT are as follows. Bohm et al. [3] propose generalized trace JIT compilation approach that consider not only the paths through holes, but all frequently executed paths in a program. Rompf et al. [16] allows programs to invoke JIT compilation explicitly, as well as the JIT compiler to call back into the program to perform compile-time computation. In industry, Google's V8 [9] and Apple's JSC [2] are industry-leading VM and JIT compilers for JavaScript. PyPy [4] is a trace JIT framework written in Python.

---

[1] https://www.enlightenment.org/.

JavaScript with Types. Recently, a few techniques on extending JavaScript with types for better performance are proposed. TypeScript [14] is a superset of JavaScript that extends JavaScript with explicit types. Flow [8] is a subset of JavaScript that adds type-checks. SJS [7] shares the same concept as Flow, but it generates C++ code and supports AOT compilation. SJS integrates Wala [13] to perform type inference. Ahn et al. [1] propose how to derive an object type from its inherited prototype and method binding.

JavaScript VM and a Browser. A few techniques are proposed to run native code inside a browser. Doppio [17] is a JavaScript-based runtime system that allows C++ code and JVM programs run inside a browser. asm.js [15] converts C++ code to JavaScript to run on any JavaScript VM. However, it is not designed to support objects and prototype. Nacl (and PNaCl) [10] runs natively-compiled C++ code in a Chrome web browser.

3 Design of Typed JS

Typed JS utilizes type annotations, offers the usage of dynamic and static features, and an AOT compilation to increase the performance and yet reducing memory footprint on mobile platforms than current industry-leading JavaScript engines. The design principles of Typed JS are as follows.

- **Type Annotation**: Dynamicity of objects is one of major performance bottlenecks of JavaScript, as they require type-checked during runtime. Typed JS enforces types of objects to be specified when they are declared. It extends JavaScript syntax to accept type-annotated objects, and do not allow such objects to change its type during runtime. Figure 1 shows an example of a function written in Typed JS. In this example, the function is type-decorated.
- **Object Model**: Dynamically adding/deleting a property causes another performance decrease during runtime. To support dynamic objects, current JavaScript engines must check for the existence of a property during runtime. In addition to traditional dynamic objects in Typed JS, Typed JS supports sealed classes, which prevents users to change properties declared in sealed classes during runtime. Hence, sealed classes can be used if one prefers runtime efficiency over object dynamicity.
- **AOT Compilation**: Typed JS is compiled to a target-specific, optimized binary executable. Moreover, Typed JS can utilize modern compiler optimization techniques, as it annotates types and supports static classes. In our prototype, Typed JS compiler transpiles Typed JS source code into C++11, and it is natively compiled with g++'s optimization techniques.
- **Robust and Secure**: Typed JS follows the strict mode of JavaScript, and redefines a set of dynamic features that can be efficiently implemented. Also, Typed JS does not support evaluating source code during runtime, i.e., *eval*(), eliminating security holes.

```
var hanoi =
  function(disc: int, src: string,
           aux: string, dst: string): void {
    if(disc > 0) {
      hanoi(disc-1, src, dst, aux);
      console.log("Move disc " + disc +
                  " from " + src + " to " + dst);
      hanoi(disc-1, aux, src, dst);
    }
  }
hanoi(5, "src", "aux", "dst");
```

Fig. 1. Tower of Hanoi in Typed JS

4   Architecture of Typed JS

Figure 2 shows the architecture of Typed JS. It consists of two major parts—compiler and runtime. The compiler part takes Typed JS source code as input, and generates C++11 code that heavily depends on internal data structure and Typed JS runtime library. The runtime part provides the implementation of the internal data structure and runtime library. The auto-generated C++11 code is compiled, and executed natively on a low-end Samsung mobile phone. This phone operates with Tizen[2] OS. In our implementation, C++ code is compiled with g++ found in Tizen-SDK-2.3.[3] This version of g++ generates binary for ARM architecture. Additionally, binding API, a selection of Tizen EFL graphics library wrappers, is also implemented to allow GUI components to be integrated with Typed JS. Each part further consists of smaller components, and they are explained in the following sections.

4.1   Compiler

Compilation is a 3-phase process, and each phase is explained as follows.

Parser. First, the parser generates an abstract syntax tree (AST) from Typed JS source code. The AST is extended from Mozilla JavaScript AST[4] to represent type-specific information as well as Typed JS extensions such as type-annotated objects and sealed classes. We also extend esprima,[5] an open source ECMAScript 5.1 parser to validate Typed JS syntax and generate an AST with Typed JS extensions. Figure 3 shows an AST of hanoi() from Fig. 1. The figure shows that new entries are added to type-annotate function parameters and return

---

[2] https://www.tizen.org.
[3] https://developer.tizen.org/.
[4] https://developer.mozilla.org/en-US/docs/Mozilla/Projects/SpiderMonkey/Parser_API.
[5] http://esprima.org/.

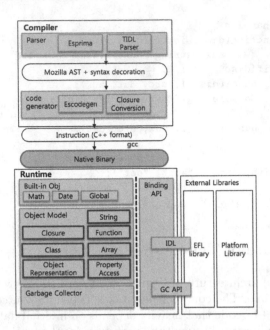

Fig. 2. Architecture of Typed JS

types (indicated by <---). Additionally, the Tizen EFL API written in Tizen IDL (TIDL) is parsed and validated, and corresponding API calls are also added to the AST (omitted in Fig. 3 due to complexity).

Code Generator. Second, the code generator takes an AST as input, performs semantics validation, and generates C++11 code. We modified escodegen,[6] which generates JavaScript code from an Mozilla JavaScript AST, to generate C++11 code with Typed JS runtime library. Furthermore, we modified escodegen to perform type inference by deriving and applying a set of type inference rules during the semantics validation to deduce unknown variable types before reporting a missing/invalid type error. Our type inference algorithm is a simplified version of Hindley-Milner.

The overview of type inference algorithm in Typed JS is given as follows. Given an expression of unknown type, its type is determined by deriving the type of right operand first, and assigning a compatible type (or subtype) to the left operand. Then, the type of the expression becomes the type of its left operand. This type resolution step is recursively applied from bottom up by traversing the AST until root is reached. For example, given an expression, *var x = 1*, the type of right operand is derived, which is a number by definition, and the same type as 1 is assigned to *x*. For an expression, *var y = x*, similar resolution process is performed once the type of its right operand, *x*, has been determined. The same process is applied to all different kinds of expressions in Typed JS

---
[6] https://github.com/estools/escodegen.

```
            . . .
            "body": [{
              "type": "VariableDeclaration",
              "declarations": [{
                "type": "VariableDeclarator",
                "id": {
                  "type": "Identifier",
                  "name": "hanoi"
                },
                "init": {
                  "type": "FunctionExpression",
                  "params": [{
                    "type": "VariableDeclarator",
                    "id": {
                      "type": "Identifier",
                      "name": "disc"
                    },
                    "idType": {          <---
                      "type": "Type",
                      "name": "int"
                    },
                  },
                  . . .
                  "returnType": {        <---
                    "type": "Type",
                    "name": "void"
                  },
            . . .
```

Fig. 3. An AST of hanoi()

whose types are not explicitly given by users. If the Typed JS function shown in Fig. 1 were written without explicitly declaring function parameter types, correct types would still be determined by the type inference rules. The type inference rules are still in preliminary phase, and further extension is left as future work.

Figure 4 shows a snippet of auto-generated C++ code of hanoi() shown in Fig. 1. The code shows that it utilizes Typed JS runtime library such as JSValue and JSStringRef to represent JavaScript number and string, respectively, while keeping the overall control flow intact (such as recursion and if-statement). A description of runtime model is provided in detail in Sect. 4.2.

Compilation. Finally, the auto-generated C++ code is compiled with g++ to produce an object binary (i.e., *.o). This binary is linked with Typed JS runtime library to produce an executable binary. Furthermore, when Tizen EFL bindings are required, the EFL wrapper API is also compiled and linked. Note that, the auto-generated C++ code is not necessarily optimal, but we implicitly apply compiler optimization (e.g., -O3) by using a state-of-the-art AOT compiler such as g++.

```
...
JSValue hanoi;
hanoi = JSValue([&](JSValue This, JSValue ___disc,
                   JSValue ___src, JSValue ___aux,
                   JSValue ___dst) mutable -> JSValue {
    int disc = (___disc).asInt32();
    JSStringRef src = (___src).asStringRef();
    JSStringRef aux = (___aux).asStringRef();
    JSStringRef dst = (___dst).asStringRef(); {
    if (disc > 0) {
        hanoi(JSValue(disc - 1), (src).asJSValue(),
              (dst).asJSValue(), (aux).asJSValue());
        console::log((JSStringRef("Move disc ") + disc +
                      JSStringRef(" from ") + src +
                      JSStringRef(" to ") + dst).asJSValue());
        hanoi(JSValue(disc - 1), (aux).asJSValue(),
              (src).asJSValue(), (dst).asJSValue());
    }
}   return undefined;
});
hanoi(JSValue(5), (JSStringRef("src")).asJSValue(),
      (JSStringRef("aux")).asJSValue(),
      (JSStringRef("dst")).asJSValue());
console::log((JSStringRef("success")).asJSValue());
...
```

Fig. 4. hanoi() in C++11 (auto-generated)

4.2   Runtime

Runtime further consists of four components, and each component is explained below.

Object Model. In Typed JS, two object models are cohesively existed—dynamic object and sealed class models. Dynamic object model is the typical prototypical model found in ECMAScript 5.1, while sealed class model is the class-oriented model found in C++. Former is to be compatible with ECMASript 5.1 specification, while latter is designed to give better performance. The difference between dynamic and sealed class models is that, dynamically adding/deleting properties is removed in the sealed class model, and all property types are finalized in the compilation time. A sealed class is specifically designed to directly map a JavaScript object to a C++ class to gain further performance.

Typical JavaScript objects cannot be simply transpiled to C++ objects due to not supporting prototypical models in C++. To support dynamic objects, additional data structures are required, and these are explained as follows.

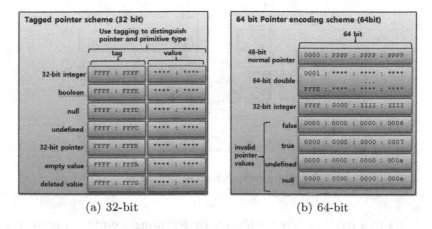

(a) 32-bit   (b) 64-bit

Fig. 5. JSValue

Object Representation. Figure 5 shows a *JSValue* data structure used to represent an object in Typed JS. The tagged pointer scheme that JSValue uses allows either an object (regardless of its type) or a primitive value to be stored in a 64-bit block. It also allows itself to convert one type to another dynamically in runtime. For example, a variable of type boolean can be converted to a pointer type by updating the tag and value. JSValue is implemented differently depending on target machines. For 32-bit machines, it uses two 32-bit spaces. The first 32-bits are used to store a tag of an object, and the last 32-bits are used to store an actual value (either a primitive value or a pointer). An exception is when double is stored. On 64-bit machines, tagging is not explicitly used but similar approach applies. The physical size of JSValue is 64-bit for both 32 and 64-bit machines.

JS Object, Prototype and Sealed Classes. JS objects are connected to each other to represent a prototype chain in Typed JS. Figure 6 shows an example of JS objects, and how they are connected to represent a prototype chain.

An JS object is represented by a combination of JSValue and JS*x*Impl, where *x* is either Object, SealedClass, Function, String or Array, if the object is neither a number, null nor undefined. As discussed above, JSValue is a generic data container from which its value is used to retrieve the actual data that JSValue represents. For example, the JSValue for "tom" object in Fig. 6 points to an JSObjectImpl where properties of "tom" are implemented. Similarly, the JSValue for function *eat*() points to an JSFunctionImpl. For security reasons, JS*x*Impl objects cannot be directly accessed from Typed JS.

An JSObjectImpl implements a typical (*key, value*) map to allow property reads and writes. The *key* and *value* is of type JSValue. Hence, a JSValue of any type can be stored as a property. For example, in Fig. 6, "tom" object contains three properties of type string, number and function, and they are all encapsulated in JSValues. Every JSObjectImpl contains a special _*proto*_ as a key

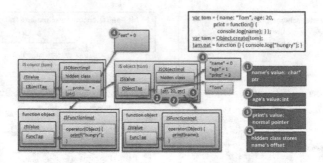

Fig. 6. Prototype chain in Typed JS

that points to a parent prototype object. By following __proto__, a prototypical model can be implemented. A property lookup of an object o can be performed as follows. First, a property x is searched in the (key, value) map in o. If a property x is found, its value is returned. Otherwise, the parent object y as indicated by __proto__ is retrieved, and the same process is recursively applied. When __proto__ is null, it indicates that, there is no parent prototype object, so the process terminates. Furthermore, to optimize property lookup, map is implemented using hidden class and inline caching techniques. Further description is given in Sect. 4.3.

An JSSealedClassImpl represents non-dynamic object. It contains a pointer that points to a typical C++ object. A sealed class is generated when a `class` is defined in Typed JS. For sealed classes, typical class-based inheritance is supported.

Function, Closure, and Polymorphic Functions. A function object (i.e., closure) is implemented by using the lambda function introduced in C++11. The lambda function allows us to define an anonymous function object that can be invoked and passed as an argument to a function. Given a Typed JS function, our code generator generates a lambda function accordingly. Polymorphic functions are supported by combining JSValue and lambda functions. A polymorphic function takes JSValues as input parameters, and the operation to perform on JSValue is determined by the type of the JSValue, which is determined in runtime. Figure 4 also shows how a function is represented by a C++11 lambda function with JSValues as input parameters. For the functions in sealed classes, it is not required to use JSValues, as types are not dynamic.

Supporting Modules. Runtime further consists of a number of supporting modules, and they are as follows.

– **Built-in Object**: Typed JS provides a number of built-in objects specified in ECMAScript 5. Some examples include Math, Date, Global, etc. These built-in objects can be used from both dynamic and static objects.

- **Garbage Collector**: In Typed JS, automatic memory management is provided when objects are allocated or deleted. In our prototype, we adopted Boehm-Demers-Weiser conservative garbage collector,[7] when objects are allocated and removed. For future work, we plan to implement reference counting-based memory management, as it gives less overhead on mobile platforms.
- **A Graphics Binding API**: The graphics binding API gives us many opportunities to use Typed JS on mobile devices. In our prototype, the binding API wraps a number of EFL graphics library on Tizen. This allows us to access Tizen's graphics components, and we successfully reimplemented mobile demo applications that came with Tizen SDK 2.3 originally written in C++ in Typed JS. This provides a way of writing native Tizen application in JavaScript-like style. A possible future work is to let the binding API wrap a web browser's canvas API to run web applications natively on Tizen.

4.3 Optimization

Noticeable optimization techniques that Typed JS currently implements are as follows.

- **Fast Property Access**: For fast property access, we implemented hidden class and inline caching technique used in V8. This technique caches a property offset when a property in an object is accessed frequently, and when the same property is accessed after caching, it improves the property access performance by quickly reading the value located in the offset without performing any string operation, as long as the layout of the object that contains the property is not changed. This allows us not to perform string hashing every time when a property is accessed.
- **Fast String Operation**: Poor string implementation significantly affects the overall performance of Type JS. Currently, we implemented string interning and rope string to improve basic string operations.

4.4 Limitations

Current implementation of Typed JS poses the following limitations.

- **Debugging Symbols**: Since Typed JS transpiles JavaScript code into C++ code and compiles using g++, generating and maintaining debugging symbols and supporting a debugger becomes a challenging problem. To address this problem, in future work, we are planning to generate LLVM[8] IR instead of C++ code from Typed JS. In this way, we can maintain a debugging symbol table and add debugging information between LLVM IRs to allow us to use any LLVM-supported debugger.

---

[7] http://www.hboehm.info/gc.
[8] http://llvm.org.

- **Supporting Existing JavaScript Libraries**: While Typed JS supports most of JavaScript operations, it is often insufficient to support existing JavaScript libraries as-is such as the libraries found in node.js.[9] This is because many libraries use unsupported patterns such as *eval()*, which requires the code to be rewritten without using such patterns. To address this problem, in future work, we are planning to generate a Typed JS pattern analyzer that can detect unsupported patterns in existing JavaScript code and even suggests valid code for Typed JS.
- **Security**: The current approach of generating and compiling C++ code from Typed JS can pose a security risk, as the auto-generated code can be altered before it is compiled. Using LLVM instead of g++ can solve this problem, as LLVM IR is not written to disk when it is compiled.

5   Experimental Results

We now present experimental results. Experiments were conducted on a prepro-duction, low-end Samsung mobile phone running Tizen 2.3. Tizen is an open source mobile operating system currently developed by Samsung Software R&D Center. In addition, to compare the performance and memory usage of Typed JS in an unlimited-resource environment, the same set of experiments were repeated on a 3.5 GHz Linux desktop with 16 GiB of memory. Typed JS is compiled using Tizen SDK 2.3 and executed on the Samsung mobile phone. For Linux desktop, g++ was used to compile Typed JS.

For performance measurement, Sunspider JavaScript Benchmark[10] was used. Memory usage was measured by checking the RSS size used by each test suite process. Binary size was measured by adding all shared libraries required to run each test suite. To compare the performance and memory usage of Typed JS against existing JavaScript engines, the same test suites were executed on V8 and JSC. When measuring the performance of V8 and JSC, the initial loading time for JavaScript virtual machine were excluded. Furthermore, the same test suites were also ported to C and executed. The ported C test suites were compiled with -O3 optimization. In the experiments, this C implementation defines the practical upper bound for both performance and memory usage.

Figure 7 shows the runtime performance and memory usage of Typed JS against V8, JSC, and C on the Tizen mobile phone (Note the log scale in Fig. 7(b)). Typed JS outperforms V8 and JSC by up to 3.5x while consum-ing up to 20x less memory. Smaller memory usage is largely due to not using a virtual machine unlike others. Typed JS is outperformed by JSC (and V8) on `recursive` and `math` test suites due to inefficient lambda functions in C++11 and lack of JIT compilation, respectively.

Figure 8 repeats the same experiments on the Linux desktop. Similar results are observed, but the performance gap between Typed JS and other engines are much reduced due to more powerful CPU. Furthermore, we observe that,

---

[9] http://nodejs.org.
[10] http://www.webkit.org/perf/sunspider/sunspider.html.

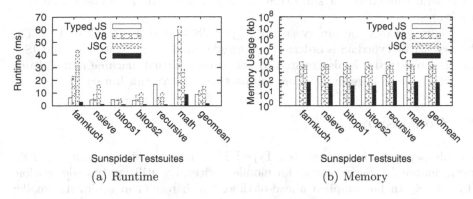

(a) Runtime

(b) Memory

Fig. 7. Tizen phone

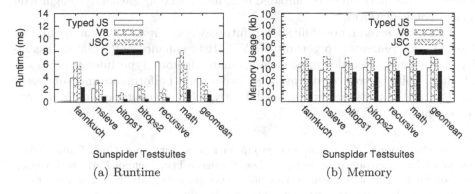

(a) Runtime

(b) Memory

Fig. 8. Linux desktop

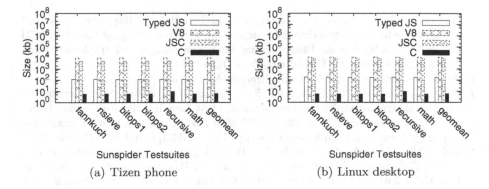

(a) Tizen phone

(b) Linux desktop

Fig. 9. Binary size

in general, the same test suite runs up to 10x slower on a mobile phone than desktop.

Figure 9 shows the binary size of Typed JS against V8, JSC, and C. The binary size of Typed JS is orders of magnitude smaller than that of V8 and JSC. Smaller binary size is also related to not using a virtual machine and utilizing C library, which is generally more compact than JavaScript library.

6   Conclusion

In this paper, we have presented Typed JS, a memory efficient but yet high-performance JavaScript engine for mobile devices. By utilizing type-decoration, Typed JS can be compiled ahead-of-time, which results in achieving smaller memory footprint and high-performance than traditional virtual machine-based JavaScript engines without scarifying much of core JavaScript concepts, such as objects, prototype, etc. Experiments show that Typed JS is memory-efficient and achieves better performance compared to industry-leading JavaScript engines on Tizen mobile platform.

There are several possibilities for future work. First, we plan to update C++11 code generator to generate LLVM IR to enhance performance, usability, and security. Second, implementing more rigorous type inference rules is planned. Third, power consumption evaluation and performance measurements on other mobile platforms are planned. Lastly, reference counting-based memory management is also planned.

Acknowledgment. We thank our group members Junyoung Cho, Eunji Jeong, Saebom Kim, Wonyong Kim, Sanggyu Lee, Seungsoo Lee, Jaeman Park, and Young-soo Son for their contributions to this paper. We are also grateful to the anonymous reviewers for their constructive comments on this paper.

References

1. Ahn, W., Choi, J., Shull, T., Garzarán, M.J., Torrellas, J.: Improving javascript performance by deconstructing the type system. In: Proceedings of the 35th ACM SIGPLAN Conference on Programming Language Design and Implementation, p. 51. ACM, Edinburgh, United Kingdom, June 2014
2. Apple.Javascriptcore (2005). http://trac.webkit.org/wiki/JavaScriptCore
3. Böhm, I., von Koch, T.J.K.E., Kyle, S.C., Franke, B., Topham, N.P.: Generalized just-in-time trace compilation using a parallel task farm in a dynamic binary translator. In: Proceedings of the 32nd ACM SIGPLAN Conference on Programming Language Design and Implementation, pp. 74–85. ACM, San Jose, CA, June 2011
4. Bolz, C.F., Cuni, A., Fijalkowski, M., Rigo, A.: Tracing the meta-level: Pypy's tracing JIT compiler. In: Proceedings of the 4th Workshop on the Implementation, Compilation, Optimization of Object-Oriented Languages and Programming Systems, pp. 18–25. ACM, Genova, Italy (2009)

5. Bracha, G., Griswold, D.: Strongtalk: typechecking smalltalk in a production environment. In: Proceedings of the Eighth Annual Conference on Object-Oriented Programming Systems, Languages, and Applications, pp. 215–230. ACM, Washington, DC, October 1993
6. Chambers, C., Ungar, D., Lee, E.: An efficient implementation of SELF, a dynamically-typed object-oriented language based on prototypes. Lisp Symb. Comput. 4(3), 243–281 (1991)
7. Choi, P.W., Chandra, S., Necula, G., Sen, K.: SJS: a typed subset of javascript with fixed object layout. Technical report UCB/EECS-2015-10, EECS Department, University of California, Berkeley, March 2015
8. Facebook.flow (2014). http://flowtype.org/
9. Google.Chrome v8 (2008). https://developers.google.com/v8/
10. Google.NaCl and PNaCl (2013). https://developer.chrome.com/native-client/nacl-and-pnacl/
11. Hölzle, U., Chambers, C., Ungar, D.: Optimizing dynamically-typed object-oriented languages with polymorphic inline caches. In: Proceedings of European Conference on Object-Oriented Programming, pp. 21–38. Schloss Dagstuhl - Leibniz-Zentrum fuer Informatik, Geneva, Switzerland, July 1991
12. Hölzle, U., Chambers, C., Ungar, D.: Debugging optimized code with dynamic deoptimization. In: Proceedings of the ACM SIGPLAN Conference on Programming Language Design and Implementation, pp. 32–43. ACM, San Francisco CA, June 1992
13. IBM.Wala (2006). https://wala.sourceforge.net
14. Microsoft.TypeScript (2012). http://www.typescriptlang.org/
15. Mozilla.asm.js (2013). http://asmjs.org/
16. Rompf, T., Sujeeth, A.K., Brown, K.J., Lee, H., Chafi, H., Olukotun, K.: Surgical precision JIT compilers. In: Proceedings of the 35th ACM SIGPLAN Conference on Programming Language Design and Implementation, p. 8. ACM, Edinburgh, United Kingdom, June 2014
17. Vilk, J., Berger, E.D.: Doppio: breaking the browser language barrier. In: Proceedings of the 35th ACM SIGPLAN Conference on Programming Language Design and Implementation, pp. 52. ACM, Edinburgh, United Kingdom, June 2014

Pervasive Context Sharing in MAGPIE: Adaptive Trust-Based Privacy Protection

Chenguang Liu$^{(\boxtimes)}$ and Christine Julien

Department of Electrical and Computer Engineering,
The University of Texas at Austin, Austin, TX, USA
{liuchg,c.julien}@utexas.edu

Abstract. Today's mobile and pervasive computing devices are embedded with increasingly powerful sensing capabilities that enable them to provide exceptional spatio-temporal context acquisition that is not possible with traditional static sensor networks alone. As a result, enabling these devices to *share* context information with one another has a great potential for enabling mobile users to exploit the nearby cyber and physical environments in *participatory* or *human-centric* computing. However, because these mobile devices are owned by and sense information about *individuals*, sharing the acquired context raises significant privacy concerns. In this paper, we define MAGPIE, which implements an alternative to existing *all-or-nothing* sharing solutions. MAGPIE integrates a decentralized *context-dependent* and adaptive trust scheme with a privacy preserving sharing mechanism to evaluate the risk of disclosing potentially private data. The proposed method uses this assessment to dynamically determine the sharing strategy and the *quality* of the context shared. Conceptually, MAGPIE allows devices to actively obfuscate context information so that sharing is still useful but does not breach user privacy. To our knowledge this is the first work to take both trust relationships and users' individual privacy sensitivities into account to balance sharing and privacy preservation. We describe MAGPIE and then evaluate it in a series of application-oriented experiments running on the Opportunistic Network Environment (ONE) simulator.

Keywords: Context sharing · Privacy preserving · Adaptive trust

1 Introduction

With the rapid development of the *Internet of Things* (IoT), everyday consumer devices have become more connected to one another [1]. This offers a chance for these devices to collaborate, which brings opportunities for new applications that can exploit the surrounding environment, especially when these devices are carried by people. By sharing local contextual information, mobile devices can help us to avoid traffic on the road (e.g., Waze[1]), improve recreational sports experiences (e.g., BikeNet [2]), and even monitor air pollution (e.g., P-Sense [3]

[1] https://www.waze.com/.

© Institute for Computer Sciences, Social Informatics and Telecommunications Engineering 2015
S. Sigg et al. (Eds.): MobiCASE 2015, LNICST 162, pp. 122–139, 2015.
DOI: 10.1007/978-3-319-29003-4_8

and Citisense [4]). With this shift in the usage comes a shift in how pervasive computing applications view context beyond simple *egocentric* views [5], collected by a single device or user for consumption by a that device or user. The collective or cumulative feature of a set of shared contexts is increasingly valued because of applications in *participatory* or *human-centric sensing* [6]. However, sharing the context information sensed by a user's personal mobile device poses a significant threat to the user's privacy if it is not under proper control.

Given the privacy concerns raised when collecting and sharing information using personal devices, there has been substantial research on two related topics: dynamic trust management and schemes to obfuscate and protect potentially personal data. The goal of dynamic trust management in pervasive computing is to select generally reliable candidates with which to interact (i.e., share information) based on previous experience or general recommendations [7–9]. On the privacy preservation side, the focus is identifying and perturbing sensitive information to protect an individual from being identified [10–12]. In isolation, neither of these is effective enough for a context-sharing scenario like *Social Cycling* [2], where the mobile devices carried by a group of cyclists should be able to efficiently provide context data to other participants in the group in order to share up-to-date and reliable information about the availability (and potential availability) of shared bicycles. Such an application requires sharing individual's location traces with other users; most people are not eager to share detailed raw information about their spatiotemporal trajectories with just anyone.

We introduce MAGPIE, a trust-adaptive and privacy-preserving approach for pervasive context sharing applications in which mobile and heterogeneous sensor-equipped devices *opportunistically* work together to increase awareness of the environment. MAGPIE facilitates device-to-device context sharing (i.e., without assistance from an infrastructure), as opposed to an approach that relies on dedicated sensors deployed in the environment that are often designed to intentionally provide context information for users without raising privacy concerns. In MAGPIE, the interaction experience that comes from sharing context information also serves as evidence for later trust establishment. MAGPIE provides an alternative to traditional *all-or-nothing* sharing approaches by potentially disclosing some obfuscated but still useful context information. A key challenge is to address the privacy concerns of the participants about whom the context is collected while ensuring that the *quality* of context shared is sufficient. Therefore our approach leverages trust relationships established among pervasive computing participants and privacy sensitivities of the individuals together to design the obfuscating process into our context sharing mechanism. MAGPIE also utilizes *context similarity factors* and *situational trust* to fit the context sharing behavior to the situations of the pervasive computing devices and their users.

To our knowledge this is the first work to use both trust relationships and an individual's privacy sensitivities to estimate the *risk* of context sharing; we use this risk to dynamically select sharing strategies and to affect the *quality* of shared context. To evaluate MAGPIE, we perform application-oriented experiments on the Opportunistic Network Environment (ONE) simulator [13].

We evaluate the effectiveness of our trust establishment scheme and privacy protection by analyzing the changes in participation in sharing activities as well as the empirical error percentage in the information shared. In Sect. 2 we outline the related works addressing privacy and trust issues in pervasive computing. The overview, design, and implementation details of MAGPIE are presented in Sect. 3, followed by the evaluation of our work in Sect. 4.

2   Related Work

By sharing context information acquired by a *set* of devices, a group of opportunistically interconnected devices with disparate sensing capabilities is able to be more adaptive to its nearby physical and cyber environments [14,15]. MAGPIE is motivated by this new type of application, and we aim to provide a balance between preserving privacy and facilitating context sharing participation. Before describing our approach in detail, we overview related projects establishing trust among distributed pervasive computing participants, addressing privacy in pervasive computing, and supporting context sharing in these environments.

Establishing Trust Among Pervasive Computing Participants. Users distinguish their expectations of their systems into *familiarity, confidence,* and *trust* [16], where the latter uniquely depends not on actual or inherent danger but on the user's perceived *risk*. These perceptions emerge as a part of decision and action. With respect to expectations for sharing context in pervasive computing, trust is fundamental for establishing the sharing relationship between the participants and for selecting the means of the sharing behavior.

Our setting demands a decentralized approach to trust management that can operate without persistent connectivity to the Internet infrastructure. Three branches of decentralized trust management systems exist in the literature: (1) approaches that rely on encounters with trusted third parties and focus largely on cryptographic issues in the authorization process [17]; (2) reputation mechanisms that use social control to store and disseminate reputation information [18–20]; and (3) purely decentralized trust management systems that establish trust relationships between the devices in pervasive environments based only on inter-device interactions [7,9]. Because we do not wish to limit the applicability of our approach, we target situations like the latter. However, these existing trust schemes are not tied to determining when and how to share context information, so they require some updating to address the needs of MAGPIE.

Privacy Preservation in Pervasive Computing. On the other hand, protecting privacy of users' personal information is also a well-studied area. One of the widely accepted works is to use *k-anonymity* [21] for statistical disclosure control; *k-anonymity* aims to render a particular piece of data indistinguishable among the aggregation of $k - 1$ other pieces. These approaches are commonly used to protect individuals from being identified given a large amount of aggregated information like medical record data. Approaches that are perhaps more appropriate to pervasive computing environments are based on the idea of adding noise to personal data on the *client-side* to ensure individual privacy. These systems then use community-wide reconstruction techniques to restore knowledge about a shared group context [11,22]. Even these latter approaches assume one or more dedicated and honest aggregators within the network, which is limiting for general-purpose pervasive computing environments.

Distributed differential privacy methods [10], derived from classical differential privacy [12], can be applied to allow applications to learn only some important statistics but no additional information and thus satisfy privacy guarantees. These approaches generally require a very large number of data items to be able to provide reasonable privacy while maintaining correct information. Therefore differential privacy based approaches do not suit our needs for sharing context among sparsely connected devices.

More recently, efforts related to data preprocessing in smart grids has demonstrated the ability to obfuscate individual users' behaviors [23]. MAGPIE is inspired by the latter and by distributed differential privacy, but we introduce new noise models to eliminate the characteristics of individual data without losing its inherent meaning. We do assume the availability of a context specific privacy sensitivity manager [24,25] on each user's device. This privacy manager is able to offer a quantified sensitivity value $\varepsilon \in (0,1)$ for each type of context, which provides an individualized perception of how private the particular context type is. For instance, a particular user may deem his location context information to be highly private while his ambient sound level context may be less private.

Sharing Context. MAGPIE provides capabilities that allow mobile devices to share their sensed context with one another. The potential applications of this work include systems like BikeNet [2] or P-Sense [3], or generally mobile and pervasive computing applications that take advantage of directly sharing context information (e.g., workout companion applications like "Run with a buddy"). Our approach can also be used to extend participatory sensing systems (e.g., a crowd-sourced transit information system [26] or CarTel [27]), especially the ones collaborating in a device-to-device fashion [28–30]. MAGPIE is primarily motivated by our own previous work on the Grapevine context framework [5], which was developed for succinctly summarizing and efficiently sharing context information in pervasive computing environments.

3   MAGPIE: Adaptive Trust- and Privacy-Based Context Sharing

We consider a network of users with smart devices that are connected to one another by an opportunistic mobile network of device-to-device links[2]. Users' applications collect and act on context information that describes the user's state and situation; this information comes both from the user's own device

---

[2] We use "device" and "user" interchangeably because we assume that every participant is associated with a single device through which he collaborates.

and through opportunistic sharing with connected devices of other users. For example cyclists can increase energy efficiency or data accuracy if their devices are wisely and effectively sharing information about the riders' trips [2] (e.g., sharing compass information with users in a traveling group whose devices lack that particular sensing capability or taking turns collecting motion statistics to distribute sensing costs). We assume devices operate under a shared context ontology, i.e., we assume that there is a well known set of context types and that the names of these types are shared among all of the participants *a priori*.

We introduce MAGPIE, which facilitates context sharing activities to make it possible for users to adjust their behavior based on the sensed context while maintaining the privacy of the users about whom the context information is collected. Consider a classic context-awareness scenario [31] in which smart devices are able to adjust themselves and thereby the ambient environment by collecting and actuating on high-level situational knowledge (e.g., the start of a meeting or a social event like a coffee break) inferred from the shared context acquired from multiple devices. MAGPIE has two key components: adaptive trust evaluation and privacy preserving context sharing.

A key principle of MAGPIE is that users share multiple types of context information with several other users. For this reason, both the trust evaluation scheme and the privacy sensitivity are *context-dependent*. This reflects the fact that, simply because a coordinating partner is a good source for one type of context information (e.g., local weather) does not necessarily imply he is trustworthy with some particularly personal data (e.g., raw location). MAGPIE assumes that each user is associated with an individualized specification of their privacy sensitivities for each type of context information shared and maintained by a privacy sensitivity manager (see Sect. 2). These sensitivity values range over $(0, 1]$, where larger values indicate higher privacy requirements.

Figure 1 shows an overview of MAGPIE, specifically in the process of responding to a neighboring device's request for a piece of context. Upon receiving a request from user u_i for a specific type of context information, m (top center of the figure), the request passes to the adaptive trust management module to evaluate how trustworthy u_i is regarding the type m. Intuitively, the device

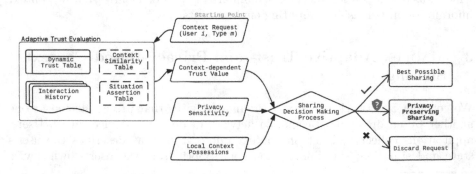

Fig. 1. System Overview

determines whether u_i is trustworthy enough to share the raw context information with. If not, the device needs to determine whether it is possible to share
any knowledge about this context type with u_i, e.g., in an obfuscated form. The
quantified result $\tau_{i,m}$ of trust evaluation is considered, together with the user's
privacy sensitivity for the context type m (ε_m) and the local context possession
C_m, to assess the potential *risk* of sharing the requested context information
with u_i. The context sharing module uses this risk to select a sharing strategy that maximizes the possibility of participation while keeping any potential
privacy breach under control. Figure 1 shows three possibilities: (1) there is no
risk, so the request can be fully satisfied with the raw data; (2) there is some
mitigable risk, and MAGPIE shares some obfuscated context data; and (3) the
risk is intolerable, and the request is discarded. The rest of this section provides
the details of MAGPIE's two essential components.

3.1   Adaptive Trust Management

In MAGPIE, the sharing decision is made based on several factors as described
earlier, but the foundation is an established level of trust between the recipient
of the request and the peer initiating the request. MAGPIE makes it possible to
potentially disclose some obfuscated but still useful context information, even if
the requesting peer is not fully trustworthy. Therefore the trust a potential sharer
of context information has in the requesting peer not only partially determines
which option to take, but also relates to how useful the information will be. As
such, having an expressive and effective mechanism to dynamically evaluate the
trust that a participant has in some requesting peer is essential to MAGPIE. We
define trust (as perceived by a particular user u_i) as follows:

Definition 1. *Trust. For a given user u_i, the value of Trust, $\tau_{j,m}^i \in (0,1)$ indicates to which extent a context requester u_j can be trusted with respect to a
particular context type, m.*

   We build on the wealth of mathematical models of trust and incorporate
decentralization, personalization, and specificity to the type of context information being shared. To start, we use the *Pervasive Trust Management* model [7]
based on Luhmman's idea [16] as a foundation. This definition of trust relies on
a log of user i's satisfaction (or dissatisfaction) in his historical interaction experience $a_{j,k}^i$ with a particular peer u_j. To account for these dynamics, we extend
the above definition of trust with a notion of timestep. In this extended model,
user i's trust in user j for context type m after interaction k is defined as:

$$\tau_{j,m,k}^i = \begin{cases} \tau_{j,m,k-1}^i + \omega \cdot V_{a_{j,k}^i}(1 - \tau_{j,m,k-1}) & V_{a_k} > 0 \\ \tau_{i,m,k-1}^i(1 - \omega + \omega \cdot V_{a_{j,k}^i}) & else \end{cases} \tag{1}$$

where $V_{a_{j,k}^i}$ is the product of the satisfaction (a^+) and dissatisfaction (a^-) of
the past behaviors. Satisfaction and dissatisfaction can be measured in a variety
of ways. In MAGPIE, we count satisfaction (a^+) as the percentage of times in

which a request from i to j for context type m resulted in a response and dissatisfaction as the percentage of times in which such an interaction did not result in any response. This is a simple scheme that could easily be extended, but this is not the primary focus of this work. The updated trust value is also weighted according to a user- or system-defined weight (ω).

In MAGPIE, the actions through which users can learn about others' trustworthiness involve context requesting and sharing, thus it is natural to make $V_{a^i_{j,k}}$ also be context dependent. Specifically, with regard to context type m, a $V_{a^i_{j,m,k}}$ can be calculated independently for each type of context that may be requested (and context-specific satisfaction measures) using the equation below[3]:

$$V_{a^i_{j,m,k}} = \Theta_m \cdot \frac{(a^+ - a^-)((a^+ - a^-) \cdot \delta)^{2s}}{(a^+ + a^-)((a^+ - a^-) \cdot \delta)^{2s} + 1} \tag{2}$$

where δ and s are inversely proportional values that determine the individualized trust increment or decrement based on satisfaction and dissatisfaction with interactions. Based on the general frequency of the sparse interactions in an opportunistic network [7] and the empirical evidence from our experiments, this δ should be in the range of $(0, 0.05]$, and it is mapped to the individualized privacy sensitivity of the context type m, ε_m, ($\delta \in (0, 0.05] \mapsto \varepsilon_m$). The value Θ_m weights the value for context m as shared by j based on the cost of retrieving the particular context value. Intuitively, this gives more "credit" to users or devices that share context that is more expensive to acquire in the first place.

As the topology of a pervasive computing network can be sparse and frequently changing, there is a considerable chance that no previous interaction will have occurred between two users regarding the context type m. It is also possible that the resulting trust level is a value that will likely lead to an undesired sharing option later in Eq. 4. To bootstrap sharing in such circumstances, MAGPIE considers a *context-similarity* parameter $\Re(m, n)$. This metric provides a measure of similarity between m and n, a second type of context; such a metric could be based on the comparison of the distinct keywords used to describe them [19]. As an example, school information and field-of-study could be considered similar because they both relate to one's educational background. Thus, Eq. 2 can be refined as:

$$V'_{a^i_{j,m,k}} = \Re(m, n) \cdot \Theta_n \cdot \frac{(a^+ - a^-)((a^+ - a^-) \cdot \delta)^{2s}}{(a^+ + a^-)((a^+ - a^-) \cdot \delta)^{2s} + 1} \tag{3}$$

where a^+ and a^- are the interaction satisfactions with user u_j regarding to context type n. Of course, a given context type m may be "similar" to more than one other context type; we capture this in MAGPIE through multiple applications of Eq. 3 for different values of n.

At last, we provide support for *situational trust* as a short term trust boost [32,33]. This short-term situational trust is applied to increase the trustworthiness between a group of users by some adaptive percentage β_k when they

---

[3] In the equation, $a^+_{j,m}$ and $a^-_{j,m}$ haven been replaced with a^+ and a^- for simplicity.

are perceived to be in some special shared situation. For example two users with a mutual friend may both attend a party hosted by this friend where their joint attendance at the party can bootstrap sharing some context types when the interacting parties are in the same situation.

Considering this last piece of trust determination, Algorithm 1[4] shows the complete procedure of calculating the trust value of a context requester.

Algorithm 1. Instantaneous Trust Calculating Procedure

input : j, peer making request; m, context type; k, current time step

output: $\tau_{j,m}^*$, instantaneous trust value for peer j

1 initialization: $\tau_{j,m}^*, \tau_{max} \leftarrow 0$;

2 $V_{a_{j,m,k}} = \Theta_m \cdot \frac{(a_{j,m}^+ - a_{j,m}^-)((a_{j,m}^+ - a_{j,m}^-) \cdot \delta)^{2s}}{(a_{j,m}^+ + a_{j,m}^-)((a_{j,m}^+ - a_{j,m}^-) \cdot \delta)^{2s} + 1}$;

3 **if** $V_{a_{j,m,k}} > 0$ **then**

4 $\quad | \quad \tau_{j,m,k-1} + \omega \cdot V_{a_{j,m,k}}(1 - \tau_{j,m,k-1})$;

5 **else**

6 $\quad | \quad \tau_{j,m,k-1}(1 - \omega + \omega \cdot V_{a_{j,m,k}})$;

7 **end**

8 $\tau_{max} \leftarrow \tau_{j,m,k}$;

9 **if** *sharing option* $o_{i,m} < 2$ **then**

10 $\quad |$ **foreach** c_n where $\Re(m, n) > thld$ **do**

11 $\quad | \quad | \quad V_{a_{j,n,k}} = \Re(m, n) \cdot \Theta_n \cdot \frac{(a_{j,n}^+ - a_{j,n}^-)((a_{j,n}^+ - a_{j,n}^-) \cdot \delta)^{2s}}{(a_{j,n}^+ + a_{j,n}^-)((a_{j,n}^+ - a_{j,n}^-) \cdot \delta)^{2s} + 1}$;

12 $\quad | \quad | \quad \tau' \leftarrow \tau_{j,n,k-1}(1 - \omega + \omega \cdot V_{a_{j,n,k}})$;

13 $\quad | \quad | \quad$ **if** $\tau' > \tau_{max}$ **then**

14 $\quad | \quad | \quad | \quad \tau_{max} \leftarrow \tau'$

15 $\quad | \quad | \quad$ **end**

16 $\quad |$ **end**

17 **end**

18 **if** *Situation k perceived* **then**

19 $\quad | \quad \tau_{j,m}^* \leftarrow (1 + \beta_k)\tau_{max}$

20 **else**

21 $\quad | \quad \tau_{j,m}^* \leftarrow \tau_{max}$

22 **end**

23 **return** $\tau_{j,m}^*$

Line 2 of Algorithm 1 applies Eq. 2 to compute the aggregate prior satisfaction and dissatisfaction of user i sharing context type m with peer j. Based on whether this prior is positive, i computes a preliminary trust value for j (specific to context type m) based on Eq. 1 (lines 3–8). If this value is likely lead to an undesired sharing option later in Eq. 4 (line 9), the algorithm successively applies Eq. 3 for each context type n that is "similar" to m (with a similarity value above some specified threshold, *thld*). If this results in a larger trust

---

[4] We omit the i as super script for variables; each step in Algorithm 1 shows the perspective of the user i who is responding to a request from peer user j.

value than the calculation based on the experiences just with context type m, Algorithm 1 updates the working trust value for peer j. Finally, Algorithm 1 checks whether i and j are in any special shared situation that would boost the trust level that i has computed for j (lines 18–22).

The instantaneous trust value $\tau^*_{j,m}$ returned from the last step (line 16 to 20) is different from the stored trust value that user i maintains for peer j. This returned trust value may indirectly impact the stored trust value in the long term, since it will be used to support interactions, and the user's satisfaction (or dissatisfaction) may cause an update to $\tau^i_{j,m,k}$ for some later value of k.

3.2 Privacy Preserving Sharing of Context

Above, we described how MAGPIE expressively determines a trust value for a collaborating peer requesting access to a potentially sensitive piece of context information. In this section, we describe how MAGPIE uses this value to determine what strategy to use when sharing the particular type of context information with the given requester. MAGPIE's options range from the best possible sharing, which shares the complete raw context information, to sharing no information at all, with MAGPIE's novel privacy-preserving sharing mechanisms providing a middle ground. The latter can share an obfuscated version of context that considers both the device's context-dependent privacy sensitivity and the trust level that the device has in the particular requesting peer.

Intuitively, the only way to completely avoid any risk of privacy breach is to reject every request for context sharing. But this negates any possible advantage that may come from sharing context information, including learning more broadly about one's surroundings or distributing the costs associated with context sensing. To balance the potential for leaking private information with the benefit to be garnered by sharing context information requires a rational calculation to keep the risk within acceptable limits. MAGPIE achieves this balance by exposing options that disclose blurred versions of context information when the recipient is not trusted enough to receive the raw data.

Consider a simple example in which a lunchtime line forms at a food truck outside a large office building. Someone still inside the building wonders how long the line currently is in an effort to determine whether it is a good time to get lunch. The device of someone in line could respond to this request in a variety of ways. A naïve user might choose benevolence and be perfectly willing to share information about the line. However, even sharing just this simple piece of information might leak very sensitive private information. For instance, if the user is in line, he is obviously not in his office. This could be sensitive if his coworkers or supervisers expect that he is in a meeting right now. On the other hand, someone else who also knows where his office is might know that now is a good time to steal some of his candy stash. A more cautious user may then want to carefully consider whether the risk of sharing the context information is worth the benefit. There are a few things to consider before participating in the potentially risky behavior. First is the question of *who* is making the request. In real life, if the requester is a buddy of the person in line, they may be completely trustworthy. In the digital world of MAGPIE, we assume that if the requester is another user who has proven to be a reliable information source for similar types of information in the past, then a user is may be more willing to reciprocate and provide the requested context information. This is a basic overview of how MAGPIE's adaptive trust management component informs the context sharing actions that users' devices take. As described previously, this process also depends on the particular *type* of context being requested and how sensitive the owner of that data is to sharing it. MAGPIE introduces a *privacy sensitivity* factor to capture this notion.

These first two aspects (i.e., the identity of the requester and the type of context information requested) relate only to the request for the context information. Determining *what* and *how* to share also depends on how well MAGPIE can obfuscate the context information that is shared. In MAGPIE, we achieve obfuscation by adding noise to context information, which can be better achieved when a device has similar context values from other users into which it can *blur* the individual data. In MAGPIE, all such noise additions are computed entirely on the user's personal device using only context information the device has collected or received through other device-to-device interactions. Such an approach is inspired by *differential privacy* and enables MAGPIE to share a blurred version of data with the requester only if the system has enough data to blend the raw data in and make its individual presence appear irrelevant. A similar approach has been used to solve the problem of indirect inference [34], where a composition of pieces of context information that have individually low sensitivity but, when associated with one another could jeopardize a user's privacy. By demanding strict trust in context recipients and offering somewhat inaccurate values, MAGPIE makes it harder to infer such knowledge.

MAGPIE's process for determining what context information to share and how to share it starts with the reception of a request from a peer. Consider the situation when the local MAGPIE system has received a request $r_{j,m}$ from user u_j asking about context type m. Using the algorithm in the previous section, assume that the trust management component determined an instantaneous trust value for this request to be $\tau_{j,m}^*$.

Given a privacy sensitivity for the context type m of ε_m, MAGPIE compares the inner product of $\tau_{j,m}^*$ to ε_m to determine the sharing option:

$$o_{i,m} = \begin{cases} 2 & \text{if } \langle \tau_{i,m}, 1 - \varepsilon_m \rangle \geq \theta, \\ 1 & \text{if } \langle \tau_{i,m}, 1 - \varepsilon_m \rangle \geq \eta, \\ 0 & \text{if } \langle \tau_{i,m}, 1 - \varepsilon_m \rangle < \eta. \end{cases} \tag{4}$$

where θ is the threshold for being considered as trustworthy as possible for the context type m and η is the threshold for accepting the request; $\theta, \eta \in (0,1)$, and $\theta \geq \eta$. In Eq. 4, option codes 1 and 2 indicate that the system will try to accept the sharing request, while code 0 indicates that the request will be discarded. In option 2, the requester exceeds θ, and MAGPIE will simply share the raw context data with the requester. For option 1, meeting or exceeding the threshold η indicates that the requester can be trusted with an obfuscated form of the data, where the level of obfuscation will be further based on the magnitude of the trust in user j for context type m. For the purposes of this paper, MAGPIE uses a straightforward approach for both options 1 and 2. For option 2, MAGPIE simply shares the values generated by the context sensors directly. For option 1, MAGPIE shares some locally generated statistics, which include aggregating information from other nearby users and adding randomly generated noise.

MAGPIE's approach builds a trust development ladder, which is important in preventing the overall performance of the MAGPIE (distributed) system from degrading because devices do not learn to trust one another. Without support from third party relationship sources like social networks [35, 36] (which we aim to avoid), this trust development ladder is essential. That is, an essential component of MAGPIE is the fact that users can learn to trust each other in *semi-trust* situations as long as the risk can be kept within acceptable limits.

Next we show the basic algorithm that MAGPIE uses to generate obfuscated context based on aggregating the user's local information with others' information for the same context type and adding random noise. In the end, as we will show, the amount of obfuscation is dependent on the trust value generated for the particular requester and particular context type. Given the sensing neighborhood at the time, let N be the number of recently connected participants for which a reasonably up to date value of context type m is known by the local device; we assume that these peers have identifiers $1 \ldots n$. Let c^m be the device's value for context type m and $C'^m = (c_1^m, c_2^m, \ldots, c_n^m)$ be the vector of values of context type m for the N peers. Let $C^m = C'^m \cup c$ represent an aggregate of the local context value with the values of the neighboring nodes. In [11] the authors emphasized that knowledge of the exact community distribution (which they refer to as $f_k^e(x)$) is unrealistic because it requires an infinite population. We use a similar notation $f_k^m(x)$ to represent the approximate neighborhood distribution of the local knowledge of context m with limited population at the time instance k. That is, $f_k^m(x)$ is a *statistic* that is *representative* of C^m. To ensure obfuscation commensurate with the required instantaneous trust level for peer j, we further obfuscate $f_k^m(x)$ as shown in Algorithm 2. Our goal here is to perturb the aggregation to achieve context-dependent privacy protection and then randomly select a context value to share given a range whose size is determined by the trust value $\tau_{j,m}^*$, while ensuring the noise being added is controlled by the privacy sensitivity ε_m, which is particular to the context type m.

Algorithm 2 computes the distribution of local context aggregation $f_k^m(x|\mu, \sigma)$ in its initialization stage, where μ and σ are the mean and standard deviation, as usual. For example, a continuous context *temperature* (shown in Fig. 2, where c^m is the self-perceived context) results in the $f_k^m(x)$ shown in Fig. 3. At line 2 Algorithm 2 first determines how many pieces of noisy context (n_p), based on the product of a *perturbing factor* $\lambda \in (0, 2]$ and the cardinality of local aggregation $|C^m|$, should be mixed into the perturbed distribution. In the next step (lines 3–8), n_p pieces of *white Gaussian noised* contexts will be *independently* generated and added into the perturbed set. In line 9 the algorithm calculates the new statistic of the blurry distribution $f_k^m(y)$ before selecting a random variable from the perturbed distribution within the range of $2(1 - \tau_{i,m})$ in line 10.

Algorithm 2. Obfuscating Procedure

input : C^m, set of context values for type m;

$\tau^*_{j,m}$, instantaneous trust value for peer j and context type m;

ε_m, privacy sensitivity for context type m

output: c^m_o, obfuscated context value of type m

1 initialization: $f^m_k(x|\mu, \sigma) \sim C^m$;

2 $n_p = \lambda|C^m|$;

3 **while** $n_p \neq 0$ **do**

4 $\quad \rho \leftarrow E^{n_p}_W(0,1)$;

5 $\quad c_g = \mu + (1 + \varepsilon_m)\sigma\sqrt{2}erf^{-1}_{p_n}(2\rho - 1)$ $C^m \leftarrow C^m \cup c_g$;

6 $\quad n_p = n_p - 1$;

7 **end**

8 $f^m_k(y|\mu', \sigma') \sim C^m$;   // *perturbed pdf*

9 $c_o = \mu' + \sigma'\sqrt{2}erf^{-1}_y(2E_W(0, 1 - \tau_{i,m}) - 1)$;

10 **return** c_o

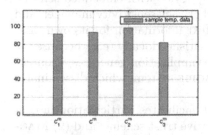

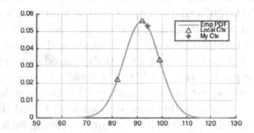

Fig. 2. Local Contexts   **Fig. 3.** Empirical Distribution

The loop in lines 3–8 adds n_p pieces of noisy data into the aggregation. Within this perturbed aggregation, the scale of the noise is calibrated to the device's privacy sensitivity for context type m. The error function used in line 5 is from the standard Gaussian statistical noise model except the standard deviation is stretched to $(1 + \varepsilon_m)$:

$$P_N(n) = \frac{1}{\sigma'\sqrt{2\pi}}e^{-\frac{(n-\mu)^2}{2\sigma'^2}}, \ where \ \sigma' = (1 + \varepsilon_m)\sigma \qquad (5)$$

Note that in the process of generating noise, we use the Weibull distributed random numbers [37] ($E_{Weibull} \in (0, 1)$); however using other transformation methods should work as well. We also tried the Laplacian noise with $b = \Delta f/\varepsilon$ to determine which perturbation suits our purpose better (Fig. 4). The result complies with the findings in [38] in the sense that the level of noise generated by using the Laplacian model may be so large as to make responses meaningless for many queries for *small data sets* such as a set of evanescent context information; this is why we evaluate MAGPIE using the Gaussian noise model.

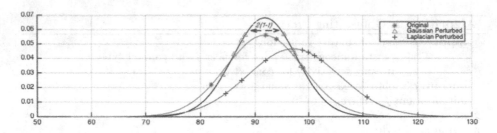

Fig. 4. Perturbed Contexts

4   Experimental Evaluation

To evaluate our proposed approach, we implemented a pervasive context-sharing application as an application protocol in the Opportunistic Network Environment ONE simulator [13]. Each of the Delay-Tolerant Networking (DTN) hosts in the simulation simulates a mobile computing device with embedded sensors, MAGPIE's adaptive trust evaluation module and privacy sensitivity manager, and an application that periodically *consumes* context information for its own task. When the application's context need cannot be satisfied locally (e.g., because the local host does not have the required sensor) the application generates a context request that it sends to the locally running MAGPIE system, which disseminates the request to any connected MAGPIE devices.

Our contributions are two-fold: (1) MAGPIE facilitates participation in context sharing activities by implementing an adaptive trust scheme; and (2) MAGPIE protects a context provider's privacy by adding controllable noise into the context being shared according to provider's privacy sensitivity policy and the level of trust between provider and the peer initiating the request. We performed two sets of experiments to evaluate these two contributions.

In our first experiments, we compare the sharing participation of four different schemes: (*a*) traditional *all-or-nothing* sharing based on a static trust policy; (*b*) traditional *all-or-nothing* sharing with privacy consideration based on a static trust policy; (*c*) traditional *all-or-nothing* sharing with MAGPIE's dynamic trust establishing mechanism; and (*d*) the full MAGPIE approach, with both privacy preserving sharing and dynamic trust establishment. To capture the performance in real pervasive computing environments, we conducted the experiments under two settings that entail heterogeneous connectivity protocols, mobility models, and transmit ranges. Table 1 gives the detailed simulation settings.

We ran two different situations: one with 30 nodes and one with 60 nodes. In each, the set of nodes was divided into six equally sized groups as indicated in the table. Nodes were allowed to communicate with other nodes regardless of group. In the table, BT refers to the BlueTooth connection protocol, WiFi refers to standard WiFi links, and highspeed indicates a high-speed and long range wireless interface. The mobility models listed are all built into the ONE simulator, and their names are relatively self-descriptive. The world size parameter in

Table 1. Simulation Settings

	Protocols	Mobility	TX range (m)	Speed (m/s)	Description
Group 1	BT	Roads	10	(0.5, 1.5)	Slow pedestrian
Group 2	BT	Pedestrian-path	10	(2.7, 13.9)	Car
Group 3	BT &WiFi	tram4	20	(0.5, 1.5)	Pedestrian
Group 4	BT &Highspeed	Mainroads	500	(7, 10)	Super connectivity
Group 5	BT	tram10	10	(7, 10)	Commuter
Group 6	BT	Shops	10	(6, 12)	Shop runner

ONE was set to the same size in both settings (4500 m × 3400 m), resulting in a *denser* network in the second (i.e., 60 node) case.

We first demonstrate the success of MAGPIE in facilitating the sharing of context information among peer devices. We recorded the sharing interactions of the experiments under the four schemes described above to compare how different aspects of MAGPIE affect the community participation in the sharing activity. During the experiment, we simulated five types of context information including three that are continuous measures of ambient context (temperature, light intensity, and noise level), one that is categorical data (power switch) and one that is discrete data (office floor). We run the experiments for 20,000 s to ensure that the schemes with trust establishing mechanisms run for a period of time after reaching their stable stages.

In Fig. 5, we show the sum of the number of completed sharing interactions in an experiment lasting 20,000 s. There is a noticeable increase (approximately 4×) when MAGPIE's dynamic trust is used (schemes c and d). This suggests that our dynamic trust establishing mechanism explores significantly many more sharing interactions for upper-layer context-aware applications. We can also see that the schemes that employ MAGPIE's privacy sensitivity metrics have slightly lower participation than their counterparts. This indicates that MAGPIE is succeeding in reducing the sharing for privacy preservation by making the decision of selecting the *best possible sharing* strategy context-dependently harder. Finally, it can also be seen that context sharing becomes approximately 10 % more frequent in the more densely connected community, which hints at situations in which MAGPIE will be particularly useful.

We next plot the evolution of trust values during the above experiments to understand how the increase in interactivity occurs. We measured the mean trust levels of the context recipients of the same sharing interactions recorded by a single experiment in 10 s intervals. The result is shown in Fig. 6. As this graph shows, the trust level in schemes a and b stays constant throughout the experiment as expected (they both use a static trust model). In schemes c and d, the trust levels oscillate at the beginning and then gradually rise until relatively stabilizing. This observed trends indicate that MAGPIE's privacy preserving sharing helps pervasive devices to become familiar with their surroundings and to establish meaningful trust relationships; this matches our daily social experience: we

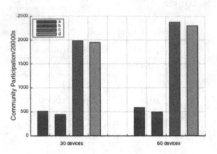

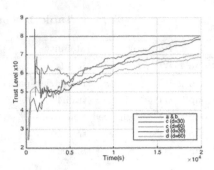

Fig. 5. Sharing Activity Participation   **Fig. 6.** Trust Establishing Process

need to be a little extroverted when we arrive in a new place in order to know those who can we get along with and those with whom we cannot.

MAGPIE's primary goal is to balance an individual's privacy protection against the community's context availability. In our second set of experiments, we take a joint view of a two day long simulation with 60 devices in a larger area (6000 m × 4500 m). We recorded changes in trust levels, sharing interactions, and quality of shared contexts (as measured by the empirical error [10]) for three context types (with privacy sensitivity (i.e., ε) selected from among $\{0.4, 0.6, 0.8\}$) to investigate how these settings affect each other from an application's view.

Figure 7 shows the results. The x-axis of all three plots show the elapsed time of the simulation. The middle plot shows the sum of the number of interactions that happened for each type of context in the immediately preceding 600 s. The context for which the provider has a low privacy sensitivity (red in Fig. 7) is shared more frequently than medium (green) or high (blue). They have been shared 7.0486, 6.8625, and 5.4722 times per interval on average, respectively. By comparing to the trust level graph in the top of Fig. 7, we can explain this difference as it is apparent that the context with high privacy sensitivity requires a higher level of trust for the provider to participate in this risky behavior.

If we take a closer look at the corresponding trends in the context quality graph (at the bottom of Fig. 7), the least shared type of context (blue in the figure) also results in the highest percentage of error when it is shared. This is because MAGPIE shares the obfuscated version of this context in lieu of sharing the raw data, and the privacy sensitivity requires a higher degree of obfuscation than for the other two context types. Note also that the error percentage for all three context types declines over time; this is a result of the gradually increasing trust levels, which result in higher quality sharing as the participants get to know one another better.[5]

---

[5] Code and full results at: https://github.com/liuchg/OneSim_PCSharing.git.

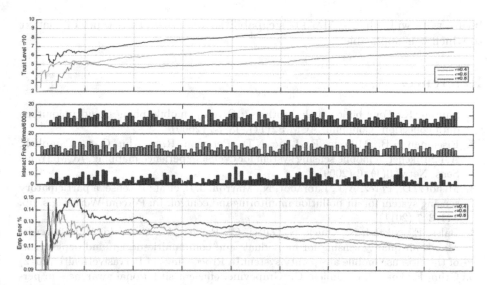

Fig. 7. Joint results from Experiment 2 (Color figure online)

5 Conclusions and Future Research

Through collaboration, mobile and pervasive computing devices can enjoy unprecedented context availability and help users to exploit the nearby environment. However, sharing context information sensed by a user's personal device poses threats to the user's privacy and must be controlled. We introduced MAG-PIE which, by dynamically evaluating the *risk* of disclosing potentially private data based on the level of trust between the participants and the individualized context-dependent sensitivity, helps users to select sharing strategies for context. In MAGPIE we assumed trustworthiness to be reciprocal relationship. Future work will explore additional factors to determining the trustworthiness of a collaborating peer, including relaxing this assumption. In our initial work with MAGPIE, we have demonstrated that there are context types amenable to our simple data perturbation mechanisms. This may not be true for all types of context information; future work will look at specialized ways to add noise to common types of context data to increase the applicability of MAGPIE. Currently, MAGPIE responds to each context request individually; it is possible that multiple neighboring devices may request the same or similar information from a user. Optimizations to MAGPIE's behavior could save some processing overhead by using results of previous computations.

In this paper, we built a prototype of our current vision of MAGPIE. Given this prototype, we performed a series of application-oriented experiments performed on the ONE simulator. Even without the enhancement discussed above, this evaluation validated that MAGPIE can effectively facilitate context sharing activities by implementing an adaptive trust scheme and can protect a context provider's privacy by adding controllable noise into the context. We expect that future work will enhance MAGPIE's capabilities and extend the types of context to which it is applicable.

References

1. Shilton, K.: Four billion little brothers?: Privacy, mobile phones, and ubiquitous data collection. Commun. ACM **52**(11), 48–53 (2009)
2. Eisenman, S.B., Miluzzo, E., Lane, N.D., Peterson, R.A., Ahn, G.-S., Campbell, A.T.: Bikenet: a mobile sensing system for cyclist experience mapping. ACM Trans. Sens. Netw. **6**(1), 6 (2009)
3. Mendez, D., Perez, A.J., Labrador, N., Marron, J.J., et al.: P-sense: a participatory sensing system for air pollution monitoringand control. In: Percom Workshops, pp. 344–347 (2011)
4. Bales, E., Nikzad, N., Quick, N., Ziftci, C., Patrick, K., Griswold, W.: Citisense: Mobile air quality sensing for individuals and communitiesdesign and deployment of the citisense mobile air-quality system.In Proceedings of PervasiveHealth (2012)
5. Grim, E., Fok, C.-L., Julien, C.: Grapevine: efficient situational awareness in pervasive computingenvironments. In: Proceedings of Percom Workshops (2012)
6. Srivastava, M., Abdelzaher, T., Szymanski, B.: Human-centric sensing. Philos. Trans. Royal Soc. Lond. Math. Phys. Eng. Sci. **370**(1958), 176–197 (2012)
7. Almenarez, F., Marin, A., Díaz, D., Sanchez, J.: Developing a model for trust management in pervasive devices. In: Proceedings of Percom Workshops (2006)
8. Wang, X., Cheng, W., Mohapatra, P., Abdelzaher, T.: Artsense: anonymous reputation and trust in participatory sensing. In: Proceedings of INFOCOM (2013)
9. Xiong, L., Liu, L.: Building trust in decentralized peer-to-peer electronic communities. In: Proceedings of ICECR-5 (2002)
10. Shi, E., Chan, T.-H., Rieffel, E.G., Chow, R., Song, D.: Privacy-preserving aggregation of time-series data. In: Proceedings of NDSS (2011)
11. Ganti, R.K., Pham, N., Tsai, Y.-E., Abdelzaher, T.F.: Poolview: stream privacy for grassroots participatory sensing. In: Proceedings of SenSys, pp. 281–294 (2008)
12. Dwork, C.: Differential privacy. In: Encyclopedia of Cryptography and Security, pp. 338–340 (2011)
13. Keränen, A., Ott, J., Kärkkäinen, T.: The one simulator for dtn protocol evaluation. In: Proceedings of SimuTOOLS, pp. 55 (2009)
14. Christin, D., Reinhardt, A., Kanhere, S.S., Hollick, M.: A survey on privacy in mobile participatory sensing applications. J. Syst. Softw. **84**(11), 1928–1946 (2011)
15. Pelusi, L., Passarella, A., Conti, M.: Opportunistic networking: data forwarding in disconnected mobile ad hoc networks. IEEE Commun. Mag. **44**(11), 134–141 (2006)
16. Luhmann, N.: Familiarity, n.confidence, trust: problems and alternatives. Trust Mak. Breaking Coop. Relat. **6**, 94–107 (2000)
17. Li, H., Singhal, M.: Trust management in distributed systems. IEEE Comput. **40**(2), 45–53 (2007)
18. Babu, S.S., Raha, A., Naskar, M.K.: Trust evaluation based on nodes characteristics and neighbouring nodes recommendations for WSN. In: Wireless Sensor Network 2014 (2014)
19. Uddin, M.G., Zulkernine, M., Ahamed, S.I.: Cat: a context-aware trust model for open and dynamic systems. In: Proceedings of SAC, pp. 2024–2029 (2008)

20. Selcuk, A.A., Uzun, E., Pariente, M.R.: A reputation-based trust management system for p2p networks. In: Proceedings of CCGrid, pp. 251–258 (2004)
21. Sweeney, L.: k-anonymity: a model for protecting privacy. Int. J. Uncertainty Fuzziness Knowl. Based Syst. 10(5), 557–570 (2002)
22. Bilogrevic, I., Freudiger, J., De Cristofaro, E., Uzun, E.: What's the gist? privacy-preserving aggregation of user profiles. In: Kutyłowski, M., Vaidya, J. (eds.) ICAIS 2014, Part II. LNCS, vol. 8713, pp. 128–145. Springer, Heidelberg (2014)
23. Reinhardt, A., Englert, F., Christin, D.: Averting the privacy risks of smart metering by local data preprocessing. Pervasive Mob. Comput. 16, 171–183 (2015)
24. Pallapa, G., Das, S.K., Di Francesco, M., Aura, T.: Adaptive and context-aware privacy preservation exploiting user interactions in smart environments. Pervasive Mob. Comput. 12, 232–243 (2014)
25. Hengartner, U., Steenkiste, P.: Avoiding privacy violations caused by context-sensitive services. Pervasive Mob. Comput. 2(4), 427–452 (2006)
26. Tomasic, A., Zimmerman, J., Steinfeld, A., Huang, Y.: Motivating contribution in a participatory sensing system via quid-pro-quo. In: Proceedings of CSCW (2014)
27. Hull, B., Bychkovsky, V., Zhang, Y., Chen, K., Goraczko, M., Miu, A. Shih, E., Balakrishnan, H., Madden, S.: Cartel: a distributed mobile sensor computing system. In: Proceedings of SenSys, pp. 125–138 (2006)
28. Shokri, R., Theodorakopoulos, G., Papadimitratos, P., Kazemi, E., Hubaux, J.: Hiding in the mobile crowd: locationprivacy through collaboration. IEEE Trans. DSC 11(3), 266–279 (2014)
29. Liu, Y., Rahmati, A., Huang, Y., Jang, H., Zhong, L., Zhang, Y., Zhang, S.: xshare: supporting impromptu sharing of mobile phones. In: Proceedings of MobiSys (2009)
30. Golrezaei, N., Molisch, A., Dimakis, A.G., Caire, G.: Femtocaching and device-to-device collaboration. IEEE Commun. Mag. 51(4), 142–149 (2013)
31. Oulasvirta, A.: Finding meaningful uses for context-aware technologies: thehumanistic research strategy. In: Proceedings of the SIGCHI Conference on Human Factors in ComputingSystems, pp. 247–254 (2004)
32. Stephen, M.: Formalising trust as a computational concept. Ph.D. dissertation. University of Stirling, Scotland (1994)
33. Duma, C., Shahmehri, N., Caronni, G.: Dynamic trust metrics for peer-to-peer systems. In: Proceedings of DESA, pp. 776–781 (2005)
34. Jiang, X., Landay, J., et al.: Modeling privacy control in context-aware systems. IEEE Pervasive Comput. 1(3), 59–63 (2002)
35. Lu, Y., Wang, Z., Yu, Y.-T., Fan, R., Gerla, M.: Social network based security scheme in mobile information-centric network. In: Proceedings of MED-HOC-NET (2013)
36. Parris, I., Bigwood, G., Henderson, T.: Privacy-enhanced social network routing in opportunistic networks. In: Proceedings of Percom Workshops, pp. 624–629 (2010)
37. Belyaev, Yu.K., Chepurin, E.V. (originator): Weibull distribution.http://www.encyclopediaofmath.org/index.php?title=Weibull_distribution&oldid=18906
38. Sarathy, R., Muralidhar, K.: Evaluating laplace noise addition to satisfy differential privacy for numeric data. Trans. Data Priv. 4(1), 1–17 (2011)

Middleware

Panorama: A Framework to Support Collaborative Context Monitoring on Co-located Mobile Devices

Khaled Alanezi[1]([✉]), Xinyang Zhou[2], Lijun Chen[1,2], and Shivakant Mishra[1]

[1] Department of Computer Science, University of Colorado,
Boulder, CO, USA
{Khaled.Alanezi,mishras}@colorado.edu
[2] Interdisciplinary Telecom Program, University of Colorado,
Boulder, CO, USA
{Xinyang.Zhou,Lijun.Chen}@colorado.edu

Abstract. A key challenge in wide adoption of sophisticated context-aware applications is the requirement of continuous sensing and context computing. This paper presents Panorama, a middleware that identifies collaboration opportunities to offload context computing tasks to nearby mobile devices as well as cloudlets/cloud. At the heart of Panorama is a multi-objective optimizer that takes into account different constraints such as access cost, computation capability, access latency, energy consumption and data privacy, and efficiently computes a collaboration plan optimized simultaneously for different objectives such as minimizing cost, energy and/or execution time. Panorama provides support for discovering nearby devices and cloudlets/cloud, computing an optimal collaboration plan, distributing computation to participating devices, and getting the results back. The paper provides an extensive evaluation of Panorama via two representative context monitoring applications over a set of Android devices and a cloudlet/cloud under different constraints.

Keywords: Collaborative computing · Pervasive computing · Multi-objective optimization

1 Introduction

In the field of context-aware computing, a wealth of clever mobile applications that monitor user environment to detect and react to events of special interest have recently been proposed; see, e.g., [11,19,20]. However, a major obstacle towards wide adoption of context-aware applications is the requirement of continuous context monitoring. User context can change at any time and it is crucial for the application to detect those changes promptly. This requirement is difficult to accommodate due to limited smartphone resources, particularly the battery resource. Moreover, despite significant advances in smartphone processing power, context computation latencies remain prohibitively high for several interesting applications such as cognitive assistance [17]. For these reasons, users tend to avoid using context-aware applications.

© Institute for Computer Sciences, Social Informatics and Telecommunications Engineering 2015
S. Sigg et al. (Eds.): MobiCASE 2015, LNICST 162, pp. 143–160, 2015.
DOI: 10.1007/978-3-319-29003-4_9

Different offloading techniques have been proposed recently to address these issues of limited battery life and long computation latency. These techniques fall into two broad categories. In the first category, resource-hungry tasks are off-loaded to powerful servers residing in the cloud, leading to both computation speedup and energy efficiency. However, accessing the cloud incurs additional cost for the user in terms of cloud access fee and cellular data plan. In addition, access latency for cloud can be quite high. To address this, researchers are introducing cloudlets, acting as a middle-tier to bridge the gap between the mobile devices and the cloud [17].

In the second category, mobile applications use nearby mobile devices to share tasks, thereby minimizing the need for accessing cloud resources [6,10]. This helps with avoiding cloud and ISP charges, as nearby resources can be personal devices, or mobile devices of family members and coworkers. This also eliminates redundant sensing and computation, if several nearby mobile devices are interested in the same (shareable) context [10]. In addition, collaborative context monitoring extends sensor modalities and tackles the smartphone position problem [1]. However, this technique suffers from uncertainties due to the ad hoc nature of the network, lack of any apparent incentives for participation, security and privacy, varying device capabilities and device mobility.

It is clear that both of these offloading techniques have their pros and cons with one of them suitable for one scenario and the other one for a different scenario. At present, offloading solutions to cloud, cloudlet or nearby mobile devices exist in isolation. With proliferation of mobile devices, increased availability of (nearby) computing servers that can operate as cloudlets, and improved connectivity to the cloud, a highly likely scenario is one where a user has access to multiple computing resources whenever she/he needs to perform a context computation. Figure 1 illustrates four common scenarios in a typical user's (Alice) life. In the morning, Alice takes a bus to go to her work (*Bus scenario*). During her bus ride, she can perform collaborative computing with mobile devices of other bus riders. Later, in her work place (*Work Place scenario*), she can perform collaborative computing with mobile devices of co-workers as well as an office server (cloudlet) accessible within one network hop. During lunch time (*Lunch Break scenario*), Alice goes to a restaurant, where she can perform collaborative computing with mobile devices of other restaurant customers as well as a cloudlet provided by the restaurant. Finally, in the evening or on weekends, Alice goes for shopping in a mall with her family members and friends (*Shopping Mall scenario*), where she can use their mobile device for collaborative computing.

In this paper, we present a middleware framework called *Panorama* that enables mobile applications to reap the benefits of every computing opportunity (cloud, cloudlets, and other mobile devices) available at runtime. Panorama runs on multiple mobile nodes, and builds an optimized collaboration plan taking into consideration the users' performance objectives and the participants' preferences and constraints. A key challenge addressed in Panorama is to ensure an optimal partitioning of the computation task among available mobile devices, cloudlet, and cloud. Panorama considers important and practical constraints in

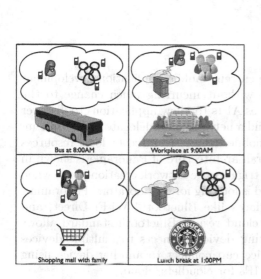

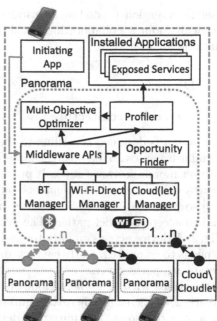

Fig. 1. Alice's typical day   **Fig. 2.** Panorama's architecture

collaboration planning, such as the energy constraints of mobile devices, and their computation and communication capabilities. It also considers the costs involved in accessing nearby mobile devices vs. cloudlets/cloud. It also takes into consideration security, privacy, and trust relationship of the participating devices. At the heart of collaboration planning in Panorama is a versatile multi-objective optimization framework that takes into account various constraints of available computing opportunities and efficiently computes a collaboration plan that optimally trades off different performance objectives such as minimizing the overall cost, minimizing the energy consumption, and minimizing the execution time. Panorama provides support for both parallel and sequential (pipeline) task structures, two most common structures in context monitoring applications.

We have prototyped and extensively evaluated Panorama under a variety of scenarios in the presence of several different network configurations of mobile devices, cloudlet and cloud and under different device constraints. We have experimented with two representative context-aware applications: speech recognition (a parallel task) and ambiance sound monitoring (a sequential task). Experimental results show that Panorama can achieve both reduced computation time and decreased energy consumption while working within the constraints set by the collaborators, such as limits on the contributed energy, cost budget, and privacy requirement. Experimental results also show that Panorama is expressive and flexible in realizing different tradeoffs between completion time, energy consumption, and/or cost. Panorama is completely automated with no user intervention needed after installation. A device with Panorama can automatically join a collaboration network when needed, and run tasks that are suitable for it.

2   Design

2.1   Overall Architecture

Panorama is designed according to the current mobile application development standards, and can be easily adopted without incurring much change to the current mobile software stack. It provides APIs to allow applications to discover nearby devices, cloud and cloudlets, build a network, and delegate tasks to them. It also provides APIs to allow other mobile devices to discover local resources and to accept task delegation. The overall architecture of Panorama is shown in Fig. 2. A device acts as an initiator and triggers the network creation phase when it needs to compute a costly context and is looking for collaborators. Panorama's design supports diverse network interfaces like Bluetooth, Wi-Fi Direct, and connections with IPs where cloudlets/cloud reside. Bluetooth standard allows creation of Piconets where the initiating device connects to multiple devices in a star topology. The initiating device can connect to another device using WiFi-Direct and to previously defined IPs for cloudlets/cloud.

Panorama is implemented as a background service that exposes the middleware APIs to applications looking for collaboration opportunities. The main component is the *middleware APIs component*. This component contains the APIs that the applications can call to use the framework's services. The *Bluetooth Manager* and *Wi-Fi Direct Manager* components implement technical details of short-range communication channels. Panorama defines the behavior that every communication channel must provide to support task collaborations like searching for other devices, connecting to other devices, accepting connections from other devices, accepting and responding to resource inquiry messages, and finally accepting and processing task delegation. Panorama currently supports two communication interfaces with other mobile nodes: Bluetooth and Wi-Fi Direct. With this design, it would be easy to plug in new communication interfaces (e.g., NFC or ZigBee) without any significant change in Panorama.

The *Cloud(let) Manager* component implements technical details of connecting with cloudlets/cloud. Currently, we pre-configure the IP addresses where the implementation for specific context monitoring task exists. However, we expect that network resource discovery techniques can be utilized to discover cloudlets/cloud efficiently.

The *Profiler* component gathers collaboration-relevant information about the mobile node Panorama is running on and provides it to other nearby mobile devices through Panorama's APIs. The initiating node delegates different context sub-tasks to different devices based on the profiler information. Currently, this component provides two types of information: available set of services on the device along with their performance metrics and constraints of the mobile device. Available services here refer to context derivation code that applications expose so that other mobile devices can execute their context-aware task on the device. In the current design, the required code should be available on the device before collaboration can take place. Device constraints include energy quota, time quota, and incentives, etc.

The *Multi-Objective Optimizer* component employs multi-objective optimization to find the best collaboration plan that conforms to the device constraints and achieves the initiator's objectives. Currently, we optimize for energy consumption, execution time, and cost. However, due to its flexibility, the optimization model can be easily extended to accommodate for other parameters when required. Details of this component are discussed in Sect. 2.3. Finally, the *Opportunity Finder* component performs regular scanning for nearby devices using Bluetooth and maintains a list of recently discovered devices to be utilized whenever collaboration is required.

2.2   Application Partitioning and Profiling

Collaborative context monitoring involves changing the application execution model from standalone execution on a single mobile device to distributed execution on multiple mobile devices, clouds and cloudlets. This requires partitioning the application and making the code for calculating context available on collaborating nodes before the collaboration. Panorama's design requires the context code to be available on other mobile devices before the collaboration. This design choice is reasonable since Panorama targets shareable contexts that will be of common interest. For example, a programmer will write a speech recognition component that takes an audio as input and returns text as a result. This component can then be made available for other applications running on the device as well as for nearby collaborators by being exposed as a service through the operating system. Note that this design choice is consistent with research in the field that proposes contextual data units [4] and envisions sharing them among collaborators [8]. Technically, Panorama utilizes the Android service component to support this design (see Sect. 3). For servers, we envision a future where popular shareable context is exposed by server APIs analogous to web APIs.

For application profiling, Panorama tracks the required execution time and energy consumption for exposed services and provides this information through the API to other mobile devices. Panorama uses information gathered from previous invocations to build a linear regression model similar to the work in [7] that predicts the execution time and energy consumption for future tasks delegated to the node. We choose to use file size as the input to this regression model. This choice has proven accurate for speech recognition tasks in our current implementation. The energy profiling is done manually by taking measurements from an external power source. This workaround solution is required due to the lack of an accurate API that exposes energy consumption of the device to solutions like Panorama.

2.3   Optimization Models

Consider a system where n devices, indexed by $i = 1, \cdots, n$, collaborate on a certain task with a total workload of w. Let $x = (x_1, \cdots, x_n)$ denote the allocation of the task, with device i being allocated an amount $x_i \geq 0$ of workload. Obviously, $\sum_{i=1}^{n} x_i = w$. Denote by e_i the energy consumption for processing one unit of workload by device i. We assume that each device i has an energy budget b_i that it is willing to expend for collaboration, i.e., $e_i x_i \leq b_i$. Denote by c_i the payment received by device i for processing a unit of workload, and B the initiator's total budget on payment. So, $\sum_{i=1}^{n} c_i x_i \leq B$. We further assume that each device i takes an amount f_i of time to process one unit of workload. We aim to minimize both the energy consumption and the completion time, which is formulated as the following multi-objective optimization problem:

$$\min_{x \succeq 0} \;(\text{w.r.t } R_+^n)\; \left(\sum_{i=1}^{n} e_i x_i, \quad \max_i \{f_i x_i\} \right) \tag{1}$$

$$\text{s.t. } e_i x_i \leq b_i, i = 1, \cdots, n \tag{2}$$

$$\sum_{i=1}^{n} x_i = w \tag{3}$$

$$\sum_{i=1}^{n} c_i x_i \leq B. \tag{4}$$

Introducing a weight $\gamma \geq 0$ to specify the tradeoff between energy consumption and execution time, we can solve the above problem by scalarization, which can be reformulated as a linear program (LP):

$$\min_{x \succeq 0} \; \sum_{i=1}^{n} e_i x_i + \gamma t \tag{5}$$

$$\text{s.t. } e_i x_i \leq b_i, i = 1, \cdots, n \tag{6}$$

$$f_i x_i \leq t, i = 1, \cdots, n \tag{7}$$

$$\sum_{i=1}^{n} x_i = w, \quad \sum_{i=1}^{n} c_i x_i \leq B. \tag{8}$$

A larger (smaller) γ means a higher preference/priority on short completion time (low energy consumption). In practice, the value of γ is set based on the initiator's preference.

Notice that in the above optimization problems, we impose a hard constraint on the initiator's budget; see Eq. (4). But we can also make the payment an objective to optimize. For example, we can optimize both the initiator payment and the completion time under the energy budget constraint, i.e.,

$$\min_{x \succeq 0} \; \sum_{i=1}^{n} c_i x_i + \gamma t \tag{9}$$

$$\text{s.t. } e_i x_i \leq b_i, i = 1, \cdots, n \tag{10}$$

$$f_i x_i \leq t, i = 1, \cdots, n \tag{11}$$

$$\sum_{i=1}^{n} x_i = w. \tag{12}$$

The above modeling framework can be easily extended to incorporate different performance objectives or concerns. For example, for certain reason such as privacy concern, we may require certain portion of workload u to be processed at a subset $i = 1, \cdots, m$ of devices such as those that can be trusted. This can be ensured by imposing an additional constraint $\sum_{i=1}^{m} x_i = u$ to the above optimization problems.

In practice, the values of e_i and f_i can be measured/estimated as described in Sect. 2.2. The value of c_i will be determined by each device/collaborator based on its resource scarcity or abundance as well as incentive. The total number n of collaborating devices is usually a small number less than 10, resulting in a small LP problem. The LPs (5), (6), (7), (8), (9), (10), (11) and (12) can be solved on smartphone using existing LP solvers, e.g., Apache for Java, in tens of millisecond. We have implemented a customized solver especially for Panorama.

2.4 Discovery Protocol

For collaboration, Panorama needs to know what devices are available nearby and how long those devices are expected to stay within the collaboration range. Under Bluetooth v3.0, Panorama needs to scan its surroundings regularly, which results in significant energy overhead. To minimize this overhead, Panorama utilizes adaptive scanning based on discovered number of peers as described in [9]. The new Bluetooth Low Energy (BLE) protocol provides lightweight mechanism for broadcasting device capability beacons in a connectionless mode called advertising. Panorama can leverage this feature for efficient service discovery and switch to classic Bluetooth for sending files at higher rates. Unfortunately, none of our Android devices support BLE peripheral mode required for advertising. We plan to incorporate BLE in Panorama as part of future work.

3 Implementation

We have implemented Panorama as a background service on the Android platform, which can be installed as a user-space application. After installing Panorama, context-aware applications running on the same mobile device can use Android IPC to call its APIs. Panorama's simple interface has a start/stop button that can be used by users to indicate their willingness to engage in collaboration. Once Panorama is started, it can automatically accept Bluetooth connections from co-located devices that also run Panorama. Bluetooth connection between Panorama copies running on different mobile devices can take place automatically without user intervention. In order to support this requirement, Panorama uses a specific Bluetooth UUID as an identifier and connects using Bluetooth insecure channel. This design allows for automatic creation of connections with co-located devices which is a mandatory requirement for systems such as Panorama to work. However, it introduces security risk from an adversary with access to the UUID. Techniques to secure mobile ad hoc networks such as reputation systems [2] and secure key management [3] can be employed to secure Panorama. We are considering implementing these techniques in Panorama as part of future work. Panorama also utilizes Wifi-Direct as an additional communication channel. However, the connection has to be accepted by the receiving party since this is the only supported scheme on Android implementation of Wifi-Direct. When the communication network is established, devices can discover resources and delegate tasks to each other.

3.1   Panorama's Programming Interface

Method signatures of Panorama's APIs are defined using the Android Interface Definition Language. In order for third-party applications developers to call Panorama's APIs, they will need to include a copy from the .aidl file in their application package and bind to Panorama's middleware service. Table 1 lists method signatures from this file. The group of APIs handling Bluetooth, Wifi-Direct and Cloudlet perform the required functions for creating the network using the communication channels. To create the Bluetooth network, a device checks the freshness of recently discovered devices list using *get_bt_devices*, then invokes the *create_piconet* API. The latter API automatically connects to nearby devices running Panorama. An application can also connect to a device through WiFi-Direct and a cloudlet/cloud server through Wi-Fi using the Wifi-Direct APIs and cloudlet APIs respectively. For generic APIs, the *discover_nw* API sends a discovery message for all connected devices with the required service name. Panorama's design utilizes the Android service component for code discovery. That is, application developers will write context derivation code in an Android service and expose it under a unique identifier through the Android OS. Accordingly, whenever a device receives a discovery message, it triggers the *get_local* API, which checks whether the required service is installed on the device by checking exposed services against the provided *service_name* string. After gathering information about connected devices, the application can trigger the optimization process and perform the collaboration using the *perform_optimization* and the *execute_optimization* APIs respectively. Upon receiving task delegations, collaborating devices can process their portions of the task using the *process_local* API.

Table 1. Method signatures from Panorama's aidl file

Generic APIs	Bluetooth, Wifi-Direct & Cloudlet APIs
`List<Device> discover_nw(service_name)`	`List<Device> get_bt_devices`
`Device get_local(service_name)`	`create_piconet`
`Plan perform_optimization(task)`	`start_wd_discovery`
`Result execute_optimization`	`List<Device> get_wd_devices`
`Result process_local(task)`	`connect_wd(device_name)`
	`connect_to_cloudlet`

In the description above, we have provided detailed APIs from Panorama for clarity. However, we note that these APIs can be combined to shield collaboration logic from the application logic and make task delegations happen automatically. For example, we have implemented an API that both connects to nearby devices and discovers them for a specific service in one step.

3.2 Experiment Testbed

To evaluate the utility of Panorama, we have implemented two context-aware applications representing two different application structures: parallel structure and pipeline structure. A speech recognition application that is based on PocketSphinx [15] to perform speech recognition from a dictionary represents a parallel task. This task is computation-intensive, making it a good candidate for collaboration. For the pipeline structure, we implement the sound ambiance monitoring task from [12]. We define three stages and run them in three different Android services components to distribute the application. First, an audio recording stage, which represents the sensing stage. Second, a stage that calculates FFT for the audio window and generates features to classify sound as either music or speech. Finally, a third stage that takes the FFT as input and generates MFCC vector, which is then used to identify the gender of the speaker. This is only used when the sound is detected as speech. We also implement both applications using Java to be able to run them on cloudlets and clouds. We integrate these applications with Panorama and run experiments on four Android mobile devices running different versions of the Android OS and a laptop to emulate a cloudlet compute box. We also rent an Amazon EC2 server to use for experiments involving the cloud. The Android devices used are Galaxy S4, Galaxy Note, Galaxy Tab 3, and Galaxy Nexus. Galaxy Note, Galaxy Tab 3 and Galaxy Nexus have dual-core processor while Galaxy S4 has a quad-core processor.

4 Evaluation

4.1 Methodology

We have evaluated Panorama for a variety of scenarios under different collaboration opportunities, resource restrictions, and incentives. The experimental settings are chosen to reflect real-life scenarios that a system like Panorama may face. Collaboration opportunities include cloudlets/cloud as well as multiple mobile devices belonging to the user, his/her friends and family members, and/or strangers. The initiator may have different objectives, and the collaborators may have different constraints in terms of energy, time, cost, and privacy.

The execution time reported in the experiments is the total time to execute the required task using a collaboration, including the time for connecting with other devices or cloudlet, devising an optimal task partitioning plan, shipping subtasks, and gathering the results back. The energy consumption reported is

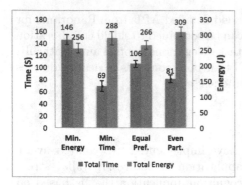
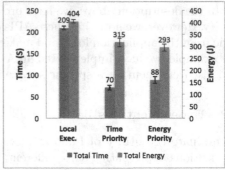

Fig. 3. Tradeoff between energy consumption and execution time by Multi-objective optimizer (3 collaborators).

Fig. 4. Impact of privacy on energy and time optimization (3 collaborators).

the sum of energy consumed in all mobile devices (not cloudlet) that participate in the collaboration. It takes into consideration the energy consumed in all stages from the creation of network for collaboration to the gathering of the results back to the initiating device. To measure energy consumption of different activities, we log the device electric current drain indicated by the power supply unit, and then subtract the average current drain observed before the measured activity starts in order to obtain the additional current drain caused by the collaboration activity. We multiply the additional current with the voltage applied at the battery terminals of the mobile device to get the instantaneous power consumption of the activity in Watt and then integrate it over time to obtain the energy consumption of the activity in Joule. We ensure that there are no other applications running in the background. We repeated each experiment five times and report the average of the measurements from these five trials. We also report standard deviation, which is rather low in all experiments.

4.2 The Utility of Multi-objective Optimizer

We use speech recognition to evaluate the adaptability of Panorama to different participant preferences and resource restrictions. Speech recognition is a good candidate for task collaboration because of its compute-intensive nature, and is used as an example context-aware task that can be distributed in parallel. We envision Panorama integrating with context-aware applications that require general speech recognition. In the experiments, we consider a scenario where an audio file of 4 MB is recorded and requires performing speech recognition.

Tradeoff Between Energy Consumption and Execution Time. We first demonstrate that Panorama provides support for appropriate partitioning to achieve the desired tradeoff between energy consumption and execution time. Such a tradeoff is needed in a Bus or a Shopping Mall scenario described in

Fig. 1, where only mobile devices may be available for collaboration and the user does not have access to a power source. Due to the lack of access to power source, the remaining battery level dictates how important it is to minimize energy consumption during computation.

In this experiment, we assume that there are two mobile devices available in the user's vicinity in addition to the user's own mobile device. We also assume that the speech data does not contain any sensitive information and so privacy is not a factor in optimization. In the next experiment, we will take into consideration the privacy concern when certain parts of the speech data are sensitive in nature. Recall from Subsect. 2.3 that different choices of weight γ correspond to different tradeoffs between energy consumption and execution time. Figure 3 shows the comparison between $\gamma = 0$ (minimize energy consumption, corresponding to a situation with relatively low remaining battery level), $\gamma = \infty$ (minimize execution time, corresponding to a situation with relatively high remaining battery level), and $\gamma = 1$ (equal preference over energy and time, corresponding to a situation with moderate remaining battery level). We also contrast this with a naive partitioning strategy that divides the task evenly over all the participants. Figure 7 shows the corresponding partitioning of speech data for each of the collaborators for these different cases. For brevity, we report in the same figure the file partitioning of speech recognition tasks for other experiments as well that are described later.

We see that in the case of minimum energy (low remaining battery level), bigger chunks of file are sent to the participating device with low energy consumption without any emphasis on exploiting parallelism to achieve computation speedup, leading to slow execution. The opposite trend is observed for the case of minimum time (high remaining battery level). Here, the total execution time is minimized at the expense of increased energy consumption. The equal preference case represents a compromise between the previous two cases, with execution time and energy consumption in between those of these two cases. Finally, the even partitioning scenario is able to exploit parallelism to achieve a good performance in time. However, it consumes the most energy because of the lack of any planning in this aspect.

Notice that in the previous experiment, the task distribution is same whether the user is in a Bus scenario or a Shopping Mall scenario, because the speech data does not contain any sensitive information. We now consider the case where some parts of the speech data contain sensitive information (1.5 MB out of the total 4 MB is sensitive). In the Bus scenario, since the mobile devices other than the initiator's are untrusted, the sensitive parts of the data cannot be shipped to them. As a result, only 2.5 MB of (non-sensitive) speech data is available for collaboration in this case and the remaining 1.5 MB of (sensitive) data must be processed at the initiator's device. Figure 4 shows the results of this case. We see that in both time and energy priority cases, the achieved time gain from exploiting other mobile nodes is more than 50 %. In the case of energy priority, 27 % energy is saved compared to local execution due to shifting of the (non-sensitive) portion of the task to a more efficient mobile node. Also, when we

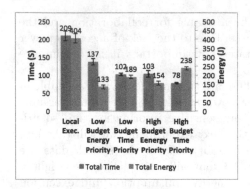
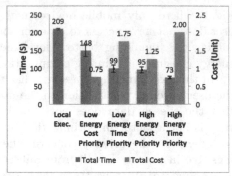

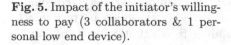

Fig. 5. Impact of the initiator's willingness to pay (3 collaborators & 1 personal low end device).

Fig. 6. Impact of the collaborators' energy budget (3 collaborators & 1 personal low end device).

compare the energy priority and time priority cases, we see that Panorama is able to devise the best plan for executing the non-sensitive part of the file. For the time priority, Panorama divides the file efficiently (see Fig. 7) to save 20 % of time when comparing to the energy priority case. As for the energy priority, Panorama sends the file chunks to the more energy efficient device thereby saving 7 % more energy. For the Shopping Mall scenario, since all devices are trusted, the presence of any sensitive data does not make any difference in task distribution. The results are same as those reported in Fig. 3.

Impact of Collaborator Constraints. We now evaluate the capability of Panorama to optimize for different objectives under different constraints specified by the participants. Consider the Bus or the Shopping Mall scenario with three mobile device collaborators and an additional mobile device (which is a tablet in the experiment) that belongs to the initiator. This corresponds to a situation where the initiator has two mobile devices, one of which is a low end device that has poor performance but is "free" in terms of cost and energy. The user may want to use the low end device to save time and energy or meet a cap on cost. We consider a situation where the initiator pays the collaborators, and the payment is proportional to the amount of work done.

We first consider a scenario in which the initiator has a budget on the total amount she is willing to pay. We experiment with two budget levels: a low budget of 2 units of payment and a high budget of 4 units of payment.[1] We consider two situations, one that aims to minimize energy consumption, and the other that aims to minimize execution time. The preference/priority on energy or time is represented by choosing a small or large weight γ in problem (5), (6), (7) and (8). Figure 5 shows the results of this experiment, and the corresponding partitioning can be found in Fig. 7.

---

[1] Notice that here the word "payment" is used in a general sense. It can be a monetary payment, or virtual payment such as credit for reputation.

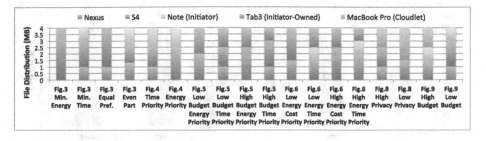

Fig. 7. File distribution for the 4 MB task in experiments of Figs. 3, 4, 5, 6, 8 and 9.

We see that, with low budget and if energy is of high priority, Panorama sends most of the task to the free initiator-owned low end device, in order to save energy in other devices and meet the payment cap while incurring a long execution time. When execution time is of high priority, Panorama sends the task more to the devices that are fast, which leads to 25 % reduction in time while costing much more energy. On the other hand, with high budget, if time is of high priority, Panorama achieves a large reduction in time by shifting larger portion of job to fast but costly devices. When energy is of high priority, the energy consumption goes up compared to the low budget case. This is because the large reduction in time from faster computing allowed by higher budget compensates the increase in energy consumption. As expected, compared to local execution, collaboration reduces execution time and saves energy.

We now consider a scenario where the collaborators have a restriction on the amount of energy they are willing to expend for collaboration, and investigate the tradeoff between execution time and initiator's cost/payment under different energy budgets; see problem (9), (10), (11) and (12). Figure 6 shows the results of an experiment with a low, 100 Joules energy budget for each mobile device, and a high, 200 Joules energy budget for each device; and the corresponding partitioning of speech data can be found in Fig. 7. We see that, compared with low energy budget case, high energy budget leads to shorter execution time when comparing both the cost and time priority cases to their corresponding low energy cases. This is because higher energy budget allows for longer use of faster devices. Also, notice that, with low energy budget and if the cost is of high priority, Panorama sends larger portion of the task to the free initiator-owned low end device, resulting in large execution time and the lowest cost. We also compare with the case of local execution. As expected, collaboration leads to shorter execution time while incurring cost as a result of utilizing other nodes.

Presence of Cloudlets. We now consider scenarios where a cloudlet is available in addition to some mobile devices for collaboration, as in the Work Place and Lunch Break scenarios shown in Fig. 1. In a Work Place scenario, a user has high trust in the available mobile devices as they belong to her/his co-workers. In addition, in some Work Place scenarios, the user may also trust the cloudlet,

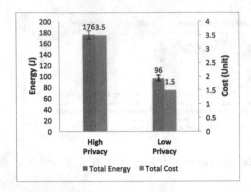
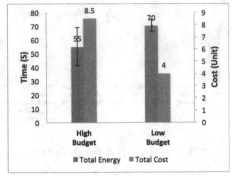

Fig. 8. Impact of privacy requirement of the task (3 collaborators & cloudlet).

Fig. 9. Impact of collaborators cost budget requirement of the task (3 collaborators & cloudlet).

while in other cases, she/he may not trust it. On the other hand, in the lunch break scenario, neither the cloudlet nor the other mobile devices may be trusted.

In the first experiment reported here, we consider a Work Place scenario that involves three mobile devices and an untrusted cloudlet. An audio file is divided into sensitive and insensitive parts. We consider two cases here: a high privacy case with 2.5 MB out of the total 4 MB file marked as sensitive, and a low privacy case with only 1.5 MB marked as sensitive. As shown in Fig. 8 (and Fig. 7), imposing higher privacy leads to higher energy consumption and higher cost. This is because only a small portion of the speech data is sent to the faster and energy-cost-free cloudlet. For lower privacy case, a much larger portion of the speech data is sent to the cloudlet, thus reducing energy consumption and execution time. We conduct two additional experiments for the cases when the cloudlet is trusted and when there is no sensitive data in the audio file. In both cases, Panorama offloaded almost the entire file to the cloudlet. This is because the cloudlet is significantly faster than the mobile devices and does not contribute to energy overhead. We do not report the results of these experiments here due to space limitation.

Next, we consider the Lunch Break scenario where both the cloudlet and the collaborating mobile devices are untrusted and there may be a cost associated with using them. In such a situation, the user has no choice other than executing sensitive parts of the task locally. Yet, Panorama can still optimize for the remaining non-sensitive portion of the task to devise an efficient plan, thereby, minimizing the burden on the initiator as much as possible. Figure 9 reports the results of an experiment where the user would like to process 4 MB of insensitive speech while minimizing the execution time (i.e., $\gamma = \infty$); and the corresponding partitioning of data can be found in Fig. 7. In contrast to the previous experiment, we gave the cloudlet here a higher cost of 4x compared to 1x for other nodes. In the case "high-budget," the user allocates a budget of 10 units to the task, whereas, in the "low-budget" case only 5 units are allocated. We see from the figures that when the budget is high, Panorama was able to shift a big portion of the task to the cloudlet achieving better computation speedup

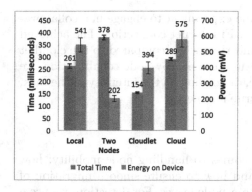

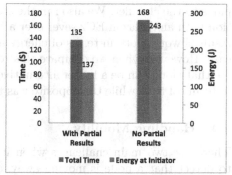

Fig. 10. Benefits of collaboration for sound ambiance monitoring.

Fig. 11. Impact of leaving node on Panorama's performance.

compared to low budget scenario. However, the low budget scenario was not as slow as we expected when compared to the high budget scenario. The reason is that Panorama was able to exploit parallel execution (see Fig. 7 for file distribution) with other collaborators within the allocated low budget without worrying about energy consumption since it is not considered in this scenario.

4.3 Benefits of Collaboration for Sequential Tasks

To demonstrate the utility of Panorama in handling sequential task structures, we have implemented the sound ambiance monitoring application proposed in [12], and employed Panorama to enable collaboration. The results of the collaboration experiments are then compared to the local execution on a single device with Panorama turned off. For collaboration, we conducted three experiments. In the first experiment, the initiator collaborates with two other mobile devices, and in the second and third experiments, the initiator collaborates with a cloudlet sitting on the same network and a cloud server accessed through a Wi-Fi Internet connection. Recall from Sect. 3.2 that the sound ambiance monitoring task can be viewed as a pipeline consisting of three subtasks. Those can be split among collaborators. From Fig. 10, we see that in case of collaboration with two other mobile devices, there is a reduction in power consumption at the initiator's device from 541 mW to 202 mW, a more than 50 % energy reduction by delegating the calculation to the other collaborator. However, this comes at the cost of an increased completion time from 261 ms to 378 ms. Completion time here is the time between when the audio recording is completed and when the gender classification result has arrived at the initiator from the collaborator (or calculated locally in case of local execution). The increase in completion time is due to the time needed to set up the collaboration task and transfer the data and results between the collaborators.

Interestingly, the second experiment involving cloudlet does not show an increase in completion time. Instead, a time saving of 40 % is achieved in addition to the energy saving of 27 %. Here, the overhead introduced by Panorama is offset by the significant gain in execution time when delegating the compute-intensive parts to the cloudlet. We also ran the same experiment to engage in a collaboration with an Amazon EC2 sever over a Wi-Fi Internet connection. The achieved result is worse both in terms of energy and time when compared to the cloudlet case. However, when we compare this result to a nearby node collaboration, we see that cloud can be a better alternative, depending on the intensity of the task, in terms of time while the opposite was true for energy.

4.4   Handling Mobility

There are two main challenges when it comes to handling node mobility: how to detect that a node is moving away, and how to ensure smooth migration of unfinished sub-task to other devices when a node leaves. For detection, we use a method proposed in [13] where we sense the accelerometer during collaboration to detect the starting of a physical activity as an indicator for a collaborator eventually leaving the scene. Once Panorama detects such activity, it sends a message to the initiator to handle mobility. We use accelerometer due to its relatively cheap energy cost and the fact that it can detect mobility promptly. Handling of interrupted collaborations depends heavily on the nature of the computation. In some situations a partial result can be migrated back to the initiator, whereas in others the whole computation need to be reprocessed. We performed two experiments with the aforementioned cases and report the results in Fig. 11 to reflect the impact of each on performance. The experiment considers a scenario where a node delegates a 4 MB task equally to two other nodes and one node moves away from the initiator. In the first case, we deliberately divided the received file and let the moving node finish the first 1 MB before moving away. Upon moving away, the node sends the partial result back to the initiator, which processes the remaining 1 MB locally. In the second case, we let the moving node report its movement without sending any partial results, so the initiator will process the whole 2 MB. Figure 11 reports the total time for completing the 4 MB task and the consumed energy at the initiator. As expected, the first scenario of partial result migration is better in terms of both energy and time when compared to the second scenario, since the initiator only needed to process half of the load assigned to the moving node. Notice that in our current implementation, when a collaborating node is leaving, the initiator picks up the unfinished work. We can also re-distribute the unfinished work among the remaining devices, which we plan to explore in future.

5   Related Work

Our work is closely related to [10,14]. However, [10] focuses on collaborative context monitoring between co-located mobile devices only, while Panorama leverages more opportunities by involving not only co-located devices but also cloudlets/cloud and performing an optimization to devise an optimal collaboration plan for the task. The main goal of [14] is to enhance the reliability of the application, while the goal of Panorama is to automate and optimize collaboration for continuous context monitoring.

The work in [18] studies generic computation offloading between co-located mobile devices, and presents three algorithms to serve three different possible applications' structures while taking into consideration connectivity in distributing jobs. The implementation in [18] is limited to a prototype that performs offloading between two devices only. Panorama's design involves more opportunities by including cloudlets/cloud in addition to co-located mobile devices. We also provide an extensive Android implementation and evaluate it on multiple mobile nodes and a cloudlet/cloud. The recent work in [8] focuses on building a conceptual model to facilitate context sharing between groups of mobile devices. Such model can be leveraged by Panorama to increase the chances of meeting peers and building more beneficial collaborations.

There are several vision papers that advocate the concept of collaboration among co-located mobile devices [6,13,21] and we have used some of their ideas to motivate our work. Also, a rich body of literature exists for augmenting smartphones with resources from cloud and cloudlets; see, e.g., [5,7,16,17]. The ideas in these works have helped in guiding our design.

6   Conclusion

Panorama is a middleware framework that addresses a key question in offloadling computations to nearby mobile devices and cloudlets/cloud: when should a device offload its context computing task and how? Panorama utilizes all available collaboration opportunities from co-located mobile devices and cloudlets/cloud, and devises a collaboration plan to optimize for and trade off different objectives such as minimizing execution time or minimizing energy consumption. The optimization algorithm considers limits set by participants such as contributed energy, paid incentives, and privacy exposure. Evaluation results show that Panorama is rather practical, is able to cope up with varying device constraints, and devises collaboration plans within those constraints to optimally trade off multiple objectives.

There are a number of future directions we plan to pursue. First, we plan to incorporate Bluetooth Low Energy in our opportunity discovery protocol. While none of the Android devices we test run in peripheral mode at present, we expect that Bluetooth-enabled smartphones will increasingly support Bluetooth LE. Second, we plan to expand on handling node mobility. At present, Panorama provides basic support for ensuring that the context computation task is completed despite some of the devices moving away. We plan to explore smart ways to efficiently cope with various mobility patterns. Third, a limitation in Panorama is to rely on collaborators to come up with privacy and efficiency requirements. An interesting research direction we plan to pursue is to automate the process of generating these requirements to enhance the practicality of Panorama. Finally, we plan to conduct user studies to evaluate Panorama in the real-world setting.

References

1. Alanezi, K., Mishra, S.: Enhancing context-aware applications accuracy with position discovery. In: Stojmenovic, I., Cheng, Z., Guo, S. (eds.) MOBIQUITOUS 2013. LNICST, vol. 131, pp. 640–652. Springer, Heidelberg (2014)

2. Buchegger, S., Le Boudec, J.-Y.: A robust reputation system for mobile ad-hoc networks. Technical report (2003)
3. Buttyán, L., Capkun, S., Hubaux, J.-P.: Self-organized public-key management for mobile ad hoc networks. IEEE Trans. Mob. Comput. 2(1), 52–64 (2003)
4. Kansal, A., Liu, J., Chu, D., Zhao, F.: Mobile apps: it's time to move up to condos. In: HotOS (2011)
5. Chun, B.-G., Maniatis, P.: Augmented smartphone applications through clone cloud execution. In: HotOS (2009)
6. Conti, M., Kumar, M.: Opportunities in opportunistic computing. Computer 43(1), 42–50 (2010)
7. Cuervo, E., Balasubramanian, A., Cho, D.K., Wolman, A., Saroiu, S., Chandra, R., Bahl, P.: Maui: making smartphones last longer with code offload. In: MobiSys (2010)
8. de Freitas, A.A., Dey, A.K.: The group context framework: an extensibletoolkit for opportunistic grouping and collaboration. In: CSCW (2015)
9. Han, B., Srinivasan, A.: eDiscovery: energy efficient device discovery for mobile opportunistic communications. In: ICNP (2012)
10. Lee, Y., Ju, Y., Min, C., Kang, S., Hwang, I., Song, J.: Comon: cooperativeambience monitoring platform with continuity and benefit awareness. In: MobiSys (2012)
11. Lu, H., Frauendorfer, D., Rabbi, M., Mast, M.S., Chittaranjan, G., Campbell, A.T., Gatica-Perez, D., Choudhury, T.: Stresssense: detecting stress in unconstrainedacoustic environments using smartphones. In: UbiComp (2012)
12. Lu, H., Pan, W., Lane, N.D., Choudhury, T., Campbell, A.T.: Soundsense: scalable sound sensing for people-centric applications onmobile phones. In: MobiSys (2009)
13. Miluzzo, E., Cáceres, R., Chen, Y.-F.: Vision: mClouds-computing on clouds of mobile devices. In: MCS (2012)
14. Miluzzo, E., Cornelius, C.T., Ramaswamy, A., Choudhury, T., Liu, Z., Campbell, A.T.: Darwin phones: the evolution of sensing and inference on mobilephones. In: MobiSys (2010)
15. CMU PocketSphinx
16. Ra, M.-R., Sheth, A., Mummert, L., Pillai, P., Wetherall, D., Govindan, R.: Odessa: enabling interactive perception applications on mobiledevices. In: MobiSys (2011)
17. Satyanarayanan, M., Chen, Z., Ha, K., Hu, W., Richter, W., Pillai, P.: Cloudlets: at the leading edge of mobile-cloud convergence. In: MobiCASE (2014)
18. Shi, C., Lakafosis, V., Ammar, M.H., Zegura, E.W.: Serendipity: enabling remote computing among intermittently connectedmobile devices. In: MobiHoc (2012)
19. Wang, R., Chen, F., Chen, Z., Li, T., Harari, G., Tignor, S., Zhou, X., Ben-Zeev, D., Campbell, A.T.: Studentlife: assessing mental health, academic performance andbehavioral trends of college students using smartphones. In: UbiComp (2014)
20. You, C.-W., Montes-de Oca, M., Bao, T.J., Lane, N.D., Lu, H., Cardone, G., Torresani, L., Campbell, A.T.: Carsafe: a driver safety app that detects dangerous driving behaviorusing dual-cameras on smartphones. In: UbiComp (2012)
21. Zhang, W., Wen, Y., Wu, J., Li, H.: Toward a unified elastic computing platform for smartphones with cloud support. IEEE Netw. 27(5), 35 (2013)

Jouler: A Policy Framework Enabling Effective and Flexible Smartphone Energy Management

Anudipa Maiti[✉], Yihong Chen, and Geoffrey Challen

University at Buffalo, Buffalo, USA
{anudipam,ychen78,challen}@buffalo.edu

Abstract. Smartphone energy management is a complex challenge. Considerable energy-related variation exists between devices, apps, and users; and while over-allocating energy can strand the user with an empty battery, over-conserving energy can unnecessarily degrade performance. But despite this complexity, current smartphone platforms include "one-size-fits-all" energy management policies that cannot satisfy the diverse needs of all users. To address this problem we present Jouler, a framework enabling effective and flexible smartphone energy management by cleanly separating energy control mechanisms from management policies. Jouler provides both imperative mechanisms that can control all apps, and cooperative mechanisms that allow modified apps to adapt to the user's energy management goals. We have implemented Jouler for Android and used it to provide three new energy management policies to 203 smartphone users. Results from our deployment indicate that users appreciate more flexible smartphone energy management and that Jouler policies can help users achieve their energy management goals.

Keywords: Smartphone energy management · Smartphone platforms

1 Introduction

Effective smartphone energy management requires responding to an enormous amount of diversity. Devices have different battery capacities, users have different battery lifetime expectations determined by their charging habits, and apps consume[1] different amounts of energy depending on what they do and how well they are developed. Despite these differences, today's smartphone platforms manage energy using "one-size-fits-all" policies. For some users, the result is battery lifetimes that are too short, and this has remained a top complaint about smartphones [1,15]. For other users, the result is battery lifetimes that are unnecessarily long and degraded performance due to unneeded energy conservation.

Recent research efforts have succeeded in improving smartphone energy measurement [4,20], characterization [16] and modeling [5,6,12,24]. They have also provided new energy control hardware [9,10] and software [17,21] mechanisms.

---

[1] To avoid confusion between device usage and energy usage, we use *consumption* to denote energy usage and *usage* to denote user-device interaction.

© Institute for Computer Sciences, Social Informatics and Telecommunications Engineering 2015
S. Sigg et al. (Eds.): MobiCASE 2015, LNICST 162, pp. 161–180, 2015.
DOI: 10.1007/978-3-319-29003-4_10

However, more accurate measurements and more effective mechanisms will not improve smartphone energy management if they are not joined with a range of different *policies* reflecting the differences between devices, users, and apps.

This paper introduces *Jouler*, a system enabling effective and flexible smartphone energy management. Jouler delegates the energy management policy decisions currently embedded in smartphone platforms to unprivileged apps called *energy managers*. Energy managers use Jouler's interface to access energy measurements and energy control mechanisms. Because energy managers encapsulate energy management policies inside normal smartphone apps, they are easy for developers to create and distribute, and for users to find, try, and rate. They can also interact with the user, monitor the environment, and access all other capabilities provided to apps.

To enable flexible policies, Jouler provides energy managers with a variety of information about running apps. Energy models provide overall and per-app energy consumption measurements, broken down by component and between foreground and background operation. Jouler also provides information about how apps use the device, such as the amount of time they spend in the foreground and their usage of the network, output devices, and sensors.

To enable effective policies, Jouler provides energy managers with both energy control carrots (cooperative mechanisms) and sticks (imperative mechanisms). Jouler's cooperative mechanisms enable cooperation with modified apps that can adapt their own energy consumption when needed, making existing energy-aware apps simpler and more effective by allowing them to offload energy management policy decisions to the energy manager. When cooperation fails, energy managers can utilize imperative mechanisms—such as per-app processor frequency throttling—to force unmodified or uncooperative apps to adjust their energy consumption. Imperative mechanisms also help encourage developers to modify their apps to take advantage of Jouler's cooperative mechanisms.

After motivating our approach using results from a detailed energy consumption measurement study, we present Jouler's design and several potential energy managers. We then evaluate an Android implementation of Jouler in two ways. First, we demonstrate the effectiveness of Jouler's imperative and cooperative control mechanisms on a benchmark app. Second, we present the results of deploying Jouler and three energy managers to 203 PHONELAB participants. Our results show that Jouler is effective and that users appreciate more flexible energy management.

2   Motivation

Jouler's design is motivated by the results of two IRB-approved measurement studies performed on the PHONELAB public smartphone platform testbed [13] located at the University at Buffalo. PHONELAB consists of several hundred students, faculty, and staff who carry instrumented Android smartphones. PHONELAB participants are balanced between genders and distributed across ages, and thus are representative of the broader smartphone user population. Our study both (1) logged battery level changes for 105 users for 6 months

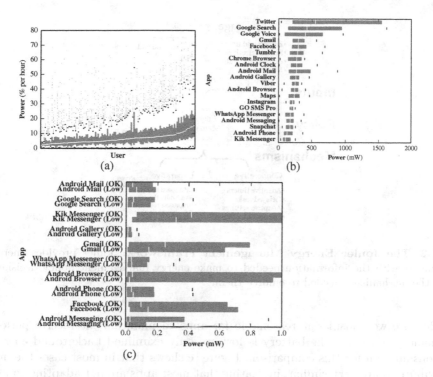

(a)

(b)

(c)

Fig. 1. Aspects of Energy Consumption Diversity. In all plots the white line shows the median, shaded bars show upper and lower quartiles, whiskers are positioned at 1.5 times the inner quartile range, and small dots show outliers. Plots show large amounts of interuser (a) and interapp (b) variation, and that apps are not successfully adapting to low battery conditions (c).

and (2) modified the Android platform to record more detailed per-app energy consumption statistics for 107 users for 2 months. Because our results largely match a previous measurement study [3], we summarize them only briefly:

- **Interuser variation.** Figure 1a shows per-user distributions of discharging rates (in percent per hour) for all discharging sessions in the six-month trace. A factor of four separates the fastest and slowest users, and a great deal of intrauser variation is visible.

- **Interapp variation.** Figure 1b shows user distributions of per-app energy consumption for the top 20 apps used by PHONELAB users. Because many apps include background services, we compute power by dividing each app's total energy consumption—including both background and foreground—by its foreground time. The data shows a large amount of interapp variation, and, for many apps, a great deal of interuser variation.

- **Apps don't adapt.** To investigate whether apps adapt to low battery levels, we separate measured app energy consumption into low battery ($< 10\%$) and OK battery states and compared these two distributions for the top 10 apps.

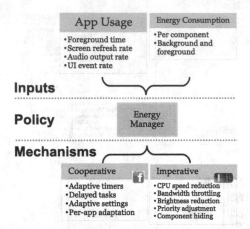

Fig. 2. The Jouler Energy Management Framework. Jouler provides energy managers with the information needed to make energy management policy decisions and the mechanisms needed to enforce them.

Because we consider it reasonable for apps to maintain interactive performance even when the battery is low, we only examined background energy consumption for this comparison. Figure 1c shows that in most cases the distributions are very similar, indicating that most apps are not adapting to low battery levels.

In summary, analysis of our two datasets confirms the well-known energy consumption differences between users and apps, and motivates the need for more flexible smartphone energy management to respond to this diversity.

3   Design

We continue by describing Jouler's design. Jouler consists of two parts: unprivileged apps called energy managers that implement energy management policies, and a privileged platform service providing an interface to the information and mechanisms used by energy managers to accomplish their goals. We describe each in turn.

3.1   Energy Managers

Enabling flexible energy management requires allowing policies to be easily created and distributed by developers and easily installed, configured, and evaluated by end users. To accomplish this, Jouler utilizes the same solution that has worked so successfully for millions of smartphone apps: app marketplaces like the Google Play Store. Jouler removes energy management policies from within the platform where they cannot be altered and replaces them with category of apps called *energy managers* implementing a variety of different energy management policies. As shown in Fig. 2, energy managers use Jouler's interface to access app usage and energy consumption statistics and control per-app and overall device energy consumption.

Because Jouler energy managers are just normal smartphone apps, we have similar expectations for their development and use. We expect a small group of app developers to develop a variety of energy managers to be used by millions of smartphone users. We expect both good, user-friendly, effective as well as complicated, ineffective, malicious energy managers to co-exist. We also expect users to try different energy managers before deciding on one or more making few energy managers more popular than others.

Energy managers are only distinguished from other smartphone apps in two ways. First, they must request and be granted permission to use Jouler's interface. During installation, energy managers request permission to access these features using the platform's standard permission dialog. Second, to prevent multiple energy managers from interfering with each other, Jouler enforces that only one energy manager can be active at any point in time—even if the user has installed several.

To continue, we provide two vignettes presenting energy managers first from the perspective of an energy manager developer and second from that of an end user.

Energy Manager Developer Experience. Alice is an experienced app developer. From personal experience she noticed that while traveling a user is most likely to decrease smartphone usage due to limited charging opportunities to avoid running out of energy too quickly. So she developed a Jouler energy manager that prompts an user to enter her travel plans when it detects her arriving at an airport. It uses her predicted arrival time to determine an appropriate lifetime target, while also prioritizing energy consumption by travel-related apps such as navigational aids. Once Alice is satisfied with her new energy manager, she publishes it to the Google Play Store for other travelers to try.

End User Experience. Dave and Bob are coworkers who travel together frequently. Dave is a heavy smartphone user and frequent charger and normally uses an energy manager that adapts to his charging habits to provide high performance. Bob, on the other hand, is a light user and forgetful charger and normally uses an energy manager that meters out energy to meet his target lifetime and aggressively reminds him to charge when his battery is low.

Both users, however, have been frustrated by their smartphones' energy consumption when traveling. Searching on the Google Play Store, Bob locates Alice's energy manager which has become popular with travelers. On their next trip, he tries it and finds it effective enough to recommend to Dave, who begins to use it regularly as well. While traveling they enable Alice's energy manager, and when they return home they again enable their normal energy managers.

3.2   Energy Manager Inputs

To enable a variety of effective energy management policies, Jouler provides energy managers with as much information about app usage and energy consumption as possible. To measure energy consumption, Jouler tracks total system and per-app energy consumption, breakdowns of energy consumption between device components (processor, network interfaces, screen, GPS), and breakdowns of energy consumption between screen foreground, audio foreground, and background sessions. While some of this information can be obtained by Android apps through Java introspection, this approach is brittle and not officially supported. Jouler's interface standardizes access to detailed energy consumption information.

To measure interaction, Jouler tracks the number of and length of each app foreground session; rates of click, type, and swipe interactions; screen redraw and audio sampling rates; and notification delivery and click times. This collection of information is sufficient to support the variety of energy managers described later, but Jouler may eventually provide more information if it proves useful to promising new energy management approaches.

3.3   Cooperative Mechanisms

To enable effective energy management policies, Jouler provides energy managers with two types of mechanisms: cooperative mechanisms that rely on collaboration with apps, and imperative mechanisms that do not. Cooperative mechanisms allow apps to guide the process of aligning their own energy consumption with the energy manager's and user's goals. Jouler's collaborative mechanisms combine a simple set of signals with a library of useful energy management primitives based on common app design patterns.

However, imperative mechanisms can always be used to control the energy consumption of apps that either have not been modified to use Jouler or are not cooperating effectively. As a result, no changes to existing apps are required to use Jouler. In addition, because apps have no control over the imperative mechanisms applied to them by the energy manager, imperative mechanisms also serve to incentivize developers to modify their apps to use Jouler's cooperative mechanisms.

Cooperative Signals. Jouler's cooperative mechanisms are driven by three simple signals that energy managers can send to apps:

- Reduce indicates the app must reduce its energy consumption. If it does not, the energy manager may apply an imperative mechanism. This signal is also sent whenever an imperative mechanism is applied.
- OK indicates that the app's energy consumption is acceptable to the energy manager.
- Increase indicates that the app can increase its energy consumption. This signal can be sent when an imperative mechanism is removed or the device begins charging.

So a cooperative app should immediately reduce its energy consumption on receiving single or repeated *Reduce* signal. Unmodified apps that have chosen not to cooperate with the energy manager will ignore these signals, and it is safe for any app to do so—except for the fact that cooperative mechanism will be followed by imperative ones if the app's energy consumption remains at odds with the energy manager's policy. Once we gain more experience with Jouler, we may consider delivering more information along with cooperative signals— such as the apps' current energy consumption rate and the energy manager's target—if cooperative apps find additional information useful.

Cooperative apps may connect cooperative signals to app-specific choices affecting energy consumption. For example, an email client may reduce the number of folders that are periodically synchronized and a browser may request lower-quality content. Because Jouler's cooperative signals directly reflect a user's energy manager's policies, they are much more powerful than ad-hoc triggers—such as low battery level—at enabling app energy awareness. A user may want an infrequently-used app to always limit its energy consumption and a frequently-used app to never limit its energy consumption, regardless of the current battery level.

Cooperative Library. Apps are free to respond to cooperative signals directly, but there are also a set of energy-aware design patterns common across many apps. To further encourage apps to collaborate with the energy manager, Jouler includes a library of cooperative mechanisms driven by its cooperative signals.

- **Energy-adaptive timers.** Background operations performed by smartphone apps are often driven by timers. For example, an email client may periodically contact a server to check for new mail. Unfortunately, the energy consumption resulting from a static rate may not be appropriate for all users or in all scenarios.

  Jouler provides *energy-adaptive timers* that adjust their firing rate in response to cooperative signals. Apps configure a maximum and minimum firing rate and step size when initializing the energy-adaptive timer. When they receive the Reduce signal, energy-adaptive timers reduce their firing rate by one step until they reach the minimum; when they receive the Increase signal, they increase their firing rate by one step until they reach the maximum.

  Using adaptive timers is easy. Developers can simply replace calls to existing timer interfaces with the new adaptive timers provided by Jouler.

- **Energy-delayed tasks.** Some tasks performed by smartphone apps are delay tolerant and can be deferred until conditions are favorable. For example, a music client may only download requested music to add to a local cache when an energy-efficient Wifi network is available and not over 4G. Unfortunately, it is difficult for apps to determine under what conditions tasks should be delayed.

Jouler's provides *energy-delayed tasks* that use cooperative signals to determine when to run. Apps register an energy-delayed task with a maximum delay. The task will not run until the app receives the OK or Increase signal or the maximum delay is reached.

Using energy-delayed tasks is also easy. Assuming that developers already have their task in a separate module so that it can be deferred, they need only to wrap the task in the new energy-delayed task object provided by Jouler.

We do not claim either of these mechanisms to be novel, and Jouler's cooperative library borrows freely from previous systems, such as Eon, which also adjusted timer rates to control sensor network node energy consumption [19]. However, to our knowledge Jouler is the first system to integrate these approaches into a smartphone energy management framework. The cooperative library also allows apps to factor out complicated and error-prone decision making concerning when to conserve energy, and instead focus on responding effectively to signals issued by the energy manager.

3.4   Imperative Mechanisms

Jouler's cooperative features encourage apps to manage their own energy consumption. However, there are many cases where cooperation will fail. First, as Jouler is introduced, most apps will not have been modified to cooperate with the energy manager. Second, some apps may not want to cooperate, either to selfishly gain performance or to maliciously waste energy. Finally, an app's attempts to cooperate may be insufficient to meet the energy manager's and user's goals. These limitations require that Jouler provide imperative mechanisms that force—rather than ask—apps to reduce their energy consumption. Imperative mechanisms both ensure that energy managers can control all apps while also encouraging apps to cooperate with the energy manager to manage their energy consumption more intelligently.

Jouler ties all imperative mechanisms to cooperative signals. Any time an energy manager applies an imperative mechanism to an app it is also sent the Reduce signal. When the imperative mechanism is removed, the app is sent the Increase signal—but only after a delay to avoid feedback loops. Coupling cooperative signals to imperative mechanisms allows cooperative apps to continue to attempt to adjust their energy consumption while imperative mechanisms are applied.

To enable effective energy management policies, Jouler provides energy managers access to as many imperative mechanisms as possible to limit overall and per-app energy consumption. Most of these mechanisms other than screen brightness cannot be accessed by unprivileged apps in general.

Jouler currently provides energy managers with the following imperative mechanisms reflecting energy-saving features available on current smartphones:

- **CPU tuning.** Energy managers can change CPU governors and adjust the CPU frequency of dynamic voltage and frequency scaled (DVFS) processors by selecting either performance-boosting higher frequency or energy-efficient lower frequency.

- **App priorities.** Energy managers can set app scheduling priorities which affect the relative performance of multiple running apps. For example, an unthrottled app may achieve equivalent performance at a lower CPU frequency if its priority is increased relative to a throttled app.
- **Bandwidth throttling.** Energy managers can control per-app and global usage of available network interfaces.
- **Brightness adjustment.** Energy managers can control per-app and global screen brightness.

To allow energy managers to apply per-app policies, Jouler delivers a signal to the energy manager each time any app comes to the foreground. Energy managers can use this signal to adjust global settings such as the CPU frequency on a per-app basis while also enforcing background settings. Energy managers may also want to adjust per-app settings such as priorities to distinguish between foreground and background operation.

In some cases imperative mechanisms may have varied effects on apps. For example, slowing the CPU frequency may cause certain apps to consume more energy due to other components being active for a longer period of time. These complicated app interactions argue for the increased policy flexibility provided by Jouler, particularly given that default platform policies frequently ignore these complexities.

Intentionally Omitted Imperative Mechanisms. Because Jouler's goal is to enable flexible and effective energy management of apps that users want to continue using, it does not allow energy managers to uninstall apps or kill app services, which can cause apps to misbehave. Jouler energy managers are free to suggest these actions to users if they could be beneficial.

3.5 Privacy Concerns

To manage energy effectively, energy managers have access to information about the apps running on their smartphone that some users may prefer not to reveal. Currently, Jouler uses a single permission mechanism to inform users of this risk during installation, but we are exploring more fine-grained permissions that could allow users to anonymize the app information provided to energy managers. This would affect policies that rely on identifying apps, but might alleviate some privacy concerns.

4   Example Energy Managers

Jouler is designed to allow flexible and innovative energy management policies to be implemented as energy managers. In this section, we describe few such policies.

Lifetime Targeting. Many previous approaches to energy management focus on meeting a target lifetime. By monitoring energy consumption and the remaining battery level, the energy manager can determine whether the user's lifetime target will be met. If their smartphone may run out of energy too soon, the energy manager can decide to use Jouler mechanisms in a way that reduces energy consumption with minimal performance degradation. On the other hand, if their smartphone may run for hours more than the expected target lifetime, due to less usage or short term unexpected charging sessions in between, then the manager can use Jouler mechanisms to boost performance for better user experience.

While lifetime targeting is conceptually simple, dynamically deciding the trade off between conserving energy and boosting performance is difficult. It is also hard to predict hours before if the target can be met or not due to possible fluctuations in app usage. Although we are not sure what lifetime targeting approach will prove most effective, by enabling the distribution and testing of new approaches Jouler accelerates the process of developing effective solutions.

App Based Throttling. Smartphone users generally install a large number of apps over the time they use their device, some of which they use regularly and are clear favorites—such as a default email client, browser, messaging app and social networking client. There are also those apps which a user has installed but has hardly used or would not care if there is a slight performance degradation to reduce energy consumption. An energy manager can allocate a major chunk of energy to the regular apps and monitor the energy consumed by most favorite apps and least favorite apps. If the non-favorite apps consume more energy than desired, the energy manager can start throttling them to allow the user to access the regular apps for longer period. By observing users' app usage over a period of time, the energy manager may be able to suggest what apps should be on their list of favorites.

Reward Efficient Content Delivery. To determine appropriate per-user settings the energy manager needs better understanding of app energy consumption. A common challenge faced by many energy management approaches is distinguishing between two apps: one that uses a great deal of energy because it is poorly written, and a second that inherently needs a great deal of energy to function properly. Without more information about what the apps are doing, these two very different apps are indistinguishable. Moreover app background energy consumption varies widely between apps, and between the same app used by different users. Whether legitimate or not, the variation in background energy consumption weakens the connection between how much the smartphone is used and how much energy it consumes.

For this reason, Jouler provides energy managers with app usage and interaction information. An energy manager could combine energy consumption with the amount of data delivered through the screen and audio port to determine how efficiently the app is delivering content to the user. In the example above, this would allow the energy manager to distinguish between a streaming video client (inherently-high consumption) and a poorly-written chat client (buggy consumption). This will also help the manager to determine whether the energy consumed for background work is required or is a waste. We anticipate that the Jouler framework will lead to more intelligent energy management policies that observe a variety of aspects of app and user behavior.

5 Implementation

We have implemented the design, we just discussed, by modifying the Android Open Source Platform (AOSP) version 4.4.4 named KitKat. The detailed information about app usage and energy consumption are collected by a lightweight privileged service `JoulerPolicyService` running in the platform from boot time. This information includes overall, per-app, per-component, foreground and background breakdown of usage and energy consumption. These inputs can be accessed by the energy managers through the custom apis `JoulerStatistics` and `JoulerPolicy`. The later api also provides an interface for using all the imperative mechanisms discussed in Jouler design. For example, AOSP in LG Nexus 5 uses the `online` governor as a default CPU governor which jumps between low and high CPU frequencies based on predetermined workload thresholds. Using Jouler, an energy manager, if it chooses, can select the `userspace` governor and set the highest frequency to boost performance of a heavyweight app which is also a favorite of the user. But in order to access Jouler's framework, the energy manager apps need to use the new `CAN_MANAGE_ENERGY` android permission. For stability reasons, Jouler allows only one energy manager to run at any given time even if multiple energy managers are installed in a single device.

The cooperative signals and mechanisms are also implemented in a manner that is intuitive and easy-to-use for existing community of app developers. The easiest way to send signals in an Android environment is to broadcast intents. So, we defined a new intent `ACTION_ENERGY_ALERT` having three separate lists of package names of installed apps, each list corresponds to apps who need to reduce energy consumption, or apps who are doing okay or apps who can boost their performance as they are below the threshold determined by a particular energy manager. Cooperating apps only have to register to listen to this broadcast intent and decide whether they should reduce their energy consumption or not. For other cooperative mechanisms like adaptive timers, we have stayed true to the current AlarmManager implementation in Android. We added a new `setAdaptive` method to the existing android.app.AlarmManager that is similar to existing methods like setInexactRepeating but accepts an extra input to determine the longest deadline till which the work can be delayed if needed. On the other hand the wrapper for delayed task is found in the Jouler api we have mentioned earlier.

Overall our experience of implementing Android Jouler suggests that it should be straightforward to implement Jouler for other smartphone platforms, allowing cross-platform distribution of effective energy management policies.

Jouler's cooperative library will need to be reimplemented, but the service mainly exposes statistics and control mechanisms provided by operating systems for decades. However, without access to sources for iOS or Windows Mobile we can only speculate about the development burden on these other smartphone platforms.

5.1   Energy Manager Implementation

We implemented and distributed three simple and straightforward energy managers:

- The **Favorites Manager** allows users to select a list of favorite apps. Periodically, it compares the total energy consumption of the favorite apps and that of the other apps. If the later is higher, then the energy manager restricts network usage by the non-favorite apps when they run in the background and reduces brightness to reduce screen energy consumption when they run in the foreground.
- The **Blacklist Manager** is identical to the *Favorites* manager except that it asks users to choose the apps they like the least. Accordingly, it tries to reduce energy consumption by the blacklisted apps when they run in the screen foreground or background.
- The **Lifetime Manager** attempts to achieve at least the target lifetime hours configured by the user. With every alternate battery level drop, the manager compares the current battery discharge rate with the expected discharge rate. Accordingly, the manager gradually throttles the CPU, app priorities, network usage and screen brightness. If it is still unable to reach the target, it notifies the user how many hours left before the device runs out of energy. Currently the energy manager does nothing if the achieved lifetime is much more than what the user has asked for.

6   Evaluation

Our evaluation of the Android prototype demonstrates that Jouler provides both effective and flexible energy management policies. We evaluate Jouler in two steps. First we use energy benchmarks to show that Jouler's mechanisms are effective. Second, we perform a ten day deployment of Jouler's platform modifications and of three simple but different energy managers on the PHONELAB testbed.

6.1   Energy Benchmark

First, we wanted to test if Jouler's privileged system service, running continuously in the platform to collect detailed app usage and energy consumption information, causes any overhead. We fully charged two LG Nexus 5 smartphones, flashed a clean Android build on one of them and flashed an image with Jouler

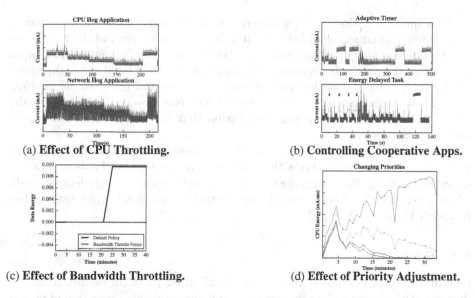

(a) **Effect of CPU Throttling.**

(b) **Controlling Cooperative Apps.**

(c) **Effect of Bandwidth Throttling.**

(d) **Effect of Priority Adjustment.**

Fig. 3. Effects of few Jouler Mechanisms on Energy

modifications on the other. We kept these phones unplugged with display screen off for 8 hours. The same battery level drop for both phones assured us that there is no perceptible overhead for Jouler. Next, we wrote a simple Android energy benchmark which is configurable to hog the processor and network either continuously in the screen foreground or periodically in the background. We tested the imperative mechanisms using this benchmark and some of those results are presented in this section. To test the cooperative mechanisms, we wrote one client app which uses both adaptive timer and energy delayed task wrappers to cooperate with our simple energy manager which can send *Reduce*, *OK* and *Increase* signals to the client app.

6.2   Jouler Mechanisms

To verify that Jouler's mechanisms were having the intended effect on our benchmark, we measured the current output of a Samsung Galaxy Nexus smartphone using a Monsoon Power Monitor [2]. Figure 3a shows the effect of reducing the processor frequency in steps when the benchmark is hogging both the CPU and network. As expected, CPU throttling reduces the power consumption of both hogs.

Figure 3d shows the effect of adjusting the Linux priorities of four instances of our energy benchmark running as CPU hogs and competing together for the processor. As the priorities of two hogs are raised—the yellow hog to the highest priority and the red hog to an intermediate level—their share increases, and the shares of the two other hogs are decreased as their priorities are lowered.

It is important that Jouler's imperative mechanisms do not force existing, non-cooperative apps to misbehave. In a Nexus 5 with pre-installed apps, we ran a whitelist energy manager that throttles bandwidth of all non-favorite apps running in the screen background. Figure 3c shows that bandwidth throttling saves power consumption by limiting Gmail background energy consumption. During the experiment, we verified that Gmail continued to behave normally and did not crash, confirming our expectation that well-written apps can handle resource limitations.

Our evaluation of Jouler's cooperative mechanisms is shown in Fig. 3b. The power monitor output confirms that Jouler's cooperative mechanisms work as expected, slowing the energy-aware timer and stopping energy-delayed tasks when receiving the *Reduce* signal and restarting energy-delayed tasks when receiving the *Increase* signal.

6.3   Deployment

Our final step of evaluation consists of distributing platform modifications for implementing Jouler and an integrated app which provides a selection of energy managers to the participants of the PHONELAB testbed as an over-the-air update. The integrated app offers 4 choices to users - Lifetime Energy Manager, Favorites Energy Manager, Blacklist Energy Manager and No Energy Manager. The last choice allows users to continue using or go back to the default Android energy management. These energy managers are chosen because they are simple to use and understand. Users can also switch between energy managers multiple times. We did not advertise or try to influence the testbed participants to use the app or configure it in a particular way. This is done to evaluate if the energy managers are intuitive and easy to understand and use. 203 participants received the update and 173 participants access the app at least once. Table 1 shows the breakdown of users who used one energy manager for the longest period during the experiment lifetime. After 10 days a short survey was distributed to collect their overall impressions of the Jouler system. PHONELAB's built-in platform instrumentation and logging capabilities were used to collect data generated by the platform and energy managers. The entire experiment was reviewed and approved by the University at Buffalo's Institutional Review Board (IRB).

Table 1. Energy Managers preferred by Users.

Preferred Energy Manager	Users
Lifetime Energy Manager	44
Favorites Energy Manager	31
Blacklist Energy Manager	10
Default Android Energy Manager	88

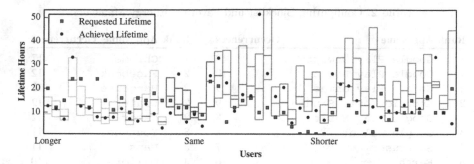

Fig. 4. Lifetime Energy Manager Comparison. The red line shows the median while the upper and the lower edges of each box shows upper and lower quartiles of the expected lifetime hours distribution for each user. The different colored boxes labeled as longer, same and shorter signify users requesting lifetime hours greater than, equal to or slightly less than and much lesser than the median respectively. **This analysis aims to compare the expected, requested and achieved lifetimes for each user** (Color figure online).

Lifetime Energy Manager. To understand the lifetime expectations of different users, first we need to know for how long can a device stay off the plug on any given day. We have recorded battery related details for all PHONELAB participants since September 2014. Using this data, we computed the average battery drain per hour for each user and the expected lifetime hours based on that rate. In Fig. 4 for all the participants who selected the lifetime manager we show the distribution of expected lifetime hours. Users did not always request lifetime hours close to what is expected of their device. So we group the users based on whether the requested lifetime hours is shorter, longer or equal to the lifetime hours they usually experience. It needs to be pointed out that the energy manager has a constraint that does not allow users to select a lifetime goal beyond 24 hours. The energy manager failed badly for most of the users in the first group, who requested a comparatively longer lifetime. Thus, our *Lifetime* energy manager is not a good fit for users running heavyweight apps frequently or having heavy device usage because this manager cannot decrease the discharge rate by only following global policies. Rather *Blacklist* or *Favorites* energy manager can be a better choice in these cases. The energy manager fared slightly better for the group of users who requested similar lifetime hours. In the last group, a large number of users requested a shorter lifetime either due to the constraint imposed by the energy manager or because they do not care about very long lifetime hours. In these cases, a good energy management policy will be one which can boost performance instead of being too conservative about saving energy while reaching the lifetime target. Though our energy manager did not fare well across all categories of users, it provided us with interesting insights to improve lifetime management policies in future.

Table 2. Configuring Blacklist and Favorites Energy Managers.

Rank	App Name	Occurrences	Rank	App Name	Occurrences
1	Google Play Newsstand	10	1	Chrome	17
1	Google Play Books	10	2	Facebook	12
2	Google Play Games	9	2	Hangouts	12
2	Android Movie Studio	9	2	Dialer	12
3	Google Play Music	8	2	Camera	12
3	Google Wallet	8	3	Youtube	11
4	Superuser	7	3	Maps	11
5	Earth	6	4	Gallery	10
5	News & Weather	6	4	Clock	10
5	Google	6	5	Gmail	9

(a) **Most Common Blacklisted Apps.**   (b) **Most Common Favorite Apps.**

Blacklist and Favorites Energy Manager. The other two energy managers we distributed are app based. At the beginning, users, who selected one of these managers, are prompted to choose one or more apps to put in the blacklist or whitelist for *Blacklist* and *Favorites* energy managers respectively. In Table 2 we found pre-installed google apps to be most commonly blacklisted. On the other hand, users were more likely to select browsers and social media apps as favorites.

Survey. Continuing with the evaluation, we distributed a short survey among the participants. Our goal is to determine if users are interested in using energy manager apps in the future. We asked users if they found understanding and configuring our energy managers easy and if they appreciated having more control over how energy is managed in their devices. We asked users to list which energy manager they preferred the most and to state problems they faced while using any of the energy managers. We also asked for any suggestion they might have to improve our energy managers. 88 participants responded, 80 % of whom appreciated having this extra control over energy management. But 25 % of the participants reported facing problems while the energy manager was running. The most common complaint was about the harsh decrease in the display screen's brightness by the energy managers which hampered user-experience. Some users did not find the energy managers to be perceptibly effective. Many users also pointed out lack of instructions from our end to be a key factor for not knowing how to use the app, which might be the reason why a majority of the participants did not use any of the three energy managers. Some also suggested instead of their having to select their favorite apps manually, it would be more helpful if the energy manager could internally decide which are the preferred apps from usage related information.

7 Related Work

We divide related work into projects related to Jouler's inputs, its mechanisms, its policies, before briefly discussing other Android apps that attempt to help users manage their smartphone's energy consumption. While some portions of Jouler draw on similar work in the sensor network and mobile systems areas, to our knowledge no existing system provides the capabilities and flexibility of Jouler.

Jouler Inputs. Effective energy management relies on accurate energy measurement and attribution. Previous tools such as PowerTutor [24] have demonstrated model-driven approaches to determining per-component and per-app energy usage, with this approach being largely replicated by Android's internal Fuel Gauge component. Because many modeling approaches struggle with limited visibility of aggregate energy consumption, VEdge [20] uses only measurement of the battery voltage to infer current draw and therefore energy consumption. Other recent projects have provided improved approaches incorporating temporal variation in exogenous factors such as network signal strength into models to make them more accurate [5]. Jouler's energy managers will benefit from future improvements in this area.

Jouler Mechanisms. Multiple systems have attempted to establish new operating system energy management mechanisms or encourage more adaptive app energy consumption. ECOSystem proposed a system where each process was given an energy budget to spend and would use this "currentcy" to schedule tasks [23]. Both Pixie [11] and Eon [19] provided the ability for sensor network programs to adapt to changing energy availability, but did so by relying on special languages or program structure that would be infeasible to apply to smartphones. Odyssey [7] focuses largely on enabling per-app resource adaptation, a capability complementary to Jouler. Recently the Cinder [18] OS based on HiStar [22] proposed new mechanisms enabling explicit resource allocation and accounting which would help Jouler control uncooperative apps. The battery virtualization proposed by PowerVisor [25] would also be useful as a Jouler mechanism but does not by itself address the policy problem.

Jouler Energy Managers. Recent work on smartphone energy management has used measurements from large user communities to categorizing apps based on energy consumption. Carat has been installed by over 500,000 devices, and attempts to identify two energy anomalies: *bugs* and *hogs* [14]. Carat is a notable attempt to address smartphone energy management but suffers from several drawbacks that Jouler could help address. First, Carat's app generalizations fail to consider the differences in smartphone users our data has demonstrated, which render an app that one user considers acceptable a hog to another user. Second, Carat has the same heavy-handed mechanisms available to it as all other current energy management approaches: remove the app or stop using it. Jouler's mechanisms would provide Carat with more tools to enforce its classification. PowerLet [8] is another system that suffers a similar weakness in that it relies on users to take energy saving actions, rather than creating an interface as Jouler does which allow these actions to be performed programmatically.

Existing Energy Management Apps. The Google Play Store provides Android users with multiple options for controlling their energy consumption but many of them require root privileges. JuiceDefender[2] controls the underlying smartphone hardware such as enabling and disabling wireless interfaces to attempt to keep energy consumption under control. Easy Battery Saver[3] offers users the choice of multiple energy modes and a variety of battery lifetime estimation tools. Unfortunately, both these apps have to apply policies across the entire phone and cannot control individual apps. The mechanisms currently available to these tools are too blunt to effectively control apps with varying usage patterns. But we expect that such approaches may be more effective with the additional app information and fine-grained mechanisms Jouler provides. Tools such as Mr. Nice Guy[4] which allows per-app priority adjustments, force users to manually fiddle with priorities and act as energy managers to implement specific policy goals.

8   Future Work and Conclusions

To conclude we have presented the Jouler policy framework which enables flexible and effective smartphone energy management benefiting both developers and end users. With the Jouler service running on the PHONELAB testbed, we are planning several next steps. Based on the lessons learned from our evaluations, we plan to improve our energy managers by having policies that do not hinder user experience. For example, brightness level needs to be changed more intuitively. We also plan to add new mechanisms to the existing framework that allow the energy manager to effectively enhance device performance for users who do not mind shorter lifetime hours. Lastly, we are working to modify several apps with sources available as part of the AOSP to allow them to use Jouler's cooperative library. We expect that the continued evaluation on the PHONELAB testbed will lead to new results and hope to eventually prepare a patch allowing Jouler to be considered for inclusion in the AOSP.

References

1. Battery Life: Is That All There Is? http://www.jdpower.com/resource/jd-power-insights-i-battery-life-all-there
2. Monsoon power monitor. http://www.msoon.com/LabEquipment/PowerMonitor/

---

[2] http://www.juicedefender.com.
[3] http://goo.gl/GfcI2q.
[4] http://goo.gl/8utSxe.

3. Banerjee, N., Rahmati, A., Corner, M.D., Rollins, S., Zhong, L.: Users and batteries: interactions and adaptive energy management in mobile systems. In: Krumm, J., Abowd, G.D., Seneviratne, A., Strang, T. (eds.) UbiComp 2007. LNCS, vol. 4717, pp. 217–234. Springer, Heidelberg (2007)
4. Brouwers, N., Zuniga, M., and Langendoen, K. Neat: a novel energy analysis toolkit for free-roaming smartphones. In: Proceedings of the 12th ACM Conference on Embedded Network Sensor Systems, pp. 16–30. ACM (2014)
5. Ding, N., Wagner, D., Chen, X., Pathak, A., Hu, Y. C., Rice, A.: Characterizing and modeling the impact of wireless signal strength on smartphone battery drain. In: Proceedings of the ACM SIGMETRICS/International Conference on Measurement and Modeling of Computer Systems SIGMETRICS 2013, New York, pp. 29–40. ACM (2013)
6. Dong, M., Choi, Y.-S.K., Zhong, L.: Power modeling of graphical user interfaces on oled displays. In: Proceedings of the 46th Annual Design Automation Conference, DAC 2009, New York, pp. 652–657. ACM (2009)
7. Flinn, J., Satyanarayanan, M.: Energy-aware adaptation for mobile applications. SIGOPS Oper. Syst. Rev. **33**(5), 48–63 (1999)
8. Jung, W., Chon, Y., Kim, D., Cha, H.: Powerlet: an active battery interface for smartphones. In: Proceedings of the 2014 ACM International Joint Conference on Pervasive and Ubiquitous Computing, UbiComp 2014, New York, pp. 45–56. ACM (2014)
9. Lin, F.X., Wang, Z., Zhong, L.: K2: a mobile operating system for heterogeneous coherence domains. In: Proceedings of the 19th International Conference on Architectural Support for Programming Languages and Operating Systems, ASPLOS 2014, New York, pp. 285–300. ACM (2014)
10. Liu, J., Priyantha, B., Hart, T., Ramos, H.S., Loureiro, A.A., Wang, Q.: Energy efficient gps sensing with cloud offloading. In: Proceedings of the 10th ACM Conference on Embedded Network Sensor Systems, pp. 85–98. ACM (2012)
11. Lorincz, K., Chen, B.R., Waterman, J., Werner-Allen, G., Welsh, M.: Resource aware programming in the pixie OS. In: ACM Conference on Embedded Networked Sensor Systems, SenSys 2008, November 2008
12. Mittal, R., Kansal, A., Chandra, R.: Empowering developers to estimate app energy consumption. In: Proceedings of the 18th Annual International Conference on Mobile Computing and Networking, Mobicom 2012, New York, pp. 317–328. ACM (2012)
13. Nandugudi, A., Maiti, A., Ki, T., Bulut, F., Demirbas, M., Kosar, T., Qiao, C., Ko, S.Y., Challen, G.: Phonelab: a large programmable smartphone testbed. In: Proceedings of 1st International Workshop on Sensing and Big Data Mining, SenseMine 2013, November 2013
14. Oliner, A.J., Iyer, A.P., Stoica, I., Lagerspetz, E., Tarkoma, S.: Carat: collaborative energy diagnosis for mobile devices. In: Petrioli, C., Cox, L.P., Whitehouse, K. (eds.) SenSys (2013), p. 10. ACM (2013)
15. Punzalan, R.: Smartphone Battery Life a Critical Factor for Customer Satisfaction. http://www.brighthand.com/default.asp?newsID=18721
16. Qian, F., Sen, S., Spatscheck, O.: Characterizing resource usage for mobile web browsing. In: Proceedings of the 12th Annual International Conference on Mobile systems, Applications, and Services, pp. 218–231. ACM (2014)
17. Ravindranath, L., Agarwal, S., Padhye, J., Riederer, C.: Procrastinator: pacing mobile apps usage of the network. In: Proceedings of the 12th Annual International Conference on Mobile Systems, Applications, and Services, pp. 232–244. ACM (2014)

18. Rumble, S.M., Stutsman, R., Levis, P., Mazières, D., Zeldovich, N.: Apprehending joule thieves with cinder. In: Proceedings of the 1st ACM Workshop on Networking, Systems, and Applications for Mobile Handhelds, MobiHeld 2009, New York, pp. 49–54. ACM (2009)

19. Sorber, J., Kostadinov, A., Brennan, M., Garber, M., Corner, M., Berger, E.D.: Eon: a language and runtime system for perpetual systems. In: ACM Conference on Embedded Networked Sensor Systems, SenSys 2007 (2007)

20. Xu, F., Liu, Y., Li, Q., Zhang, Y.: V-edge: fast self-constructive power modeling of smartphones based on battery voltage dynamics. In: Proceedings of the 10th USENIX Conference on Networked Systems Design and Implementation, NSDI 2013, Berkeley, pp. 43–56. USENIX Association (2013)

21. Xu, F., Liu, Y., Moscibroda, T., Chandra, R., Jin, L., Zhang, Y., Li, Q.: Optimizing background email sync on smartphones. In: Proceeding of the 11th Annual International Conference on Mobile Systems, Applications, and Services, pp. 55–68. ACM (2013)

22. Zeldovich, N., Boyd-Wickizer, S., Kohler, E., Mazières, D.: Making information flow explicit in histar. In: Proceedings of the 7th Symposium on Operating systems Design and Implementation (2006), pp. 263–278. USENIX Association (2006)

23. Zeng, H., Fan, X., Ellis, C.S., Lebeck, A., Vahdat, A.: ECOSystem: managing energy as a first class operating system resource. In: Proceedings of the Architectural Support for Programming Languages and Operating Systems (ASPLOS), San Jose, CA, October 2002

24. Zhang, L., Tiwana, B., Qian, Z., Wang, Z., Dick, R.P., Mao, Z.M., Yang, L.: Accurate online power estimation and automatic battery behavior based power model generation for smartphones. In: Proceedings of the 8th IEEE/ACM/IFIP International Conference on Hardware/Software Codesign and System Synthesis, CODES/ISSS 2010, New York, pp. 105–114. ACM (2010)

25. Zhang, N., Ramanathan, P., Kim, K.-H., Banerjee, S.: Powervisor: a battery virtualization scheme for smartphones. In: Proceedings of the Third ACM Workshop on Mobile Cloud Computing and Services, MCS 2012, New York, pp. 37–44. ACM (2012)

CSSWare: A Middleware for Scalable Mobile Crowd-Sourced Services

Ahmed Abdel Moamen and Nadeem Jamali[✉]

Department of Computer Science, University of Saskatchewan, Saskatoon, Canada
ama883@mail.usask.ca, jamali@cs.usask.ca

Abstract. The growing ubiquity of a variety of personal connected computational devices – each with a number of sensors – has created the opportunity for a wide range of crowd-sourced services. A busy professional could find a restaurant to go to for a quick lunch based on information available from smartphones of other people already there. Sensors on smartphones could detect whether their owners are having lunch, waiting to be seated, or even heading there.

Although the programming required for offering a new service of this sort can be significant if done from scratch, we identify core communication mechanisms underlying such services, which can be implemented as part of a middleware. Service designers can then launch novel services over this middleware by plugging in small pieces of service-specific code.

This paper describes the multi-origin communication mechanism which we believe to underlie many crowd-sourced services. It presents our design and prototype Actor-based implementation of middleware for crowd-sourced services, CSSWare. We present the code for a realistic crowd-sourced service to illustrate the ease with which new services can be specified and launched. Finally, we present our experimental results demonstrating scalability, performance and data-contributor side energy efficiency of the approach.

Keywords: Crowd-sourced · Middleware · Actors · Programmability · Power

1 Introduction

With the growing ubiquity of personal computational devices such as smartphones and wearable devices, has also come the ubiquity of sensors on these devices, as well as the potential for triggering actions virtually anywhere. This opens up an opportunity to offer a variety of services which rely on the state of the context in which devices are located, such as a person or a group of people carrying the devices, their geographical location, etc. We broadly refer to these as crowd-sourced services.

Consider a restaurant recommendation service which samples data collected about experiences of clients at a number of restaurants in a neighborhood and ranks them according to the service experience of these clients. The source of

© Institute for Computer Sciences, Social Informatics and Telecommunications Engineering 2015
S. Sigg et al. (Eds.): MobiCASE 2015, LNICST 162, pp. 181–199, 2015.
DOI: 10.1007/978-3-319-29003-4_11

the data could be sensor feeds on clients' smartphones, used to guess whether they are waiting, seated, enjoying their meals, paying or leaving. There could be a similar service for recommending hospital emergency services to people. Social media applications (Twitter, etc.) also appear to follow a similar pattern, where crowds contribute to collective messages by contributing free-form short messages.

We are interested in an opportunity created by the similarity in the patterns of communication required for many of these services, which we refer to as multi-origin communication. This is the type of communication where a group of senders contribute to a group message, without any of them necessarily *taking the lead*. Contrast this with a single-origin (multi-sender) communication [7], which is initiated by a single party which solicits interest from other parties to join together in sending a particular message. An example of the latter would be a workplace petition drafted by an individual and presented to others to sign. In multi-origin (implicitly also multi-sender) communication, the expectation is that there is no single party that takes the lead. In other words, multiple parties may autonomously launch messages which could then be aggregated in order to create a group message.

It turns out that unlike single-origin multi-sender messages, multi-origin messages require a setup in advance. Consider a public square where a number of citizens spontaneously begin to gather to party or protest. In this context, the physical space of the square serves as part of a setup which allows mutual observation, an opportunity to join in or leave, to endorse, reject or refine the collective message or experience over time. The closest electronic equivalent of such a physical space would be social media services such as Twitter, which allow people to observe others' tweets in an aggregate form (which is quite natural in physical space, but requires filtering and counting mechanisms in electronic space), endorse them by adopting hashtags, improve upon the message, and so on. In general, for a crowd (or mass) - conceived communication to happen, there is a need for a mechanism to be in place to coordinate the generation of the group message by soliciting individual messages, receiving them, and then aggregating them into a group message. The solicitation lays out the rules to be followed for selection of the potential senders, receiving their messages, and aggregating them. The communication could be one-time, periodic, or continual. There may or may not be a time-out for responding to the solicitation. All these aspects would be laid out in the original solicitation.

Multi-origin communication [1] serves as the core mechanism underlying many such crowd-sourced services. In other words, key coordination mechanisms can be provided in a platform over which a class of crowd-sourced services could be implemented relatively easily. Here, we present our efforts in realizing that potential by implementing a middleware for crowd-sourced services, CSSWare. Using CSSWare, all that a service designer needs to do to launch a new service is to identify a constituency of potential contributors, and to provide a few lines of service-specific code for specifying the nature of contributions and for aggregating them when they arrive. Additionally, we try to (opportunistically) optimize the data contributor side energy consumption of crowd-sourced services for the situation where a number of services are being contributed to simultaneously. An optimizing sampling scheduler schedules the sampling of sensors based on the sensing requirements received from services running concurrently. The scheduler opportunistically optimizes the effective sampling rate of each sensor, exploiting opportunities for different services to share sensor samples when possible.

The rest of paper is organized as follows: Sect. 2 presents the related work. Section 3 describes our general approach to supporting crowd-sourced services using multi-origin communication. Sections 4 and 5 present our design and prototype implementation respectively. Section 6 evaluates the work by illustrating the ease with which new services can be implemented over our platform. It also presents our experimental results showing scalability, performance and energy efficiency of the approach. Finally, Sect. 7 concludes the paper.

2   Related Work

The term crowd-sourced can refer to two types of services: participatory sensing services and crowdsensing services. Participatory sensing involves explicit participation of human beings in possession of mobile devices, whereas crowdsensing relies on sensor feeds automatically flowing from devices to servers.

Participatory crowd sensing has been used in applications ranging from assisting drivers in making routing decisions based on real-time data (e.g., Waze [11] and TrafficPulse [12] to helping response to medical emergencies (e.g., CrowdHelp [5]) to disaster relief (e.g., in the aftermath of the 2010 Hatian earthquake [18]).

Among crowdsensing services, the real-time traffic information displayed on Google Maps is arguably the most widely used one, which now also has a participatory sensing aspect since Google's acquisition of Waze [11] in 2012. Uga et al. [15] have used crowdsensing to develop an earthquake warning system, which uses data from accelerometers present in many modern mobile devices to detect seismic vibrations.

Our work is more closely related to research focused on supporting crowd-sourced applications. Existing efforts have taken different approaches to supporting such applications in terms of programmability and generality.

Medusa [14] is a programming framework for crowd-sourced applications. A task (such as video documentation or citizen journalism) is launched by a requester, and *workers* are solicited through Amazon's Mechanical Turk (AMT) service. These workers – volunteering smartphone users – then provide raw or processed data to be used as part of a social or technical experiment. An XML-based programming language, MedScript, is used to specify the required task as a series of several stages, from the initial recruitment of volunteer workers, to the workers' (say, for a video documentation task) recording videos on their smartphones, summarizing them, and then sending them back. The stages can involve actions selectable from a library of executables, which are downloaded to mobile devices from a cloud server. Because Medusa requires that tasks pick from a limited set of activities, it suffers from limited programmability and generality, and is not applicable to a large class of crowd-sourced services.

AnonySense [6] is another framework for collecting and processing sensor data, which pays particular attention to privacy concerns. AnonySense allows a requester to launch one of a selected group of applications with their parameters. The application then distributes sensing tasks across anonymous participating mobile devices (referred to as carriers), and finally aggregates the reports received from the carriers. Achieving anonymity relies on separating sensor data from identifying features (such as homes or workplaces in GPS traces) to obscure individual identities. Similarly to Medusa, AnonySense has limitations in programmability and generality because of its limited focus on collection of sensor data and in-network processing.

CDAS [13] is an example of participatory crowd-sensing frameworks. It enables deployment of various crowd-sensing applications which require human involvement for simple verification tasks to deliver high accuracy services. Similar to CDAS, MOSDEN [10] is a collaborative mobile sensing framework that operates on smartphones to capture and share sensed data between multiple distributed applications and users.

The MECA (Mobile Edge Capture and Analysis) middleware for social sensing applications [16] focuses on efficient data collection from mobile devices. It uses a multi-layer architecture to take advantage of similarities in the data required for different applications to lower the demand on devices on which data is being collected. MECA's focus is limited to a narrow class of applications, and does not address wider programmability challenges. Furthermore, MECA – like other similar frameworks – uses the smartphone as a dumb data generator, offloading all processing to the server layer. This increases communication cost and does not allow applications to take advantage of data collected while the mobile device is not connected.

In summary, existing frameworks for crowd-sourced applications focus on narrow application areas or specific concerns, making it difficult to utilize them for a wider class of services. Also, none of them support concurrent execution of multiple services from within one service platform, which precludes taking advantage of opportunities to optimize for shared sensing requirements.

3   Supporting Crowd-Sourced Services

It turns out that a large class of crowd-sourced services exhibit a similar pattern of interaction, where members of a *crowd* contribute bits of information from their respective contexts, which are then aggregated to create useful information for clients. We have identified this pattern of interaction as *multi-origin (multi-sender) communication*, which involves aggregation of the messages received from a group of senders (referred here to as the constituency) into a *group message* to be sent on behalf of the group to one or more intended recipients.

Most examples of crowd-sourced services fit the *continual* type of multi-origin communication, where members of the constituency send messages on a continual basis rather than just once; this would be useful for a service provided over the web or through a mobile application where site visitors or application users seek up-to-date information (say) on restaurant waiting times in a neighborhood. The *one-off* type of interaction soliciting only one message from each member of the constituency is a special case of this general case; this would be the type of communication used to serve one-time requests, such as to hold a census or an election, or to satisfy a one-off request to recommend a restaurant with a short waiting time. For some services, such as the one for restaurant recommendations, the choice between the continual and the one-off type of communication would depend on the frequency of requests, the number of potential senders of messages, etc. For instance, it would not be useful to be maintaining up-to-date information about all restaurants when there are very few requests for recommendations; however, it would be wasteful to solicit one-off communications for frequent requests.

From here on, we will refer to continual multi-origin communication as simply multi-origin communication.

3.1 Multi-origin Communication

To be precise in our presentation of continual multi-origin communication, we specify it in terms of the Actor model [3]. Actors are autonomous concurrently executing primitive agents (i.e., active objects) which communicate using asynchronous messages.[1] We represent the different parties involved in a multi-origin communication using actors, and define the required communication in terms of asynchronous actor messages.

The requester of a multi-origin communication makes a function call in order to launch the communication. The call passes two parameters, the first specifying the potential contributors – the constituency – to be invited to participate in the communication, and the second specifying an aggregation method. As illustrated in Fig. 1, an invocation of this function results in the creation of a new coordinator actor capable of coordinating the communication, which is next told to invite the constituency to participate. The coordinator then sends invitations to the members of the constituency (the contributors) to send their messages; when applicable, it also sends them parameters advising on how to construct their contributions (such as by tapping into a set of sensors, or soliciting input from the user), how often to send them (once or periodically, how frequently), etc.

As the contributors send their messages, the messages are aggregated by the coordinator as specified in its own behavior, to generate group messages on behalf of the contributors. When a contributor's message arrives at the coordinator, it checks whether the message warrants an update, or whether the interval for which it was to collect messages has passed. In both cases, it forwards an aggregate of messages received since the beginning of the interval to the requester. For example, a restaurant recommendation service available over the web would collect periodically sent updates from various restaurants and offer up-to-date information to site visitors.

---

[1] Actors are emerging as the model of choice for large-scale communication systems. Among others, Twitter and Facebook Chat have been implemented using Actor systems [4].

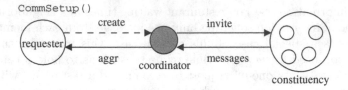

Fig. 1. Multi-origin communication setup

4   Middleware Design

Our design of a crowd-sourced service (CSSWare) middleware builds on the mechanism for multi-origin communication described in the previous section. As illustrated in Fig. 2, the sensing crowd becomes the constituency whose input is solicited. The service continually aggregates the feeds arriving from the crowd to create up-to-date custom views for various types of clients. For example, if the service were for recommending restaurants, one interface could be for prospective diners, another for the restaurant managers making real-time staffing plans, yet another could be for a vehicular routing system interested in improving downtown traffic flow at lunch time.

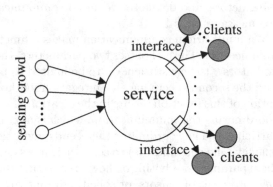

Fig. 2. Crowd-sourced service

Figure 3 illustrates how the distributed run-time system for the middleware is organized with parts executing on the service platform, on devices of members of the constituency, as well as client devices. In the rest of this section, we discuss these three parts separately.

4.1   Service Platform Side

The service designer uses the service creation API to create and launch a new crowd-sourced service. A set of parameters stating service specifications is passed through the API. These specifications identify the contributors to be invited

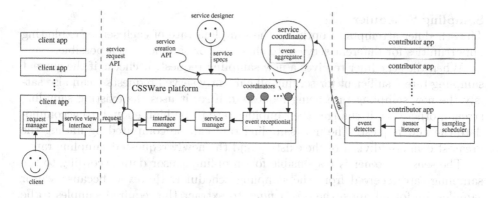

Fig. 3. System architecture

to participate in the service, the aggregation method to be used, as well as a description of the feeds solicited from the contributors in terms of specific events of interest, such as arrival at a restaurant, being seated at the table, etc.

To launch a new service, the service manager (see server in Fig. 3) creates a new service coordinator to coordinate the communication between the contributors and the CSSWare platform, which is capable of coordinating the communication between the contributors and the CSSWare platform. Next, it sends invitations to the contributors to send their events – when one is detected – to the coordinator. It also sends them parameters advising on how to detect events, construct their messages, and how often to send them (once or periodically, how frequently, etc.).

Contributor events received by a service coordinator are handled by its event aggregator, which in turn reports the events in aggregate form to the CSSWare platform's event receptionist. The aggregated events are then passed on to the service manager, which processes them to update the service's state, which is forwarded to the service interface manager to deliver appropriate views requested by clients through custom interfaces.

4.2 Contributor Side

To launch a service, the platform's service manager sends invitations to contributors to participate in the service. It also sends them parameters advising on how to detect events and construct their messages (i.e., sensing parameters). Event detection is carried out by dedicated *event detection actors*, who generate event feeds using relevant sensor feeds, which are then sent to the service coordinator.

An optimizing *sampling scheduler* schedules the sampling of each sensor based on the sensing requirements received from the service coordinator for each service being served at the time.

Sampling Scheduler

The scheduler attempts to optimize the sampling rate of each sensor exploiting opportunities for different services to share sensor samples when possible.

When the scheduler receives a new sampling request, it checks if the current sampling rate – sufficient for serving all currently served requests – can also satisfy the new sampling rate being requested; if so, it uses the existing sampling stream; otherwise, it changes the sampling rate to be high enough to accommodate the new request. The new sampling rate can be computed by finding the greatest common divisor of the existing and the newly requested sampling rates.

The sensor listener is responsible for sampling sensor data according to the sampling rate received from the sampling scheduler. However, because sensor samples are for all apps, there is a *filter* to extract the required samples to be sent to the different apps.

Algorithm 1 shows the steps followed by the scheduler to find the optimal sampling rate for sensing requests being served at the time. Each sensing request specifies the sensor to be sampled, as well as the rate at which it should be sampled. When a new request is received, the scheduler checks if the sensor is already scheduled; if so, it merges the current sampling rate with the GCD of the inverse of the current sampling rate and the new rate; otherwise, it sets up a new sensor listener to the requested sensor.

A more detailed presentation of the sampling scheduler can be found in [2].

Algorithm 1. Sampling Rate Adaptation Algorithm

1: **procedure** SENSOR SCHEDULING
2: **Input:** sensor name (s) and sampling rate (r)
3: **Output:** sensor data stream
4: */* check if s is already scheduled */*
5: **if** SamplingScheduler.isSensorFound (s, r) is false **then**
6:     SamplingScheduler.add(s, r);
7:     *create a new sensor listener actor for s*
8: **else** */* if s is already scheduled */*
9: */*find the GCD between r and current sampling rate*/*
10:     newRate = GCD(SamplingScheduler.currentRate, r);
11: */* adapt the sampling rate */*
12:     SamplingScheduler.adaptSamplingRate(s, newRate);
13: **end if**
14: *filter sensor data*
15: *send sampling streams to services when the sensor listener detects an event*

4.3   Client Side

A service can have various types of clients subscribed to different views of the service's state, each provided by a custom interface. When a client requests subscription to a particular type of view, the request manager inside the client app constructs a custom view subscription request. This request is passed on to the service view interface, which is transmitted through the service request API of the CSSWare platform (see Fig. 3). The platform adds the client to a list of subscribers to that view of the service, and begins sending it all updates.

5 Middleware Implementation

A prototype of CSSWare has been implemented as an actor system. The prototype has two parts: a server implementing a crowd-sourced service platform (about 7,500 lines of code), and a mobile app supporting both client and contributor functionalities (about 4,600 lines of code).

Our implementation is built using the CyberOrgs [8] extension of Actor Architecture (AA) [9], a Java library and runtime system for distributed actor systems. Crowd-sourced services run over CSSWare, which runs over the CyberOrgs runtime system.

For the client and contributor side, we have ported AA to Android OS for supporting the mobile app.

5.1 Service Platform Side

To launch a new service, first, the requested service's meta data (i.e., its title and description) is added to the list of published services, which lists active services visible to contributors. Next, the service manager creates a service actor which invites potential contributors to send their events to the service's coordinator. It also sends them parameters advising on how to construct their contribution messages. After inviting the contributors, a new service view is created in the service request API in order to serve clients' requests.

As contributors to a service detect and send events, the events are aggregated by the coordinator and reported to the service manager through the event receptionist (see Fig. 3). The service manager collects aggregated events until a sufficient number of them have been received (as determined by a sufficiency condition provided by the service designer in the form of a function) and then updates the service state, revising the custom service views available to the clients.

5.2 Contributor Side

For the contributor (and client) side, we have ported CyberOrgs to Android OS, and implemented a self-contained application over it which runs on the Android OS (ver. 5.1). The current implementation supports contributions based on feeds from the GPS, accelerometer, microphone, magnetometer, gyroscope, pressure, humidity, temperature and light sensors. A set of high-level sensor events has been pre-implemented in terms of these (low-level) sensor events – as executable specifications – which a service designer can draw from and customize by providing parameters. These high-level events form the basis for service events. For each high-level sensor event feed, the list of required low-level feeds is provided in the form of a list, where each entry identifies a sensor and specifies the rate at which it should be sampled. These specifications are typically only a few lines of code, varying between 7 and 18 lines of code for the triggers used in the example service prototypes. The code for using high-level sensor events to generate the service events is typically even shorter. The current prototype does not have a way for a service designer to add completely new high-level sensor or service event types; ongoing work is developing a way to allow that.

As shown in Fig. 4, the runtime system executing on the Android device has two components: the sampling scheduler and the event detector.

Sampling Scheduler. As described in Sect. 4.2, the sampling scheduler sets a sampling rate for each sensor based on the received sensing parameters. The scheduler first parses the service parameters to extract the coordinator name and the list of the service's event feeds.

Sensor listeners are responsible for sampling sensor data according to the sampling rate received from the sampling scheduler. The scheduler optimizes sensor sampling feeds by opportunistically sharing them between different service feeds.

Event Detector. Because the data sampled from a sensor can be for multiple event feeds, the data is filtered to extract the sub-feed pertinent to each event feed being served, and only that sub-feed is forwarded to the relevant event detection actor. An event detection actor monitors the sensor feed it receives for event triggers; when it sees one, it fires the event off to its service coordinator.

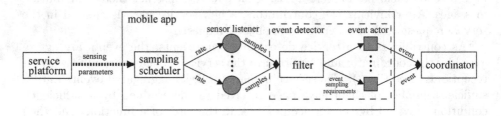

Fig. 4. Contributor side

An event detector does not maintain a local record of the triggered events itself; all events are sent to the service coordinator.

Because the contributor side of the system will likely execute on battery-operated mobile devices, it is important that contributors have the ability to either develop or adopt simple resource consumption policies to avoid undesired battery drain. We hope to utilize the fine-grained resource management features already present in the CyberOrgs [8] extension of Actor Architecture which we have used in our prototype. For now, we have implemented a feature allowing a service designer to specify resource limits after reaching which the contributor device would stop contributing feeds.

5.3 Client Side

Client side of the platform is implemented as part of the Android application implementing the contributor side. When a new service is launched, each client receives a notification about the launch. Multiple views are supported through custom interfaces installed by the service designer. A client interested in subscribing to a service can examine available views using the *service view interface* (see Fig. 3), and then use the service request API to subscribe to the desired view.

There is a collection of four general purpose view interfaces pre-implemented in the platform, which average at about 85 lines of code (the largest at about 100 and the smallest at 75 lines).[2] Although these interfaces are sufficient for the examples we have implemented, and for services with similar client side requirements, additional interfaces would need to implemented for different types of services. In our current prototype, there is no way for service designers to program these interfaces themselves; however, we plan to provide a way for new (general purpose or custom) interfaces developed by service designers or other parties to be installed or added to a repository from which they could be installed.

6 Evaluation

In this section, we present our evaluation of CSSWare for both the programmability of new services, as well as our experimental evaluation for performance, scalability and energy efficiency.

6.1 Programmability

The main programmability advantage of using CSSWare is in the orders of magnitude lower number of lines of code required for launching a new service. The prototype restaurant recommendation service presented in this section required 41 lines of code for the server and contributor side combined; in comparison, an equivalent standalone service we implemented required 6,142 lines of code. A twitter-like messaging service we implemented, which is not discussed in greater detail because of space constraints, similarly required 46 lines of code instead of 4,768 lines for an equivalent standalone service. For reference, the server and contributor end of the CSSWare platform required 7,473 and 4,622 lines of code respectively.

Restaurant Recommendation Service
Consider the type of restaurant recommendation service previously described in Sect. 1, where mobile devices of people visiting restaurants in a neighborhood automatically send real-time updates about the service they are receiving to a

---

[2] These 350 lines of code are included in the previously mentioned roughly 4600 lines of code for the Android application's implementation.

service provider, which then aggregates this information for people searching for restaurants. We assume that information required for generating these feeds can be gathered automatically by the devices by tapping into various sensors to determine when someone arrives at a restaurant, when they are waiting to be seated, when they sit down, when they are served, when they finish eating, and when they leave. The information could be coarser or finer grained depending on the device, usage habits, quality of the behavior detecting software, etc. These updates from personal mobile devices could then be aggregated by a service provider to rank restaurants according to criteria such as the amount of wait time before being seated, the length of time taken dining (shorter or longer, as preferred), the total amount of time that the user could expect to travel to the restaurant, dine, and be back at work. The ranking could also consider the server's meta-knowledge about the number of people being sent to various restaurants by the service.

Figure 5 presents our code implementing such a service as a `createSensor-Service()` method. First, a number of service variables are initialized: the list of restaurants (i.e., their names and coordinates), `restaurantList`, a method to be used by the coordinator to aggregate contributions, `aggrMethod`, and the sampling rate to be used for sensor feeds when a rate is not explicitly specified, `Default_SamplingRate`. `aggrMethod` is initialized here to a general purpose method for computing the average; it is to be used by the coordinator to compute average waiting time. Other services could use other available aggregation methods; our prototype provides a selection of them. There is currently no way for a service designer to add a new aggregation method, but we plan to provide that functionality in the future. Although here we hardcode the restaurants, functionality can be easily added to the mobile app to allow contributors to add previously unknown restaurants.

A sensor is set up for each of the sensor feeds required for any of the service feeds, following which the two types of service events are defined. The first, `locationEvent`, is defined to require the GPS sensor feed and is defined in terms of a number of parameters. The "trigger" parameters identify high-level sensor events, which become the basis for service events. For example `enterPlace` recognizes entering a location (a restaurant in this service). The "output" parameters identify the service events to be sent to the coordinator; here, `visitTime` computes the difference between `enterPlace` and `departPlace`. Additional parameter types are parameters that are available to the various methods; for example, `updateInterval` is available to `visitTime` as a parameter to decide the frequency of feeds to send to the coordinator.

Similarly, `activityEvent` specified a different sensor feed related to observations of the restaurant client's activity. It uses various sensor feeds. The triggers detect activities of "sitting down" or "being still," the latter using the `stillTime` parameter, which are then used as the basis for a `waitingTime` service event to be sent to the coordinator.

Finally, the service is created as an instance of the `CrowdService` class, and launched. The constructor for `CrowdService` takes as parameters a `title`, a

```
void createSensorService()
{
  /* initialize service variables */
  String placeList = "Restaurant1,52.1269,-106.7618;
           Restaurant2,52.1156,-106.5997; .......";
  int aggrMethod = ServiceEnum.average;
  int Default_SamplingRate =
      SensorManager.SENSOR_DELAY_NORMAL;

  /* defining sensors */
  Sensor GPS = new Sensor (ServiceEnum.GPS,
                              Default_SamplingRate);
  Sensor accelerometer = new Sensor(
  ServiceEnum.accelerometer, Default_SamplingRate);
  Sensor gyroscope = new Sensor(
      ServiceEnum.gyroscope, Default_SamplingRate);

  /* define a service event */
  ServiceEvent locationEvent = new ServiceEvent
  (ServiceEnum.sensorEvent, new List<Sensor>(){GPS},
    new List<EventParam>(){
      createParam("trigger",ServiceEnum.enterPlace),
      createParam("trigger",ServiceEnum.departPlace),
      createParam("placeList",placeList),
      createParam("updateInterval",30),
      createParam("output",ServiceEnum.visitTime),
   });

  /* define a service event */
  ServiceEvent activityEvent = new ServiceEvent
  (ServiceEnum.sensorEvent, new List<Sensor>(){
                     accelerometer,gyroscope},
    new List<EventParam>(){
      createParam("trigger",ServiceEnum.sitDown),
      createParam("trigger",ServiceEnum.still),
      createParam("stillTime",1),
      createParam("output",ServiceEnum.waitingTime),
   });

  /* create and launch the service */
  CrowdService service = new CrowdService(title,
          description, new List<ServiceEvent>()
    {locationEvent, activityEvent}, aggrMethod);
  service.launch();
}
```

Fig. 5. Restaurant recommendation service

description, the list of events (i.e., locationEvent and activityEvent) and the aggregation method aggrMethod. Once the service has been created, launch is called to launch the service.

6.2 Experimental Evaluation

We experimentally evaluated CSSWare in terms of performance, scalability and energy efficiency. Our experiments were conducted on a prototype Actor-based implementation of CSSWare. On the contributor side, we used a Samsung Galaxy Note II phone with a 1.6 GHz quad-core processor and 2 GB of RAM running Android OS ver 5.1. The server ran on a Windows 7 laptop equipped with a 2.6 GHz quad-core Intel i7 processor and 8 GB of RAM.

We installed instrumentation in the server and mobile application (i.e., contributor and client) parts of our prototype restaurant recommendation service to measure the processor time taken to perform various tasks. Instrumentation was also added to the contributor side to measure energy consumption of sensing.

Performance and Scalability
Service Platform Processing Demand. To evaluate the scalability of the server, we measured the resources required to host a service.

We created and launched a set of instances of the previously described restaurant recommendation service with their required frequencies of event feeds distributed over a normal distribution function. Specifically, we picked 150 random values with an average of 6.7, which added up to 1,000. We created 150 services with the randomly chosen feed frequency requirements, adding up to a cumulative feed frequency of 1,000 feeds per second. Each service received feeds from 10 restaurants. Note that the event feeds here are feeds of higher level events detected at the contributor end; these are not the raw data received at a high frequency from the sensors. In other words, the average frequency of 6.7 events per second per service would mean that something interesting is observed at some contributor device related to the service at the rate of 6.7 per second. Furthermore, we used a window size of 20 for recently received feeds for any window, this is the number of recent feeds which were used to compute a score for the restaurant. For this local aggregation, we simply maintained the average wait time for the restaurant, which required $O(1)$ amount of time to maintain. These local aggregates for restaurants fed into the creation of a global aggregate in the form of a ranked list of the restaurants based on their scores, which amounted to a single step of *insertion sort* to maintain a sorted list, with an $O(n)$ cost.[3]

Table 1 separately shows the one-time processing costs involved in creation of a new service as well as on-going processing costs as each event feed is received and processed. Creating service and coordinator actors – the former also including parsing the service's meta data (i.e., title and description) and adding the new service to the published service list – took 13.04 ms and 11.67 ms on average,

---

[3] Although this performs well for the small number of restaurants, it would be more efficient to use a binary search tree to keep a large number of restaurants sorted.

respectively. Initializing the global view for the service required 7.84 ms. In terms of on-going costs, receiving and parsing an incoming event feed required 7.35 ms on average. The cost of local aggregation to keep track of the average of the last 20 waiting times for a restaurant was 0.024 ms on average. This aggregation has $O(1)$ complexity. We also measured costs for $O(\log n)$, $O(n)$ and $O(n^2)$ complexity local aggregation functions as shown in the table. The global aggregation for ranking the 10 restaurants incurred an average processing cost of 0.95 ms.

To put these numbers in some context, given the 8.325 ms required per feed on an on-going basis, about 120 event feeds could be processed by a server of our configuration per second. This could support a single service where 120 events are being collectively detected by the contributors every second, or 10 services which are each receiving about 12 feeds per second on average, and so on. In a broader context still, assuming 40 % of the population dines out at a meal time[4], assuming the diners are distributed somewhat evenly over a period of two hours, and each diner's device is sending 3 events over the course of their meal (indicating arrival, seating, departure) a server of our modest configuration could process 288,288 diners' data, equivalently data for a city of about 720,720 people. In practice, data from a small fraction of the diners could be used, allowing service for an order of magnitude higher population.

That said, our global aggregation function assumed only 10 restaurants. Although this may be reasonable because individuals requiring restaurant recommendations are not likely to be close to hundreds of restaurants, narrowing down the selection before aggregation would mean custom global aggregations, each costing the 0.95 ms. However, this custom aggregation could happen on the client's own device, without impacting the server's scalability. Alternatively, for a truly global aggregate for a city with (say) 10,000 restaurants, an $O(\log n)$ binary search tree could be used to keep the restaurants sorted; only the top few would ever need to be fetched, limiting the fetching cost.

Contributor Processing Demand. On the contributor side, again, we separately measured the initial cost of handling a new service's request for contribution, as well as the on-going cost of serving the service. The average total of measured one-time cost was 54.87 ms (SD 3.57). The on-going costs measured were per sensor feed: every time a piece of raw data was received from a server, its average total processing cost amounted to 8.68 ms (SD 1.02).

To put this on-going cost in perspective, about 115 sensor feeds per second could be handled on a device of our configuration (assuming no other computations executing). If an average service requires as many as 10 data samples per second (from a variety of sensors), 11.5 of such services could be supported; if an average of 1 data sample per second is required per service, a more likely scenario, 115 services could be simultaneously contributed to.

Client Processing Demand. For the client side as well, we measured the one-time processing costs of accessing a new service, as well as the on-going costs of receiv-

---

[4] Zagat 2014 restaurant survey reported that an average American ate out or bought 47 % of their lunches or dinners.

Table 1. Average processing time at the server side in ms

One-Time Per-Service Costs	Mean	SD
Create a service actor	13.04	2.63
Create a coordinator actor	11.67	1.74
Create a service view	7.84	0.98
Total processing time	32.55	5.35
Per-Event-Feed Costs	**Mean**	**SD**
Process an event feed	7.35	1.11
Local aggregation ($O(1)$ cost)	0.024	0.0021
Local aggregation ($O(\log n)$ cost)	0.078	0.0083
Local aggregation ($O(n)$ cost)	0.280	0.0349
Local aggregation ($O(n^2)$ cost)	0.680	0.0987
Global aggregation (10 Restaurants)	0.95	0.17
Total processing time ($O(1)$ local aggregation)	8.325	1.28

ing updates. The average total of measured one-time costs was 35.53 ms. The total of measured per-refresh on-going costs amounted to 60.9 ms on average, with 28.7 ms (SD 3.9) for processing the update, and 32.2 ms (SD 6.4) for display. In other words, a client could be simultaneously subscribed to and receive updates from 16 services every second. This is not very meaningful considering that more than half of the processing cost is for graphically displaying the update, which is not likely to happen simultaneously for more than only a few services. If we assume that only one service's updates are actually displayed at a time, more than 30 services could be supported in the background where interesting updates could lead to notifications, invitations to display, etc.

Energy Consumption of CSSWare vs. Standalone Services

Finally, a set of experiments was carried out to measure the overall improvement achieved in energy consumption by using CSSWare's sampling scheduler on the contributor device. We used the PowerTutor software [17] for our energy measurements.

To measure the overall improvement in energy consumption, we made measurements of energy used by CSSWare and identical standalone services implemented without using CSSWare. The sampling scheduler improved energy consumption of accelerometer and gyroscope sensors by up to 24.60 % and 26.63 %, respectively. However, the percentage savings depend entirely on the number of requests being served, because although the energy used is roughly linear in the cumulative sampling rate of all requests for the standalone services, for CSS-Ware, it depends almost entirely on the highest frequency being requested at the time, from which other requests are also served.

Overhead Analysis. In order to determine the non-sensing overhead of CSS-Ware, we measured the energy consumed by the contributor device side of the framework, albeit without the actual sensing. The average energy consumed was measured to be 72.9 mJ for the accelerometer, and a very similar 81 mJ for the gyroscope sensor. In percentage terms, this was roughly 4 % of the total energy consumed in the accelerometer experiments, and 0.8 % for the gyroscope sensor, the difference explained by the order-of-magnitude larger overall energy demand of the gyroscope sensor itself.

7 Conclusions

With the growing ubiquity of sensors and mobile devices, it is more possible than ever to offer innovative services based on both what the millions of sensors on people's devices are sensing, as well as what individuals are willing to actively contribute. However, the barriers to offering such services continue to be prohibitive for most: not only must these services be implemented, they would inevitably compete for resources on people's devices.

We have argued in this paper that many crowd-sourced services, including prominent social media services (if we consider their role of helping evolve collective messages), require similar communication mechanisms. We focus on one such mechanism – multi-origin communication – which allows a number of autonomous participants to contribute messages which can then be aggregated to create group messages on behalf of all. We introduced an approach to supporting crowd-sourced services using multi-origin communication, and presented our design and implementation of an Actor-based middleware for crowd-sourced services as a platform for launching such services. We illustrated the ease with which new services can be launched by presenting code for a prototype implementation for a crowd sensed restaurant recommendation service requiring fewer than 50 lines of main service specification code, with less than 100 lines of additional relevant code from available libraries of aggregation functions, feed specifications and service view interface. Finally, we experimentally evaluated the scalability of the approach. Most notably, even our modestly configured server could potentially provide a restaurant recommender service to a population of millions; contributor devices could contribute to tens if not hundreds of services simultaneously; client devices could monitor tens of services.

We have additionally addressed the challenge of satisfying the energy needs of a potentially large number of services requiring sensor data continuously. Use of the sampling scheduler takes advantage of the overlap in sensing requirements of various applications to achieve significant energy savings when there are overlapping requirements, with minimal overhead.

In on-going work, we are developing mechanisms for service designers and third parties to add new service feed specifications, custom service view interfaces, and aggregation functions. This will allow a larger variety of services to be implemented. We are also working on further simplifying programmability of services through web-based graphical interfaces. Finally, we would like to apply our approach for fine-grained resource coordination to refining the sensor sampling scheduler, and more generally to manage the resource demands that a larger number of services may place on resource-constrained mobile devices.

Acknowledgments. Support from NSERC and CFI is gratefully acknowledged.

References

1. Abdel Moamen, A., Jamali, N.: Coordinating crowd-sourced services. In: Proceedings of IEEE Mobile Services, Alaska, pp. 92–99 (2014)
2. Abdel Moamen, A., Jamali, N.: ShareSens: an approach to optimizing energy consumption of continuous mobile sensing workloads. In: Proceedings of IEEE Mobile Services, NY, USA, pp. 89–96, June 2015
3. Agha, G.: Actors: A Model of Concurrent Computation in Distributed Systems. MIT Press, Cambridge (1986)
4. Agha, G.: Actors programming for the mobile cloud. In: Proceedings of ISPDC, pp. 3–9, June 2014
5. Besaleva, L., Weaver, A., CrowdHelp,: a crowdsourcing application for improving disaster management. In: Proceedings of GHTC, California, USA, pp. 185–190 (2013)
6. Cornelius, C., Kapadia, A., Kotz, D., Peebles, D., Shin, M., Triandopoulos, N., AnonySense: privacy-aware people-centric sensing. In: Proceedings of MobiSys, Breckenridge, USA, pp. 211–224 (2008)
7. Geng, H., Jamali, N.: Supporting many-to-many communication. In: Proceedings of AGERE!@SPLASH, Indiana, USA, pp. 81–86 (2013)
8. Jamali, N., Zhao, X.: Hierarchical resource usage coordination for large-scale multi-agent systems. In: Ishida, T., Gasser, L., Nakashima, H. (eds.) MMAS 2005. LNCS (LNAI), vol. 3446, pp. 40–54. Springer, Heidelberg (2005)
9. Jang, M.-W., Ahmed, A., Agha, G.: Efficient agent communication in multi-agent systems. In: Choren, R., Garcia, A., Lucena, C., Romanovsky, A. (eds.) SELMAS 2004. LNCS, vol. 3390, pp. 236–253. Springer, Heidelberg (2005)
10. Jayaraman, P., Perera, C., Georgakopoulos, D., Zaslavsky, A.: Efficient opportunistic sensing using mobile collaborative platform MOSDEN. In: Proceedings of the 2013 International Conference on Collaborative Computing: Observation of Strains: Networking, Applications and Worksharing (2011). Infect Dis Ther. 3(1), 35–43
11. Levine, U., Shinar, A., Shabtai, E., Shmuelevitz, Y.: Condition-based activation, shut-down and management of applications of mobile devices. United States Patents, US 8,271,057 (2009)
12. Li, R.-Y., Liang, S., Lee, D.-W., Byon, Y.-J.: TrafficPulse: a mobile gisystem for transportation. In: Proceedings of MobiGIS, California, USA, pp. 9–16 (2012)
13. Liu, X., Lu, M., Ooi, C., Shen, Y., Wu, S., Zhang, M.: CDAS: a crowdsourcing data analytics system. J. PVLDB 5(10), 1040–1051 (2012)
14. Ra, M.-R., Liu, B., La-Porta, T., Govindan, R.: Medusa: a programming framework for crowd-sensing applications. In: Proceedings of MobiSys, pp. 337–350 (2012)
15. Uga, T., Nagaosa, T., Kawashima, D.: An emergency earthquake warning system using mobile terminals with a built-in accelerometer. In: Proceedings of the 2012 IEEE Conference on ITS Telecommunications (2012)

16. Ye, F., Ganti, R., Dimaghani, R., Grueneberg, K., Calo, S.: MECA: mobile edge capture and analysis middleware for social sensing applications. In: Proceedings of the Conference Companion on WWW, pp. 699–702. ACM, Lyon (2012)
17. Zhang, L., Tiwana, B., Qian, Z., Wang, Z., Dick, R.P., Mao, Z.M., Yang, L.: Accurate online power estimation and automatic battery behavior based power model generation for smartphones. In: Proceedings of CODES+ISSS, Arizona, USA, pp. 105–114 (2010)
18. Zook, M., Graham, M., Shelton, T., Gorman, S.: Volunteered geographic information and crowdsourcing disaster relief: a case study of the Haitian earthquake. World Med. Health Policy 2(2), 7–33 (2010)

Interactive Applications

Quality Assurance in Additive Manufacturing Through Mobile Computing

Sam Hurd[✉], Carmen Camp, and Jules White

Vanderbilt University, Nashville, TN 37235, USA
{sam.p.hurd,carmen.camp}@vanderbilt.edu, jules@dre.vanderbilt.edu

Abstract. The increase in use of consumer 3D printers for in-home or small business manufacturing may signal the start of an additive manufacturing revolution, but unfortunately these printers are often error prone. In order to remedy the time and materials lost when a failed print continues on a low-end 3D printer, a cost-effective method is needed to monitor the quality of a print and stop it when an error occurs. This paper presents an approach to using a commodity smartphone and computer vision to perform quality assurance on selected layers of a 3D print. Our results indicate that a commodity mobile device using our technique is capable of accurately detecting printing errors and then effectively determining whether or not a print should continue.

Keywords: Consumer 3d printers · Cost-effective · Quality assurance · Computer vision

1 Introduction

Emerging Trends and Challenges. Additive Manufacturing (AM) is the process of constructing a 3D object from a model design file by joining together solid materials [12]. A 3D model of the object is created and then translated into a series of instructions, such as GCode, which dictate the movements of an AM machine to construct the physical object layer by layer [1]. For example, a Fused Filament Fabrication 3D printer (FFF) works by moving a heated nozzle that extrudes thin layers of plastic to build a 3D object layer by layer as shown in Fig. 1.

AM machines are being used increasingly as their capabilities develop. They minimize waste and can create lighter, yet sturdy, parts more quickly for some applications. Additionally, they provide a method of building objects with complex interiors, a challenging task that few machines can accomplish accurately. For example, General Electric is creating a new fuel nozzle for aircraft engines, and these parts are being created using AM machines to make the fuel nozzles lighter, simpler to craft and more durable [2]. In addition to creating useful parts for aircrafts, AM machines are also beginning to be used for medical purposes. For example, researchers are beginning to create organs through the AM of human tissue [4] which would allow for failed organs to be replaced. As AM machines continue to develop, their potential continues to grow.

© Institute for Computer Sciences, Social Informatics and Telecommunications Engineering 2015
S. Sigg et al. (Eds.): MobiCASE 2015, LNICST 162, pp. 203–220, 2015.
DOI: 10.1007/978-3-319-29003-4_12

Fig. 1. The heated nozzle extruding filament to produce the sides of a square.

Recently, inexpensive AM machines have become more available allowing consumers to bring manufacturing into the home [3]. While printing is still not fast as it can take over an hour to print even a small box, consumer 3D printing is increasingly becoming a viable option for the future of small-scale, in-home manufacturing. There is a large and growing "maker" community that is using consumer AM machines to design and print complex parts at home and in small businesses.

Open Problem ⇒ Low-cost Quality Assurance for 3D Printers. Low-cost AM machines that are used by consumers for in-home or similar small scale printing are error-prone. With current consumer-focused devices, when an error occurs, the machine continues working wasting time and materials. Additionally, errors that occur early may not be detectable on the finished product and could compromise the structural integrity of the final object, especially in machines that are lower-cost, but also not necessarily professional or commercial grade [10].

Quality assurance and detection for 3D printing is still in early stages, and while some processes have been developed for industrial uses [5] or for analyzing the instructions' data points for correctness before the print [6], there are no automated mid-print quality control processes for low-end or home scale 3D printers. This paper focuses on addressing this gap in low-cost quality assurance systems.

Solution Approach ⇒ Mid-print Quality Assurance with a Commodity Mobile Device. To address the print quality detection problem with 3D printing, we created a cost effective mid-print quality assurance process using a mobile device that can easily be utilized alongside commercial FFF printers to detect when the printer has made an error through the use of image analysis. This solution uses a mobile device mounted above a 3D printer to capture images of selective layers after their completion, perform computer-vision based analysis of the layers, and if an error has occurred, stop the print and notify the user. The approach relies on automated pre-print analysis of the 3D model to predict what each layer should look like when printed and rewriting of the GCode sent the printer to insert quality assurance checks in the print instructions.

In Sect. 5, we present empirical data that we have gathered from experiments with a MakerGear M2 printer showing that our solution is able to effectively identify errors through a smartphone or tablet's camera with a high level of accuracy. These experiments centered on examining the accuracy of smartphone-based visual quality control for AM. This paper provides the following contributions to the study of using mobile computing for mid-print quality control in AM:

- We provide a method for extracting a 2D representation of what layer should be printed and where this layer should be printed.
- We provide an image based analysis of the printed object that can pinpoint errors through use of a mobile device's camera.
- We present empirical data comparing the accuracy and speed of two different image analysis approaches for AM quality assurance.
- Overall, we provide a mobile device-based architecture for quality control on consumer AM machines.

The remainder of the paper is organized as follows: Sect. 2 describes typical problems that arise during a 3D print, which we use as a motivating example throughout the paper; Sect. 3 describes the challenges of creating an effective mid-print quality assurance process; Sect. 4 presents our technique for analyzing a manufactured object mid-print and determining when an error has occurred; Sect. 5 presents empirical results demonstrating the ability of our process to effectively distinguish between failed prints and good prints; Sect. 6 compares our work with related research; and Sect. 7 presents concluding remarks.

2   Motivating Example

The need for a quality assurance process can easily be demonstrated using a commercial 3D printer using Polylactic Acid (PLA) as the printing filament [17]. Several types of errors can occur when printing with this setup and watching the print to manually catch errors is time consuming. To print a very basic one-inch cube takes approximately two hours, resulting in much lost time and effort if the print must be redone.

Figure 2 illustrates two errors that are common in commercial 3D printing. When printing a curved area, the PLA sometimes does not effectively stick to the previous layer and creates a chord between two points on the curve. Additionally, present in the figure is an internal error caused by the filament not properly sticking to the printerbed and being pushed around by the nozzle as it continues to print. 3D printing is becoming increasingly utilized in areas from manufacturing aircraft parts to printing organs, but unfortunately errors still occur often during prints. It is important that an effective error detection mechanism is developed to locate the error, save materials and prevent structurally unsound objects from being printed.

3   Challenges

In order to develop a mobile image-based approach to quality control, a number of key challenges must be overcome:

Fig. 2. The beginning of a failed print. Internal error caused by PLA not sticking to the printerbed, and external error caused by PLA not sticking to the previous layer.

3.1   Challenge 1: Generating a 2D Representation of a Print Layer

In order to effectively detect errors in a 3D printed object, the monitoring device must know what the object should look like at different stages of the manufacturing process. That is, the imaging process must be able to predict what the 3D model will look like in the physical world when printed on a specific 3D printer's bed with the chosen printing materials. For example, different plastics may be varying colors and printer beds vary in design and color. However, the image analysis must be able to predict what a layer is expected to look like while taking into consideration each of these factors. Figure 2 illustrates internal and external errors in printing, but without the monitoring device knowing what is supposed to be printed, it would not be able to identify this error. This challenge appears in all prints. With the extensive variety of objects available to print, it is impossible to assume internal gaps or thin filaments around the outline are errors.

3.2   Challenge 2: Time Synchronization with the Printer

During printing, the printerbed moves constantly along two axises as filament is extruded to build the object. Because the object's position relative to the monitoring device is constantly changing, it is difficult to know where the object will be at any given time to begin the quality analysis. To perform effective quality analysis, it is crucial that the monitoring device and the printer are time-synchronized so that the monitoring device runs the quality analysis check at the right time.

The challenge of synchronization manifests itself in every print as the movement of the printer bed occurs during every print to build the object. If the printer and the monitoring device are not in sync, error could be detected simply because the object is not where the monitoring device expects it to be due to printerbed movement.

3.3   Challenge 3: Accurate Positioning of the Monitoring Device

Effective quality analysis of a 3D print relies on the print monitoring device knowing where the print should occur. If the monitoring device is not aligned perfectly with the printer bed, a good print could be deemed erroneous simply because the print is not where the device believes it should be. Errors identified through the incorrect positioning of the monitoring device manifest themselves in various manners. If the device is too close or too far from the print, it may believe the print is an incorrect size. If the device is tilted or not in line with the printer bed, it may believe the print is warped or printed askew.

3.4   Challenge 4: Identifying When a Print has Failed

Identifying where an error has occured in the print is only one step towards generating effective quality assurance. All prints may contain some level of error due to natural process variation. An effective monitoring solutions needs to be able to differentiate between prints that have an acceptable amount of error and prints that should be stopped.

A failed print from commercial 3D printers is typically easily detectable to the human eye since we can see large internal gaps or filament outside the area the object should be printed in. While it is easy for humans to visually process whether a print is good or bad, it is difficult for a monitoring device to know how much error is too much. Section 4 describes how we address this challenge by running experiments to arrive at accepted threshold values.

4   Print Quality Assurance with a Mobile Device

The solution we propose is a process for detecting the print quality using a mobile device. Developers can utilize our approach to remotely monitor the quality of a 3D print, and the process can autonomously stop a failed print. The basic setup for the approach is shown in Fig. 3a. A small stand is used to position a mobile device's camera over the printer bed. As the printer constructs the 3D object, time-synchronized quality control checks are performed to verify the integrity of printed layers. The overall architecture is based on 4 components: (1) the 3D printer, (2) the host computer that is controlling the printer by sending GCode commands over USB, (3) a mobile device performing the visual quality assurance using an Android app, and (4) a back-end server that coordinates communicating between the host computer and the mobile device.

The workflow of the approach is shown in Fig. 3b. The initial step in the process is to generate 2D representations of the layers that are being checked for quality. The set of 2D reference images, $r_{it} \in R$, is produced by analyzing the 3D model, which is typically an STL file, at a monotonically increasing series of time steps S_t, and producing a 2D rendering of the expected top-down perspective on the model at each time step s_{ti}:

$$\forall s_{ti} \in S_t, r_{ti} = r(M, P, S_t)$$

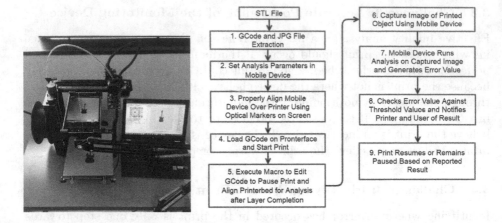

(a) Mobile device positioned above printerbed for analysis.

(b) Step-by-step description of analysis process.

Fig. 3. The effectiveness of the analysis relies on device positioning and a nine step process.

A set of process parameters, P, provides information about the printer and materials being used, such as the color of the plastic filament. With these R 2D reference images, the mobile device will be able to compare the printed layers to what the printed layers should look like and then determine if they are acceptable. To implement $fx(M, P, S_t)$ and extract a 2D image from a 3D file, we used a transcoder provided by the Batik library. During step 1 of Fig. 3b, this transcoder turns a SVG file into a 2D format, such as PNG or JPEG [7]. These files are used for comparison to the actual imagery of the printed layers later in the process.

The most common standard for controlling AM equipment is GCode. In order to print an object, a 3D model, M, needs to be converted into a series of "slices" or layers that the printer is instructed to print:

$$G = slice(M, P)$$

These successive layers are represented as a series of GCode instructions, G, that tell the printer how to move the print head, how much material to extrude, etc. to produce the layer. The combined GCode for all of the layers is sent to the printer to produce the final object. The slicing process also relies on the process parameters, P, in order to calculate appropriate GCode for the print.

Another parameter that must be determined is the offset, $o_i \in O$, where the $i_t h$ layer will be printed on the printer bed. The same 3D object can be printed at different offsets on the printer bed and this must be accounted for in the visual quality control process. To determine the print offset information, an extraction function is applied to the GCode that finds the offset of the layer printed at time s_{ti}:

$$o_i = o(G, P, s_{ti})$$

The next step in the process is to setup the mobile device, which is not assumed to be permanently attached to the printer, so that it can capture imagery of the print. An important step in this process is aligning the mobile device's camera with the print bed so that accurate image analysis can be performed. We added a white rectangle to the camera viewfinder fragment used in our Android quality control application. This white rectangle's dimensions are proportional to the dimensions of the printerbed, so during step 3 of Fig. 3b the user can adjust the position of the mobile device using a stand like the one pictured in Fig. 3a until the printerbed lies inside the rectangle when the printerbed is in the resting position.

To solve the time synchronization issue of coordinating the printer and the mobile device imaging, we apply a program transformation to the GCode, G, to generate a modified set of instructions that include specific synchronization points. The modified GCode, G', stops the printer at specific points in time, s_{ti}, and moves the printer bed to specific coordinates for imaging and waits for feedback from the image analysis process (described later) that the print should proceed. The transformed GCode is produced via a program transformation function that takes the original GCode and a series of synchronization time steps as input:

$$G' = \omega(G, S_t)$$

At each of these synchronization points, the printer moves the printer bed into positioning for imaging and the host computer controlling the printer sends a message to the back-end server in the cloud to send a push notification to the mobile device to begin the imaging process. The mobile device captures an image, I_t, of the printer bed and then runs one of the image analysis algorithms, $\delta(R, I, L)$, described in Sect. 4.1, to calculate an error value, e:

$$e = \delta(r_{it}, I_t, o_i, P)$$

$$\beta = b(M, o_i, I_t)$$

If e is above a configurable threshold, β, then the device sends a message back to the back-end server to notify the host computer to stop the print. Optionally, the back-end server also can send a notification to the user's mobile device (one not being used for the quality control) to allow for a decision on whether or not to continue the print. If the print is stopped, the host computer sends terminating GCode instructions to the printer to end the print.

4.1   Algorithm to Discover Misprinted PLA

To begin addressing the challenge of identifying when a print should fail, which is discussed in Sect. 3.4, we developed two algorithms to implement $\delta(r_{it}, I_t, o_i, P)$ that would be able to find and highlight error in an image of the 3D printed object during step 7 of Fig. 3b. The first algorithm we used to implement δ involves image subtraction and the second algorithm we use involves searching a single picture. These two algorithms use a similar process at the end to arrive at the number of erroneous pixels, and they both depend on using black PLA and a blue or dark gold background.

Image Subtraction. The first algorithm to detect errors in a print involves an image difference method, which is applied following the completion of a layer that should be analyzed for error. The error detection by image subtraction involves two input images $I_{t-x}(o_i, P)$ and $I_t(o_i, P)$ taken x seconds apart where x is the print time up to the point the analysis is run. A classical image subtraction is performed to identify where PLA has been printed:

$$I_d(o_i, P) = |I_{t-x}(o_i, P) - I_t(o_i, P)|$$

The obtained image, $I_d(s)$, is a light color where the object has been printed while the remainder of the printerbed is dark. We can then compare the light spot in this image to r_{it}, the corresponding 2D slice, to produce the image I_f:

$$I_f = \rho(I_d, r_{it})$$

This function iterates through I_d and inserts the slice r_{it} into the image by changing the appropriate pixels in I_d to white. At the conclusion of this function, where the object should be located is entirely white, while error appears as a light color and the background remains white. As this function runs, another function to determine internal error, e_y is performed concurrently. This function analyzes all pixels p_{ab} in I_d that should contain PLA according to slice r_{it}. If this pixel is dark and therefore does not contain PLA, it is perceived as erroneous. The function to determine the number of internal erroneous pixels can be defined as:

$$s_y = \phi(I_d, r_{it}, p_{ab})$$

After these methods have finished running, the mobile device iterates through image I_f. Since the background is dark and where the object should be is white, the device can use a function s_x to find external error by searching all pixels p_{cd} in the image for light, but not white pixels. This function to find the number of external erroneous pixels can be defined as:

$$s_x = \upsilon(I_f, r_{it}, p_{cd})$$

The total number of erroneous pixels, S, can then be defined as:

$$S = s_x + s_y$$

Image Searching. The second algorithm to detect errors in printed objects is a simple image searching algorithm. This algorithm initially inserts the correlating slice, r_{it}, into the image $I_t(o_i, P)$ by iterating through the pixels of the image and changing pixels where PLA should be printed to white. This function creates a new image, I_f:

$$I_f = \varphi(I_t, r_{it})$$

While this algorithm runs, the mobile device concurrently searches for internal error, s_y by searching each pixel p_{ab} that should have PLA according to r_{it} but does not. This error is identified by checking if the pixel p_{ab} is black before changing it to white per $\varphi(I_t, r_{it})$:

$$s_y = \psi(I_t, r_{it}, p_{ab})$$

After $\varphi(I_t, r_{it})$ has completed, a new function iterates through I_f and searches the image for external error s_x. Since the printerbed is blue, the allocated location for the object is now white, and the PLA is black, we can search each pixel p_{cd} of the image and count the number of black pixels as those indicate PLA outside of the acceptable area:

$$s_x = \varrho(I_f, r_{it}, pcd)$$

The total number of erroneous pixels, S, can therefore be defined as:

$$S = s_x + s_y$$

While the image searching algorithm is similar to the subtraction algorithm, the subtraction algorithm provides the benefit of the background being very dark if not black. When simply searching the image of the object, a color similar to the color of the PLA may be present in the image and cause the mobile device to falsely detect that as error.

4.2 Identifying Failed Prints

As discussed in Sect. 3.4, a necessity for effective quality assurance is determining a threshold value for β when the print should fail. In Sect. 4.1 we began to address this challenge by describing two processes to discover the number of pixels that contain error in an image of the printed object. The mobile device calculates the error value e using the number of pixels that contain error and the total number of pixels in the slice r_{it}:

$$e = \delta(r_{it}, I_t, o_i, P) = \frac{S}{\sum p_{ab}}$$

While calculating this error value is a crucial first step towards determining the quality of a print, this value alone is not enough. The device needs to know what error values should be passing and what error values should be failing, and then it can compare the calculated error value of a print to these reference values β to determine the quality of the print during step 8 of Fig. 3b.

By visually determining whether or not a print should pass and recording the calculated error value as well as the analysis parameters used, we could experimentally discover threshold values that marked the line between a passing print and a failing print. After discovering these values and reporting them to the mobile device, a simple comparison between the calculated error e for any given print and the appropriate reference value β based on the analysis parameters can determine whether or not the print should continue.

5   Empirical Results

5.1   Experimental Platform

An important consideration in this research was the real-world performance of a mobile device in detecting errors on 3D prints. We conducted a series of experiments to compare the performance, in terms of accuracy and speed, of both image analysis approaches. We also provide data on how effective functions for calculating the error threshold, β, can be determined.

To conduct the experiments, we used a Samsung Galaxy Tab 3 running Android 4.4.2. The device has 8.0 GB of ROM and 1.0 GB of RAM and features a 3.0 megapixel camera. The screen is 7 in. and 1280 pixels by 800 pixels [18]. To hold the device over the printerbed, we used a modified desk lamp.

The 3D printing device we used for making the objects is a Makerbot M2 printing with black PLA. The nozzle was set to 200°C and the printerbed temperature was set to 70°C for all of the tests. The glass of the printerbed was also covered with blue painters tape that has gold lettering to easily contrast with the black PLA.

5.2   Experiment 1: Image Subtraction Analysis

First, we tested our algorithm that uses image subtraction on various prints of differing qualities to experimentally discover threshold error values that indicate when an object has too much error. Discovering these values allows us to solve Challenge 6 presented in Sect. 3.4 as we can compare a calculated error value to our threshold error values to determine the quality of a printed object. The data collected in this experiment will also show the ability of the subtraction algorithm to consistently produce similar error values for similar quality prints.

Hypothesis: Threshold Error Values. Our hypothesis was that there is a threshold error value for each permutation of subtraction analysis parameters that can be used to distinguish between passing and failing prints.

Experiment 1 Results. To experimentally discover the various error threshold values for different parameters, we collected data by executing the image subtraction algorithm on objects we printed and recording the calculated error value as well as whether or not the print should pass. Figure 4a illustrates the results of varying the buffer parameter while keeping the internal search parameter false. While there is not a clear division between accepted prints and not accepted prints, we were able to determine a threshold line, indicated by the dotted line on the graph, that most accurately divides the two. When performing subtraction analysis not searching for internal error, we found that $error = -0.0057x+.0365$, where x is the buffer value, is a good indication of print quality with error values below that line passing and error values above that line not passing.

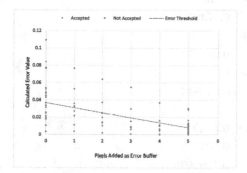

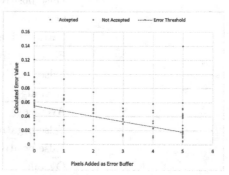

(a) Only searching for external error.   (b) Searching for internal and external error.

Fig. 4. Passing and failing prints when using the subtraction algorithm

Similarly, we collected data to discover the threshold error values when running the subtraction algorithm, processing the image for internal error and varying the error buffer. Figure 4b shows the results of these tests. Once again, there is not a clear division between accepted prints and not accepted prints, but we are able to determine a threshold line, the dashed line on the graph, that most accurately divides the two. When performing subtraction analysis and processing for internal error, we found that $error = -0.0074x + .055$, where x is the buffer value, is a good indication of the print quality. Prints with error values above this line are not accepted, and prints with error values below this line are passing.

From this experiment we discovered that we can use our subtraction algorithm to distinguish between good and bad prints with some accuracy. Table 1 contains various percent error values that signify that the algorithm is most successful when a 5 pixel buffer is added. This buffer allows our algorithm to be more robust to account for positioning errors discussed in Sect. 3.3. Additionally, Table 1 also indicates that false positives are not very likely when using this algorithm meaning that prints that should fail typically do fail, which indicates that this algorithm effectively stops failed prints.

5.3   Experiment 2: Image Searching Analysis

Next, we tested our algorithm that uses an image searching process to find error in printed objects to experimentally discover threshold error values that indicate

Table 1. Percent errors when using the subtraction algorithm with at least 25 samples for each calculation.

0 Error Pixels	
False negative	0.214286
False positive	0.125
Overall	0.173077
5 Error Pixels	
False negative	0.074074
False positive	0
Overall	0.040816
Average	
False negative	0.178947
False positive	0.101266
Overall	0.156069

when an object has too much error. We are also able to compare the results of using this algorithm to the results of using the image subtraction algorithm discussed in Sect. 5.2 to see which algorithm does a better job identifying the quality of a print. The data collected in this experiment will also help to solve Challenge 6 presented in Sect. 3.4 as we are experimentally finding values that can help us determine the quality of a print.

Hypothesis: Error Threshold Values. Our hypothesis was that there is a threshold error value for each permutation of searching analysis parameters that can be used to distinguish between passing and failing prints and that the results of using the searching analysis will be similar to results when using the subtraction analysis.

Experiment 2 Results. To experimentally discover the various error threshold values for different parameters when using the image searching algorithm, we printed out various objects and ran the image searching algorithm on them. By varying the parameters of the search - whether or not to search inside the object for internal error and adding an error buffer - we were able to collect data that helps us to determine the threshold values that indicate an erroneous print. Initially we ran tests where the image searching algorithm did not search for internal error, and we only varied the error buffer parameter, and by recording whether or not a print should pass as well as the calculated error value, we were able to generate the graph pictured in Fig. 5a. While accepted prints and not accepted prints are not clearly divided from each other, we were able to determine a threshold line, indicated by the dotted line n the graph, that can be used to most accurately predict the quality of a print. When running the image searching algorithm and not searching for internal error, we found that $error = -0.0063x + 0.039$ where x is the buffer value, is a good indication of print quality with error values below that line passing and error values above that line not passing.

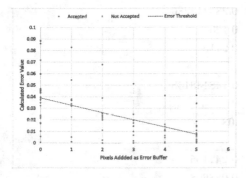

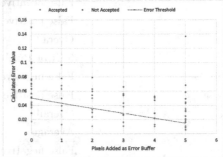

(a) Only searching for external error.   (b) Searching for internal and external error.

Fig. 5. Passing and failing prints when using the searching algorithm

After collecting the appropriate data for figuring out threshold values when not searching objects for internal error, we then conducted the same tests, but this time we did search for internal error. Figure 5b illustrates the results of searching the internal and external areas of the object for error using the image searching algorithm and varying the error buffer. Once again, the accepted prints and not accepted prints are not clearly separate, but we can find a threshold line - the dotted line in the graph - that most accurately defines an appropriate boundary. We found that $error = -0.007x + 0.05$, where x is the error buffer, is a good indication of print quality where error values above this line are not accepted and error values below this line are accepted

From this experiment, we did discover threshold values that can be used with some accuracy to differentiate between prints that should be accepted and prints that should not be accepted. Table 2 contains various percent error values that help show the accuracy of this method. Similarly to the results found in Experiment 1 in Sect. 5.2, using the image searching algorithm produces relatively low percent error especially in terms of false positives meaning that this algorithm only rarely continues a print that is of low quality. These results also indicate that both the image subtraction analysis and the image searching analysis are valid ways to detect errors in a print.

5.4   Experiment 3: Correlations Between Size and Analyzation Speed

Finally, we determined the cost of running the analysis program and whether the searching or subtraction method was faster. Each time a test is run over the

Table 2. Percent errors when using the searching algorithm with at least 25 samples for each calculation.

0 Error Pixels	
False negative	0.285714286
False positive	0.125
Overall	0.2115
5 Error Pixels	
False negative	0.148148148
False positive	0
Overall	.08
Average	
False negative	0.242105
False positive	0.088608
Overall	0.201149

printed object, x amount of time is added to the process, with x being dependent upon the size of the object printed and the parameters for error allowance entered by the user.

Hypothesis: Time Increase with Added Size and Error Pixels. We hypothesized that through running these experiments, we would find that more error pixels and larger objects result in a slowing down of the analysis.

Experiment 3 Results. There are three main components that consume time:

1. Moving from the final location of printing to the home position required to run analysis provides a constant, baseline amount of time that does not change with variation of the parameters. The average time during our experiments was 4.718 s, with a range from 4.24 s to 5.16 s.
2. Actually running the analysis may vary based on the size of the object, and the number of error pixels added to the outside of the object. The graphs shown in Fig. 6a and b detail results of the time taken to perform search and subtraction, with varying size and parameters. Our results indicate that, from a time standpoint, simply using the searching algorithm is better, especially for larger objects.
3. Lastly, returning to the print after analysis provides another constant time. The average time calculated during our experiments was 9.145 s with a range from 7.94 s to 10.56 s.

Adding each of the formerly stated three process steps together returns the total time cost of the entire procedure. Figure 6a and b show the distinct correlation between the upward trends of both the search and subtraction methods based upon increasing numbers of error pixels that must be searched during the analyses. Comparing the two graphs also leads to the conclusion that the image

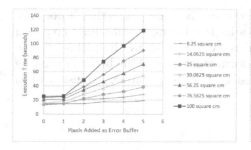 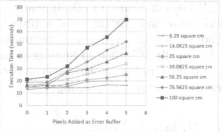

(a) Subtraction Algorithm.   (b) Searching Algorithm.

Fig. 6. Algorithm execution times based on object size and error buffer.

searching algorithm is faster than the image subtraction algorithm, especially on larger prints and when the error buffer increases.

5.5   Analysis of Results

The data we collected during testing indicates that our process can effectively and consistently identify error location in a print. Additionally, using this identification, it can then identify with fairly high accuracy whether or not a print should continue.

We experimented with two different algorithms, and the results of those experiments indicate that the image searching algorithm is a better algorithm than the image subtraction algorithm. While comparison of the results from Experiment 1 in Sect. 5.2 and Experiment 2 in Sect. 5.3 leads to the conclusion that the two algorithms produce similar results in determining the quality of a print, Experiment 3 in Sect. 5.4 indicates that the image searching algorithm is a faster method.

In all experiments we printed out objects of different shapes and sizes to run the tests. While the different sizes had a large impact on execution time as outlined in Sect. 5.4, the size of the object seemingly had very little bearing on the calculated error value. Results from Experiments 1 and 2 in Sects. 5.2 and 5.3 show that all sizes of objects have the same error threshold value that can be used to determine the quality of a print.

We completely solved the problem because we were able to develop an easy to use process that accurately identified 3D printing errors. While some prints during testing stopped when they could have continued, very few failed prints continued, and this was the goal of our work. We are able to stop failed prints with our work.

Our data also shows that we are better than existing approaches. Most quality assurance processes are either industrial solutions or analyze finished product, but we were able to design a cost-effective mid-print quality assurance process.

While our solution works in many instances, there are places that it does not perform as well. As the print approaches its last layers, it sometimes creates a shadow and this shadow is sometimes perceived as error by the mobile device. Additionally, it is time consuming to perform analysis, and the break in printing that occurs during the analysis can occasionally cause improper extrusion when the device returns to printing.

6   Related Work

Although three dimensional printers have been available since the late 20th century, little research has been done to ensure the quality of a product while printing [13].

Though the taxonomy of our research is nebulous on account of the many uses and possibilities for additive manufacturing, it is clear that all research utilizing three dimensional printers face the same issue of security and needing a guarantee that precious time and resources will not be wasted in making a faulty object. Other examples of similar work number very few, revealing the necessity for a sort of quality assurance when printing [14]. Developers have begun to integrate sensors into their additive manufacturing processes to maintain constant, perfect conditions. Others detect structural insecurities in designs and fix them prior to printing. Areas such as those in the medical industry troubleshoot until theyve built a quality product, then design it with renewing chemicals to repair itself should any damage occur after its been created.

Monitoring Manufacturing Conditions During Print. Sigma Labs [5] patented a program in spring 2014 that balances the amount of energy entering the powder layer of an additive manufacturing machine to maintain a constant, ideal temperature for the product. While their controlling sensor monitors the object and fabricating conditions throughout the process, our analyzation runs after a certain time interval or number of layers, depending upon user input. Instead of controlling situational parameters, we test the freshly manufactured hardware to determine whether or not it is a quality product and thus whether the build should be terminated.

Structural Security in Design. Benes [8] collaborated with Adobes Advanced Technology Labs to develop a software that detects weaknesses in initial STL-type files that are sent to printers. Instead of spending time and resources to fabricate large, layered designs, their program identifies weak and structurally unsound areas on the design template, then fixes these frailties so that the printer is sent a stronger, more durable construction.

Self Renewing Materials Post-construction. Lewis and White et al. [9] began researching printable materials to self-healing organs or vessels made of tissue similar to that found naturally in the human body [19]. Their approach to mending damaged or flawed printed products is to implant chemicals within them to detect a change in the structure and release healing cells when erosion occurs. Though our project detects flaws during the building process to create an ideal result, it is not specific to a need such as medical implantation, and thus does not require a self-mending feature.

Optical Assessment of Print with Robot. The most similar design to ours appeared recently from Alcona in the form of a multi-axis robot attached to a sensor [20]. This setup requires the purchase of the robot and sensor, and is not mobile as ours is; however, the design allows a live, constantly updating look at the quality of a print throughout the printing process. While printers are not updated as to whether the print is performing well or not if they are not present and observing the setup, it is indeed a powerful tool to quickly and accurately provide quality assurance without pausing the print after a certain number of layers or amount of time as ours does.

7   Concluding Remarks

It is challenging to determine the quality of a 3D printed object. This paper describes how we were able to use a mobile device and computer vision to identify errors in a print and then distinguish between prints that should be continued and prints that should stop.

The following are lessons learned from our efforts thus far:

- By adding an error buffer, we created a robust analysis process that could accurately identify printing errors and then determine the quality of a print even when the mobile device's positioning is slightly off.
- In future work, we plan to develop a faster algorithm for determining error to reduce the time cost of using the analysis during a print.

This research has been supported in part by the National Science Foundation and Department of Homeland Security through Grant #CNS1446303.

References

1. Gibson, I., Rosen, D., Stucker, B.: Additive Manufacturing Technologies: 3D Printing, Rapid Prototyping, and Direct Digital Manufacturing, 2nd edn. Springer, New York (2015)
2. 3D Printing Creates New Parts for Aircraft Engines. GE Global Research, Web. 13 July 2015
3. Rega, S.: How 3D Printing Will Revolutionize Our World. Business Insider. Business Insider Inc., 22 August 2014, Web. 27 July 2015
4. Mironov, V., Boland, T., Trusk, T., Forgacs, G., Markwald, R.R.: Organ printing: computer-aided jet-based 3D tissue engineering. Trends Biotechnol. 21(4), 157–161 (2003)
5. Sigma Labs, Inc.: Announces Patent Filing of Unique Sensor Invention That Helps Both Process Development and Quality Assurance in Additive Manufacting of Metal Components. Sigma Labs Inc. , 25 March 2014, Web. 10 July 2015
6. Millsaps, B.B.: Trinckle 3Ds Free Error Detection Service: No More Misprints!. 3DPrintcom, 17 October 2014, Web. 10 July 2015

7. DeWeese, T., Hardy, V.: Introduction to the Batik Project [PDF document]. http://old.koalateam.com/ftp/batik/apacheCon.pdf
8. Walton, Z.: Purdue University Professor Fixes Major Flaw In 3D Printing - WebProNews. WebProNews. 19 September 2012, Web. 21 July 2015
9. Groopman, J.: Print Thyself. New Yorker, 24 November 2014, Web. 7 July 2015
10. Cel Robox 3d Printer Review. IT Pro, Web. 29 July 2015
11. FAQ: CubeX 3D Printer. Cubify, Web. 28 July 2015
12. Gibson, I., Stucker, B., Rosen, D.: Additive Manufacturing Technologies, 2nd edn. Springer, New York (2015)
13. History of 3D Printing: 3D Printing Industry. May 2015, Web. 29 July 2015
14. Molitch-Hou, M.: EOS Partnership Signals 3D Printing Quality Assurance for Aerospace. 3D Printing Industry, 21 January 2015, Web. 29 July 2015
15. Parse: Parse, Web. 29 July 2015
16. PrintRun: Pronterface, Web. 29 July 2015
17. Royte, E.: Corn Plastic to the Rescue. Smithsonian. August 2006, Web. 29 July 2015
18. Samsung Lays Out Which Devices Will Get Android 4.4.2 KitKat. Android Central, Web. 29 July 2015
19. Soft Tissue Repair and Healing Review. Electrotherapy, Web. 29 July 2015
20. Woodcock, J.: 3D Metrology Robot for Automated Optical Quality Assurance. TCT, 27 July 2015, Web. 30 July 2015

Interactively Set up a Multi-display of Mobile Devices

Peter Barth[✉] and Manuel Pras

Hochschule RheinMain, University of Applied Sciences,
Kurt-Schumacher-Ring 18, Wiesbaden 65197, Germany
peter.barth@hs-rm.de, mail@manuelpras.de

Abstract. We provide a method to interactively set up a multi-display using a combination of multi and single device gestures. An initial setup provides a coarse grained model. Test pictures and user judgement based on the human visual system then guide a fine grained interactive process. This allows the user to move and rotate single screens until differences between physical and model position are no longer perceived. To this end, a central computer holds the model and connects among all participating smartphones and tablets with different physical dimensions and display resolutions. In addition, it evaluates gestures and prepares as well as distributes images on the multi-display.

Keywords: Multi-display · Interaction · Smartphone · Visual system · Network graphics

1 Introduction

The sheer number of smartphones and tablets pushed into the market makes mobile devices available in large quantities. Each device has a high resolution display and provides touch interaction. However, each individual display is still comparatively small and typically supports interaction with one user only. With a comparatively small investment or being a group of people, many devices are available. These devices may be joined to provide one large display, a multi-display, for interactive applications or just the visualisation of single screens. To set up a flexible multi-display, we need to know the position of each individual device that constitutes the multi-display.

We propose an interactive method to quickly reconstruct the position of many devices that form a multi-display. Instead of relying on cameras and computer vision techniques [8], we employ the error detection capabilities of the human visual system until perceived accuracy satisfies the user. We can then display any image on the modelled multi-display. Typical applications include image and slide shows as depicted in Fig. 1, as well as tickers, games and videos [9]. These applications all depend on having a single canvas where each devices shows just a portion of one large image.

© Institute for Computer Sciences, Social Informatics and Telecommunications Engineering 2015
S. Sigg et al. (Eds.): MobiCASE 2015, LNICST 162, pp. 221–238, 2015.
DOI: 10.1007/978-3-319-29003-4_13

Fig. 1. Multi-display showing an image

2   Related Work

Most often multi-displays are found in fixed installations where the location and position of the often homogeneous displays are known. Systems range from the Nintendo DS over laptops with slide out screens such as the Gscreen Spacebook to expensive commercial multi-displays to be used in fairs and exhibitions consisting of many large monitors or even many projectors joined together [8]. While these setups offer an harmonic user experience, they require dedicated hardware and do not support spontaneous scenarios or reusing a multitude of different displays at hand.

Traditionally, forming multi-displays relies on computer vision techniques [2, 3, 5–7]. These techniques suffer from external conditions of the surrounding environment and can most often not be used in sunlight or other direct light from above. In contrast, they do not require interacting with the device and are thus less likely to change the position of the devices during setup.

Schmitz et al. [8] were first to realise that smartphones and tablets are well suited to support multi-displays. They propose to combine a collection of heterogeneous devices to form a single screen multi-display. Their main contribution is a calibration process relying on computer vision combined with manual fine tuning and supporting any possible distribution of the devices on a flat surface. They have already realised, that a manual calibration procedure using gestures is not only useful, but may be sufficient. Although they favour the automatic camera based calibration, they support skipping it altogether. They chose communication over Wi-Fi instead of Bluetooth to achieve acceptable latency and high bandwidth. As test image during manual calibration they use a checker board which has concentric circles as overlay. User tests indicated that centring

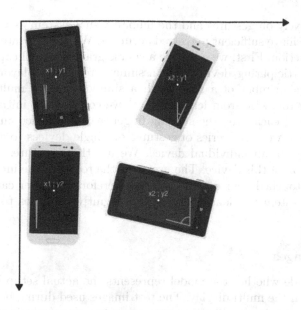

Fig. 2. Model of a multi-display with position and rotation angle

the test image on the device currently being adjusted helps the users to focus. They provide user evaluation setting up a multi-display consisting of four devices and report using up to seven mobile devices with displays using different resolutions.

3 Interactive Multi-Display Setup

We support any non-overlapping distribution of mobile devices on a flat surface. We distribute an image on the devices constituting the multi-display once the layout is known. Here, we concentrate on setting up the model. An accurate representation needs to know the exact position of each device as depicted in Fig. 2. For each device we need to know the physical width and height as well as the number of pixels in x and y direction of its screen, assuming classical portrait mode. Using any origin on the surface, it is sufficient to know the x and y coordinates of the centre of each display as well as its rotation angle. We opted for right rotation with 0 degrees for a device in upright portrait mode. We always use an origin such that all mobile devices are to the right and under the origin. Thus, each centre point has positive values in millimetres and rotation angles are between 0 and 360 degrees. We differentiate between the device model and one physical instance of it. Of the device model we know the physical dimensions and pixels. Of the physical instance we know its centre point position and rotation. Thus, to alter a model we adjust only three values per participating device instance.

Our main contribution is an interactive procedure to adjust the computer model of the position of the participating devices to the actual physical setup.

We rely exclusively on gestures and the human visual system as well as human judgement to achieve sufficient perceived accuracy. We differentiate between two modes of interaction. First, we compute a coarse grained model capturing alignment of the participating devices. We assume a row based layout, such that each device is a member of a row. With a simple series of multi-device gestures – swiping row-wise from left to right – we compute an initial model. We update the model each time the swiping finger leaves a device and refresh the test image. Then, we use a series of gestures on single devices to express movement or rotation of an individual device. We use these gestures to adjust the modelled position of this device. The user sees the result of the interaction with each currently touched device immediately. Therefore, the user can employ the human visual system to identify errors and cognitive abilities to improve the model.

3.1   Test Images

Users shall decide whether the model represents the actual setup based on test images shown on the multi-display. The test images used during both the coarse grained and fine grained calibration step serve two purposes: identify a device that needs to be adjust and correct the positional error of that device. To identify a device that needs to be adjusted, we need a global test image, that allows to spot any offset in position or rotation. We propose to use intersecting lines combined with coloured concentric circles such as in Fig. 3. The concentric circles help best to spot position offsets as even small errors are identified as oval by the visual system. In addition, the lines serve to identify rotation errors, which appear as bend. Test images are always shown on all devices and if necessary centred to the barycentre and scaled in advance to cover the entire multi-display. Furthermore, the central computer visualises the current model on its screen to mimic the setup. Thus, the user may compare again visually the current model to what is laid out on the surface as in Fig. 3. This is helpful to spot very large offsets.

In the correction phase the current position in the model of the individual devices is manually corrected. We propose an alternative test image as in Fig. 4. A collection of equidistant coloured lines is used, that intersect on the first touch point of the device to be adjusted. Thus, the user can concentrate on the device being positioned and perceives errors in its position and rotation angle more easily.

3.2   Coarse Grained Initial Position

For initial setup, we assume that all devices are members of a row, but the devices need not be aligned. For the gesture, the user swipes over all devices from left to right, row by row from top to bottom. For each device, we compute a straight line from the touch points using linear regression. Based on the entry and exit points on each device of a row, we can compute its absolute position as in Fig. 5. For this, we postulate that the user performed a straight line with

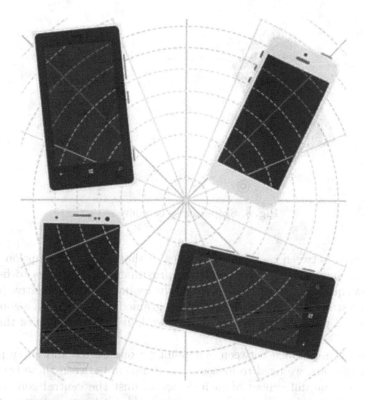

Fig. 3. Test image of coloured concentric circles and intersecting lines (Color figure online)

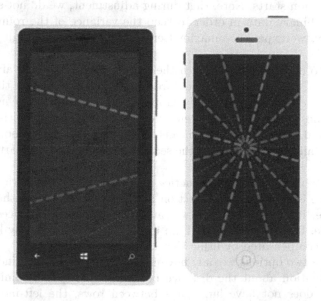

Fig. 4. Test image to adjust single device

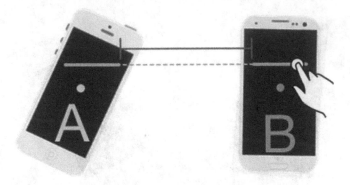

Fig. 5. Swipe across two devices

constant speed between each pair of devices. Although this assumption will not hold exactly, it gives us a near enough approximation and allows to build our initial model quickly. Thus, the devices are always in the correct relative position. Showing a test image allows to start the fine grained calibration on a good basis. The horizontal position is never off more than half the dimension of the device screen.

To guess the distance between exit point on one device and entry point on its right neighbour, we need to measure the duration between these two events. We compute time differences of each device against the central computer and thus adjust device times to an absolute time. This adjustment uses standard techniques [4] and is not visible to the user. It is performed before any multi-display calibration starts. Note, that during adjustment, we do not send images or other bulk binary data in order to keep the variance of the round trip time low. Typically, we experience maximal errors within a single digit millisecond range.

We need to detect when we reach the right end of a row and after that the next row starts. One option is to measure the (adjusted) absolute time between device exit and device entry. We only support initial layouts where neighbouring devices have no huge gaps in between, which is sensible for a multi-display. We set the maximal gap to 7 cm. This means that if two devices are more than 7 cm apart horizontally, we assume that the second device marks the start of the next row.

However, while this works in practice, the approach is not always adequate. An alternative is changing the direction at each row. Although that approach is very stable, it implicitly assumes that orientation of all devices is upright portrait mode. If a device is flipped, an incorrect row change may be detected. This may be compensated by using the compass.

With these two options we only have information about each individual row but no information about the distance between two rows. Assuming that the multi-display does not have huge gaps between rows, the left-most device of each row gets vertically aligned using the lower border of the previous row as in

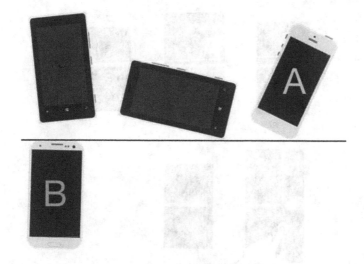

Fig. 6. Vertical alignment using row borders

Fig. 6. This means that the upper border of the left-most device equates with the lower border of the previous row. To accommodate for frames of the mobile devices, we can either assume a fixed average frame border or use dedicated device specific information. Note, that we assume the left-most devices to be left aligned in order to determine the horizontal position of the left-most device of each row. Again, we think that this is a plausible assumption for most multi-display setups.

We may relax that assumption and only require that there is a left-most column. Then we would add as final step a swipe on the left-most column of the devices from top to bottom as in Fig. 7. The computation is similar to the one we did per row. With the resulting distance between the centre points of all devices in vertical direction, the initial model can be build again.

3.3 Fine Grained Absolute Position

Given a model, we rely on the visual system of the user to spot errors and his or her cognitive abilities to manually improve the model. These two steps are repeated until the final model matches the physical setup with good enough perceived accuracy. To do so, the user can adjust the position and the rotation angle of each individual device. It is important, that the feedback of gestures happens immediately in order to employ the visual system of the user. Thus, we do not distribute images over the network. Instead, we compute the corrected image on the device that is being adjusted and show the correction effects locally as quickly as possible. Therefore, we do not suffer from lagging screen updates impairing the direct interaction cycle. We visualise a dedicated device centred test image as in Fig. 4 on the entire multi-display as soon as a manipulation gesture starts on a device. To save bandwidth, we currently only distribute the

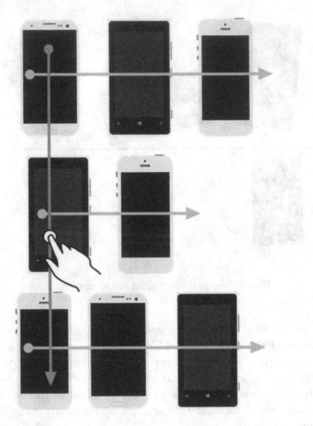

Fig. 7. Additional vertical swipe for row detection and alignment

image to the nearest four neighbours as they are the ones the visual system most likely uses as reference to detect errors. Typically, the test image with device centred lines on the four nearest neighbours allows users to spot and quantify offsets accurately.

We support changing position or rotation with different gestures as depicted in Fig. 8. We change position using a single touch point as in Fig. 8 left and rotation using two touch points as in Fig. 8 right.

To this end, we evaluate the gestures on the device and translate and rotate the image on the device. During a gesture, we need to cover the entire display with a single test image. Therefore, we use a test image that is 100 percent larger in each direction than the actual screen of the device. This allows to show complete images during all single stroke adjustments.

The translation gesture is straightforward. The user touches the device and moves the image around until the image fits the idealised image. After releasing the finger, we compute the offset and send the offset to the central computer. There, the model is updated and freshly generated parts of the test image are distributed. Note, that the model visualised on the central computer screen is

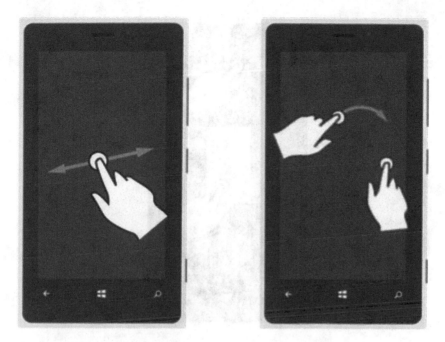

Fig. 8. Translation and rotation gesture

not updated during adjustment. This is not necessary. The user shall concentrate on the manipulated and nearest devices while having the finger on the device.

The rotation gesture is slightly more complex. We may use two fingers of different hands or two fingers of one hand as with a typical pinch gesture. To fluently switch between translation and rotation we suggest to use one finger of one hand to translate. To rotate, keep on finger on the screen and touch it with a finger of the other hand. Moving the second touch point while holding the first manipulates the rotation angle. The distance between the two fingers is used to calibrate the effect of rotation. Bringing them closer together allows for a more coarse grained rotation, while moving them apart allows for a finer grained rotation adjustment. We amplified this natural effect to allow for better control. The further apart the two fingers are, the less is the effect of the circular arc on the rotation angle.

3.4 Differentiate Among Gestures

One challenge is to differentiate among the different gestures. We have three different gestures in two phases. In the initial phase there is swiping entire devices. In the correction phase there is translation with one finger and rotation with two fingers. We differentiate between the translation and the rotation gesture using the current finger count. As long as there is only one finger touching the screen it is a translation gesture. As soon as another finger joins the device screen the gesture changes to a rotation gesture.

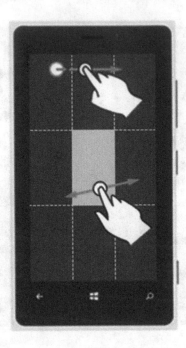

Fig. 9. Display sections to differentiate between initial and fine grained gestures

We may want to differentiate between the coarse grained initial phase and the fine grained correction phase. Note, that after the start of a fine grained phase there won't be a coarse grained phase again. This may only happen, if the user wants to start over because the device layout has changed dramatically, was wrong to start with, additional devices have joined, or the results are unsatisfactory. Based on the location of the first touch point (as shown in Fig. 9), we can reliably recognise coarse a grained setup during the entire gesture. Note, that we expect the user to swipe the complete screen of the device in the coarse grained phase. Thus, the user will start a swipe gesture on the border of the mobile device. Furthermore, the user will naturally – and if not by training – put a translation or rotation start point in the centre of the device to retain more degrees of freedom. Thus, we can partition the device screen into an inner and an outer area. We recognise a coarse grained calibration in the outer area and a fine grained calibration in the inner area. A working setup is to divide the display area into three equally sized parts in horizontal and vertical direction as depicted in Fig. 9, but that may be changed. Therefore, users can do a fine grained adjustment or start over by executing at any time any gestures they have in mind without being forced to use meta commands.

Fig. 10. Single steps for creating an image portion

4 Image Preparation and Distribution

The central computer holds the multi-display model and the image to be shown on the multi-display. The image will be shown on the bounding box of the individual displays of the multi-display. First, the bounding box and thus the individual display positions are scaled to fit the image. For example, we start with the left-most image in Fig. 10. Next, we need to construct the correctly sized and rotated image parts per individual display. To this end, we cut out rectangular pieces. We make sure that any later rotation will be covered by using the diameter as side length of the rectangular piece. This results in the second picture in Fig. 10. Next, we rotate the image by the screen's negated rotation angle to compensate for the device rotation in the physical setup. This gives the third picture in Fig. 10. Finally, we cut out the rectangular image and scale it to the resolution of the target device. We get the right-most picture in Fig. 10. This image is then sent to the device and there shown without any further processing.

We base our data communication on Blaubot [1], which provides distributing messages among a collection of mobile devices and potentially connected central machines. Blaubot supports both Bluetooth and Wi-Fi out of the box and the underlying transmission technology can be selected by configuration. During the production phase most often high resolution images are regularly distributed to all devices. Because of the high bandwidth requirements, we rely on Wi-Fi.

5 Evaluation

We evaluated the simplicity and accuracy of the proposed calibration method through user tests. With adequate test images an accuracy within a 1–2 mm error margin is routinely attainable by untrained users in 2 min on average.

5.1 Participants and Setup

We run the tests with six participants, two female and four male. All participants own a smartphone for at least two years and are between 21 and 29 years old.

The different tasks of the evaluation are performed using three different smart-phone models running Android 4.0 or higher (HTC Desire, HTC Legend, and Motorola Milestone). The mobile devices were released between 2009 and 2010 and represent the low end of the currently running Android devices. While the screens of those devices have about the same dimension, they vary in resolution.

5.2   Tasks

The participants had to solve three different tasks, two of which were divided into two sub tasks. This gives a total of five sub tasks. As part of the first task the participants were asked to build a 2 × 3 device matrix and set up a multi-display as in Fig. 11 left. After the participants had finished the calibration, the multi-display showed a checker board pattern, which allowed them to rate the accuracy.

Fig. 11. 2 × 3 matrix for a checker board (left) and swapped and flipped devices (right)

The second task focused on the ability to detect and fix large errors between physical setup and the multi-display model using different test images. The coloured concentric circles image was compared with an alternative image, consisting of a coloured grid as in Fig. 12 left. In order to compare those two test images the second task was divided into two sub tasks. In both sub tasks the participants were asked to identify and fix two large errors in the multi-display as in Fig. 11 right. The first error consisted of a random swap of two devices in the setup. The second error was a 180° rotation of one of the remaining devices.

While the first sub task used the concentric circles as test image, the second sub task used the alternative grid image.

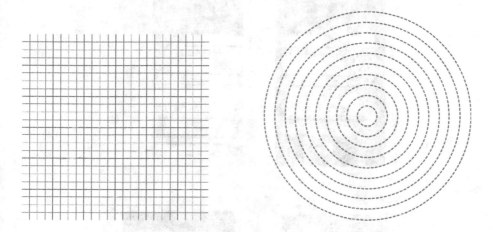

Fig. 12. The two test image alternatives used in the evaluation

The third task evaluated the adequacy of the test image for the fine grained calibration step. We compared equidistant coloured lines with monochrome concentric circles as in Fig. 12 right. The participants were asked to build a 2 × 2 matrix for displaying a picture showing buildings as in Fig. 13.

Due to its geometric patterns, this type of subject is suitable for judging the accuracy of the multi-display setup. Again, this task consisted of two sub tasks. One sub task used the equidistant coloured lines as test image, the other sub task used monochrome concentric circles.

5.3   Procedure

After filling in personal background information, the participants watched a tutorial video in order to learn the basic steps of the multi-display setup. To familiarise themselves with this process, they set up a 2 × 2 matrix under the supervision of an expert before processing the five sub tasks. Following each processed sub task the participants rated the difficulty of solving the task as well as the accuracy of the multi-display setup. The accuracy rating of the multi-display setup was done for all participants by one neutral observer. The rating was done on a Likert scale between one (least agreement) and four (most agreement).

In addition to those subjective ratings we were also interested in the measured offsets between the physical setup and the multi-display model. After the test was over, we measured the remaining offsets of the multi-display. We showed a generated test pattern consisting of horizontal and vertical lines with a distance of 1 cm as in Fig. 14. We then took a picture of the multi-display setup and used

Fig. 13. Final image shown in production phase

it to measure the offset using image processing tools between each neighbouring pair of devices.

5.4 Results

The evaluation of the first and the third task shows that the resulting model of the actual physical layout can be adjusted to satisfy users for most common visualisation tasks. To achieve such a result, it is crucial to use adequate test images for both the coarse as well as for the fine grained calibration phase. This claim is supported by the results of the second (Fig. 15) and the third task (Fig. 16). The test image consisting of equidistant coloured lines is best suited for

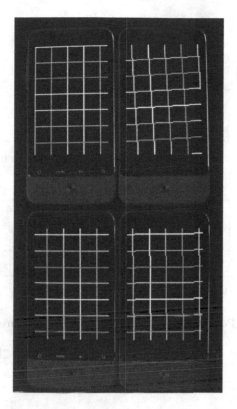

Fig. 14. Test pattern for measuring the offsets of the multi-display setups

the fine grained phase. The test image consisting of coloured concentric circles is best suited for the coarse grained calibration phase.

With the test image consisting of equidistant coloured lines all participants found the calibration of a multi-display to be easy or very easy (Fig. 17). In addition, they rated the perceived quality of the display setup to be accurate or very accurate (Fig. 16). With the monochrome concentric circles as test image the participants found calibration to be hard or very hard. They rated the quality of the display setup to be only 2–3. These results reflect the need of using adequate test images for an easy to use and accurate interactive setup of a multi-display.

As the results of the second task show this does not only apply for the fine grained calibration step but also for the coarse grained calibration step. With the test image consisting of coloured concentric circles the participants found the task of identifying the permutation and rotation of the devices to be very easy. But with the test image consisting of coloured grids the participants only identified and fixed half of the offsets (Fig. 15). In this case they found the task of identifying the offsets to be hard or very hard. Moreover the participants only identified and fixed half of the offsets in the multi-display setup compared to the test image consisting of coloured concentric circles.

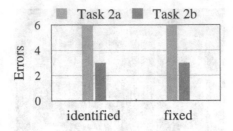

Fig. 15. Identified and fixed errors, second task (Color figure online)

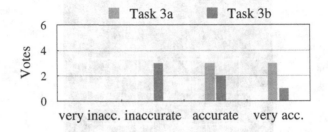

Fig. 16. Perceived accuracy, third task (Color figure online)

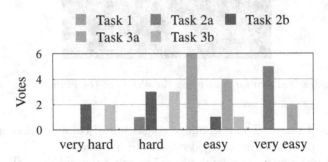

Fig. 17. Complexity of solving the five tasks (Color figure online)

In addition to evaluating perceived accuracy we also photographed the generated test pattern and measured accuracy of the multi-display model. The measured offsets between model and physical setup for each pair of individual devices were mostly between 1 and 2 mm. There have been few exceptions of up to 8 mm, depending on participant and task (Fig. 18). With the proposed test images the offsets turned out to be significantly smaller compared to the multi-displays which were set up using one of the alternative patterns.

The average processing time of the three tasks was 116 s as in Table 1. The individual processing time not only depends on the participant but also on the task as well as the test image used for setting up the multi-display. With the alternative test image the processing time was 15–50 % higher in comparison to the proposed test images.

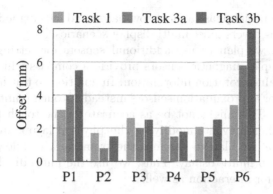

Fig. 18. Measured accuracy per participant (Color figure online)

Table 1. Average processing times in seconds

Task	1	2a	2b	3a	3b
min	55	43	63	68	54
Ø	102	107	164	98	113
max	142	300	256	181	241

Note, that the user may unintentionally move the device physically while applying the gestures. This may happen if the friction between device and surface is very small, which is not the case for typical office tables (medium-density fibreboard), or the users applies too much force. We have experienced these issues only during the coarse grained phase, if the devices are too far apart. If that happens, the users adjust the physical layout to the intended layout by moving the devices physically. After that the fine-grained gestures are applied, which is possible without unintentionally moving the devices physically.

6   Conclusion

The visual system of human users paired with their cognitive capabilities can be used to quickly build a multi-display consisting of heterogeneous mobile devices including smartphones and tablets. The resulting model of the actual physical layout on a flat surface can be adjusted to comply with enough perceived accuracy for most common visualisation tasks.

The main contribution is a two phased interactive method to first build a coarse grained model followed by a fine grained correction phase. Users do not need to leave the interaction mode and can continuously use any of the three offered gestures. This allows them to quickly set up a multi-display consisting of many devices and correct them accurately with dedicated test images and immediate feedback on their actions. The setup is limited to multi-displays that are at least in the initial phase almost row-based and left-aligned. In the opinion of the authors this covers most multi-display scenarios.

In the future, we plan to use additional sensors for setting up the multi-display. For example, magnetic sensors provide a compass which already gives at least coarse grained rotation information. In addition to touch points, we may use light sensors or approximation sensors instead of touch points for computing the initial layout. This might not be as accurate as the touch points, but it is contactless and thus prevents modifying the physical layout during the initial phase. In addition, we plan to enhance the framework to allow touch interactions on the set up multi-display. Thus, we use the multi-display not only for visualisation but for interaction as well.

References

1. Barth, P., Groß, H., Pras, M.: Blaubot middleware, March 2015. https://github.com/Blaubot
2. Chen, H., Sukthankar, R., Wallace, G., Li, K.: Scalable alignment of large-format multi-projector displays using camera homography trees. In: IEEE Visualization, pp. 339–346 (2002)
3. Chen, Y., Clark, D. W., Finkelstein, A., Housel, T.C., Li, K.: Automatic alignment of high-resolution multi-projector displays using an uncalibrated camera. In: IEEE Visualization, pp. 125–130, October 2000
4. Cristian, F.: Probabilistic clock synchronization. Distrib. Comput. 3(3), 146–158 (1989)
5. Li, M., Kobbelt, L.: Dynamic tiling display: building an interactive display surface using multiple mobile devices. In: 11th International Conference on Mobile and Ubiquitous Multimedia, MUM 2012, pp. 24:1–24:4. ACM, New York (2012)
6. Rädle, R., Jetter, H.C., Marquardt, N., Reiterer, H., Rogers, Y.: Huddlelamp: Spatially-aware mobile displays for ad-hoc around-the-table collaboration. In: Proceedings of the Ninth ACM International Conference on Interactive Tabletops and Surfaces, ITS 2014, pp. 45–54. ACM, New York (2014). http://doi.acm.org/10.1145/2669485.2669500
7. Raskar, R., Brown, M. S., Yang, R., Chen, W. C., Welch, G., Towles, H., Seales, W., Fuchs, H.: Multi-projector displays using camera-based registration. In: IEEE Visualization, pp. 161–168 (1999)
8. Schmitz, A., Li, M., Schönefeld, V., Kobbelt, L.: Ad-hoc multi-displays for mobile interactive applications. In: Eurographics, vol. 29, p. 8 (2010)
9. Shen, G., Li, Y., Zhang, Y.: Mobius: enable together-viewing video experience across two mobile devices. In: Knightly, E., Borriello, G., Cceres, R. (eds.) MobiSys, pp. 30–42. ACM (2007)

SURFLogo - Mobile Tagging with App Icons

Chadly Marouane[1]([⊠]) and Andre Ebert[2]

[1] Virality GmbH - Research and Development,
Rauchstraße 7, 81679 Munich, Germany
marouane@virality.de
[2] Ludwig-Maximilians-Universität München,
Oettingenstraße 67, 80538 Munich, Germany
andre.ebert@ifi.lmu.de

Abstract. Mobile tagging became more and more popular in commercials, magazines, newspapers, and other applications during the last years. In context of commercials, a bar code containing the advertisers internet address is often used to refer a customer to related online content. Due to their robustness as well as their comparably high fault-tolerance in case of low quality pictures, QR-Code systems are commonly used for that task. Connected to that topic we present a special procedure for mobile tagging, which uses a distinct logo or image in order to refer to certain information instead of a QR-Code. Our procedure was optimized to work with a conventional smartphone – the only prerequisite for usage is the possession of a smartphone capable of capturing and analyzing the different logos with our smartphone application. To match the logos with related information and to determine their uniqueness we introduce a new similarity measure on basis of SURF feature points and a contour comparison.

Keywords: Mobile tagging · Mobile marketing · QR-code · Computer vision · App stores

1 Introduction

When talking of mobile tagging, an advanced process of associating real world items with digital information is meant [11]. In this context, this association represents an exciting as well as complex section in the area of current media developments [1,5,24]. Therefore, objects marked with tags are scanned with a smartphone's camera and the information encrypted within the tag can be processed. 2D codes, e.g., QR-Codes or Data-matrix codes are enriched with information which can be used and displayed on mobile devices like mobile phones, smartphones, or tablets. Hereby, new chances for enriching advertisements on posters, for pointing to localities on Google Maps, or to apps in app stores as well as for linking to profiles in social media networks are opened – the physical world becomes linked to its virtual counterpart. Contents of mobile tags are mostly conventional unique resource identifiers (URL) which get recognized

S. Sigg et al. (Eds.): MobiCASE 2015, LNICST 162, pp. 239–256, 2015.
DOI: 10.1007/978-3-319-29003-4_14

as the corresponding hyperlink though they are only represented by a simple string. Moreover, mobile tags also get used more and more for the advertisement of mobile apps by displaying a QR-Code in range of the app's print or its digital advertisement. As soon as a customer is curious about the app, he can become linked directly into the app store for downloading it.

But despite all of these advantages, there are major issues with the usage of QR-Codes. Besides their lack of an attractive visual appearance there is also a shortage of customer acceptance. A QR-Code often looks misplaced, especially when it takes up more space than the actual commercial. Related to that, there were developments for encoding additional information without a visual tag, e.g., under the usage of radio transmission technologies. Near Field Communication (NFC) is often used as a mobile tag in the tourism business [14], as well as in the smart home area [7] and the mobile payment sector [22]. Furthermore, the Bluetooth 4.0 standard became more attractive due to its energy efficient functioning. Technologies like Apple's iBeacons and Google's Eddystone are already deployed in the range of proximity marketing with great success [8,9].

But there are also disadvantages coming with these technologies. Compared to visual procedures, they tend to be expensive in purchase and their operational area is limited, e.g., they cannot be printed on a commercial poster or being displayed in a television advertisement. Another way for mobile tagging are Microsoft's Custom Tags. These are offering the possibility to use individual logos, brandings or photographies for mobile tags. Therefore, with the help of a specifically for this purpose developed treatment they are repainted with a matrix of dots. This treatment enables a special image scanner, which can be installed on a smartphone in form of an app, to recognize the custom tag [15]. Thus, the usage of QR-Codes can be prevented completely and the question is raised, if an app logo itself could be enough for linking additional content.

Driven by that idea and related to Microsoft's concept, we present an approach which enables us to identify apps distinctly by only analyzing their app logo. Similar to a bar code scanner for smartphones, a mobile application was developed to accomplish this. Therefore, we developed a multi-layered decisioning process for app logo identification, which is introduced and evaluated in the frame of this work. Additionally we present SURFLogoApp, a smartphone application consisting of a request server and a smartphone application which is capable of implementing our multi-layered decisioning process.

The contribution of this work is a system that can identify logos of an app store distinctly. Especially when using images of poor quality, taken by a smartphone camera, the system still returns a unique result. In this context, we present and evaluate a scanner that provides an easy and fast identification of app logos as well as a method that returns a unique result. Therefore, it uses a fine granular search and comparison process, a so-called multi-layered decisioning process. In contrast to a conventional search of images, such as Google Image Search, the method can also be applied to poor image quality. This paper is structured as follows: In Sect. 2 we explain some fundamentals of image processing relevant for the following application. Subsequently, we elucidate our general concept in Sect. 3, consisting of the multi-layered decisioning process as well as the SURFLogoApp system. Section 4 evaluate our approach and provide some insights into our test results. Afterwards, we sum up our findings in Sect. 5 and give and outlook towards open issues and possible future work.

2 Image Processing

In the following we present some conceptual fundamentals concerning the main components of SURFLogo, i.e., image representation, feature point extraction and image comparison.

2.1 Representing Images with Feature Points

Many tasks and applications in the computer vision domain require a representation of images, which is detached from their raw pixels. For example, recognizing objects or identifying similar images based on raw pixel values gets unusable when images differ in color, illumination, scaling, or rotation. A solution to this problem is to compute so-called feature points which represent very characteristic and therefore highly distinctive points or areas of an image. Depending on the employed algorithm, feature points are robust against common transformations and varying contrast situations.

The Speeded Up Robust Features (SURF) algorithm by Bay et al. [3] can be used to compute feature points. It applies an approximation of the Gaussian blur filter to the image and then looks for local extrema to identify scale- and rotation-invariant feature points. Subsequently, these points are described via a 64-dimensional vector which, is computed from the Haar-Wavelet response of the feature point's surrounding region. Similarities between two feature points can be calculated with the help of the Euclidean Distance between them.

There are also techniques for identifying and describing feature points [6,17,18]. Recently, there is a trend towards binary descriptors (e.g., [2,4,13,19]), which can be compared to each other more efficiently (e.g., using Hamming Distance).

2.2 Image Comparison

In order to select the image out of the test set, which is most similar to a test candidate, image comparison techniques are necessary. All images are represented by feature points which are pre-computed in the first and become stored in a database in the following. In general, there are two different classes of matching techniques: Those working directly on feature points and those using so-called *visual words*.

Comparison Directly Based-on Feature Points. These approaches compare images using their respective feature points. Each feature point of the query image votes for a reference image out of the database, which contains the most similar feature point. The image with the most votes is selected as the one with the highest similarity [16,20].

A disadvantage of this concept is its inefficiency due to a huge amount of feature points to be considered as well as the high dimensionality of their descriptors. Even with moderately large databases, comparisons to a complete set of reference images can be unfeasible. Thus, a scalability to big amounts of data is not given.

Based on Visual Words. The second class of algorithms tries to overcome this shortcomings by virtually pre-computing matches of individual feature matching by quantizing feature descriptors. For that purpose, the existing feature points or a subset of them are clustered, e.g., with the k-Means algorithm. Thus, every feature point is assigned to its nearest cluster center. As a consequence, an image is represented by a histogram of cluster frequencies, whose comparison can be undertaken much more efficiently. Since most of these approaches originate from domains of text processing and document retrieval, the clusters are also called visual words, a set of all words is called the *vocabulary* and an image representation is called *bag-of-words*. One of the first approaches in that category was introduced by Sivic and Zisserman [21]. Additionally, Turcot and Lowe showed that it is possible to discard up to 96 % of all feature points without reducing the matching precision [23].

3   Concept

In the following we introduce our system's components as well as further information about these. Moreover, our multi-layered decisioning approach is explained in detail.

3.1   Control Concept

The core idea of SURFLogoApp is to link additional content, e.g., a hyperlink to an app store, to a physical as well as to a digital advertisement while completely resigning conventional methods like QR-Codes. Instead, we only use the apps own logo. The logo is detected and scanned by the smartphone's built-in camera and links the user to the commercials counterpart in the app store as well as it enables its download. In the following, we call this referencing logos SURFlogo.

The control concept of SURFLogo from the user's point of view is designed as follows (see Fig. 1): (1) the users recognizes a SURFLogo related to a specific app in a commercial, which is bounded by a quadratic twin framed box, (2) if SURFLogoApp was downloaded and installed on the user's device, the SURFLogo gets scanned with it and, (3) the user becomes redirected to an app store with the opportunity to download the associated app.

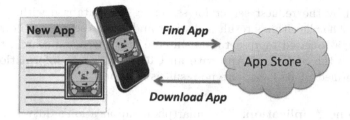

Fig. 1. Control concept of the SURFLogoApp - the SURFLogo which links to an associated app becomes scanned with the smartphone application

3.2 Components of SURFLogoApp

The distributed SURFLogoApp system consists of three different components, which are a request server, a database and a smartphone application. The communication between these components is established by the use of a conventional internet connection.

Database. The database components contains all registered SURFLogos in the form of a sequence of feature points $Seq_{Feature}$, a quantized vector of these feature points $Quant(Seq_{Feature})$ (*bag-of-words*), a sequence of contour points $Seq_{Contour}$, and a uniform resource identifier URL_{App} associated with an app in an app store.

$$AppIc_i = \begin{pmatrix} Seq_{Feature} \\ Quant(Seq_{Feature}) \\ Seq_{Contour} \\ URL_{App} \end{pmatrix}, i \in Database_{AppIc}$$

Furthermore, the database component contains a vocabulary, which enables the calculation of a quantized vector out of an image's sequence of feature points (bag-of-words). This procedure as well as the extraction of feature points and the contour extraction is undertaken for every SURFLogo in the database.

The vocabulary consists of all clustered feature points' cluster centers, which are available in the database. Related to that, the component can possess multiple vocabularies bound to specific areas of operation. The database's creation takes place in the so-called offline phase, scheduled prior to the system's operational phase. Still, the database can always be extended during the operational phase (online phase). On updating an existing SURFLogo, all related references in the database are also replaced.

Request Server. The request server receives and processes all requests for the SURFLogo system via a REST service.

A request consists of a sequence of feature points as well as of a sequence of contour points, which represent and describe a SURFLogo image. The sequences are needed by the request server for searching the database with a matching algorithm. The algorithm's result is distinct and is represented by a direct hit or no existing associated representation. In case of a successful search, the server responses to the SURFLogoApp with an URL pointing to information related to the identified SURFLogo, else no result is returned.

Smartphone Application. The smartphone application's duty is to identify images marked as SURFLogos with its camera, to scan them and in the following to analyze them. In order to support a SURFLogo's distinct an automatic identification, it is marked with a quadratic, black, twin frame (see Fig. 2).

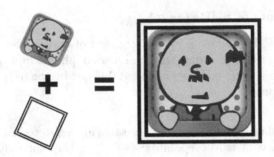

Fig. 2. Example of a SURFLogo – an app icon and a black twin frame for automated recognition by the smartphone's camera

For recognizing a SURFLogo, the frames needs to comply with the following requirements: (1) the corner points of one quadratic frame need to be within the other quadratic frame's corners, (2) the ratio of both of the quadratic frames needs to be within a defined area, and (3) both of the quadratic frames need to have a minimum size.

As soon as a SURFLogo becomes detected by a smartphone application, it gets scanned and rotated in dependence of its surrounding frames. The time needed to scan a SURFLogo is comparable to the time needed by a conventional QR-Code scanner.

After the frame became removed, all feature points are extracted out of the image and consolidated in a sequence $Seq_{Feature}$. In the next step, all two dimensional coordinates which are describing the images contour are also becoming aggregated in a sequence $Seq_{Contour}$. These sequences are now sent to the request server, which responds with an URL URL_{App} if the database search was successful. The URL references to the an apps download page within an app store.

3.3 Matching Algorithm

The matching algorithm serves for comparison of features and therefore distinct recognition of SURFLogos – it is one of the most important components for the SURFLogoApp. During the comparison process it determines individual characteristics of a SURFLogo on basis of the given features. These characteristics allow a explicit distinction between different SURFLogos and false positive results in context of the searching process can be suspended. In a positive case, a distinct data entry related to the given features is found in the database, in a negative case no entry is available. The algorithm consists of two different steps: a preprocessing step followed by a matching step.

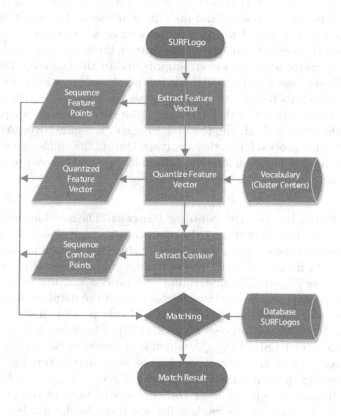

Fig. 3. Preprocessing: (1) Extraction of feature points and vectors, (2) quantization of feature vectors, (3) extraction of contour points. At least all information from (1), (2) and (3) will be used for the multi-layered decisioning process.

Preprocessing. The preprocessing step is needed during the offline phase at the database's creation as well as afterwards during the online phase. Especially for the extraction of an image's features and the SURFLogo's appending to the database, an effective preprocessing is crucial (see Fig. 3). Therefore, all feature points and their corresponding vectors are extracted out of a SURFLogo and saved temporarily. For the extraction routine the robust SURF process is used [3]. Subsequently, the extracted feature vectors become quantized with the help of a vocabulary which was created at the forefront. The quantization itself is crucial for the process of searching in order to speed it up. The vocabulary is created by computing clusters, e.g., with the k-Means algorithm, out of a large range of feature points. Ideally this range represents the full number of all SURFLogos contained by the database. During the quantization each feature vector is matched with the cluster center it has the least distance to. Thus, each SURFLogo can be represented by a histogram of cluster frequencies. These histograms - so-called bag-of-words - are easy and efficient to compare to each other. Because of the fact that lots of these and related processing concepts are originated in text processing and document retrieval, the resulting clusters are also referred to as visual words, the number of all words is referred to as dictionary, and the associated image representation is referred to as bag-of-words. The quantized vector also gets saved temporarily. In the last step, the contour of the SURFLogo described by SURF feature points and consisting of x- and y-coordinates gets extracted and temporarily saved as a sequence. Afterwards, all temporarily saved data gets either transferred into the database for permanent storage together with an URL and the SURFLogo or is handed over to the multi-layered decisioning process for further analysis. During the online phase, requests from a smartphone application already contain feature and contour points, which is why the first and the third step can be skipped.

Matching: Multi-layered Decisioning Process. The multi-layered decisioning process is only necessary during the operational online phase. Thereby, temporarily saved information from the preprocessing step as well as the database are used for data input. All in all, the matching step consists of three comparing processes (see Fig. 4). The first comparing process considers the quantized vector. For this purpose, all quantized vectors out of the database are compared to the given quantized feature vector. The k closest possible matches are used for the second comparison process $k \in \{2, .., 25\}$. The value k is defined as a chosen threshold $\text{THRESHOLD}_{\text{Quant}}$, which is evaluated in Sect. 4.3. Otherwise, the k next possible matches are compared on basis of their feature points and are ranked descending by their number of successful matched features. For the last comparison process, which considers the contours of both of the entries, only the first two entries out of the ranked list are used. Is the number of feature matches for both entries below a chosen threshold $\text{THRESHOLD}_{\text{Surf}}$, the whole process is canceled again. Else, the sequences containing the contour points are analyzed by the Hausdorff distance. The winning sequence is the one with the smallest Hausdorff distance. Again, if the Hausdorff distance is above a chosen threshold $\text{THRESHOLD}_{\text{Hausdorff}}$ for both contours, the comparison process is canceled without a successful result.

4   Evaluation

In this section, we evaluate our SURFLogoApp system concerning its performance and provide detailed information about the evaluation's results.

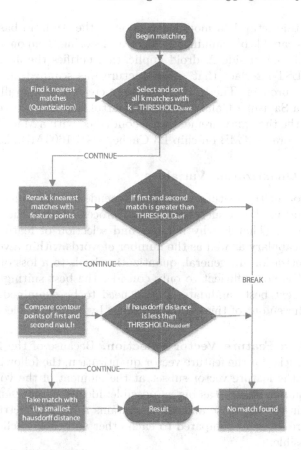

Fig. 4. Multi-layered decisioning process: (1) Find k nearest matches with quantized feature vectors, (2) rerank all matches with his feature points, (3) compare reranked matches with contour points.

4.1   Setup Configuration

We used one set of test data during the whole evaluation phase. Therefore, a database containing 5541 different SURFLogos was created. The logos itself were crawled and downloaded randomly out of Google's PlayStore and all in all we extracted more than 2118240 SURF feature points and stored them in our database.

A higher number of SURFLogos - so e.g., all 1.6 million logos from the Google PlayStore - has only a small influence on the duration of the query of the first sub-process of the multi-layered decisioning process and increases linearly with increasing number of SURFLogos.

In order to evaluate the multi-layered decisioning process, we generated 759 test images. In this context, a browser-based JavaScript application for sequential displaying of different SURFLogos in different sizes within one browser tab was developed. Additionally, the displayed SurfLogos were noted in a log file. The counterpart of this setup is a modified version of the Android-based SURFLo-goApp, which is capable of scanning the logos and storing them on a smartphone. Subsequently, the client-side Android application notifies the Javascript application via a REST-interface that a new picture was scanned and needs to be displayed in the browser. The test images were created by overall 6 volunteers equipped with a Samsung Galaxy S5 mini smartphone. The clustering calculations as well as the time measurement were conducted with a Mac Book Air 2013 (1,7 GHz Dual-Core i7, 4 MB on-chip L3 Cache, 8 GB 1600 MHz LPDDR3).

4.2   Critical Quantization Variables

The quantization of the feature vectors is dependent from different variables, which are important for a successful search process during the multi-layered decisioning process. That is why number and selection of feature vectors for generating a vocabulary as well as the number of words within a vocabulary are crucial for quantization. In general, quantization leads to a loss of information, which is why it is not sufficient to only consider the best suiting vector alone. Moreover, the next best candidates k also need to be examined. The correct result can be chosen out of this candidate range by a further selection step.

Subset Size and Feature Vector Selection. Because of the fact, that the vocabulary is crucial for the feature vector quantization, the following conditions must apply for the feature vector subset at the moment of the vocabulary creation: (1) the subset must be as big as possible; ideally it represents all feature vectors stored in the database and (2) it contains a broad spectrum of feature vectors; they are different compared to each other and their euclidean distance is as big as possible.

In order to create the vocabulary, the subset of feature vectors needs to be clustered. Therefore, a simple k-Means algorithm capable of clustering the whole subset is used [10]. When analyzing a large amount of vectors, placed in a vast vector space, e.g., a SURF feature vector with 64 dimensions, the clustering tends to be CPU- and time-intensive. That is why we evaluated different sizes of subsets while generating the vocabulary.

Table 1 shows the different time spans for subsets containing 10 %, 20 %, and 100 % of the existing feature vectors which complies to the whole amount of existing feature points.

Table 1. Time needed for clustering - 3 cluster sets with a subset of 10 %, 20 %, and 100 % from the database's feature vectors with a cluster size of 512.

Subset	10 %	20 %	100 %
Time	4 h 1 m 11 s	15 h 39 m 37 s	4 d 12 h 2 m 29 s

The larger the vector amount for the vocabulary's generation is selected, the longer takes the process of clustering. The time span between the usage of 10 %, which was 4 h, 1 min, and 100 %, which was 4 days, 12 h and 2 min, is extraordinarily significant. Furthermore, when examining the results from Fig. 5, it is clearly visible that the success rate of clusters generated with a subset of 20 % of all feature points is not particularly better than the one corresponding to clusters generated with a 100 %. In case of our 20 % subset, it is even worse. That is why for our evaluation we generated the clusters with a subset of only 10 % of all existing feature points from our database.

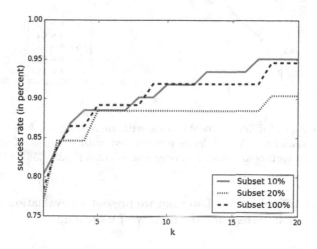

Fig. 5. Success rate of different vocabularies with increasing k – k is the number of possible result candidates. Vocabularies are created with a subset of 10 %, 20 %, and 100 % from the database's feature vectors and with a cluster size of 512.

Vocabulary Size. Besides the right amount of feature vectors for vocabulary generation, the number of clusters, which are representing a word, is also vital for the result's quality. If the size of a cluster is chosen to be to small, the loss of information due to the quantization process is larger and the quality of the results is smaller. In contrast, if the cluster size was chosen to be to large, the desirable time-saving due to the quantization process is narrowed.

Figure 6 shows, that with a rising number of clusters the result's quality is comparably high, even with a lower ranked k candidate. It is notable, that the discrepancy between the cluster sizes of 32 and 512 with $k = 1$ is already almost 30 %. Admittedly, it decreased with a growing k, but even with a candidate size of $k = 20$ it is still 10 %. Subsequently, we use a cluster size of 512 because of the superiority of its result's quality compared to cluster sizes of 32, 64, 128, and 256.

4.3   Multi-layered Decisioning Process

In context of our multi-layered decisioning process, we first examined some vital factors and variables within the procedure's sub-processes because of their

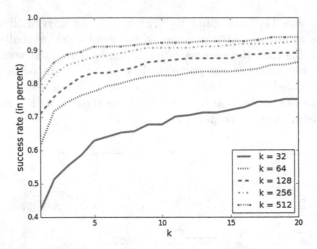

Fig. 6. Success rate of different vocabularies with increasing k - k is the number of possible result candidates. Vocabularies are created with a subset of 10 % from the database's feature vectors and with a cluster size of 32, 64, 128, 256 and 512.

influence onto our final results. Later on, we present an evaluation covering and examining our whole system and the quality of its results.

Quantization: Numbers of k Candidates. The identification of the right number of k candidates, which are the output of the quantization process, influences the following sub-process of feature vector comparison significantly. Moreover, the number of k candidates is heavily influencing the search and comparison time while matching the features of the SURF vectors. Because of the fact that all feature vectors are compared for each single candidate, a high number of candidates can slow down this sub-process noticeable. That is why it is important to identify the right amount of candidates in order to acquire an accurate result within an appropriate time span.

Figure 6 shows distinctly, that an increasing k also raises the success rate, independently from the chosen cluster sizes. The success rate itself already converges towards a maximum value for all different cluster sizes if $k = 18$. E.g., for a cluster size of 512, an amount of $k = 18$ candidates converges to an average of 94 %. That is why we use a candidate number of $k = 18$ with an additional buffer of 2 for the following evaluation, so we use all in all a $k = 20$. This k represent the THRESHOLD$_{\text{Quant}}$ like in Sect. 3.3 is described.

SURF Feature Matching. The following sub-process is a comparison search based on the actual SURF feature vectors. Therefore, the SURF feature vectors of all k candidates, which where determined in previous subprocesses are examined. In the easiest case all SURF feature vectors of the SURFLogo we want to analyze are compared to all k candidates and their feature vectors, respectively.

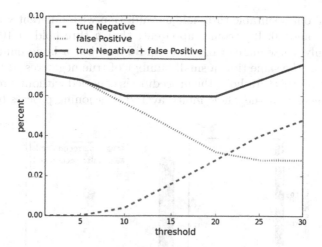

Fig. 7. Threshold's evaluation with different values of 0, 5, 10, 15, 20, 25 and 30. The sum of false positives and true negatives has its minimum between a threshold of 10 and 20. In order to have a small number of true negatives, a threshold of 10 is most ideal.

In contrast to the comparison process used during the quantization, the procedure used at this step of the analysis is much more complex. In that context, the complexity of the quantization's comparison procedure is about $O(1)$, the complexity of SURF's comparison procedure is $O(n)$. For that reason, a small number of comparison candidates is desirable at this step. As stated before, we use a candidate input of $k = 20$ for our evaluation. After comparing the 20 candidates on basis of their SURF feature descriptors, they are sorted anew with the goal of bringing the candidate with the most similar feature descriptors to the top. Our results are, that the correct logo is placed on the first two positions with a probability of 93 %, the correct result is on top of the list with a probability of 91 %. All in all it turned out, that after a quantization and the subsequent comparison search under the usage of feature points leads to a positioning of correct results in first place with a probability of 99 %. That is why the input for the last sub-process is limited to the first two results of the newly ordered candidate list. This limitation has positive effects in regarding the last sub-process, which is the process with the most computational costs. Furthermore, the 1 % of results ordered aback in our list can be neglected because of their little impact onto the overall result.

In order to better the result additionally, all possible false positives are about to be eliminated in the forefront. Therefore, candidates become rated false positive as soon as the sum of the number of all matched feature points is below a threshold of 10. This value represent the THRESHOLD$_{Surf}$ like in Sect. 3.3 is described.

An additional evaluation showed, that a value of 10 is already sufficient in order to exclude as much false positive candidates as possible. Figure 7 provides information about a suitable threshold's evaluation with different values of 0, 5, 10, 15, 20, 25 and 30. It becomes apparent, that a threshold of 10 is suitable to sort out only a few number of valid candidates, but a large number of false positives and at the same time a small number of true negatives. If there are no candidates below this threshold, the procedure is canceled without a return value, which also means that the whole multi-layered decisioning process terminates.

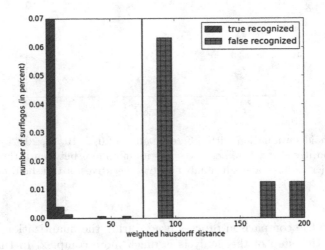

Fig. 8. Histogramms of all computed hausdorff distances: all distances with a true recognition are placed below a threshold of 75 (Black vertical line). Except for of a few outliers, the most of the true recognized results are in a range below a distance of 5.

Contour Detection and Hausdorff Distance. The last and thereby third sub-process consists of a contour comparison between two SURFLogos. The contour comparison itself is realized by using the Hausdorff distance [12]. In that context it measures the distance between two contours in a metric space, which allows us to compare them. Goal of this sub-process is the identification of the candidate among all candidates with the least contour distance – it is winning the comparison process and regarded as the correct result. For the contour we use the x- and y- coordinates of the SURF feature points which where matched in both images. With this approach it is guaranteed, that contour points created by noise or other camera effects are not included in the computation of the Hausdorff distance.

In order to prevent a better outcome for pairs with a small amount of common feature points, the distances itself become normalized. Thereby the Hausdorff distance is calculated as follows.

$$\frac{distance_{hausdorff}}{\#matches_{featurepoints}} \tag{1}$$

If there is no common feature point for a pair of candidates which is about to be compared, a maximum distance MAX_{float} is returned.

Fig. 9. A free and a purchasable version of an app logo. The hausdorff distances are really similar and difficult to distinguish.

Fig. 10. Example of a printed SURFLogo on the left side and a scanned SURFLogo with poor quality on the right side.

An evaluation on basis of this defined comparison procedure provided the following results. Figure 8 displays distinctly, that all distances are placed below a threshold of 75. So we set this value as THRESHOLD$_{Hausdorff}$ like in Sect. 3.3 is described.

Moreover, SURFLogos with small distance differences between candidate one and two are only logos which differ in small details. Figure 9 shows an example for those, where an app logo exists two times for a free and also for a purchasable version of the same application. This means, that in general the same app is referenced, but there are two existing versions of it. One which is about to be payed for and one which is available for free.

On basis of this insights, the third sub-process was extended by the following conditions:

– All distances placed above a threshold of 75 are neglected and not considered as a possible result.
– If the difference of the two comparison pair's distances is within a range from 0.5 to 1, both candidates are considered to be the correct SURFLogo.

Hence, the whole decisioning procedure of the sub-process is defined as follows: (1) the distances of the candidates 1 and 2 to the SURFlogo are computed. If both distances are placed above of a defined threshold in (2), the whole process terminates and no result is returned, else it continues. If the distances of two comparison pairs are placed within a range from 0 to 1 in (3), the process terminates and both associated candidates are returned, else the candidate with the smallest distance to the logo on the captured image is returned.

Results. After we reviewed the three sub-processes of our multi-layered decisioning process individually, the evaluation of the complete procedure is provided in the following. Therefore, the identified thresholds of the individual processes were used, the candidate pool delivered from sub-process 1 to sub-process 2 and from sub-process 2 to sub-process 3 was kept consistent.

All analysis requests with the multi-layered decisioning process are resulting a correct response in 92 %.

If the results for apps which possess two logo versions, e.g., for a free version and a purchasable version, are also taken into account the overall result rises to 93 %. Another significance of the overall result is the fact that there are no false positives occurring in the result quantity. This means, in the best case a distinct result is delivered by the multi-layered decisioning process, in the worst case no result is returned.

5   Conclusion

In the context of this paper we presented a procedure capable of replacing QR-Codes in their functionality of mobile tagging for commercials in print and digital media. Instead, the applications logo itself is used for automated identification and referral to the app store. For realization we introduced and evaluated a multi-layered decisioning process. Furthermore, we provided a distributed system called SURFLogo, which implements the procedure in form of a mobile application, a request server and a database, which supports the process's special requirements.

The evaluation of all three subprocesses of our multi-layered approach was undertaken separately for each subprocess. The first subprocess indicates, that a cluster size of 512 is suitable for the feature vectors' quantization and in order to reach a success rate of 82 % when searching for the associated SURFLogos. Because of the fact that such a result is not sufficient, we use the 20 best result candidates from subprocess 1 as input for subprocess 2. The second subprocess shows, that a search based on basis of feature points results in a better result set, which enables us to only use the two best candidates out of the second step for the third subprocess. Additionally, we introduced a threshold, which considers the sum out of successful created feature points for both candidates and cancels the process without return value if this value is placed below 10. The third subprocess identifies the correct candidate on basis of the SURFLogo contour. Therefore, we calculated the Hausdorff distance on basis of the x- and y-coordinates of all matched feature points and returned the candidates with the least distance as the correct result. In that context, we used another threshold capable of identifying distances larger than 75 as belonging to wrong candidates.

All in all, the multi-layered decisioning process has a success rate of 93 %. In 7 % of all cases we were not able to identify the right SURFLogo. There was no case of a false positive result being returned, which proves that the procedure is relatively distinct. Compared to the QR-Code procedure with a success rate of nearly 100 %, our approach is still very robust. Additionally it is based on a visually more individual content, which is easy assignable to a specific app. In contrast to image searching approaches (e.g., Google Image Search), a SURFLogo with a comparably poor quality is still identifiable (Fig. 10).

Despite the high success rate, there were some SURFLogos, which were not detected. Reasons for that may be a bad image quality due to the smartphone's camera, which can lead to interferences and inaccuracies due to noise or to blur effects conditioned by ambiguous movements. Furthermore, the procedure is colorblind, which means that it is not capable of distinguishing between SURFLogos with identical content displayed in different contrasts or intensities of colors. An advantage of that is a higher robustness during different lighting conditions. However, because of that there are restrictions regarding the discriminability of similar contours. Thereto, the procedure could be extended by a color detector.

References

1. Al-Khalifa, H.S.: Utilizing QR code and mobile phones for blinds and visually impaired people. In: Miesenberger, K., Klaus, J., Zagler, W.L., Karshmer, A.I. (eds.) ICCHP 2008. LNCS, vol. 5105, pp. 1065–1069. Springer, Heidelberg (2008)
2. Alahi, A., Ortiz, R., Vandergheynst, P.: Freak: fast retina keypoint. In: IEEE Conference on Computer Vision and Pattern Recognition (CVPR 2012), pp. 510–517 (2012)
3. Bay, H., Tuytelaars, T., Van Gool, L.: SURF: speeded up robust features. In: Leonardis, A., Bischof, H., Pinz, A. (eds.) ECCV 2006, Part I. LNCS, vol. 3951, pp. 404–417. Springer, Heidelberg (2006)
4. Calonder, M., Lepetit, V., Strecha, C., Fua, P.: BRIEF: binary robust independent elementary features. In: Daniilidis, K., Maragos, P., Paragios, N. (eds.) ECCV 2010, Part IV. LNCS, vol. 6314, pp. 778–792. Springer, Heidelberg (2010)
5. Canadi, M., Hpken, W., Fuchs, M.: Application of QR codes in online travel distribution. In: Gretzel, U., Law, R., Fuchs, M. (eds.) Information and Communication Technologies in Tourism 2010, pp. 137–148. Springer, Vienna (2010)
6. Chandrasekhar, V., Chen, D.M., Lin, A., Takacs, G., Tsai, S.S., Cheung, N.-M., Reznik, Y., Grzeszczuk, R., Girod, B.: Comparison of local feature descriptors for mobile visual search. In: 17th IEEE International Conference on Image Processing (ICIP 2010), pp. 3885–3888 (2010)
7. Darianian, M., Michael, M.: Smart home mobile RFID-based internet-of-things systems and services. In: International Conference on Advanced Computer Theory and Engineering, ICACTE 2008, pp. 116–120, December 2008
8. Gast, M.S.: Building Applications with iBeacon: Proximity and Location Services with Bluetooth Low Energy. O'Reilly Media, Sebastopol (2014)
9. Goosen, C.A.: Design and implementation of a bluetooth 4.0 le infrastructure for mobile devices, June 2014
10. Hartigan, J.A., Wong, M.A.: A K-means clustering algorithm. Appl. Stat. **28**, 100–108 (1979)
11. Hegen, M.: Mobile Tagging: Potenziale für das Mobile Business. Diplom.de (2010)
12. Huttenlocher, D., Klanderman, G., Rucklidge, W.: Comparing images using the hausdorff distance. IEEE Trans. Pattern Anal. Mach. Intell. **15**(9), 850–863 (1993)
13. Leutenegger, S., Chli, M., Siegwart, R.Y.: BRISK: binary robust invariant scalable keypoints. In: IEEE International Conference on Computer Vision (ICCV 2011), pp. 2548–2555. IEEE (2011)
14. Madlmayr, G., Scharinger, J.: Neue dimension von mobilen tourismusanwendungen durch near field communication-technologie. In: Egger, R., Jooss, M. (eds.) mTourism, pp. 75–88. Gabler (2010)
15. Microsoft: Mircosoft Tag - Creating Custom Tags (2011). http://tag.microsoft.com/what-is-tag/custom-tags.aspx. Accessed 16 July 2015
16. Mikolajczyk, K., Schmid, C.: Indexing based on scale invariant interest points. In: Proceedings of Eighth IEEE International Conference on Computer Vision, ICCV 2001, vol. 1, pp. 525–531. IEEE (2001)

17. Mikolajczyk, K., Schmid, C.: A performance evaluation of local descriptors. IEEE Trans. Pattern Anal. Mach. Intell. **27**(10), 1615–1630 (2005)
18. Miksik, O., Mikolajczyk, K.: Evaluation of local detectors and descriptors for fast feature matching. In: 21st International Conference on Pattern Recognition (ICPR 2012), pp. 2681–2684 (2012)
19. Rublee, E., Rabaud, V., Konolige, K., Bradski, G.: ORB: an efficient alternative to SIFT or SURF. In: IEEE International Conference on Computer Vision (ICCV 2011), pp. 2564–2571 (2011)
20. Schaffalitzky, F., Zisserman, A.: Automated scene matching in movies. In: Lew, M., Sebe, N., Eakins, J.P. (eds.) CIVR 2002. LNCS, vol. 2383, pp. 186–197. Springer, Heidelberg (2002)
21. Sivic, J., Zisserman, A.: Video google: a text retrieval approach to object matching in videos. In: Proceedings of Ninth IEEE International Conference on Computer Vision, pp. 1470–1477 (2003)
22. Tan, G.W.-H., Ooi, K.-B., Chong, S.-C., Hew, T.-S.: NFC mobile credit card: the next frontier of mobile payment? Telematics Inform. **31**(2), 292–307 (2014)
23. Turcot, P., Lowe, D.G.: Better matching with fewer features: the selection of useful features in large database recognition problems. In: IEEE 12th International Conference on Computer Vision Workshops (ICCV Workshops 2009), pp. 2109–2116 (2009)
24. Walsh, A.: Blurring the boundaries between our physical and electronic libraries. Electron. Libr. **29**(4), 429–437 (2011)

Mobility

Towards Indoor Transportation Mode Detection Using Mobile Sensing

Thor Siiger Prentow, Henrik Blunck, Mikkel Baun Kjærgaard,
and Allan Stisen(✉)

Department of Computer Science, Aarhus University, Aarhus, Denmark
{prentow,blunck,mikkelbk,allans}@cs.au.dk

Abstract. Transportation mode detection (TMD) is a growing field of research, in which a variety of methods have been developed, foremost for outdoor travels. It has been employed in application areas such as public transportation and environmental footprint profiling. For indoor travels the problem of TMD has received comparatively little attention, even though diverse transportation modes, such as biking and electric vehicles, are used indoors. The potential applications are diverse, and include scheduling and progress tracking for mobile workers, and management of vehicular resources. However, for indoor TMD, the physical environment as well as the availability and reliability of sensing resources differ drastically from outdoor scenarios. Therefore, many of the methods developed for outdoor TMD cannot be easily and reliably applied indoors.

In this paper, we explore indoor transportation scenarios to arrive at a conceptual model of indoor transportation modes, and then compare challenges for outdoor and indoor TMD. In addition, we explore methods for TMD we deem suitable in indoor settings, and we perform an extensive real-world evaluation of such methods at a large hospital complex. The evaluation utilizes Wi-Fi and accelerometer data collected through smartphones carried by hospital workers throughout four days of work routines. The results show that the methods can distinguish between six common modes of transportation used by the hospital workers with an F-score of 84.2 %.

Keywords: Transportation mode detection · Indoor positioning · Mobile sensing

1 Introduction

Transportation mode detection is a growing field of research, in which a variety of methods have been developed for detecting transportation modes foremost for outdoor travels. It has been employed in application areas such as public transportation, environmental footprint profiling, and context-aware mobile assistants. For indoor travels the problem of transportation mode detection has received comparatively little attention, even though diverse transportation

© Institute for Computer Sciences, Social Informatics and Telecommunications Engineering 2015
S. Sigg et al. (Eds.): MobiCASE 2015, LNICST 162, pp. 259–279, 2015.
DOI: 10.1007/978-3-319-29003-4_15

modes, such as biking, electric vehicles, and scooters, are used indoors, especially in large building complexes.

The potential applications are diverse, and may also extend beyond indoor variants of the above outdoor applications, and include, e.g., scheduling and progress tracking for mobile workers, management of vehicular resources, and navigation support. However, for indoor transportation mode detection, both the physical environment as well as the availability and reliability of sensing resources differ drastically from outdoor scenarios. Owing to these differences, many of the methods developed for outdoor transportation mode detection cannot be easily and reliably applied indoors.

In this paper, we explore indoor transportation scenarios to arrive at a conceptual model of indoor transportation modes, and then compare challenges for outdoor and indoor transportation mode detection. In addition, we explore methods for transportation mode detection we deem suitable in indoor settings, and we perform an extensive real-world evaluation of (combinations of) such methods at a large hospital complex. The evaluation presented here utilizes Wi-Fi and accelerometer data collected through smartphones carried by several hospital workers throughout four days of work routines. The results show that the methods can distinguish between six common modes of transportation used by the hospital workers with an F-score of 84.2 %.

2   Indoor Versus Outdoor Settings

In this section we discuss the challenges and opportunities provided by respectively indoor and outdoor settings, and how they relate to a representative selection of the many methods for outdoor TMD.

2.1   Transportation Infrastructure

There are significant differences between outdoor and indoor transportation infrastructures, which may influence the results of TMD. Outdoor road networks are often practically unbounded in size, and the possible distance that a tracked person or vehicle may travel is practically unlimited. Indoor travels on the other hand, are bound by a building infrastructure, which greatly limits the sensible travels that may be performed. A result of this difference is that indoor travels are typically much shorter in both distance and time, compared to outdoor travels. For TMD this means that there is less time to determine a specific transportation mode, and that changes in transportation mode will typically happen more often in an indoor setting. In addition the smaller indoor route networks are likely to cause different acceleration profiles through, e.g., more turns and more stops.

Another significant difference between indoor and outdoor transportation infrastructures, is the availability of additional information on the route networks. For outdoor route networks, data is publicly and easily available on roads, biking paths, railways as well as bus stops and routes. This information is very useful for position-based TMD, as it can help limit the number of likely transportation modes [15]. For indoor settings however, this kind of information is much harder to achieve. Floor plans for buildings are only publicly available for a very limited set of buildings, typically large shopping malls and public places, e.g. railway stations. For other types of buildings, the floor plans may only be available in simple digital formats, such as pictures, which are ill suited for extracting e.g. the route network of hallways in a building [11].

2.2   Transportation Modes

In outdoor scenarios a variety of modes of transportation are common-place; similarly, also indoors, especially in large-scale environments and scenarios, several modes are available some of which overlap with outdoor equivalents. Figure 1 lists what we consider relevant indoor transportation modes. The color of the modes listed indicates, whether they are specific exclusively to indoor (green) or outdoor settings (orange), or whether they occur in variations both in- and outdoors (blue).

Note, that many of the transportation modes (and respectively vehicles) listed could be divided further: e.g. specializations exist for some of them for indoor and outdoor settings, respectively, such as electric versus fossil-fueled forklifts. Indoor transportation modes include various and sometimes specialized electric vehicles which are used as transportation aid in places such as hospitals, airports, or factories, e.g. small electric buses and luggage carts, scooters, bed-pushers and forklifts. These may be designed for and used only indoor, or may be vehicles which can be used in both indoor and outdoor settings.

A significant challenge inherent in most indoor settings relative to outdoor settings is the significantly lower difference in speed profiles of different transportation modes—which is due to foremost the lower top speeds in indoor environments. While it's possible to distinguish between e.g. a bicycle and a car based on maximum speed [15], it's significantly harder to distinguish a bike from an indoor electric vehicle, as the typical speeds fall in similar intervals.

A second challenge in distinguishing indoor transportation modes is that the various modes (resp. vehicles) share the same route network (in contrast to trains versus cars for outdoor travels); additionally most indoor route networks do not cause significant halting patterns during travels such as traffic lights and train stops do.

A further challenge for TMD is the lack of combustion engines in indoor vehicles. Combustion engines in vehicles vibrate at specific frequencies, for example when idling. Distinguishing (fossil-fueled) motorized from other transport modes can thus be facilitated—even when speed profiles for mode candidates are similar—through picking up engine frequencies, which can be achieved even by low-grade, and sub-optimally placed accelerometers, as they are common-place in people's smart phones [23]. Note though that while most indoor vehicle types are not fossil-fueled, recent research reports that electric vehicle motors emit high-frequency sounds which can be picked up by smartphone microphones [19]. This may help in distinguishing electrical vehicles from, e.g., human-powered bikes.

Figure 1 also shows a hierarchical model of transportation modes which we discuss in this paper. Such a hierarchical model gives raise to subdividing the problem of distinguishing (groups of) transportation modes—which brings the advantage of allowing dedicated classifiers for detection decisions on individual nodes, as exploited, e.g. by Hemminki et al. [7] for outdoor TMD. In the hierarchy in Fig. 1 higher entries group similar transportation modes, and consequently neighboring modes in the lower tiers are expected to be more challenging to distinguish.

The root of the hierarchical models resembles the distinction between *stationary* from *moving* activities. For *moving* activities we distinguish two main categories, namely *motorized* and *unmotorized* transport. This distinction is made due to their different qualities with regards to speed and movement patterns, where *motorized* vehicles typically have a different acceleration and speed profile when compared to *unmotorized* vehicles. For *motorized* indoor transports, we consider foremost *electric* vehicles. This category contains general vehicles such as electric *scooters* and *bikes*, but also specialized vehicles for specific settings and applications, e.g., electric forklifts for warehouses or bed-pushers for moving beds around at hospitals. For *unmotorized* transportation, several modes, using e.g. vehicles such as *bicycles* and *scooters*, as well as *walking*, are to be distinguished. The *stationary* activity category is further subdivided into *stationary active*, which covers activities not involving transportation, e.g. performing a stationary work task, while *resting* covers idling, i.e. the absence of significant physical activity.

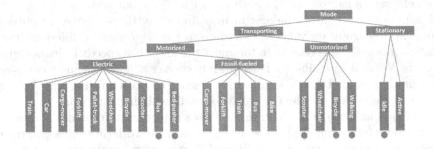

Fig. 1. Hierarchy of transportation modes. Orange: Outdoor-only modes. Green: Indoor-only modes (Color figure online).

As part of the exploration of indoor transportation modes, we collected transportation mode statistics in a real-world example scenario involving a variety of transportation mode choices, namely the daily work routines of a group of hospital orderlies throughout four days on a large modern hospital complex, covering 150,000 square meter on three floors. The statistics were collected by an assistant assigned to follow the orderlies (without interfering) throughout their work and keep record of the transportation modes they used. In total 300 transportation mode changes were collected, from 6 different modes (as marked in Fig. 1):

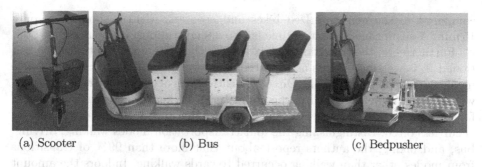

(a) Scooter   (b) Bus   (c) Bedpusher

Fig. 2. Common indoor transportation vehicles.

Stationary, walking, scooter, bike, e-bus and *e-bedpusher*, of which the last two are hospital-specific electric vehicles. The vehicles can be seen in Fig. 2. Table 1 shows the collected statistics. The upper part shows the number of transitions occurring between different transportation modes as a transition matrix, with transitions occurring from rows to columns in the matrix. The lower part lists the total number of trips made with each transportation mode, the total and relative time spent for each transportation mode, as well as the average time for a trip of the given mode.

Table 1. Number of transitions between different modes of transportation.

Transition	Stationary	Walking	Scooter	Bike	E-bedpusher	E-bus
Stationary	0	35	2	1	14	3
Walking	29	0	2	3	64	24
Scooter	2	1	0	0	1	0
Bike	1	4	0	0	0	0
E-bedpusher	16	61	0	0	0	6
E-bus	6	22	0	1	4	0
Total	54	123	4	5	83	33
Time	08:01:30	11:53:21	00:10:32	00:05:01	05:57:27	03:21:55
Percentage	27 %	40 %	0.6 %	0.3 %	20 %	11 %
Average	00:08:27	00:05:47	00:02:38	00:01:00	00:04:15	00:06:07

The table reveals that for all of the transportation modes the average trip duration is rather short (below ten minutes) as compared to typical outdoor scenarios. The mode the persons observed spent most time on during their work routine was walking, with almost 12 h over four work days. For motorized transportation, the bed pusher is used most often, with about 6 h, followed by the electric bus, with about 3 h. The motorized vehicles are clearly preferred compared to the non-motorized bikes and scooters, with in summation only 15 min. A significant amount of time is also spend stationary, about 8 h in total.

Furthermore, the transition matrix reveals that the mode most often transitioned to is walking. This is as expected since walking often serves as an intermediary transportation mode. Direct transitions do occur however, for example when changing between bed pushers and buses. When comparing with results for outdoor settings as presented, e.g., by Zheng et al. [24] the latter transitions occur less often: Distinguishing the four transportation modes walking, driving, bus, and biking, the authors report about that more than 99 % of transitions from modes other than walking occurred towards walking. Indoors the amount of direct transitions between non-walking modes is higher, which is likely due to the fact that outdoors the different transportation vehicles are spatially more separated, e.g., in roads, pavement and biking paths, as well as with regards to parking areas, which means that it is rarely possible to park right next to a bus stop. Indoors the different transportation modes share the same hallways, and to some degree also the same storage places, e.g. electric recharging stations for the electric buses and bed-pushers.

2.3   Available Sensing Technologies

As elaborated above, the sensing capabilities usable for TMD differ significantly between indoor and outdoor scenarios. Table 2 provides a generalised view of the availability and applicability of sensors in indoor and outdoor environments. In the following, we elaborate on these and their benefits and limitations. Furthermore, we provide pointers into how outdoor TMD make use of sensor modalities, before we overview in Sect. 3 methods which utilize respective sensor data methods for inferring transportation modes indoors.

Global Navigation Satellite Systems. GPS and similar satellite based systems provide—at least in most outdoor environments—ubiquitously available and precise positioning and speed estimates, on which many methods for TMD rely. GPS is not reliably available in indoor settings however, where direct signals from satellites are attenuated, refracted, and reflected by building infrastructure [9]. GPS as a data source is popular within TMD, see .e.g. [12,24], due to its comparatively reliable and direct speed data coming with accurate position samples in outdoor scenarios [22].

Radio-Based Sensing. Many radio-wave based systems, e.g., WiFi, GSM, Bluetooth and RFID, which are commonly available, e.g. on smartphones, give raise to position estimations. Apart from their use for communication, their signal's strength can be measured by the participating devices, beacons and mobile clients alike. The resulting *RSSI (received signal strength indicator)* data allows for coarse positioning, proximity detection, and for computing further features capturing motion characteristics of mobile clients. The technologies differ in wavelength and emission power, and thus also in range and accuracy. GSM provides very long ranges, up to 34 km, and is almost ubiquitously available, which makes it useful for both indoor and outdoor settings. However, as GSM also has comparatively little spatial variability, the accuracy is typically less than for shorter-range signals, such as Bluetooth or WiFi [10, 21]. With a maximum range of about 50 m the use of WiFi measurements require a nearby (and preferably dense) network, which makes it most useful for indoor (and urban) settings. Bluetooth and RFID have even lower maximum ranges, which makes them mostly useful for indoor settings or for use with specific gateways, as many beacons, resp. readers, are required to cover a large area. RFID is often used for proximity detection, and can provide very accurate positions, but only for the specific gateway locations where a reader is located. For these technologies the actual RSSI measurements can be performed either by the device or by the network. This makes it possible to track devices with no additional setup on the device, and potentially without the knowledge of the device owner. Maintenance and installation cost is an additional issue that may differ for indoor versus outdoor settings with regards to radio-based infrastructure. For covering outdoor settings, the infrastructure may need to cover a larger area, and beacons to be placed outside need to be resilient to the outdoor environment, potentially at a larger cost.

Kinetic Sensors. This covers sensors which are capable of sensing motion in different forms, e.g., accelerometers, gyroscopes and magnetometers. As these are common-place in, e.g., most modern smartphones, they can be used for a variety of application scenarios. They can help to identify movement and acceleration profiles of users to match with transportation modes, as well as be used for dead reckoning in addition to other positioning methods. Specifically for magnetometers however, issues usually arise when using it as a compass indoor, due to significant disturbances in the magnetic field caused by man-made building infrastructure.[1] Notwithstanding such issues, kinetic sensors are of use in TMD both for outdoor as well as for indoor scenarios, as they do not rely on any environmental sensor infrastructure and do not make strict assumptions about the environment. Thus, the respective TMD methods for outdoor scenarios [5, 7, 12] are useful and comparatively easy to adapt also for indoor scenarios.

Environmental Sensors. Within this category we group in-device sensors which inform about the user's (resp. the device's) current environment, e.g., microphone, light detectors and cameras. These may provide useful information relating to the transportation mode, e.g., microphones can be used to detect specific sounds of vehicles [19], as well as be used for positioning [20], while cameras can be used for positioning and object detection [2]. Such sensors are

---

[1] In fact, these disturbances are sufficiently significant that they give rise to positioning via fingerprinting instead: given a magnetic field fingerprint collection, a phone's location can subsequently be estimated within the fingerprinted environment by the local characteristics of the magnetic field as measured by the phone's magnetometer [1].

generally available in smartphones and may be used both indoors and outdoors. However, outdoor settings may provide additional challenges as the environment is less restricted and there are more potential sources of, e.g., noise and light; conversely, distinguishing vehicles outdoors is often easier than indoors due to the noisy engines in, e.g., most cars and buses, c.f. Sect. 2.2.

Table 2. Sensor types and their applicability for TMD in indoor and outdoor environments.

	GNSS	Radio-based	Kinetic	Environmental
Outdoor	✓	✓	(✓)	(✓)
Indoor	(-)	✓	✓	✓

2.4 Existing Approaches for TMD

This section discusses a representative selection of the many available methods for outdoor TMD, in order to determine their applicability for general indoor settings. Table 3 provides an overview of the selected methods, which are discussed in detail in the following.

Table 3. Selected related work on transportation mode detection.

Name	Reddy et al. [12]	Sohn et al. [14]	Stenneth et al. [15]	Hemminki et al. [7]
Modes	Stationary, walking, running, biking, motorized	Stationary, walking, driving	Stationary, walking, biking, car, bus, train	Stationary, walking, bus, train, metro, car
Sensors	GPS, accelerometer, (GSM)	GSM	GPS	Accelerometer
External Data	-	-	Bus locations, rail lines, bus stops	-

Reddy et al. [12] evaluate the usefulness of several sensors and methods for detecting five different transportation modes. They show that the methods can distinguish between those five modes with an overall accuracy of 93 %. However, these results are computed using ten-fold randomized cross-validation, which has a tendency to produce overly optimistic results, as we will elaborate on in Sect. 4. The authors conclude furthermore that the best trade-offs between energy-efficiency and accuracy are obtained by choosing GPS and accelerometer as sensors, and that supplying with WiFi and GSM sensor data is not improving accuracy significantly. Their results are instead for employing GPS for speed estimates and the accelerometer for basic statistical and frequency features. The chosen two complement each other well, since using only speed or frequency features does not allow for distinguishing between all transportation modes: E.g., distinguishing stationary mode from motorized transport moving at constant speed may be similar in acceleration patterns, but distinguishable by speed. On the opposite, running and biking can be similar in speed, but have different acceleration variances and dominating frequencies. Their methods are not directly applicable to indoor settings, due to the reliance on speed from GPS. However, on can (and we will) apply the accelerometer features they recommend also in indoor settings.

Hemminki et al. [7] rely solely on the accelerometer sensor for distinguishing still, walking, and four different motorized transport modes. They attribute their improvements in accuracy over related work mostly to a novel method for detecting the direction of gravity, and thereby of the phone's orientation. Knowing the latter is useful as it eases the comparison of acceleration patterns across phones with different orientations.

Sohn et al. [14] distinguish between three transportation modes: stationary, walking and driving. Their methods are based on collecting consecutive GSM fingerprints, between which the Euclidean distance in signal space is computed. They show that these distances correlate closely with the speed of a device, and achieve an accuracy of up to 90 % in distinguishing between the three modes. Their methods takes advantage of large expected speed differences of the considered modes—and thus it is not clear how their results generalize to further modes, and especially to indoor settings where most modes are similar in expected speed, c.f. Sect. 2.2. Their methods, however, are more or less directly applicable to WiFi fingerprints as well.

Stenneth et al. [15] use only GPS measurements, but utilize both speed and position estimates. In combination with external information on real-time bus locations, bus stop locations, and railway layouts, they are able to distinguish the motorized transportation modes into further detail, as either car, bus or train, which they are able to do with an accuracy of up to 93.5 %. The external information which they take advantage of is specific to outdoor settings, however it may be possible to employ some similar information from indoor settings, e.g., on locations of electric vehicle charging stations.

3   Features for Indoor Transportation Mode Detection

This section considers the sensing modalities which we consider most useful for indoor transportation mode detection, and presents features which we recommend to extract from the respective sensor data. While we will evaluate the respective features' usefulness solely in indoor scenarios, note that all of them are also applicable in non-indoor or mixed scenarios. Thus, the listed features can be deployed for outdoor settings without modification, by using the relevant technologies as input, e.g. GPS-retrieved positions instead of positions based on indoor positioning for the position-based features and GSM instead of WiFi for the signal-strength based features. In addition, further features will be applicable for outdoor settings, such as speed-based features from GPS speed-measurements [12].

The following description of features assumes that the input measurements are aggregated into time windows of a certain duration. We will discuss the size of the windows and other parameter values in Sect. 4.

3.1   Signal Strength Based Features

As described in Sect. 2.2, radio infrastructures allows clues about the user's position, proximity, and motion via measuring incoming signal strengths over time (either on the user device or by the beacons receiving the user device's radio messages). The signal strength measurements can stem from various sources, e.g., WiFi, Bluetooth or GSM beacons and are structured in *scans*, containing all the received signal strength values from all incoming radio transmitters measured in a single scanning. The frequency of scans, as well as the transmission power, depends on the technology and the specific device settings.

The general idea behind these signal strength based features is that due to the spatial variability of radio signals–and specifically their power loss over distance and when being attenuated by building infrastructure, the signal strength measurements received will vary when moving about—with greater variance when moving fast, e.g., on vehicles. However, variance in signal strength may also stem from other sources such as other people moving in vicinity, opening of doors, etc.

Variance. For each window of signal strength measurements, we compute the variance of the signal strength measurements for each beacon. Based on this we use as feature for the window the minimum, maximum and mean values over all beacons.

We compute variance in three forms, differing on the handling of beacons that do not occur in all scans in the window: (i) we remove beacons that are not in all scans in the window, (ii) we use a low default value for a beacon's signal strength when the beacon is missing in a scan, and (iii) we complete the computation using the values that are available, with no specific handling of missing values.

Access Points. For each window, we compute the number of beacons from which signal strength measurements have been received. To normalize for different beacon densities in different buildings or different parts of the same building, we also compute the number of beacons divided by respectively the average and total number of received signal strength measurements during each scan. The motivation behind these features is that the number of beacons from which measurements have been received serves as a measure of the size of the area covered in the time window at hand. In addition, we compute the number of changes in beacons, as the total number of either appearing or disappearing beacons in consecutive scans in the window. Given the fixed duration of the time window at hand, the above features serve as a proxy for speed.

Distance in Signal Space. For each pair of consecutive scans in each window, we compute the Euclidean distance in signal space between the samples. This is done by treating each access point as a dimension in the Euclidean distance formula, as described by Bahl et al. [3]. As features we extract the mean, minimum and maximum of the distances computed within a window.

3.2 Position Based Features

When a positioning system is available, we can use the (sequence of) timestamped position estimates to extract features. The usefulness of these features obviously depends on the accuracy of the positioning system used.

Movement Speed. We can compute an estimate of the current speed from (consecutive) position estimates. To mitigate the effects of positioning inaccuracies, we smooth the position sequence by computing the median trajectory of the given positions [4]. We then use these smoothed positions to compute the speed between each consecutive position estimates, from which we for each window compute the mean, maximum, minimum and end-to-end speed in the window, which are used as features.

3.3 Kinetic Features

Time Domain. The kinetic sensors we used include time-domain features which have been used for human activity recognition (HAR) in multiple systems, as described by Figo et al. [5]. The time-domain features include statistical measures such as mean, standard deviation, minimum and maximum values and root mean square. The full list of features used here is given by Figo et al. [5, Table 2].

For the time domain features, as for the following two classes of kinetic features, we employ accelerometer measurements from each axis x, y, z as well as the orientation-independent magnitude $\sqrt{x^2 + y^2 + z^2}$.

Frequency Domain. The kinetic features subsumed here are based on frequency analysis, which is useful for detecting (especially periodic) patters of movement, such as walking. These features include the normalized spectral coefficients from 0 to 20 Hz, the entropy of coefficients and the dominating frequency, see Figo et al. for a full list of features used here [5, Table 3].

ECDF Features. Additional to the explicitly chosen kinetic features above, we also employ feature learning in the form of *empirical cumulative distribution function (ECDF)* features, as described by Hammerla et al. [6] for accelerometer measurements. Note that while the kinetic features above can also be employed for kinetic sensors other than accelerometers, such as gyroscopes or magnetometers, ECDF features are expected to generalize even better—as they adapt to the patterns in the provided training data.

4   Evaluation

This section details the evaluations we have performed of the methods for indoor TMD described in Sect. 3. We evaluate the methods based on real-world data collected from a large hospital, as described in Sect. 4.2.

For evaluating approaches for indoor TMD, we undertook a real-world evaluation in a concrete case setting where accurate TMD provides significant value. Advantages of this choice includes the evaluation in the face of both real-world challenges, varying use-case scenarios and user behaviours, as well as a discussion of the real-world impacts of shortcomings in TMD accuracy and reliability.

4.1   Evaluation Setting

The scenario in which we evaluate indoor TMD methods lies within mHealth, specifically within hospital task logistics and focuses on the automatic scheduling and registering of tasks of orderlies. To this end, various prototypes have been evaluated in cooperation with hospital stakeholders and staff at several hospitals, including the one chosen as environment for this investigation [17]. To further improve the support of hospital work logistics, the automatic detection of which transportation modes the orderlies use promises the following improvements for the overall hospital logistics:

- *Travel time estimation:* Inferring transportation modes from collected data in real-time will provide more accurate travel time estimates for the current as well as for potential future tasks. That will in turn render task scheduling more efficient.
- *Navigation:* The available routes through a building are restricted by the transportation mode used, e.g., stairs cannot be used when on a vehicle. Thus, for navigational aids knowing the user's current mode is essential.
- *Task registration:* For automatic registration of tasks, detecting changes in transportation mode provides valuable clues for automatic trip detection—and may thus serve to detect the begin or ending of a task, or a task phase, or for determining which (sequence of) task types are being performed.
- *Vehicle management:* For managing upkeep for a fleet of vehicles, the amount, rate, and areas of use that each individual vehicle and each type of vehicle has seen can provide valuable input, both for scheduling maintenance as well as for optimizing the size of and default locations for the vehicle fleet.

4.2   Dataset

The dataset used comprises the activities of several orderlies throughout their daily work routines for four days—which include maintenance work, transporting patients, and similar tasks, which may require different transportation means, c.f. Sect. 2.2. When collecting data with an orderly, we supplied him with a smartphone which logged accelerometer and WiFi-scan signal-strength measurements, at the highest available frequencies. This was approximately 0.5 Hz for WiFi, and

200 Hz for accelerometer. The smartphone was carried in a shirt pocket where the orderlies would normally carry their phones, so we do not evaluate for different phone placement locations.[2]

Meanwhile, ground truth with regards to used transportation means was collected by a person following the orderly throughout his work. The person was following on an independent vehicle such as a bike, so as to influence neither the orderlies (and specifically: their choice of transportation means), nor the collected sensor measurements. We also had access to the WiFi network of the hospital, which allowed us to collect all signal-strength measurements made by the network for signals from the phone carried by the orderly.

4.3 Evaluation Methodology

For the evaluation, in line with standard practices in activity recognition research, we use the F_1-score, which is the harmonic mean of precision and recall [13].

The evaluations are performed using 10-fold cross-validation. However, we do not use random folds for the cross-validation, as random folding is prone to provide overly optimistic results when dealing with time-series data. Due to being collected close in time, neighbouring measurements will often be similar, but may be selected for different folds. Thus the classifier will be trained on measurements that are similar to those which are tested on. Instead we split folds on time, so that the first fold will be the first tenth of the data time-wise, etc. This ensures that the folds are completely independent, as they will stem from different trips made by the orderlies. For comparison we performed the evaluation of Sect. 4.4 also using random-fold cross-validation which resulted in an unrealistically high F-score of 99.2 %, as compared to the F-score of 84.2 % when using time-folded cross-validation.

We evaluate four different classifiers that are popular for use in human activity recognition, namely nearest neighbour classifier with $k = 5$, C4.5 decision tree, support vector machines (SVM), and random forest.

4.4 Detecting Transportation Means

In this section, we present overall accuracies for detecting different transportation modes, in different layers of the transportation mode model, as shown in Fig. 3. Two hospital-specific vehicles are included: The e-bus and the e-bedpusher. Both are electric vehicles which serve two different purposes. The e-bus is used for fast transport by an orderly, as well as up to two passengers which are typically patients at the hospital. The bed-pusher is designed for use by an orderly for fast and easy transportation of bed-bound patients - however the orderly may also use it for transporting just himself.

---

[2] While the assumptions of homogeneity in device placement and smartphone model are valid in the use scenario of this study, such homogeneity may be missing in other scenarios and lead to lower accuracies for distinguishing transportation modes, see, e.g., [7,16].

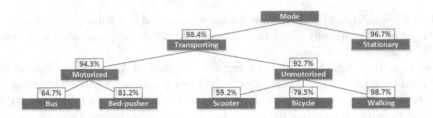

Fig. 3. Accuracy in detecting different levels of transportation means.

For the evaluation we used a random forest learner, parametrized to train 100 trees, and a window size of 10 s for accelerometer measurements, and for Wi-Fi measurements we use a hierarchy of window sizes: a short one of 10 s and a large one of 60 s. Later on we will discuss the influence of the chosen parameters, specifically for various classifiers in Sect. 4.6, and for various window sizes in Sect. 4.8. Complementing Figs. 3 and 4 shows the resulting confusion matrix. Figure 3 shows the accuracy in the different layers of the transportation mode model. Note that F-scores given at each node refer to the task of distinguishing that node's mode from just its siblings' modes. It is visible, that when only distinguishing between categories of upper-level layers, distinguishing is done accurately, e.g., for the top-level categories "transporting" and "stationary"—with an F-score of 98.6 %. Considering more specific transporting subclasses, for distinguishing between motorized and unmotorized transportation, the accuracy falls to an F-score of 92.8 %. This fall continues when distinguishing between the two quite similar motorized vehicles considered: bus and bedpusher—with an F-score of only 61.0 %. For distinguishing unmotorized transportation, results are better: walking is detected correctly 98.7 % of the time, whereas the scooter and bike transportation - for which we have only little data - are harder to detect. This may also be due to that the movements may look similar to walking, e.g. for powering a scooter. In total the modes of the unmotorized category can be detected with an F-score of 97.5 %.

To a large degree the results match the expectations. The features can accurately determine whether the user is moving or not, since the typical values of both WiFi and kinetic features are well separated for these two cases. The motorized and unmotorized categories can also be distinguished quite clearly, likely due to the fact that a person riding a motorized vehicle will be standing still on the vehicle, while a person riding a unmotorized vehicle will move in order to power the vehicle, or in order to walk - causing characteristic (and usually: periodic) movement patterns. The distinction between bus and bed-pusher, however, was likely to be hard—as both vehicles are quite similar, specifically they are both electrically-powered and drive at about the same speeds.

4.5   Evaluating Different Sensor and Feature Types

In this section, we evaluate the usefulness of the different feature and sensor types, as well as of individual features, for indoor TMD.

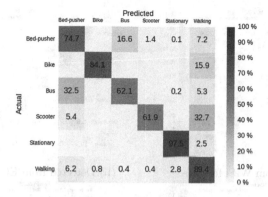

Fig. 4. Confusion matrix based on accelerometer and WiFi features

Comparing the Usefulness of Different Feature Types. We will do so by evaluating—for all the transportation modes for which we have collected data—various candidates using different combinations of feature types. Figure 5a shows the resulting confusion matrix when using only WiFi features, while Figs. 5b, c and d show confusion matrices for employing solely accelerometer features of one of the three kinetic feature types, respectively: ECDF, time-domain and frequency-domain features. Table 4 shows F-scores for use of individual feature-types as well as for any combination of features, ordered by F-scores.

For individual feature types the results show that the type providing the best results for classification of these indoor transportation modes are the kinetic time-domain features with an F-score of 78.9 %, the next best being WiFi features with an F-score of 76.0 %, followed by ECDF and frequency-domain features. These results are mirrored in the combined features, where the best results are achieved by a combination of time-domain accelerometer features and the WiFi features, with an F-score of 84.2 %. Interesting to note is that for all combinations of accelerometer-based features, the inclusion of WiFi features improves the results.

The individual figures show that accelerometer has better performance than WiFi when distinguishing walking from the motorized vehicles. As the vehicles may at times drive at speeds close to walking, it may be hard to distinguish them based on WiFi features, while the accelerometer features will be much more distinct due to the specific movement patterns from walking. On the other hand, WiFi features are significantly better for distinguishing stationary from walking, as they can distinguish shifting weight between legs or shuffling around from walking a distance. In this way the ability of accelerometers to detect very small-scale movements complement the ability of WiFi to detect major movements.

Comparing the Importance of Individual Features. In order to evaluate which particular features appear most useful, we measured accuracy changes

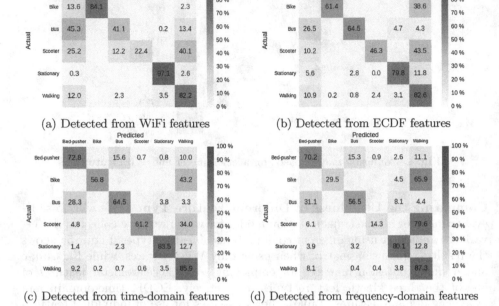

(a) Detected from WiFi features

(b) Detected from ECDF features

(c) Detected from time-domain features

(d) Detected from frequency-domain features

Fig. 5. Confusion matrices holding F-scores when using a single feature type.

Table 4. The results for different combinations of feature types

ECDF	-	-	-	✓	✓	✓	✓	-	-	✓	✓	✓	-	-	✓
Frequency	-	✓	✓	✓	-	-	✓	-	✓	-	✓	✓	-	✓	-
Time	✓	✓	-	-	✓	-	-	✓	✓	✓	✓	-	-	-	-
WiFi	✓	✓	✓	✓	✓	✓	✓	-	-	-	-	-	✓	-	-
Result	84.2	83.9	83.5	83.1	83.0	82.8	82.8	78.9	78.9	78.6	78.6	77.7	76.0	75.9	75.7

resulting from including (vs. excluding) individual features. Figure 6 shows for each of the features types—WiFi, ECDF, time-domain, and frequency-domain features— the five features which by themselves cause the highest accuracy gains. The most important ones among the WiFi features we used, are based on the number of unique access points seen in a time window—which is a rather crude proxy of the area covered in that window, and in turn for speed. Less well performing are WiFi features based on variance in signal strength measurements, or on the estimation of speed via WiFi positioning data (likely due to the inaccuracy of the latter). For the ECDF features notably the higher bins appear important, suggesting that the values in the high end of the histogram are best for distinguishing transportation modes. From the time domain kinetic features, variance and standard deviation, as well as the 75 percentile of the normalized measurements show high importance. As with the well performing ECDF features, the feature values' independence of phone orientation is likely to be helpful. Although, also useful appear the variance and standard deviation of measurements on the y-axis—which is for normal phone orientation the axis which captures upwards and downwards movement best, and is thus helpful for detecting, e.g., steps during walking. For the frequency domain features, features covering movements in the frequency range from 0 to 2 Hz are dominating, which is a bandwidth which captures well the characteristics of many common human movement patterns [18].

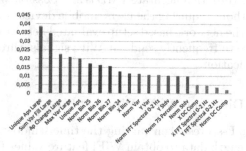

Fig. 6. Computed feature importance for the 5 most important features of each type. Blue: WiFi, Orange: Accelerometer-ECDF, Green: Acc-Time, Yellow: Acc-Frequency (Color figure online)

4.6 Evaluating Different Classifiers

We evaluate several candidate classifiers in regards to their usefulness for indoor TMD when using combined accelerometer and WiFi features. We selected candidates that are often used in similar classification tasks such as activity detection and TMD, as described in Sect. 3. For each candidate, we have experimented with the relevant parameters; we obtained best results, e.g. for $C4.5$ tree classifier when setting a max-depth of 10, and for the random forest, results did not improve when using more than 150 trees. For the K-nearest neighbours algorithm, we found $K = 3$ to work best. Table 5 presents F-scores of time-folded cross-validation for each of the classifiers. We see that random forests seem to be superior to support vector machines and K-nearest neighbour classifiers in this setup, while all are superior to the C4.5 classifiers. A likely reason is that the setup is prone to overfitting, and that thus the more resilient classifiers perform better; e.g. random forests profit from the several trained trees voting to reach a common verdict. These results and explanations are in line with those reported by Sagha et al. [13] for indoor activity recognition.

4.7 Network- Versus Client-Based Wi-Fi Signal Strength Measurements

Access to the WiFi network infrastructure at the hospital site allowed us to evaluate also (the differences between) using network-based and client-based WiFi

Table 5. F-scores when using different classifiers.

Learner	C4.5	K-NN	SVM	Random forest
F_1-score (%)	78.6	81.2	81.6	84.1

signal strength data collection. The results showed an only marginal F-score decrease of 0.2 when using network-collected instead of on-phone-collected measurements—and thus, that accurate TMD is also possible when using network-based WiFi, i.e., without requiring the users' mobile devices to perform measurements. Note that in the network-based setup evaluated here we do however depend on the mobile device to frequently send out WiFi signals, through WiFi scans or other data communication.

4.8   Evaluating Different Wi-Fi Window Size

Table 6 presents the F-scores when varying the time window size over which we aggregate signal strength data to obtain WiFi feature values from 10 up to 640 s. The accuracy improves significantly when increasing a smaller window size, but the increase lessens once sizes reach a minute, and using a window size of 10 min provides for worse results than for 5 min. The optimal choice for a window size relates to the expected trip length. As shown in Table 1, the trips performed are on average below 9 min for all transportation modes. Increasing the window size beyond yields high chances that several transportation modes are covered in a given time window. Additionally, increased window sizes also increase the response-time for detecting transportation mode changes in a real-time setting.

Table 6. F-scores for the different window sizes of WiFi features.

Window size	10 s	20 s	40 s	1 min 20 s	2 min 40 s	5 min 20 s	10 min 40 s
F_1-score (%)	66.8	69.1	72.6	77.1	78.1	81.4	80.3

4.9   Evaluating the Usefulness of Additional Tagging of Vehicles

For cases where the transportation modes are hard to distinguish due to similar movement profiles, e.g., for bus versus bed-pusher vehicles, the accuracy can be improved by fitting WiFi tags onto such vehicles. To evaluate the usefulness of WiFi tags, we fitted a bus and a bed-pusher with tags that performed WiFi scans every 10 s. These scans were collected by the WiFi infrastructure during our observation of the orderlies. From the collected scans we computed as features the Euclidean distance in signal space of the orderlies' WiFi measurements to those of respectively the bus and the bed-pusher WiFi tags—the intuition here being that when the order drives, e.g. a bus, he will be in close proximity to the bus tag, resulting in a low signal space distance. Figure 7 shows an example of the computed signal space distance before, during, and after a trip on a bed-pusher. It shows how the distance decreases when the user approaches the tag, and it is consistently low while he drives the bed-pusher. Our evaluation showed that with the addition of tags, the distinction between bus and bedpusher improved from an F-score of 49.3 % to an F-score of 82.3 %. However, this approach may not work in situations where several types of vehicles are driven in closer proximity— in which case co-movement detection could be used on sequences of position estimates for further disambiguation [8].

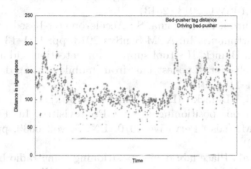

Fig. 7. Distance in signal space between the user and tag placed on bed-pusher.

5 Conclusions

Through the performed evaluations we have shown that automatic detection of transportation modes using mobile devices such as smartphones is possible also in indoor settings. The results show that accelerometer or WiFi measurements can be used individually to detect transportation modes, but that a combination of both provides for improved results: Accelerometer-based features show strength in distinguishing between walking and vehicles, while WiFi is especially useful for determining whether a user is moving or not, and for distinguishing between vehicles used in case those are WiFi-tagged. Future work includes automatic detection of transportation modes also in mixed indoor and outdoor setting, in order to support e.g., logistics in such settings. Furthermore, also additional sensors and respective fusion techniques, e.g. orientation-aware motion sensor features, may provide further accuracy gains. Finally, it is left as future work to explore the impact of different device placements and models on the classification accuracy.

References

1. Indoor Atlas. http://www.indooratlas.com. Accessed 3 August 2015
2. Asmar, D.C., Zelek, J.S., Abdallah, S.M.: Smartslam: localization and mapping across multi-environments. In: Proceedings of International Conference Systems, Man and Cybernetics (2004)

3. Bahl, P., Padmanabhan, V.N.: Radar: an in-building RF-based user location and tracking system. In: Proceedings of IEEE Conference Computer Communications, pp. 775–784 (2000)
4. Buchin, K., Buchin, M., van Kreveld, M., Lffler, M., Silveira, R., Wenk, C., Wiratma, L.: Median trajectories. Algorithmica 66(3), 595–614 (2013)
5. Figo, D., Diniz, P.C., Ferreira, D.R., Cardoso, J.M.P.: Preprocessing techniques for context recognition from accelerometer data. Pers. Ubiquit. Comput. 14(7), 645–662 (2010)
6. Hammerla, N.Y., Kirkham, R., Andras, P., Plötz, T.: On preserving statistical characteristics of accelerometry data using their empirical cumulative distribution. In: Proceedings of ISWC 2013 (2013)
7. Hemminki, S., Nurmi, P., Tarkoma, S.: Accelerometer-based transportation mode detection on smartphones. In: ACM SenSys 2013, pp. 13:1–13:14. ACM (2013)
8. Kjærgaard, M.B., Blunck, H.: Tool support for detection and analysis of following and leadership behavior of pedestrians from mobile sensing data. Pervasive Mob. Comput. 10, 104–117 (2014)
9. Kjærgaard, M.B., Blunck, H., Godsk, T., Toftkjær, T., Christensen, D.L., Grønbæk, K.: Indoor positioning using GPS revisited. In: Floréen, P., Krüger, A., Spasojevic, M. (eds.) Pervasive 2010. LNCS, vol. 6030, pp. 38–56. Springer, Heidelberg (2010)
10. LaMarca, A., et al.: Place lab: device positioning using radio beacons in the wild. In: Gellersen, H.-W., Want, R., Schmidt, A. (eds.) Pervasive 2005. LNCS, vol. 3468, pp. 116–133. Springer, Heidelberg (2005)
11. Prentow, T.S., Thom, A., Blunck, H., Vahrenhold, J.: Making sense of trajectory data in indoor spaces. In: IEEE 16th International Conference Mobile Data Management (2015)
12. Reddy, S., Mun, M., Burke, J., Estrin, D., Hansen, M., Srivastava, M.: Using mobile phones to determine transportation modes. ACM Trans. Sen. Netw. 6(2), 13:1–13:27 (2010)
13. Sagha, H., Digumarti, S., del R. Millan, J., Chavarriaga, R., Calatroni, A., Roggen, D., Tröster, G.: Benchmarking classification techniques using the opportunity human activity dataset. In: IEEE Systems, Man, and Cybernetics (SMC) (2011)
14. Sohn, T., et al.: Mobility detection using everyday GSM traces. In: Dourish, P., Friday, A. (eds.) UbiComp 2006. LNCS, vol. 4206, pp. 212–224. Springer, Heidelberg (2006)
15. Stenneth, L., Wolfson, O., Yu, P.S., Xu, B.: Transportation mode detection using mobile phones and gis information. In: Proceedings of 19th ACM GIS, pp. 54–63. ACM (2011)
16. Stisen, A., Blunck, H., Bhattacharya, S., Prentow, T.S., Kjærgaard, M.B., Dey, A., Sonne, T., Jensen, M.M.: Smart devices are different: assessing and mitigating mobile sensingheterogeneities for activity recognition. In: ACM SenSys 2015. ACM (2015)
17. Stisen, A., Verdezoto, N., Blunck, H., Kjærgaard, M.B., Grønbæk, K.: Accounting for the invisible work of hospital orderlies: designing for local and global coordination. In: ACM CSCW 2016. ACM (2016)
18. Sun, M., Hill, J.: A method for measuring mechanical work and work efficiency during human activities. J. Biomech. 26(3), 229–241 (1993)
19. Takagi, M., Fujimoto, K., Kawahara, Y., Asami, T.: Detecting hybrid and electric vehicles using a smartphone. In: ACM UbiComp 2014, pp. 267–275 (2014)

20. Tarzia, S.P., Dinda, P.A., Dick, R.P., Memik, G.: Indoor localization without infrastructure using the acoustic background spectrum. In: Proceedings of MobiSys 2011 (2011)
21. Varshavsky, A., de Lara, E., Hightower, J., LaMarca, A., Otsason, V.: GSM indoor localization. Pervasive Mob. Comput. **3**(6), 698–720 (2007)
22. Witte, T., Wilson, A.: Accuracy of non-differential GPS for the determination of speed over ground. J. Biomech. **37**(12), 1891–1898 (2004)
23. Wüstenberg, M., Blunck, H., Grønbæk, K., Kjærgaard, M.B.: Distinguishing electric vehicles from fossil-fueled vehicles with mobile sensing. In: IEEE MDM (2014)
24. Zheng, Y., Chen, Y., Li, Q., Xie, X., Ma, W.: Understanding transportation modes based on GPS data for web applications. TWEB **4**(1) (2010)

Indoor Navigation with a Smartphone Fusing Inertial and WiFi Data via Factor Graph Optimization

Michał Nowicki[✉] and Piotr Skrzypczyński

Institute of Control and Information Engineering, Poznań University of Technology,
Ul. Piotrowo 3A, 60-965 Poznań, Poland
{michal.nowicki,piotr.skrzypczynski}@put.poznan.pl

Abstract. Mobile devices are getting more capable every year, allowing a variety of new applications, such like supporting pedestrian navigation in GPS-denied environments. In this paper we deal with the problem of combining in real-time dead reckoning data from the inertial sensors of a smartphone, and the WiFi signal fingerprints, which enable to detect the already visited places and therefore to correct the user's trajectory. While both these techniques have been used before for indoor navigation with smartphones, the key contribution is the new method for including the localization constraints stemming from the highly uncertain WiFi fingerprints into a graphical problem representation (factor graph), which is then optimized in real-time on the smartphone. This method results in an Android-based personal navigation system that works robustly with only few locations of the WiFi access points known in advance, avoiding the need to survey WiFi signal in the whole area. The presented approach has been evaluated in public buildings, achieving localization accuracy which is sufficient for both pedestrian navigation and location-aware applications on a smartphone.

Keywords: Navigation · Localization · Factor graph · Data fusion · WiFi · IMU · Smartphone · Android

1   Introduction

Nowadays smartphones became a viable computation platform to implement indoor localization in GPS-denied environments. Indoor localization functionality for mobile devices is commercially available using services provided by such companies as Skyhook [22], which maintain WiFi and cellular fingerprint databases for specific locations. However, such solutions require to survey the area in order to obtain a signal strength map, which is time consuming and expensive. Moreover, the user has to have a persistent Internet connection to the database provider. Therefore, we are interested in self-localization solutions for smartphones that do not require laborious surveying of the locations, but use opportunistic sensing of signals from the ubiquitous wireless networks to enable

© Institute for Computer Sciences, Social Informatics and Telecommunications Engineering 2015
S. Sigg et al. (Eds.): MobiCASE 2015, LNICST 162, pp. 280–298, 2015.
DOI: 10.1007/978-3-319-29003-4_16

pedestrian navigation in unknown, cluttered environments. One of the possible approaches is to use WiFi fingerprinting without a presurveyed database of places. This solution can be then combined with visual appearance-based location verification algorithm, as in [19]. However, such a system is able to tell the user only his discrete location, and cannot provide a continuous pose estimate to a pedestrian. Thus, we propose a solution that combines WiFi fingerprinting with the Pedestrian Dead Reckoning (PDR) for continuous localization.

The problem we have to deal with is how to combine the user's trajectory estimate obtained from a dead reckoning algorithm exploiting the inertial sensors and magnetometer of a smartphone, and the WiFi signal fingerprinting method, which allows for detection of already visited places. Thus, the system has the ability to close a loop, if the user re-visits a location that was previously associated with a fingerprint. The information coming from both sources is very different as to the spatial uncertainty characteristics, but both sources define useful constraints as to the current location of the user. We formulate the smartphone localization problem in a graphic model, as optimization of a graph of constraints that are related to the sensory observations. The resulting factor graph has a sparse structure and can be optimized in real-time on the smartphone using the Android port of the g^2o general graph optimization library [15] applying the Preconditioned Conjugate Gradient (PCG) algorithm.

Our solution assumes that only a small fraction of the WiFi networks existing at the given area has been pre-labeled and anchored to the floor plan. We do not assume a dense distribution of the WiFi Access Points (APs), and we can work with few APs in the area. The proposed system does not need an off-line learning or calibration stage. Although full simultaneous localization and mapping (SLAM) solutions based on WiFi signals that enable to obtain a map of the APs in the area are known from the literature [9], they usually assume an environment densely populated by the WiFi networks and are computation intensive, thus they are unsuitable for implementation on a smartphone. Thus, a solution which requires to know only few APs in the area is advantageous, as the APs can be easily anchored to a known floor plan uploaded to the smartphone (we use standard building blueprints digitized to images). The WiFi nodes may be attached to known locations in the global coordinates, or can be discovered opportunistically, and treated as labelled poses. All computations are performed on a smartphone.

2   Related Work

The rapid proliferation of high-end smartphones has brought a growing interest among the researchers in using these devices for indoor navigation. One of the possibilities is to use the camera of a smartphone and a monocular visual odometry algorithm implemented on Android platform to estimate user motion. However, existing research [6] demonstrated that real-time operation of a simple visual odometry pipeline is only possible if there is no significant motion blur and there are not sudden orientation changes, which makes it an impractical solution.

Therefore, we are interested in exploring other sensing modalities for smartphone-based navigation. Various forms of dead reckoning have been considered for mobile devices, e.g. as an aid to visually impaired users [21]. Reliable pedestrian dead reckoning may be obtained by combining robust attitude estimation of a smartphone [7] with a smartphone-based pedometer [25]. The literature is also rich in papers concerning using WiFi for indoor localization. A survey of the possible localization methods is given in [17]. The WiFi triangulation uses three or more line-of-sight AP positions to determine position of the receiver based on the measured signal strength of each network [1]. To localize in areas where the signal strength from particular APs may vary due to occlusions and attenuation the WiFi fingerprinting approach is more appropriate [2]. This technique was already demonstrated to be feasible in smartphones [16], and was applied to localize elderly patients by means of Android application [10].

Also systems employing more than one sensor type and localization method have been investigated. Some researchers used sensors that were equivalent to those employed in mobile devices, but did not perform the experiments on actual smartphones/tablets, like Quigley *et al.* [20], who investigated combination of vision, accelerometer, and WiFi signal-strength measurements for localization. This approach required also to build a priori map of the environment using a mobile robot equipped with a laser scanner. The WiFi fingerprinting technique is a basis for the multimodal localization solution for smartphones presented in [18]. Dead reckoning from smartphone-embedded inertial sensors is used together with an independent position estimate from WiFi fingerprinting and a pre-built environment map to localize the user in [14]. In this system a particle filter is applied to obtain the final pose estimate. Similarly, Wu *et al.* [24] applied off-line a particle filter to fuse WiFi and inertial data from a smartphone for indoor localization. To implement SLAM relying on the WiFi strength signals also other off-line optimization frameworks have been applied. Ferris *et al.* [5] used Gaussian processes to obtain a map of WiFi signal strength in a given area, avoiding to model explicitly the radio signal propagation. A GraphSLAM-like algorithm is employed in [9] for localization using only the WiFi signal strength. However, the off-line approaches cannot be implemented on a smartphone and used for real-time indoor navigation. A more computation efficient approach for the fusion of WiFi and inertial data from a smartphone was demonstrated in [4]. This approach employs Kalman filtering and estimates the user location with respect to the WiFi APs by computing the distances upon a signal propagation model. Unfortunately, using such a model in real indoor environments usually yields highly inaccurate distance measurements, which renders this approach rather impractical.

Recently, factor graphs became an increasingly popular framework for solving real-time SLAM and similar navigation problems [8]. Although most of the applications of this framework to navigation assume a single sensor type, there are notable works demonstrating that factor graphs are also a viable solution for multi-sensor integration. Indelman *et al.* [11] used factor graph formulation for information fusion in IMU-based navigation systems with constrained computation resources. Research within the DARPA All Source Positioning and

Navigation project demonstrated that the extended, sliding-window factor graphs can be used to integrate data from many sensor types in a plug-and-play manner [3]. However, none of these works tackled the problem of modelling WiFi fingerprinting constraints in the factor graph framework, neither demonstrated real-time performance on such a low-power and resource constrained device as a smartphone.

3   Indoor Localization in a Smartphone

Modern smartphones provide a variety of sensors, but the proposed graph-based localization scheme focuses on the use of inertial sensors (accelerometer, magnetometer and gyroscope) and data from the WiFi signal scanning. The overall structure of the processing pipeline is presented in Fig. 1. The main modules include: the stepometer that uses data from accelerometers, orientation estimation based on the Adaptive Extended Kalman Filter (AEKF) that fuses data from inertial sensors and mangnetometer, and WiFi fingerprints matching that exploits WiFi signal scans provided by the Android OS. The user poses and localization-relevant constraints estimated by these modules are then used to build a factor graph, which is optimized providing to the user the current pose estimate in real-time.

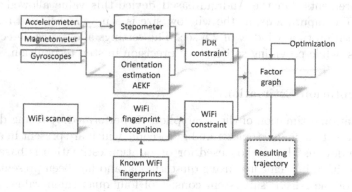

Fig. 1. Processing pipeline of the proposed navigation system

3.1   Stepometer

The stepometer, called also pedometer, is a subsystem that measures the user movement by detecting user's steps. Smartphones are a perfect platform to run stepometer processing, as the modern devices contain accelerometers and enough processing power, while the users keep them close to their bodies. In the presented system, the step detection is performed by computing the FFT of the accelerometer signal in a moving window, which is a simplified version of the algorithm presented in [12]. To reduce the influence of the device orientation on the step detection, the magnitude of the accelerometer signal is processed. The steps are considered to be detected if the dominant frequency f found by the FFT is between the values of 1.3Hz and 2.0Hz. Knowing the person's step length s (default value measured in tests for an adult male person was 0.65 m), it is possible to compute the covered distance using:

$$d_i = s \cdot f_i \cdot \frac{n}{n_w}, \tag{1}$$

where d_i denotes the covered distance in i-th iteration, f_i is the found dominant frequency for the moving window in i-th iteration, n is the number of new accelerometer measurements since the last stepometer output computation, and n_w is the number of accelerometer measurements in the processing window. If the total covered distance value d is sought, it is computed by summing up the partial distances d_i from each processing iteration.

The precision of the stepometer defined by (1) depends on the precision of step size s estimate and the moving window size n_w. Larger window sizes result in more precise frequency estimation, but with greater latency in the detection of user movement or even inability to detect sudden motion. Smaller window size gives an ability to detect those rapid movements, but results in more false-positive step detections. In the proposed system the window size is equal to 512 measurements. On the Android-based device this value allowed to easily utilize DFT computations, as the window size is a power of 2, and resulted in the computation time-window of 2.5 sec. The settings allowed to detect sudden movements, while providing satisfactory precision in step recognition.

3.2   Orientation Estimation

The orientation estimation of the smartphone is performed by fusing data from the accelerometers, magnetometer and gyroscope, which are present in any modern mobile device. The method used for orientation estimation is based on the AEKF algorithm implemented using quaternions, and has been presented in [7]. The state of the AEKF subsystem consist of four quaternion values and estimates of three gyroscope biases. The magnetometer and accelerometer data are combined to estimate the smartphone coordinate system in the ENU global reference system (X – East, Y – North, Z – Up). The covariance matrices used in the system were estimated by the PSO optimization algorithm [13], and the AEKF parameter values used here are consistent with the optimal parameters presented in [7].

3.3   WiFi Fingerprinting

In the proposed system, the WiFi fingerprint matching approach is utilized [1]. It is possible to: (i) compare the current WiFi scan to a pre-existing database of fingerprints taken at known locations, (ii) compare the current WiFi scan to the WiFi fingerprints recorded earlier during the system operation. The former method assumes that before the start of a navigation task a small set of WiFi scans is taken in known poses of the user, and these fingerprints are stored in the memory of the smartphone. The procedure to obtain these WiFi fingerprints is straightforward and fast, as only WiFi scans in few selected locations are needed. The latter operation mode assumes no prior knowledge of the environment as only the WiFi scans taken during the system operation are compared. The matching of WiFi fingerprints provides localization constraints equivalent to the loop closure mechanism in SLAM, as it detects previously visited locations (either known a priori or discovered) and allows to reduce the dead reckoning drift.

Both of the proposed modes rely solely on comparing the two WiFi scans $\mathcal{X}$ and $\mathcal{Y}$. One of the scans $\mathcal{X}$ is the currently scanned, and the second scan $\mathcal{Y}$ comes from the stored database, either created in advance, or discovered during the system operation. The Euclidean norm between signal strength values of networks found in both scans is used to compare the fingerprints:

$$d(\mathcal{X}, \mathcal{Y}) = \sqrt{\frac{\sum_{i=1}^{N}(\mathcal{X}_i - \mathcal{Y}_i)^2}{N}}, \tag{2}$$

where $\mathcal{X}_i$ and $\mathcal{Y}_i$ are the strengths of i-th shared network between both scans, $\mathcal{X}$ and $\mathcal{Y}$, while N is the number of shared networks found in both scans. It is assumed that if the Euclidean distance $d(\mathcal{X}, \mathcal{Y})$ is less than a threshold d_{WiFi} then the fingerprints match. In the proposed solution $d_{\text{WiFi}} = 8$ dBm was used. If the Euclidean distance test was passed, the number of networks N shared between the two scans $\mathcal{X}$ and $\mathcal{Y}$ is compared to the number of WiFi networks detected in each scan, N_X and N_Y, respectively. If $N > p \times N_X$ and $N > p \times N_Y$ then the WiFi fingerprint matching is considered to be correct, where p denotes an experimentally set parameter, which may vary between environments. In the proposed system it is set to 0.75.

If the WiFi scans taken during system operation are added to the database, the number of necessary comparisons grows linearly with the number of records in the database. We deal with this problem by having a dedicated thread responsible for WiFi place recognition, which compares WiFi scans prioritized in a queue according to the difference in their IDs. If the database has grown to a size that prevents real-time operation, the fingerprints with lowest priority are omitted in the comparison.

4   Factor Graph Representation

The main contribution of this paper is the data fusion scheme using the factor graph representation and non-linear least-squares optimization. This formulation of the SLAM problem is considered the state of the art in mobile robotics [8], but is novel in the context of pedestrian navigation with sparse WiFi fingerprints, and in the context of real-time, Android-based implementation.

To find the most plausible sequence of the nodes (user poses or map positions with known WiFi scans) $\mathbf{p}_i \in SE(2)$, $i = 1 \ldots n$ satisfying k constraints existing in the factor graph the following function is minimized:

$$\underset{\mathbf{p}}{\operatorname{argmin}} \ F = \sum_{i=1}^{n} \sum_{j=1}^{k} e_j(\mathbf{p}_i, \mathbf{m}_{ij})^T \mathbf{\Omega}_{ij} e_j(\mathbf{p}_i, \mathbf{m}_{ij}), \tag{3}$$

where $e_j(\mathbf{p}_i, \mathbf{m}_{ij})$ is the error function of j-th constraint $j = 1 \ldots k$, evaluated for the estimated pose of the node and the measured pose of the node stemming from the j-the measurement $\mathbf{m}_{ij}$ related to this pose. The poses $\mathbf{p}$ for known WiFi scans are anchored to the map coordinate system and cannot be moved by optimization process. The measurement means either the user motion estimate (from PDR) or the measurement resulting from two matching WiFi fingerprints. The information matrix $\mathbf{\Omega}_{ij}$ models uncertainty of the computed error.

4.1   PDR Motion Constraints

To represent the motion constraints imposed by the PDR-estimated motion of the user, it was decided to use the *EDGE:SE2* factor graph edge defined in the g^{2}o library. This edge represents the measurement between two 2D poses as: $EDGE:SE2 = (\Delta x, \Delta y, \Delta\Theta)$, where Δx and Δy are the measured distances along the X and Y axis w.r.t. the local coordinate system. The $\Delta\Theta$ is the difference between the orientations of both connected user poses. Because the PDR employs two independent subsystems to estimate the covered distance and the orientation change, the information matrix $\mathbf{\Omega}^{\mathrm{pdr}}$ was assumed to have the form:

$$\mathbf{\Omega}^{\mathrm{pdr}} = \begin{bmatrix} I_{2\times2} & 0_{2\times1} \\ 0_{1\times2} & k \end{bmatrix}, \tag{4}$$

where the k parameter was determined experimentally, to allow the g^{2}o optimization software to trust more in the pedometer distance than in the orientation estimate, which can degrade due to very sharp turns or in presence of magnetic fields in the vicinity. We got best results with $k \geq 10$.

4.2   WiFi Fingerprint Constraints

The WiFi fingerprint information represents some belief that the user is located in a vicinity of an already visited or previously mapped location, but such a constraint cannot be easily converted into an existing g^{2}o edge, due to its topological relation rather than metric measurement nature. Therefore, we propose a novel factor graph edge, which directly represents any information that can be understood as vicinity measurement. Such vicinity measurement is represented as an edge with the error function:

$$\mathrm{Err}(x) = \begin{cases} 0 & d_{\mathrm{err}}(x) < d_{\min} \\ \mathrm{Err}_{\max} & d_{\mathrm{err}}(x) > d_{\max} \\ \mathrm{Err}_{\max} \frac{d_{\mathrm{err}}(x) - d_{\min}}{d_{\max} - d_{\min}} & \text{otherwise.} \end{cases} \tag{5}$$

The error function (5) is presented in Fig. 2. The edge formulated this way is deactivated in case of small distances, which means that two nodes are close enough to be indistinguishable by means of WiFi fingerprint matching. Then, when the error considered as the Euclidean distance between the nodes is greater then the $d_{\min}$ threshold, the edge is activated. The error increases and the optimization procedure tries to reduce that error by moving the two considered nodes closer. As the uncertainty in matching WiFi fingerprints is isotropic, we set the information matrices of the WiFi-related constraints Ω^{wifi} to identity.

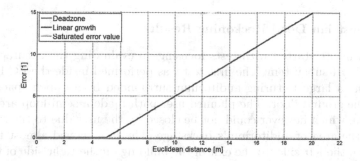

Fig. 2. The error function used for WiFi edge in graph-based optimization

4.3   Implementation Details

The proposed system was implemented for mobile devices with the Android OS (versions above 4.0), and finally tested on a Samsung Galaxy Note 3 with Android 4.4.4. The program is divided into 4 threads: (i) processing inertial data for orientation estimation and stepometer; (ii) fingerprints matching processing the WiFi scans and finding corresponding scans in the database and in the queue of scans taken in-motion; (iii) factor graph management polling data from subsystems and performing optimization; (iv) user interface. The inertial sensors data used in orientation estimation are processed with the maximal available frequency of 200 Hz whereas stepometer processing is performed at 5 Hz. The WiFi scans are performed as fast as possible (0.75 Hz). The implementation of the system is divided between JAVA and C++ (NDK) parts as it allowed us to combine C++ efficiency and possibility to use existing code with Java ease to create GUI and access available sensors.

5   Experiments

5.1   Experimental Setup

The experiments to evaluate the proposed fusion scheme were performed in two public buildings at the Poznań University of Technology (PUT) campus – the

Lecturing Center and the Mechatronics Center, shortly abbreviated to "LC" and "MC", respectively. The user equipped with a smartphone was asked to move around a building and the Android-based system was estimating the trajectory. It should be noted that the user was not stopping while moving along the trajectory to obtain the data, and therefore the WiFi scans taken in-motion cannot be easily associated with a single user position. However, the experiments conducted this way closely simulate real-life use cases of the pedestrian navigation system. The resulting trajectories are presented against the building floor plans, which allows for easy visual assessment of the correctness of the trajectories.

5.2   Pedestrian Dead Reckoning Results

The experiments started with tests focusing on evaluating the accuracy of the proposed PDR subsystem. The first test was performed inside the LC building, which hosts a large lecturing auditorium surrounded by an open space (lobby area) at the ground floor. The planned user path made a semi-loop around the auditorium, which however could not be closed by the user due to the restricted access to the area of auditorium's backstage. The user moved almost from the staircase on the left side, to the exit of the building on the right side of the floor plan (Fig. 3A). The trajectory obtained using the PDR subsystem (stepometer with orientation estimate) is presented in red, whereas the approximate ground truth trajectory, obtained by referencing to the known objects in the vicinity is depicted in yellow. The total covered distance was approximately 92 m. The trajectory obtained from the PDR subsystem is relatively good, although it can be observed that the user motion estimate is getting worse with the increasing operation time. This drift is caused by the nature of the dead reckoning principle, which accumulates small errors in estimation of the relative displacements along the trajectory. It is also evident, that even a small angle error can have a significant impact on the trajectory, and leads to large error in the Cartesian position of the user.

Due to the limited scale of the experiments in the LC building, it was decided to perform an experiment inside the MC building, which has a considerably different structure, with narrow corridors and less amount of open space. The user was asked to move twice along a rectangular trajectory and finish the experiment at the starting position, thus closing a loop. The obtained trajectory (red) is presented in Fig. 3B whereas the approximate ground truth path is denoted by the thicker yellow line. The total covered distance was approximately 178 m. This time the trajectory yielded by the PDR alone is much worse than in the LC case, due to inaccurate orientation estimation at sharp turns, and perhaps more noisy magnetometer readouts that were influenced by various electric equipment in the labs surrounding the area. The resulting PDR trajectory suffers from large drift and the second loop of the rectangular trajectory apparently does no match the first one.

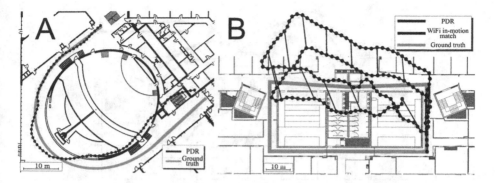

Fig. 3. PDR trajectories (red) estimated in the LC (A) and MC (B) buildings compared to the estimated pedestrian movement (yellow). The discovered WiFi-fingerprint matches (black lines) are shown for the MC trajectory (Color figure online).

5.3 PDR Supported by Matching of Discovered WiFi Fingerprints

To alleviate the odometry drift, the proposed system introduces the factor graph representation of the trajectory, which can accommodate additional information from WiFi fingerprints. The constraints stemming from WiFi fingerprints are discovered between the poses where WiFi scans were taken while the user was in motion. Unfortunately, those scans cannot be precisely associated to unique poses on the trajectory due to the long scanning time on the smartphone used in experiments. The Samsung Galaxy Note 3 scans 2.5 GHz and 5 GHz WiFi frequencies looking for WiFi APs, which takes about 4 sec. for a full scan. Therefore, for the discovered WiFi edges the deadzone parameter d_{min}^{disc} of the error function (5) was increased to 6 meters. This value captures the additional uncertainty in the location of the pose to which the fingerprint is anchored on the trajectory. Also, a discovered WiFi constraint can be spawned only to an already existing user pose. Therefore, those constraints cannot reduce the trajectory estimation drift that has mounted before the reference (revisited) pose was added to the trajectory (and the factor graph). However, the discovered constraints can keep a multi-loop trajectory more consistent, reducing the drift for motion along already covered paths. The discovered WiFi links are presented as black lines in Fig. 3B whereas the trajectory obtained after optimization is presented in Fig. 4.

From the presented trajectory, it is evident that the in-motion discovered WiFi constraints, which do not need any a priori knowledge of the environment nor the layout of the APs, reduce the trajectory estimation drift in case of longer operation with the smartphone. Unfortunately, these constraints do not guarantee a trajectory estimate that reasonably matches the ground truth path, due to the PDR errors that mounted before the first local loop closure between the fingerprints was discovered.

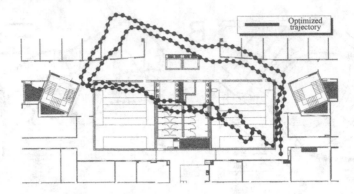

Fig. 4. Optimized trajectory estimate from PDR and WiFi links discovered in the MC experiment

5.4 Constraints from WiFi Fingerprints with Known Positions

Due to the inability of the in-motion discovered WiFi constraints to completely cancel the drift of the estimated trajectory other constraints related to the WiFi were considered. It is pretty evident that the drift in the PDR trajectory cannot be reduced significantly without prior knowledge of the locations of the APs in the environment. While these locations may be estimated by a SLAM algorithm, such an approach requires to survey the site prior to using the smartphone navigation system. We consider this too laborious and time consuming, and therefore we investigate an approach which uses only a minimal set of few APs at known positions. Those APs should be located in areas critical for PDR navigation, e.g. right-angle turns of corridors or crossroads. The few AP with known WiFi fingerprints and positions were determined prior to the experiment by a person who took 4 scans for each area of interest, and then simply pinpointed that location on the provided floor plan. The reference scans were taken with the user standing still, therefore they could be precisely associated to poses/places.

The experiments started with a trajectory taken inside the LC building as presented in Fig. 5A, where the PDR estimate (red) was presented with positions of the known WiFi fingerprints (blue crosses) and the discovered WiFi fingerprint matches (green lines) between scans taken in-motion and the known WiFi fingerprints stored in a database. The user was asked to keep moving continuously and therefore the WiFi constraints to known places could not always be detected, as in real-life scenarios.

When the factor graph of nodes and constraints is created, it is optimized on the smartphone by using the g²o library. The resulting graph, representing the best estimate of the trajectory, is presented in Fig. 5B. To distinguish the graphs before and after optimization, the used colors were reversed – the blue circles represent estimated user position whereas red crosses correspond to the positions of the WiFi fingerprints stored in database.

The obtained, optimized trajectory is similar to the PDR estimate in the initial part, as from the beginning the odometry estimate is accurate and therefore,

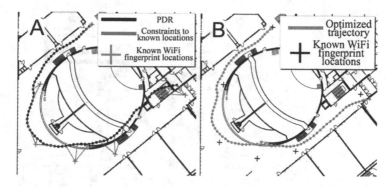

Fig. 5. PDR trajectory prior to optimization with found WiFi links (A) compared with resulting, and optimized trajectory with $d_{\min}^{map} = 6$ meters (B) in LC building

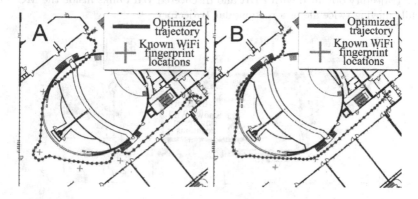

Fig. 6. Optimization trajectories obtained for differently tuned deadzone values: 3 meters (A) and 4.5 meters (B) in LC building

the WiFi constraints in the factor graph are not active. When the user moves further from the starting point, the odometry suffers from the accumulating errors, and the WiFi constraints get activated. The performed optimization results in a trajectory estimate which is close to the ground truth.

The critical parameter that needs to be properly tuned is the deadzone radius of the constraint related to the known WiFi fingerprint $d_{\min}^{map}$. Results for alternative deadzone values are presented in Fig. 6. The choice of $d_{\min}^{map}=3$ m (Fig. 6A) results in an optimized trajectory that is artificially curved around positions of the known APs. If a too strict deadzone value is selected, the WiFi constraint returns a non-zero error value even though there is no need to additionally correct the PDR estimate. A similar effect can be observed for $d_{\min}^{map} = 4.5$ meters where a single WiFi fingerprint match curves the trajectory at the beginning resulting in a trajectory estimate worse than the one using only the PDR. The proper choice of the deadzone radius $d_{\min}^{map}$ should depend on the environment

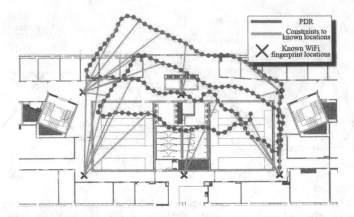

Fig. 7. Trajectory obtained with PDR and discovered WiFi links inside the MC building while moving twice along a rectangular trajectory

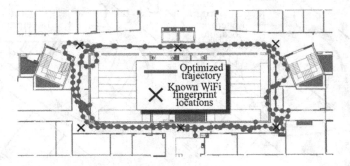

Fig. 8. Optimized trajectory with PDR and WiFi database edges inside MC building

characteristics, as in more cluttered environments smaller deadzone radius values result in better trajectories.

A similar experiment with the known WiFi fingerprints was performed in the MC building. The found WiFi constraints are visualized in Fig. 7. On the trajectory of the user, six places were chosen to record WiFi scans that can be used by the WiFi fingerprint localization system. In this experiment the in-motion discovered WiFi constraints between poses along the trajectory were neglected, in order to clearly present the benefits due to the constraints between the user pose and the WiFi fingerprints at known locations. The post-optimization trajectory is presented in Fig. 8. Again, the colors were reversed to represent optimized trajectory.

The optimized trajectory obtained from the proposed system almost perfectly resembles the real trajectory of the user. The WiFi fingerprint measurements with known positions placed on the crossroads allowed to properly constrain the trajectory. Even though the presented results are sufficient when it comes to pedestrian navigation, it is also possible to constraint the trajectory with additional in-motion discovered WiFi edges. Such a system should combine all of the possible sources of information and therefore provide a better trajectory. The trajectory recorded in the previous experiment repeated with the additional discovered WiFi links (denoted using black color) is presented in Fig. 9. In this experiment, it was decided to reduce the number of known WiFi fingerprints to four places and therefore create a more challenging environment for the proposed system.

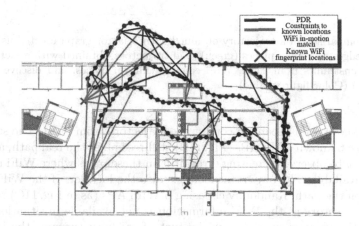

Fig. 9. Created graph with PDR edges (red), discovered WiFi edges (black), and WiFi edges to places found in the floor plan (green) (Color figure online).

Before performing the optimization, it is also important to set proper, different deadzone values of the in-motion discovered constraints and constraints to WiFi fingerprints of known position. Different parametrization has to be made due to the fact that both WiFi scans establishing a discovered constraint are taken in-motion, whereas one scan in the constraint related to a known WiFi location is static, and thus located more precisely. Therefore, we assumed and experimentally tested that the ratio of the discovered WiFi deadzone d_{min}^{motion} to the WiFi of known location deadzone d_{min}^{map} should be equal to 2. The resulting optimized trajectory with both types of WiFi constraints is presented in Fig. 10. The resulting system performs slightly better than the one using only the known WiFi locations. The discovered WiFi constraints allowed to improve the resulting trajectory, which is believed to come from the fact that the trajectory is more constrained between the repeated loops of similar shape.

The precision of the proposed system depends on the number and the location of the known WiFi positions used for smartphone localization. To demonstrate the difference in trajectory estimate, the user was asked to move for 119 meters in MC building and different configurations on known WiFi APs were tested in four experiments. The first trajectory with 15 known WiFi positions is presented in Fig. 11A. The obtained trajectory is very close to the real trajectory as there

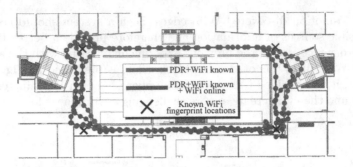

Fig. 10. Comparison of a trajectory obtained with a factor graph created using PDR and WiFi edges to known places (green), and trajectory obtained with a factor graph including constraints from PDR, WiFi edges to known places, and discovered WiFi edges (blue) (Color figure online).

is enough known WiFi scans to correct the trajectory from PDR. The same trajectory with 6 known WiFi APs (Fig. 11B) still resembles the real path, although it is possible to observe increasing error drift in these parts where WiFi information is unavailable. The important factor is also the location of the WiFi known positions on the path. Randomly choosing 6 WiFi APs (as in Fig. 11C) results in a useless trajectory as the WiFi information is not available in situations when PDR has the greatest error (especially just after sharp turns at the junctions of the corridors). Therefore, it is important to have WiFi information on possible crossroads. It is also important to have enough locations with known WiFi scan as insufficient number of those positions results in imprecise trajectory as presented in Fig. 11D. The PDR system of the proposed solution can be used to estimate the trajectory between two locations with known WiFi scans, but the lack of WiFi information (as in the end of trajectory in Fig. 11D) results in accumulation of error, mostly due to the imprecise orientation estimation inside a building.

To enable quantitative comparison between the obtained trajectories we apply the translational trajectory error metric, which is similar in concept to the ATE (Absolute Trajectory Error) proposed in [23] and commonly used in robotics. Similarly to the ATE our translational trajectory error compares the absolute distances between the estimated $\mathbf{P}$ and the ground truth $\mathbf{Q}$ trajectory. At first we map the estimated trajectory onto the ground truth trajectory by computing the rigid-body transform $\mathbf{S}$ that is the least-square solution to the alignment problem [23]. Then, the trajectory error is computed as $\mathbf{F}_i = \mathbf{Q}_i^{-1}\mathbf{S}\mathbf{P}_i$, for each i-th trajectory node. We extract the translational component of $\mathbf{F}_i$ and compute the Root Mean Square Error (RMSE) or mean error, along with the standard deviation. However, while the ATE error is computed over all time indices of $\mathbf{F}_i$ for the matching (i.e. time-synchronized) nodes of the reference and the estimated trajectory, we compute $\mathbf{F}_i$ as the error between the given node of $\mathbf{P}$ and the closest (in the Euclidean sense) point on the $\mathbf{Q}$ trajectory. This difference is caused by the fact, that working over long paths in natural

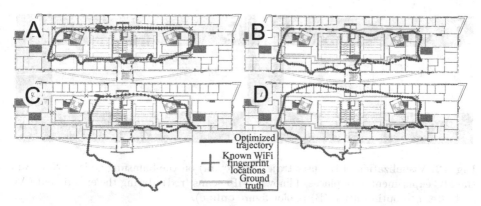

Fig. 11. Trajectories obtained with factor graphs created using PDR and WiFi edges: 15 known WiFi points (A), 6 known WiFi points anchored in critical locations of the floor plan (B), 6 randomly chosen known WiFi points (C), only 4 known WiFi points in critical locations (D)

indoor environments we cannot use an external motion capture system or GPS to obtain the ground truth trajectory, thus we cannot establish direct correspondence between the nodes of the estimated trajectory, and the ground truth path, which is surveyed manually by referencing to the walls and objects of known positions in the floor plan. The quantitative results for the experiment demonstrated in Fig. 11 are shown in Table 1.

Table 1. Accuracy of the recovered user paths with different choice of the number and location of the known WiFi Access Points

Choice of the known WiFi scan locations	Translational trajectory error			
	RMSE [m]	mean [m]	std. dev. [m]	max. [m]
15 (all known)	1.18	0.87	0.80	3.71
6 at critical places	2.33	1.74	1.54	5.38
6 chosen randomly	11.93	7.42	9.36	29.04
4 at critical places	5.60	3.88	4.05	14.92

The lowest RMSE error of 1.18 m is observed for the experiment with 15 know WiFi scans. Reducing the number of known WiFi scans to 6 yields a trajectory of RMSE error equal to 2.33 m, which is still acceptable for most of pedestrian navigation purposes. However, the maximal error increases to 5.38 m as the system depends for much longer periods on the noisy PDR estimate. The choice of 6 random locations of known WiFi scans results in the RMSE trajectory error of 11.93 m, which is useless for any application. More precise results are observed for a smaller number of known WiFi APs (only 4), but placed at locations critical for localization.

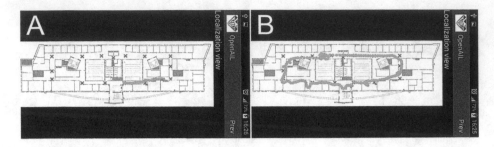

Fig. 12. Visualization of the user trajectory (cyan) on the Samsung Galaxy Note 3 in the MC experiment with places of known WiFi scans (red): during the experiment (A), and after g^2o optimization (B) (Color figure online).

All of the presented results were obtained on the real smartphone as presented in Fig. 12 and the code of the solution is publicly available.[1]

6 Conclusions

The presented graph-based representation of data coming from inertial and WiFi sensors presents an alternative, flexible and computation efficient way of data fusion when compared to typical approaches based on EKF or particle filters. The factor graph representation allows to easily model the error function to suit the uncertainty characteristics of measurements. In our system this representation allows to model the deadzone in the localization of places by using the WiFi fingerprint matching technique. The experiments proved that the stepometer with orientation estimation make a reasonable PDR system on the Android platform, but the user's position estimate from dead reckoning inevitably has a drift. The WiFi fingerprint matching approach allows to alleviate the negative effects of odometry drift and therefore provides much more precise trajectory estimates, even for long paths in complicated indoor environments.

The proposed system was evaluated when merging inertial and WiFi information, but it can be easily extended to incorporate information from additional sources, such like the smartphone's camera, which will be the main focus of further research.

Acknowledgment. This work is financed by the Polish Ministry of Science and Higher Education in years 2013–2015 under the grant DI2012 004142.

References

1. Bahl, P., Padmanabhan, V.N.: RADAR: an in-building RF-based user location and tracking system. In: Proceedings of Joint Conference of the IEEE Computer and Communications Societies, pp. 775–784 (2000)

[1] https://github.com/LRMPUT/DiamentowyGrant.

2. Biswas, J., Veloso, M.: WiFi localization and navigation for autonomous indoor mobile robots. In: Proceedings of IEEE International Conference on Robotics & Automation, Anchorage, pp. 4379–4384 (2010)
3. Chiu, H.-P., Zhou, X., Carlone, L., Dellaert, F., Samarasekera, S., Kumar, R.: Constrained optimal selection for multi-sensor robot navigation using plug-and-play factor graphs. In: Proceedings of IEEE International Conference on Robotics and Automation, Hong Kong, pp. 663–670 (2014)
4. Chen, Z., Zou, H., Jiang, H., Zhu, Q., Soh, Y., Xie, L.: Fusion of WiFi, smartphone sensors and landmarks using the Kalman filter for indoor localization. Sensors 15, 715–732 (2015)
5. Ferris, B., Fox, D., Lawrence, N.: WiFi-SLAM using Gaussian process latent variable models. In: Proceedings of International Joint Conference on Artificial Intelligence, pp. 2480–2485 (2007)
6. Fularz, M., Nowicki, M., Skrzypczyński, P.: Adopting feature-based visual odometry for resource-constrained mobile devices. In: Campilho, A., Kamel, M. (eds.) ICIAR 2014, Part II. LNCS, vol. 8815, pp. 431–441. Springer, Heidelberg (2014)
7. Gośliński, J., Nowicki, M., Skrzypczyński, P.: Performance comparison of EKF-based algorithms for orientation estimation on Android platform. IEEE Sens. J. 15(7), 3781–3792 (2015)
8. Grisetti, G., Kümmerle, R., Stachniss, C., Burgard, W.: Tutorial on graph-based SLAM. IEEE Intell. Transp. Syst. Mag. 2(4), 31–43 (2010)
9. Huang, J., Millman, D., Quigley, M., Stavens, D., Thrun, S., Aggarwal, A.: Efficient, generalized indoor WiFi GraphSLAM. In: Proceedings of IEEE International Conference on Robotics & Automation, Shanghai, pp. 1038–1043 (2011)
10. Husen, M.N., Lee, S.: Indoor human localization with orientation using WiFi fingerprinting. In: Proceedings of ACM International Conference on Ubiquitous Information Management and Communication, Siem Reap (2014)
11. Indelman, V., Williams, S., Kaess, M., Dellaert, F.: Information fusion in navigation systems via factor graph based incremental smoothing. Rob. Auton. Syst. 61(8), 721–738 (2013)
12. Inoue, S., Hattori, Y.: Toward High-level activity recognition from accelerometers on mobile phones. In: Proceedings of IEEE International Conference on Internet of Things, and Cyber, Physical and Social Computing, Dalian, pp. 225–231 (2011)
13. Kennedy, J., Eberhart, R.: Particle swarm optimization. In: Proceedings of IEEE International Conference on Neural Networks, Perth, pp. 1942–1948 (1995)
14. Kothari, N., Kannan, B., Dias, M.B.: Robust indoor localization on a commercial smart-phone. Technical report CMU-RI-TR-11-27, Carnegie-Mellon University, Pittsburgh (2011)
15. Kümerle, R., Grisetti, G., Strasdat, H., Konolige, K., Burgard, W.: g²o: a general framework for graph optimization. In: Proceedings of IEEE International Conference on Robotics & Automation, Shanghai, pp. 3607–3613 (2011)
16. Liu, H., et al.: Accurate WiFi based localization for smartphones using peer assistance. IEEE Trans. Mob. Comput. 13(10), 2199–2214 (2013)
17. Liu, H., Darabi, H., Banerjee, P., Liu, J.: Survey of wireless indoor positioning: techniques and systems. IEEE Trans. Syst. Man Cybern. Part C Appl. Rev. 37(6), 1067–1080 (2007)
18. Martin, E., Vinyals, O., Friedland, G., Bajcsy, R.: Precise indoor localization using smart phones. In: Proceedings of ACM International Conference on Multimedia, pp. 787–790 (2014)
19. Nowicki, M.: WiFi-guided visual loop closure for indoor localization using mobile devices. J. Autom. Mob. Rob. Intell. Syst. (JAMRIS) 8(3), 10–18 (2014)

20. Quigley, M., Stavens, D., Coates, A., Thrun, S.: Sub-meter indoor localization in unmodified environments with inexpensive sensors. In: Proceedings of IEEE/RSJ International Conference on Intelligent Robots & Systems, Taipei, pp. 2039–2046 (2010)

21. Richle, T., Anderson, S., Lichter, P., Whalen, W., Giudice, N.: Indoor inertial waypoint navigation for the blind. In: Proceedings of International Conference on IEEE Engineering in Medicine and Biology Society, pp. 5187–5190 (2013)

22. Skyhook. http://www.skyhookwireless.com/

23. Sturm, J., Engelhard, N., Endres, F., Burgard, W., Cremers, D.: A benchmark for the evaluation of RGB-D SLAM systems. In: IEEE/RSJ International Conference on Intelligent Robots & Systems, Vilamoura, pp. 573–580 (2012)

24. Wu, D., Xia, L., Mok, E.: Hybrid location estimation by fusing WLAN signals and inertial data. In: Liu, C. (ed.) Principle and Application Progress in Location-Based Services. LNGC, pp. 81–92. Springer, Berlin (2014)

25. Wu, S.-S., Wu, H.-Y.: The design of an intelligent pedometer using Android. In: Proceedings of International Conference on Innovations in Bio-inspired Computing and Applications, pp. 313–315 (2011)

Workshop Papers

Using Interaction Signals for Job Recommendations

Benjamin Kille[1]([✉]), Fabian Abel[2], Balázs Hidasi[3], and Sahin Albayrak[1]

[1] Berlin Institute of Technology, Berlin, Germany
`benjamin.kille@tu-berlin.de, sahin.albayrak@dai-labor.de`
[2] XING AG, Hamburg, Germany
`fabian.abel@xing.com`
[3] Gravity Research, Budapest, Hungary
`hidasi.balazs@gravityrd.com`

Abstract. Job recommender systems depend on accurate feedback to improve their suggestions. Implicit feedback arises in terms of clicks, bookmarks and replies. We present results from a member inquiry conducted on a large-scale job portal. We analyse correlations between ratings and implicit signals to detect situations where members liked their suggestions. Results show that replies and bookmarks reflect preferences much better than clicks.

Keywords: Job recommendation · Interactions · Reciprocity · Survey · Ratings

1 Introduction

Online job portals are becoming more and more popular among professionals as well as recruiters. They facilitate exchanging information. Professionals gain instant access to newly added job offers. Recruiters can spread their job advertisements to a larger base of recipients. Increasingly simple access to larger collections of data induces an information overload problem. Professionals struggle to discover interesting job offers. Recruiters struggle to discover suited candidates. The portals seek to support their members to overcome these issues. They incorporate mechanisms matching professionals and job offers based on available data. The vast set of professionals reduces to few candidates. The overwhelming collection of job offers reduces to few positions. The quality of the reduction depends on how well the system estimates recipients' preferences. Professionals expect the system to display relevant positions. Recruiters expect the system to display candidates best suited for the respective position. We refer to systems automatically learning users' preferences as *recommender systems*. Research on recommender systems has introduced a plethora of algorithms. Collaborative Filtering (CF) (cf. Koren and Bell [2]) and Content-based Filtering (CBF) (cf. Lops et al. [4]) represent two wide-spread paradigms. CF takes a collection of preferences and infers unknown (user, item)-pairs thereof. CBF additionally considers

© Institute for Computer Sciences, Social Informatics and Telecommunications Engineering 2015
S. Sigg et al. (Eds.): MobiCASE 2015, LNICST 162, pp. 301–308, 2015.
DOI: 10.1007/978-3-319-29003-4_17

features describing items. Both techniques require data expressing the preferences between user and items. Professionals include information on their general preferences in their profiles. Still, job portals lack preferences directed toward specific job offers. They have to infer such information from implicit signals. Whether professionals appreciate recommended job offers depends on a variety of aspects. For instance, they may like the job description but be unwilling to move to another location. We collaborate with the job portal XING[1]. XING is the leading job portal in the German speaking world with millions of members. There we observe professionals interacting with job postings in different ways. Types of interactions include clicking, bookmarking, and replying. Interactions have a time stamp assigned. This gives rise to temporal analysis. We look for patterns indicating situations in which professionals show interest in a job posting. Alternatively, we search for activities indicating interest toward a job posting. Our contributions are three-fold:

- we analyse interaction signals on a job portal,
- we conducted an inquiry providing ratings for job recommendations,
- we investigate the correlation between interaction signals and ratings.

First, we present previous works on job recommendation in Sect. 2. Section 3 illustrates the data we observed on a large-scale job portal. Section 4 describes the notion of relevance and how we learn correlations with interaction signals. We conclude and discuss future research in Sect. 6.

2   Related Work

Malinowski et al. [5] investigated how to automatically match professionals and open positions. Matching professionals and jobs requires a bilateral perspective. They argue that combining two recommenders promises high matching quality. On the one hand, we ought to determine relevant positions for a given professional. On the other hand, we should find the most promising candidates for an open position. Combining both yields matches satisfying both professionals and recruiters needs. Malinkowski et al. [5] conduct a user study to determine how well their recommender matches professionals and open positions. However accurate results such a study yields, a large-scale system will lack resources to apply similar evaluation protocols. Mine et al. [6] extend the idea as they consider interactions between professionals and recruiters. Their approach iteratively updates matching lists of recruiters and professionals as they exchange messages. The evaluation considers the time taken to establish matchings along with matching quality. Mine et al. [6] simulate the actions of professionals and recruiters. Behaviours of professionals and recruiters are prone to change over time. Hence, we expect to observe a more representative picture of interactions in a real, large-scale system. Paparrizos et al. [7] modell the problem as a supervised machine learning task. They take a data set of job transitions. Their method

---

[1] www.xing.com.

predicts which position a given professional will accept next. The data comprise a selection of large companies. They measure the classification accuracy. Contrarily, we consider a more comprehensive view on the labour markets. Our ability to represent the problem as classification task depends on the cardinality of potential class labels. Paparrizos et al. [7] obtain a manageable set of labels focusing on few companies. A large-scale job portal offers thousands of companies. Therefore, the classification problem would become too complex to manage. Recommender systems matching people to one another are referred to as *reciprocal recommender systems.* Online dating websites matching partners have been subject to many studies (cf. Akehurst et al. [1], Kunegis et al. [3], Pizzato et al. [8], and Zhao et al. [9]). Online dating matches exactly two persons. On the other hand, recruiters might be looking for several candidates at once to fill several positions. Thus, we face a slightly different problem. We collect observations from a large-scale job portal. Thereby, we expect to discover new insights enlightening interactions between professionals and job offers. In particular, we investigate correlations between explicitly stated preferences and implicitly observed signals.

3 Data Description

In this section, we describe the observable signals. Our data capture professionals, job offers, and interactions between both. Professionals create profiles describing themselves and their careers. These profiles include demographics, education, and interests. The job portal can track activities by identifying members. Recruiters create job offers. These offers outline required skills and portray a candidate's characteristics. In addition, they introduce the hiring company. We can track interactions with such job offers as they can be identified. Job portals let their members interact with offered jobs in different ways. Professionals may click, bookmark, or reply to suggested job postings. Additionally, they can query an integrated search engine. Details refer to random sample of more than one million members of XING. The sample has been taken over a period of several weeks in early 2015. Note that clicks, bookmarks, and replies may occur in any order. For instance, members may bookmark job postings without clicking. We highlight actions from the perspectives of professionals, job offers, and their combinations.

3.1 User Activity

We observe varying levels of activity among members. Professionals can either click, bookmark, or reply to a recommended job offer. Replies comprise three actions. First, professionals can access the job offering company's website to apply for the position. Second, professionals can request additional information about the offered position. Third, professionals can message the recruiter. Clicks require fairly low levels of cognitive effort. Conversely, replies force professionals to carefully study job offers. Our data reflect this aspect. We observe on average

95.7 % clicks, 3.3 % replies, and 1.0 % bookmarks. Our data cover a range of 3 months. Therein, professionals click on average 6.5 (standard deviation $\sigma = 15.6$) job postings. They bookmark on average 2.0 ($\sigma = 3.4$) job postings. They reply on average to 3.1 ($\sigma = 6.9$) job offers.

3.2 Item Activity

Job postings attract varying numbers of members. On average job offers obtain 87.6 ($\sigma = 219.5$) clicks. The large standard deviation indicates a popularity bias. Some job offers appear to receive much more clicks than others. Similarly, job positions obtain on average 4.2 ($\sigma = 7.2$) bookmarks. Finally, job offers attract on average 6.3 ($\sigma = 11.6$) replies.

3.3 Interaction Activity

Professionals spread limited spans of attention across the collection of job postings. Similarly, job offers target varying subsets of professionals according to their skills. Both phenomena combined cause a sparse pattern of interactions between professionals and offered jobs. We compute the density for each type of interaction. Let I refer to the number of interactions. Further, let U and J refer to the numbers of members and open positions. The density is defined as $\rho = I/UJ$. We observe densities of $\rho_{\text{clicks}} = 0.01\,\%$ for clicks, $\rho_{\text{bookmarks}} = 0.01\,\%$ for bookmarks, and $\rho_{\text{replies}} = 0.01\,\%$ for replies. In other words, if we were to pick a pair of professional and job posting at random, chances of observing any type of interactions are ≈ 1 in 10000. This implies that the job portal will struggle to estimate relevance of most combinations of members and open positions.

We notice that we observe sparse signals. We do not expect to obtain a clear picture of preferences from professionals by observing their interactions with job postings. Job portals depend on preferences to filter the most promising positions. Thus, we have to avoid misinterpreting interactions. Members might click on suggestions due to curiosity. Further, professionals might like some aspects of the position. Simultaneously, they may object to other aspects. For instance, a given position's description sounds interesting. At the same time, the position is located far from the current residence. Consequently, the position as a whole becomes irrelevant.

4 Relevance Prediction

Previous research determined the relevance of suggested jobs by simulation and small scale user studies (see Sect. 2). Large-scale job portals cannot rely on few individuals. We cannot expect preferences of thousands of members to conform to pre-defined simulation parameter. Hence, we propose to estimate preferences from signals derived from interactions between professionals and job postings. As a first step, we validate the information conveyed by these signals. We analyse the

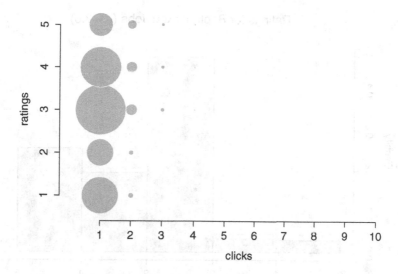

Fig. 1. Relation between clicks and ratings. The size of the circles encodes the proportion of data points. We observe that few clicks fail to indicate high relevancy. Professionals clicking once express both dislike and like toward recommended jobs. Professionals tend to click more often on relevant positions.

correlation between observed signals and ratings obtained via member inquiry. We asked professionals how they perceive job recommendations in form of an online survey. Professionals assigned stars from 1 to 5 or selected a 0 indicating they were unable to quantify their preference. Subsequently, we analysed how the responses correlate with professionals' interactions.

4.1 Clicks ~ Ratings

First, we relate clicks and ratings. We filtered all clicks of suggested job offers which professionals had rated. Figure 1 illustrates the relation. We encode proportions by the size of the circle. We observe the largest proportion referring to few clicks. Additionally, we observe that ratings vary throughout the scale with a limited number of clicks. We conjecture that few clicks fail to indicate a high level of relevance. Higher ratings dominate the range of 5 to 10 clicks. We conclude that as professionals increasingly click on suggested job offers, they become more relevant.

4.2 Bookmarks ~ Ratings

Why would professionals bookmark job postings? We suppose that bookmarking indicates a higher level of relevance than clicking. Figure 2 confirms our intuition. We filtered ratings assigned to bookmarked job offers. We observe that these job postings obtained on average 3.6 out of 5 stars. The distribution is skewed

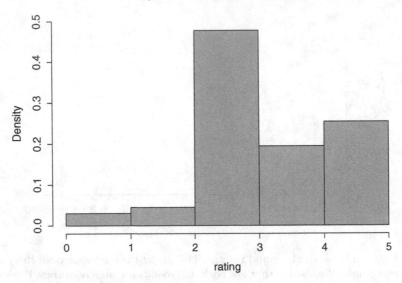

Fig. 2. Distribution of Ratings for bookmarked Job Offers. We observe that book-marked job offers obtain rather positive ratings. Professionals rated bookmarked job offers on average with 3.6 out of 5 starts.

in favour of higher ratings. Hence, we conclude that bookmarks better reflect relevance than clicks do.

4.3 Replies ~ Ratings

Replying refers to three possible actions. Professionals can either message the recruiter, request additional information, or access an external application form for the position. The systems allows multiple actions for an offered position. Figure 3 relates the number of replies with the ratings. We observe that few replies with high ratings collect the largest proportion. Thereby, we conclude that replies reliably indicate relevance.

5   Discussion

Recommending jobs is subject to vastly different requirements than recommending movies, music, or products. Recruiters require open positions to be filled within a specified time. In addition, positions are frequently open to at most one professional. In contrast, arbitrarily many users can consume movies, music, and products. Some items allow re-consumption, for instance, watching a movie several times. Users interact with recommender systems with varying motivation. Some interactions are due to information needs or decision support. Other

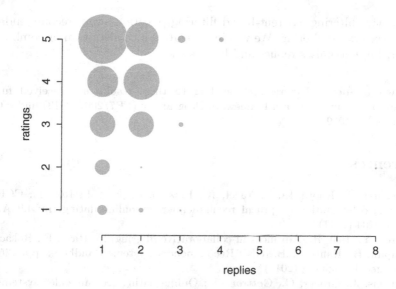

Fig. 3. Relation between Replies and Ratings. The figure encodes proportions by the size of the circle. We observe the largest proportion for a single reply and the rating 5. In addition, the next largest proportions gather around high ratings and few replies.

interactions occur as users satisfy their curiosity in exploratory fashion. Movie recommender systems tend toward explorative use. On the other hand, job recommender systems deal much more with decision support. As a result, they face users with interchanging periods of activity and absence thereof. Looking for a new position, professionals intensively interact with the system. Satisfied with their working environment, professionals scarcely interact with the system. Conversely, movie recommender systems face a more stable condition with users regularly visiting. Furthermore, movie recommender systems observe the effect of their recommendations. They can track how long their users watch a movie. Job recommender systems cannot monitor the interactions between employer and candidate outside their platform.

6   Conclusion and Future Work

Determining situations where professionals deem suggested job offers relevant is crucial to improve job recommender systems. We analysed observable signals incurring as professionals interact with job postings. We showed results of a member inquiry providing explicit preferences. We investigated how observable signals and responses from the inquiry correlate. Although, clicks are more common than bookmarks and replies, they convey less information concerning the relevance of a suggestion. Replying gives the best indication on whether a professional deemed a recommended job offer relevant.

This knowledge will support our future research. We will conduct experiments with a variety of existing recommendation algorithms. The selection includes collaborative filtering, content-based filtering, location-aware recommendation, and context-aware filtering. We will investigate which algorithm or combination of algorithm maximises replies and bookmarks.

Acknowledgement. The research leading to these results has received funding from European Union Seventh Framework Programme (FP7/2007–2013) under Grant Agreement № 610594.

References

1. Akehurst, J., Koprinska, I., Yacef, K., Pizzato, L., Kay, J., Rej, T.: CCR - A content-collaborative reciprocal recommender for online dating. In: IJCAI, pp. 2199–2204 (2011)
2. Koren, Y., Bell, R.: Advances in collaborative filtering. In: Ricci, F., Rokach, L., Shapira, B., Kantor, P.B. (eds.) Recommender Systems Handbook, pp. 145–184. Springer, Heidelberg (2011)
3. Kunegis, J., Gröner, G., Gottron, T.: Online dating recommender systems: the split-complex number approach. In: ACM RecSys Workshop on Recommender Systems and the Social Web, pp. 37–44 (2012)
4. Lops, P., de Gemmis, M., Semeraro, G., Handbook, R.S.: Content-based recommender systems: state of the Art and trends. In: Ricci, F., Rokach, L., Shapira, B., Kantor, P.B. (eds.) Recommender Systems Handbook, pp. 73–100. Springer, Heidelberg (2011)
5. Malinowski, J., Wendt, O., Keim, T., Weitzel, T.: Matching people, jobs: a bilateral recommendation approach. In: Proceedings of the Annual Hawaii International Conference on System Sciences, vol. 6, pp. 1–9 (2006)
6. Mine, T., Kakuta, T., Ono, A.: Reciprocal Recommendation for Job Matching with Bidirectional Feedback, vol. 2009, pp. 39–44 (2013)
7. Paparrizos, I., Cambazoglu, B., Gionis, A.: Machine learned job recommendation. In: RecSys, pp. 325–328 (2011)
8. Pizzato, L., Rej, T., Chung, T., Koprinska, I., Kay, J.: RECON: a reciprocal recommender for online dating. In: ACM RecSys, pp. 207–214 (2010)
9. Zhao, K., Wang, X., Mo, Y., Gao, B.: User recommendations in reciprocal and bipartite social networks-an online dating case study. IEEE Intell. Syst. **29**, 27–35 (2014)

A Spatiotemporal Approach for Social Situation Recognition

Christian Meurisch$^{(\boxtimes)}$, Tahir Hussain, Artur Gogel, Benedikt Schmidt, Immanuel Schweizer, and Max Mühlhäuser

Telecooperation Lab, Technische Universität Darmstadt, Darmstadt, Germany
{christian.meurisch,tahir.hussain,artur.gogel,
benedikt.schmidt,schweizer,max}@tk.informatik.tu-darmstadt.de

Abstract. The development of virtual personal assistants requires situation awareness. For this purpose, lightweight approaches for the processing of sensor data to derive situation information from available sensor data (e.g., mobile phone data) are required.

In this paper, we propose a spatiotemporal approach to derive situational information about social interactions only based on location and time, using data collected with off-the-shelf smartphones. We examine the approach, using location traces of 163 users collected over four weeks. The proposed spatiotemporal approach shows an average social situation recognition result of $45.8 \pm 23.2\%$ F_1-measure across the data set using Random Forest classifiers.

Keywords: Social interaction · Personal tracking · Mobility pattern · Social computing · Situation recognition · Location sensing · Smartphone

1 Introduction

Virtual personal assistants to support users in their daily lives have become more and more popular in recent years. Due to the growing use of mobile devices assistant systems are able to seamlessly track and give advices through mobile applications at any time. Examples are commercial personal assistants like Google Now or Apple's Siri which offer automatic event reminders considering related information like traffic situations. Similarly, fitness trackers offer coaching considering users' actual performance [16], can detect and even prevent health problems [4]. In all cases knowledge about the user's current situation is of utmost importance.

A major challenging problem in situation recognition is the information base. In general the fusion of already available information sources (e.g., mobile sensor data, web data) [5,20] is preferred over deploying additional static hardware (e.g., smart home sensors) [1]. After data gathering, the fusion and processing of sensor data to derive information types, granularity and quality suitable for situation follows. We propose a lightweight approach to derive social interactions based only on location and time with no additional instrumentation of the user or the environment.

© Institute for Computer Sciences, Social Informatics and Telecommunications Engineering 2015
S. Sigg et al. (Eds.): MobiCASE 2015, LNICST 162, pp. 309–316, 2015.
DOI: 10.1007/978-3-319-29003-4_18

In this paper, we examine over 24 million location traces of 163 students over four weeks to automatically infer the user's *social situation* represented by place, time and social presence. For that, we reduce the complex situation recognition problem to the detection of social interactions from mobility patterns. In our approach, a *social interaction* is defined as meeting of a group consisting of at least two persons who are co-located over a specific amount of time (e.g., five minutes). By doing this, our data model consists of three types of information: (1) *social*, (2) *spatial*, and (3) *temporal information*. We assume that each one of the three information types can be derived by using the other two. This paper focuses on inferring social interactions (class label) from spatiotemporal data (features), i.e., if we know the user's current whereabouts and the corresponding times, we are able to infer information about the social situation which means we know the exact persons a social interaction takes place with. While location and time are standard information of modern off-the-shelf smartphones, our approach is highly suitable for daily use. Training personalized classifiers for each user we get an overall classification result from $45.8 \pm 23.2\%$ F_1-measure across our user base.

In summary, the contributions of this paper are twofold:

Self-tracking Dataset. Using personal mobile devices we collected a large dataset with 24 million location values of 163 students over four weeks using our multi-device user tracking suite [17,18].

Social Situation Recognizer. Detecting social interactions only from location traces, we extract features and train personalized Random Forest classifiers for each user [3]; averaging the results over all users we get an overall classification result of $45.8 \pm 23.2\%$ F_1-measure across our users. Thus, we are able to infer the current user's social situation from spatiotemporal data stream.

The remainder of this paper is organized as follows. In Sect. 2, we provide an overview of related work in recognition users' activities and contexts. In Sect. 3, we present our approach that utilizes detection of social interactions to reveal user's social situation. In Sect. 4, the data collection process with the resulting dataset and feature extraction process are described, before we report the results. The paper closes with conclusion and future works.

2   Related Work

Most mobile phones feature a large variety of sensors [13], providing the perfect platform for activity, context and situation recognition [22] without the need of deploying additional hardware like in smart homes [1]. While simple activities (e.g., standing, walking) can be detected with a high accuracy of above 90% relying on accelerometer data only [12], the recognition of complex activities (e.g., watching tv, playing volleyball) or detecting the entire situation including social presence, only with highly available devices is still an open challenge [15]. Most approaches still need external sensors or custom wearables [9].

Our idea is based on only utilizing location traces of users to recognize social interactions (i.e., temporal co-located users) and characterize the user's current situation. Other state of the art approaches already utilize the social context inferred from mobility pattern [6] or online social networks [5] to improve their results in human activity recognition [14]. In this paper, we focus on one data source deployed in all modern mobile phones (i.e., locations) to underpin that deep insights into activity and situation can be derived only by location traces. Various works already show recognition approaches based on location traces, e.g., place detection [11,23], social relationship inferences [21] or even the recognition of mental disorders like depressions [4]. It is important to note that human trajectories show a high degree of temporal and spatial regularity [8]. Song et al. even find a 93 % potential predictability in user mobility across their user base [19], which makes human mobility an attractive data source for context and situation recognition. In the next section, we describe our spatiotemporal approach in detail.

3   Our Approach

In this section we describe our approach for deriving a current social situation (the persons interacted with) from space and time (cf. Fig. 1). For that, we only need the location sensor of the smartphone to get location (coordinates) or location traces of a user, including timestamps. In the following we explain our approach of inferring social interactions from human mobility step by step. *First*, we describe the detection of places (high-level spatial information) and place visits (high-level spatial-temporal information) inferred from location traces (low-level information) for each user. *Second*, we cluster temporal overlapping place visits of users to social interactions (high-level spatial-temporal social context). *Finally*, we represent a situation by these three information: (1) *social*, (2) *spatial*, and (3) *temporal data*.

3.1   Places and Place Visits

We define a *place* as stationary geographical location where a user stays for an amount of time. We extract a user's places from location traces by using the place detection algorithm proposed by [11] with $d_p = 25$ m and $t_p = 15$ min as distance and time threshold parameters. Within the detected places, we identify places of specific relevance throughout the daily live. Inspired by [23], we define and determine the following four meaningful place types: *home*, *work*, *university*, and *other place* (high-level spatial information). To add temporal information to that static places, we check when and how long users visit their specific places and define this as *place visit* (high-level spatial-temporal information).

3.2   Social Interactions

We define a *social interaction* as a meeting of at least two persons who are temporal co-located over a specific amount of time (*here:* at least $t_s = 5$ min).

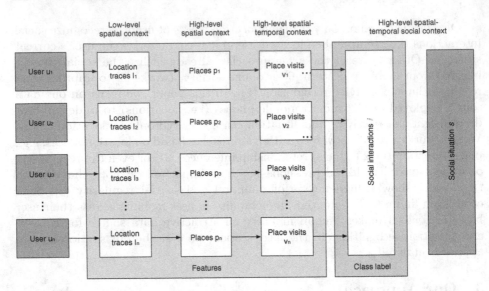

Fig. 1. Our approach utilizes location traces of users to detect higher-level information like places, place visits (features) and, finally, social interactions (class label) to characterize a situation.

Inspired by [5,6,21], we infer social interactions from co-location of users. More precisely, we consider spatiotemporal overlapping place visits of different users in a sliding window with size of t_s to detect social interactions (high-level spatial-temporal social context). For that, we use the clustering algorithm DBSCAN [7] with parameters $minPts = 2$ and $eps = 20$ m within that sliding window to cluster users to social groups.

3.3   Social Situation Recognition

A *social situation* in our approach is represented by three contexts: (1) *social*, (2) *spatial*, and (3) *temporal* context. Given a use case, we are able to sense two of these contexts and infer the third context to characterize the situation. In this paper, we focus on the recognition of the social context from spatiotemporal data. For example, if we are able to sense location values including a timestamp, our approach can infer social interactions (cf. Fig. 1), i.e., the output is the exact user group with unique persons. Utilizing well-researched *next place detection* algorithms [2], our approach could furthermore be utilized to predict the exact persons a user will meet the next or in near future.

4   Proof of Concept

To prove our approach we first conducted a user study to get real-world location data, described in the next section. Based on that dataset we extract appropriate spatiotemporal and social features (class label) to train a personalized classifier for each user to recognize user's social situations. Finally, we report and discuss the classification results.

4.1   Dataset

We conducted a self-tracking user study to collect location data from 163 students of Technische Universität Darmstadt over four weeks using our multi-device user tracking suite [17,18]. In total, we gathered over 24 million raw location values within four weeks, i.e., about 148 ± 359 thousand location values per user. The high scatter can be reasoned by dynamic sampling rates for location sensor depending on the strength of user's movement, i.e., we reduce the sampling rate if the smartphone is still, while we increase the sampling rate if the smartphone is moving, especially in vehicles.

Table 1. Obtained higher-level information from collected locations

Step	High-level information	Instances per user	Total
-	Raw locations l	$147,630.7 \pm 358,764.9$	$24,063,641$
1	Places p	14.2 ± 10.8	$2,312$
2	Place visits v	102.0 ± 59.7	$16,629$
3	Social interactions i	182.7 ± 193.7	$29,787$

Table 2. Definition of spatiotemporal features (f_p, f_w, f_d, f_t) and class label (f_s)

ID	Feature	Value range
f_p	Place type	{home, work, university, other}
f_w	Weekend	{false, true}
f_d	Day of week	{Mon, Tue, Wed, Thu, Fri, Sat, Sun}
f_t	Time of day	{morning, afternoon, evening, night}
f_s	Social interaction	$\{u_k, u_j, ..\} \subseteq U$ (users)

4.2   Feature Extraction

For the dataset, three different kinds of features were extracted: (1) *social*, (2) *spatial*, and (3) *temporal features*. For that, we proceed as described in the previous section: inferring places from raw location values (*step 1*), detecting place visits (*step 2*), and clustering social interactions (*step 3*). Table 1 shows the resulting count of instances per user and the total count of instances for each processing step. Based on this high-level information the features are extracted. Table 2 lists the resulting features and their value ranges. Feature f_p represents the place context with four possible semantic places for each user: *home*, *work*, *university* and *other places*. Finally, we have three time-based features: the binary feature f_w (weekend) with *false* for weekday or *true* for weekend as values; feature f_d (day of week) with the seven days of week as values (i.e., Monday, Tuesday,..), and feature f_t (time of day) with value range of *morning* $(6am - 12pm)$, *afternoon* $(12pm - 17pm)$, *evening* $(17pm - 22pm)$, and *night* $(22pm - 6am)$. As categorical class label, we use the feature f_s representing the social context. Its value range is an arbitrary subset of all users within the system, i.e., the smallest subset contains only the user himself and the largest subset contains all users. In total, we extracted $59,412$ instances, i.e., 364.5 ± 237.0 instances per user.

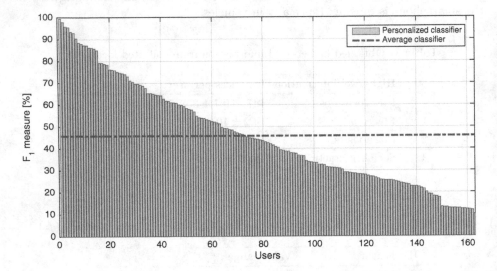

Fig. 2. Classification results (F_1-measure) of personalized classifiers for each users (*indigo*) and the average F_1-measure over all users (*green line*) (Color figure online)

4.3 Results

With the above extracted spatiotemporal features (f_p,f_w,f_d,f_t) and f_s as class to predict we train and evaluate personalized classifiers for each user. For that, we programmatically tested 26 various classification algorithms with different configurations provided by WEKA, a data mining software [10]. Avoiding overfitting, the best evaluated classifier was a *Random Forest* with 100 trees [3]. In Fig. 2, we report the results for each personalized classifier and the average F_1-measure of $45.8 \pm 23.2\%$ over our user base using the above classification algorithm. We see that social context (i.e., exact determination of present users) is highly predictable for few users, i.e., F_1-measure ranging between 70.0% and

99.3 % for about 18 % of users. For over 38 % of users our approach is able to correctly detect the exact social interactions in every second situation. For the rest of users the social context prediction out of spatiotemporal data is challenging. In future work, we plan to assign each probably presented unique person a probability of attendance, i.e., the algorithm will consider subgroups, to further improve our results.

5 Conclusion

In this paper, we proposed a recognition approach to detect user's social situation only utilizing his location traces. By analyzing these location traces we recognize social interactions (i.e., co-located persons over a specific time) to derive the social situation. Our evaluation built on a four-week self-tracking study with over 24 million location values of 163 students. We showed an average recognition result of $45.8 \pm 23.2\%$ F_1-measure across our user base using personalized Random Forest classifiers for each user. The result confirms the initial assumption that if the same group of users meets each other, the situation with respect to time and place is often the same or similar and, thus, predictable. Therefore, the presented approach can predict the persons of prospective meetings. In future work, we will also consider the relationship between social interactions, e.g., friends, classmates or colleagues, and investigate the impact of user routines versus accidental meeting. Moreover, we will build a real-time assistive system based on our situation recognition approach to support students in their daily lives.

Acknowledgments. This work has been funded by the LOEWE initiative (Hessen, Germany) within the NICER project.

References

1. Arcelus, A., Jones, M.H., Goubran, R., Knoefel, F.: Integration of smart home technologies in a health monitoring system for the elderly. In: 21st International Conference on Advanced Information Networking and Applications Workshops (AINAW 2007), vol. 2, pp. 820–825. IEEE (2007)
2. Baumann, P., Kleiminger, W., Santini, S.: The influence of temporal and spatial features on the performance of next-place prediction algorithms. In: 15th International Conference on Ubiquitous Computing (UbiComp 2013), pp. 449–458. ACM (2013)
3. Bishop, C.M.: Pattern Recognition and Machine Learning. Springer, New York (2006)
4. Canzian, L., Musolesi, M.: Trajectories of depression: unobtrusive monitoring of depressive states by means of smartphone mobility traces analysis. In: 17th International Conference on Ubiquitous Computing (UbiComp 2015), pp. 1293–1304. ACM (2015)
5. Cranshaw, J., Toch, E., Hong, J., Kittur, A., Sadeh, N.: Bridging the gap between physical location and online social networks. In: 12th International Conference on Ubiquitous Computing (UbiComp 2010), pp. 119–128. ACM (2010)

6. Eagle, N., Pentland, A.: Reality mining: sensing complex social systems. Pers. Ubiquit. Comput. **10**(4), 255–268 (2006)
7. Ester, M., Kriegel, H.-P., Sander, J., Xu, X.: A density-based algorithm for discovering clusters in large spatial databases with noise. In: 2th International Conference on Knowledge Discovery and Data Mining (KDD 1996), pp. 226–231. ACM (1996)
8. Gonzalez, M.C., Hidalgo, C.A., Barabasi, A.-L.: Understanding individual human mobility patterns. Nature **453**(7196), 779–782 (2008)
9. Gordon, D., Hanne, J.-H., Berchtold, M., Shirehjini, A.A.N., Beigl, M.: Towards collaborative group activity recognition using mobile devices. Mob. Netw. Appl. **18**(3), 326–340 (2013)
10. Hall, M., Frank, E., Holmes, G., Pfahringer, B., Reutemann, P., Witten, I.H.: The WEKA data mining software: an update. SIGKDD Explor. Newsl. **11**(1), 10–18 (2009)
11. Kang, J.H., Welbourne, W., Stewart, B., Borriello, G.: Extracting places from traces of locations. Mob. Comput. Commun. Rev. **9**(3), 58–68 (2005)
12. Kwapisz, J.R., Weiss, G.M., Moore, S.A.: Activity recognition using cell phone accelerometers. Explor. Newsl. **12**(2), 74–82 (2011)
13. Lane, N.D., Miluzzo, E., Hong, L., Peebles, D., Choudhury, T., Campbell, A.T.: A survey of mobile phone sensing. Commun. Mag. IEEE **48**(9), 140–150 (2010)
14. Lane, N.D., Pengyu, L., Zhou, L., Zhao, F.: Connecting personal-scale sensing and networked community behavior to infer human activities. In 16th International Conference on Ubiquitous Computing (UbiComp 2014), pp. 595–606. ACM (2014)
15. Lara, O.D., Labrador, M.A.: A survey on human activity recognition using wearable sensors. Commun. Surv. Tutorials **15**(3), 1192–1209 (2013)
16. Schmidt, B., Benchea, S., Eichin, R., Meurisch, C.: Fitness tracker or digital personal coach: how to personalize training. In: 17th International Conference on Ubiquitous Computing (UbiComp 2015): Adjunct Publication. ACM (2015)
17. Schweizer, I., Bärtl, R., Schmidt, B., Kaup, F., Mühlhäuser, M.: Kraken.me mobile: the energy footprint of mobile tracking. In: 6th International Conference on Mobile Computing, Applications and Services (MobiCASE 2014), pp. 82–89. IEEE (2014)
18. Schweizer, I., Schmidt, B.: Kraken.me: multi-device user tracking suite. In: 16th International Conference on Ubiquitous Computing (UbiComp 2014): Adjunct Publication, pp. 853–862. ACM (2014)
19. Song, C., Zehui, Q., Blumm, N., Barabási, A.-L.: Limits of predictability in human mobility. Science **327**(5968), 1018–1021 (2010)
20. Takata, K., Ma, J., Apduhan, B.O., Huang, R., Shiratori, N.: Lifelog image analysis based on activity situation models using contexts from wearable multi sensors. In: 2nd International Conference on Multimedia and Ubiquitous Engineering (MUE 2008), pp. 160–163. IEEE (2008)
21. Wang, D., Pedreschi, D., Song, C., Giannotti, F., Barabasi, A.-L.: Human mobility, social ties, and link prediction. In 17th International Conference on Knowledge Discovery and Data Mining (KDD 2011), pp. 1100–1108. ACM (2011)
22. Yau, S.S., Liu, J.: Hierarchical situation modeling and reasoning for pervasive computing. In: 4th Workshop on Software Technologies for Future Embedded and Ubiquitous Systems, and 2nd International Workshop on Collaborative Computing, Integration, and Assurance (SEUS-WCCIA 2006), p. 6. IEEE (2006)
23. Zhou, C., Frankowski, D., Ludford, P., Shekhar, S., Terveen, L.: Discovering personally meaningful places: an interactive clustering approach. ACM Trans. Inf. Syst. (TOIS) **25**(3), 12 (2007)

Managing Wireless Mesh Networks – A Survey of Recent Fault Recovery Approaches

Akmal Yaqini$^{(\boxtimes)}$

Department of Telecommunication Systems, Communication and Operating Systems,
Technische Universität Berlin, Berlin, Germany
Yaqini@win.tu-berlin.de

Abstract. Wireless Mesh Network (WMN) is a technology which has evolved in recent years and fits well in today's technological needs. However, due to the wireless nature of WMNs and their deployment in heterogeneous and large scale areas, wireless links often face significant quality fluctuations and performance degradation or weak connectivity. Therefore, failure detection and recovery plays crucial role in performance of WMN. This paper presents a study report on comparison of recent research and techniques developed for the issue of fault tolerance in WMNs. In this survey we present the existing techniques for fault tolerance in WMNs in categories; node failure approach, communication failure approach, routing schemes, fault tolerance techniques, and autonomous reconfiguration systems. The paper also provides an outline of areas which need further research and studies.

Keywords: Wireless mesh network · Fault tolerance · Cross-layer

1 Introduction

Wireless Mesh Network (WMN) is a specific type of Mobile Ad Hoc Networks (MANET) [12], which extends the concept of single-hop WLANs to a multi-hop network. In WMNs, nodes can automatically join or leave the network and networks can be established instantly virtually anywhere. WMNs' advantages such as low up-front cost, self-managing, robustness, and reliable service coverage encourage researchers to study their features for better and more reliable performance [2].

The main intention of WMNs is the capability of working without infrastructure. This feature and the inherit features of a wireless connectivity, such as interference, limited bandwidth, packet loss, dynamic obstacles, and fading makes WMNs not stable and reliable in all situations [6]. They may experience various failures, for example, node or link failures which may result in service interruption and degrading the performance of WMNs [8].

Hence, it is crucial to find the solutions necessary for WMN fault detection and recovery in order to make them fault tolerant. Fault tolerant function optimizes the capability of the network to deliver the data constantly and successfully during the specific time when some node or link failures happen.

© Institute for Computer Sciences, Social Informatics and Telecommunications Engineering 2015
S. Sigg et al. (Eds.): MobiCASE 2015, LNICST 162, pp. 317–324, 2015.
DOI: 10.1007/978-3-319-29003-4_19

The concept of Situation detection [16] can be used for developing a fault tolerance mechanism for WMNs. Considerable amount of event data due to changes in WMNs are produced that need to be analyzed. Gaining spatio-temporal information about the occurrence of faults enriches fault recovery mechanism. Based on the spatio-temporal data about faults, root cause and type of faults can be diagonized. Detecting faults in WMNs in time to take appropriate actions for obtaining desired QoS and save network resources can enhance WMNs performance.

Designing reliable and fault tolerant WMNs have been a hot topic of research of wireless networks during the last decade and many studies and research have been undertaken to address issues in WMNs to make them more dependable.

In this paper we present and compare the recent approaches and techniques developed for making WMNs fault tolerant against node failure, communication failure, routing protocol failure, backbone and base station failures.

2   Faults in WMNs

Based on our study, there are a number of faults that can happen in WMNs and effect the performance of the network severely. We have distinguished WMN faults in the following categories.

2.1   Node Failure

Failure in Mesh nodes occur in different ways, such as hardware failure or software issues. Node failure decreases the performance level of WMNs. More reasons which cause node failure are, deficiency in WMN coverage domain, nodes weariness after operating in a network for a long time, interruption in routing path, or reduction in node battery power [15].

2.2   Communication Failure

The wireless nature of WMNs cause their links facing quality fluctuations and performance degradation by experiencing various issues such as interference, limited bandwidth, unpredictable circumference, multi-path fading, weak signal, dynamic obstacles [10], channel overlapping and reconfiguration overhead caused by channel switching in multi channel-multi radio WMNs [5].

2.3   Traffic Overload

The other important connectivity issue is the traffic congestion (overhead). From one hand the dynamic nature of traffic demand in WMNs and also excessive throughput requested by some applications and from the other hand the limited bandwidth capacity of WMNs can cause significant traffic congestion and degrade network performance dramatically. Moreover, network traffic can be interrupted and congestion might happen due to the network structure changes or because of faults happening during the network operations.

2.4   Routing Protocol Failure

The existing routing schemes used for WMN need improvements to satisfy required QoS and to provide optimal performance level for all situations in the network. In some conditions the routing protocol messages in the network are delayed or lost and cause the routing protocol to face problems to continue operation. Moreover, the bandwidth and computing resources of communication is limited for each node, therefore wastage of time, resources, traffic overhead and bandwidth occur due to protocol decision making.

2.5   Network Scalability Issue

In wireless mesh networks the number of nodes continuously changes. The existing routing protocols work best for smaller mesh networks but cannot operate efficiently once the network is large and heterogeneous. As the network enlarges, the number of hops in the network increase, new routes are required to be established and traffic load should be calculated for different network routes. In this new condition routing mechanisms might face difficulty to find appropriate and reliable route, connections in transport protocols may weaken and MAC protocols may experience reduction in throughput. This results in increment of the number of network operations and can degrade the performance of the network [1,6].

2.6   Faults Resulting from Network Dynamics

Due to the dynamic nature of WMNs, the structure and topology of the network might stay unchanged or change often. Moreover, nodes are allowed to stay stationary or become mobile by moving around and change their location. These topological changes require WMNs for reconfiguring and reorganizing the network structure which can add more complexity and overhead.

2.7   Base Station and Backbone Failures

Mesh routers are the base stations and the connectivity among them creates a wireless multi-hop backbone for WMNs [7]. Base station and backbone faults can make network unstable and create confusion for route selection and data flow. Faults related to base station and network backbone are: weak radio frequency signal or unpredictable circumference which effect the QoS in the coverage zone, capture effect by base station with high transmission power, battery wear out, excessive energy consumption, hardware failure, gateway selection when instant changes occurs in the network.

3   Taxonomy of Approaches

This section presents the recent developed techniques for addressing current issues in WMNs. These techniques are organized in the following taxonomy: (a) Fault Diagnosis Approach, (b) Node Failure, (c) Connectivity Issues and Routing Schemes, (d) Fault Tolerance, (e) Autonomous Reconfiguration Systems.

3.1   Fault Diagnosis Approach

Xu et al., developed a fault diagnosis model for WMNs [17]. During the fault diagnosis process a shortest path spanning tree is constructed. Each node included in the tree has the shortest hop-distance to the root. In this way the delay time is reduced. Each node produces a testing request message and broadcast it to its neighbors. The reply message is not needed. Therefore, the overhead of maintaining and repairing the spanning tree is prevented and also communication and time complexity is enhanced significantly.

Li et al., propose a fault diagnosis model based on decision tree algorithm named W-C4.5-RP [9]. The developed model is basically the improvement of the C4.5 decision tree algorithm by adapting rule post-pruning mechanism. The main advantage of the developed fault diagnosis algorithm is reducing the rule set size and cutting down the rule matching time that increases the system efficiency.

3.2   Node Failure Approach

In [15] authors proposed a node recovery algorithm that replaces inactive nodes or the ones which have vacated batteries. Fault Node Recovery (FNR) algorithm allows to reuse maximum number of routing paths. As the result the network lifetime increases and on the other hand cost of node replacement decreases by consuming less power during the route discovery process.

3.3   Connectivity Issues and Routing Schemes

Franklin et al., address the problem of joint channel assignment and flow allocation in WMNs [5]. The research has proposed a static channel assignment algorithm for improving performance of WMNs by using multiple partially overlapped channels. The proposed algorithm is called Mix Integer Linear Program (MILP). The algorithm is considered load aware and deliberates increasing end-to-end throughput and decreasing queuing delay in the network.

In [4] Franklin et al., propose a solution for traffic disruption overhead that happens during channel switching in order to reconfigure the channel assignment in Multi Channel - Multi Radio (MC-MR) WMNs. The paper provides a mathematical model for reconfiguration of the network when channel switching occurs which can minimize traffic disruption and increase the throughput usage.

Papapostolou et al., proposes a simple approach for obtaining fault tolerance in WMNs [11]. Their proposed approach has three main characteristics; it adapts to changes in the network, it avoids traffic to be forwarded by unreliable nodes and selects routing path differently with a joint link metric. Their proposed link metric encapsulates distance between nodes and their inclination and vulnerability to failure. The result of the research shows certain advantages of joint link metric.

3.4   Fault Tolerance Approaches

Aizaz et al., propose a failure recovery method for TICA (Technology-controlled Interference-aware Channel-assignment Algorithm) [3]. When a failure happens the algorithm bypasses the failed node and removes its related MPNT (Maximum Power Neighbor Table). Then gateway executes the TCA (Topology Control Algorithm) to reorganize the network by making a new MPSPT (Minimum Power-based Shortest Path Tree). The new MPSPT helps gateway to recalculate the link rankings and the channel assignment. The result provided in [3] shows TICA performs well in small and large scale networks.

Ivanov et al., proposed a fault-tolerant mechanism for base station planning [7]. The developed algorithm has three steps: optimization step which finds an optimal solution for requirements and needed conditions for last mile and backbone coverage. Connectivity testing step analyzes the resulted graph for bio-connectivity. The consolidation step makes a single vertex by mapping parts of the graph that are bio-connected. In this way the algorithm generates true results after limited number of iteration during acceptable time period.

Wang et al., proposed two routing algorithms based on k-submesh concept [14]. They utilized probabilistic method on the fault tolerance of the developed algorithms. For example if nodes fail independently with given probability the algorithms are able to return a fault-free path. They provided formal proof for their algorithm's performance.

In [13] authors propose a mechanism for WMNs to recover the packets omitted by the source. The proposed mechanism is a fault-tolerant technique based on network coding and integrates the multi-path routing and random linear network coding method by enhancing the traditional coding nodes selection technique. The authors indicate the proposed mechanism has better performance in packet delivery, reducing delay, resource redundancy degree, and useful throughput.

3.5 Autonomous Reconfiguration Systems

Kim et al., propose an autonomous reconfiguration system (ARS) for WMNs in [8]. This mechanism enables a multi-radio WMN to autonomously recover local link failures by reconfiguring its local network settings, radio, and route assignment. The proposed ARS generates reconfiguration plans which satisfy applications' QoS and also needs less changes for the healthy network settings.

In [10] authors presented an Enhanced Reconfiguration System for fault recovery in WMNs. In the proposed approach the gateway is responsible for generating reconfiguration plan and process of choosing the best recovery plan by introducing the idea of cost effectiveness along with the objective of maximizing the throughput. When link failure occurs, the gateway synchronizes and reconfiguration plan is identified according to QoS which improves network utilization.

4   Discussion

The result of our survey shows there is still need for further research in the area of fault tolerance in WMNs. In this section we discuss the areas in WMNs which need further research to address the challenges of enhancing the performance of WMNs and make them fault tolerant.

Cross-Layer Design: The purpose of traditional design of layers in protocol stack is basically encapsulating each layer's information separately and maintaining levels of abstraction so that the implementation of each layer does not interfere with the others. Development of advanced and complex, systems and applications demand more sophisticated techniques to improve the network performance. In WMN there is need to develop protocols that should enable all layers to function interactively to improve quality of services by considering parameters of other layers [2].

There have been efforts to achieve cross-layer design for WMN, but these techniques are partially cross-layer and mostly consider MAC and routing protocol layers. Transport and application layers can be considered in addition to the current partially cross-layer approaches. The application layer determines which part of the missing data is important and what level of loss is tolerable. The transport layer protocols adaptively decide how to re-transmit the data. Such design improves the performance level of WMNs to obtain better QoS. Additionally, it helps the development of smarter fault recovery and self-configuration techniques for WMNs. It is important to consider and prevent the additional overhead that might happen in cross layer approaches. Cross-layer design should not induce unwanted complexity, incompatibility with existing designs and loss of protocol layer abstraction.

Network Dynamics: As WMNs have dynamic and flexible infrastructure, various changes might occur in terms of topological changes, mobility and size of the network either separately or simultaneously which can degrade network performance, cause faults or increase the faults' ratio and types.

Topological Changes: Due to the dynamic nature of WMNs the structure and topology of the network might change often or stay unchanged. Nodes can join and leave the network dynamically making the network unstable and erroneous. This results in frequent variation of connectivity, route failures and energy reduction. Therefore, there is need for adaptive routing protocols, MAC layer and channel assignment schemes, efficient topology control, and power management techniques.

Scalability: As it is discussed in Subsect. 2.4, the scalability issue in WMN is not fully solved yet. Multi-hop protocols face scalability problems when the size of network enlarges which results in network performance degradation. To make WMNs scalable, it is necessary that MAC, routing and transport layer protocols should be made scalable and collaborative. These protocols should not increase network operations exponentially and should minimize overhead and complexity.

Mobility: In order to make WMNs able to enhance mobility, sophisticated physical layer techniques should be developed which adapt to fast hand-offs and fast fading that are correlated to mobile nodes. Moreover, these techniques should be able to handle the shift in frequency, employ low latency handover and location management algorithms to enhance QoS during mobility [6].

Fault Tolerance: As it has been presented in the previous section most of the fault recovery mechanisms in WMNs deal with one type of failure. There is need for more robust approaches which help WMNs to recover from different types and composite faults such as node failure, communication failure, protocol failure, and traffic congestion. The mechanism should be able to prioritize faults in the network and assign the needed resources for recovering the more important failures first.

Most of the recovery techniques consider reliability of data delivery as a metric for performance measurement. In fact, high availability of the radio coverage and timeliness are also important for many applications. For adding these two requirements to the recovery mechanism energy efficiency should be considered and complexity should be prevented.

5 Conclusion

WMNs' advantages such as low up-front cost, self-forming, self-managing, robustness, and reliable service coverage consistently make it a promising technology for the era of mobility.

In contrast, due to the wireless nature of WMNs and their deployment in heterogeneous and large scale areas, wireless links often face various types of failures which results in significant quality fluctuations and performance degradation [7]. Therefore, designing reliable and fault tolerant WMNs have been a hot topic of research of wireless networks during the recent years.

In this paper we presented and compared the approaches and techniques which have been developed for making WMNs fault tolerant. First, we described different types of faults in WMNs, node failure, communication failure, routing failure, scalability issues, network dynamics, and base station and backbone failures. Then we discussed the recent approaches and techniques developed for fault diagnosis and recovery in WMNs. The taxonomy of the presented approaches include: fault diagnosis, node failure, communication issue, routing schemes, fault tolerance mechanisms, and autonomous reconfiguration systems. Also some of the issues to improve QoS in WMNs are mentioned for further research.

References

1. Akyildiz, I., Wang, X.: Wireless Mesh Networks, vol. 1. John Wiley and Sons Inc., UK (2009)
2. Akyildiz, I.F., Wang, X.: A survey on wireless mesh networks. IEEE Commun. Mag. **43**(9), S23–S30 (2005)
3. Chaudhry, A.U., Hafez, R.H.M., Aboul-Magd, O., Mahmoud, S.A.: Fault-tolerant and scalable channel assignment for multi-radio multi-channel IEEE 802.11a-based wireless mesh networks. In: GLOBECOM Workshops (GC Wkshps 2010), pp. 1113–1117. IEEE, December 2010
4. Antony Franklin, A., Balachandran, A., Siva Ram Murthy, C.: Online reconfiguration of channel assignment in multi-channel multi-radio wireless mesh networks. Comput. Commun. **35**(16), 2004–2013 (2012)

5. Antony Franklin, A., Bukkapatanam, V., Siva Ram Murthy, C.: On the end-to-end flow allocation and channel assignment in multi-channel multi-radio wireless mesh networks with partially overlapped channels. Comput. Commun. **34**(15), 1858–1869 (2011)
6. Gungor, V.C., Natalizio, E., Pace, P., Avallone, S.: Challenges and issues in designing architectures and protocols for wireless mesh networks. In: Hossain, E., Leung, K. (eds.) Wireless Mesh Networks, pp. 1–27. Springer, New York (2008)
7. Ivanov, S., Nett, E., Schumann, R.; Fault-tolerant base station planning of wireless mesh networks in dynamic industrial environments. In: IEEE Conference on Emerging Technologies and Factory Automation (ETFA 2010), pp. 1–8, September 2010
8. Kim, K.-H., Shin, K.G.: Self-reconfigurable wireless mesh networks. IEEE/ACM Trans. Networking **19**(2), 393–404 (2011)
9. Li, W., Li, M., Fan, R., Li, L.: A fault diagnosis method based on decision tree for wireless mesh network. In: 12th IEEE International Conference on Communication Technology (ICCT 2010), pp. 231–234, November 2010
10. Sharmila, P., Partibhan, P.A., Murugaboopathi, G., Sivakumar, R.: Feasibility based reconfiguration approach for recovery in wireless mesh networks. Int. J. Recent Sci. Res. **4**, 592–596 (2013)
11. Papapostolou, A., Friderikos, V., Yahiya, T.A., Chaouchi, H.: Path selection algorithms for fault tolerance in wireless mesh networks. Telecommun. Syst. **52**(4), 1831–1844 (2013)
12. Janes, P.: Interested in learning SANS Institute InfoSec Reading Room. In: Information Assurance and Security Integrative Project People, Process, and Technologies Impact on Information Data Loss (2012)
13. Peng, Y., Song, Q., Yao, Y., Wang, F.: Fault-tolerant routing mechanism based on network coding in wireless mesh networks. J. Netw. Comput. Appl. **37**, 259–272 (2014)
14. Qi, Q., Zili, W.: Research on fault-tolerant routing with high success probability in mesh interconnection networks and image. JATIT & LLS **48**(3) (2013). ISSN: 1992-8645, E-ISSN: 1817-3195
15. Shih, H.-C., Ho, J.-H., Liao, B.-Y., Pan, J.-S.: Fault node recovery algorithm for a wireless sensor network. IEEE Sens. J. **13**(7), 2683–2689 (2013)
16. Singh, V.K., Gao, M., Jain, R.: Situation detection and control using spatio-temporal analysis of microblogs. In: Proceedings of the 19th International Conference on World Wide Web, WWW 2010, pp. 1181–1182. ACM, New York (2010)
17. Xu, L., Ji, L., Zhou, S.M.: An efficient self-diagnosis protocol for hierarchical wireless mesh networks. Concurrency Comput. Pract. Exp. **25**(14), 2036–2051 (2013)

Threat Model Based Security
for Wireless Mesh Networks

Freshta Popalyar[✉]

Department of Telecommunication Systems, Communication and Operating Systems,
Technische Universität Berlin, Berlin, Germany
Popalyar@win.tu-berlin.de

Abstract. Wireless Mesh Network (WMN) is a technology, which has
gained popularity due to its cost effective design, robustness, and reliable
service coverage. Despite the advantages, WMNs are considered vulnerable to security breaches. Thereby, it is important to consider security
in the early design phase in WMNs. Identifying security threats helps
the system designer in developing rational security requirements. In this
paper we propose threat modeling as a systematic approach to pinpoint
the security threats for WMNs as basis for developing security requirements. We identify assets, value them and categorize possible attacks
that target the assets in a layer-wise manner. We further elucidate our
threat model by use of Attack Trees to clearly define vulnerabilities in
the system during early design phase. We take the example of Schools'
WMN in a district of Kabul City in Afghanistan as our scenario. We
briefly discuss how to assess the risks that are associated with the specified WMN based on the information that is derived from the threat
model.

Keywords: Wireless Mesh Networks · Security · Threat model · Attack
Tree

1   Introduction

Wireless Mesh Network (WMN) is a promising technology which is characterized
as a robust, scalable, resilient, cost effective and easily maintainable and manageable network technology [1]. As WMN owns such qualities it is considered
a good network solution for developing countries and organizations/institutions
with low budget. In contrast, with the advantages of WMNs there are a number
of problems associated with general performance of WMNs. One of the main
concerns regarding WMNs is security [1–3,8,9]. The vulnerabilities existing in
every layer of wireless mesh network stack pose threats and risks that need to be
mitigated. There are many intrusion detection systems available and a number
of security mechanisms and techniques have been proposed. But it is important
to realize whether the features included in the security systems are required and
whether they can fulfill the security requirements of the WMN. It is the responsibility of the system designer to resolve such doubts regarding security of the

© Institute for Computer Sciences, Social Informatics and Telecommunications Engineering 2015
S. Sigg et al. (Eds.): MobiCASE 2015, LNICST 162, pp. 325–332, 2015.
DOI: 10.1007/978-3-319-29003-4_20

system in the design phase of WMN during elicitation of the security requirements of the system. Generally considering security requirements of the system in the early design phase can save time and financial resources [4]. Therefore, before incorporating the security measures, the system designer should utilize a systematic approach that involves identifying risks, requirements, risk mitigation strategies and looking at the system from the adversary's perspective.

Threat modeling helps in rationalizing the chosen security measures for a system and verifying the security decisions of system designer [4]. Previously threat modeling was used for application security modeling [12], but recently it has been adopted by researchers in the areas of Mobile Ad hoc Networks and Wireless Sensor Networks [13–16]. There is still a lack of literature on threat modeling and attack tree definition for WMNs.

In this paper we propose Threat Modeling as a systematic approach to pinpoint the security threats for WMNs as basis for security requirements in the initial design stage of developing a WMN. We identify assets, value them and identify threats to assets. To elucidate the threat model we use Attack Tree to view the system from the attacker's perspective and develop attack trees to clearly define vulnerabilities in the system during early design phase. Moreover, the proposed approach considers a layer-wise classification of threats in WMNs, since attacks can happen in every layer of WMN network stack. The proposed approach can also be used in existing WMNs where security measures need to be reimplemented.

Obtaining spatio-temporal attack information in WMNs can help in understanding which kinds of attacks are targeting WMNs. According to [22], adapting the definition of Situation, it is implied that an attack on the WMN is an actionable event and can be observed in time. Furthermore, situation modeling is used to derive information about an occurrence, sequence of events and set of events [23]. Thereby, we use the concept of situation modeling (attack/threat modeling) to obtain information about attacks in WMNs. We take the example of Schools' WMN in a district of Kabul City in Afghanistan as our scenario. We briefly discuss how to assess the risks that are associated with the specified WMN based on the information that is derived from the threat model.

The rest of the document is structured as follows: The threat model is described in Sect. 2. Risk assessment is presented in Sect. 3 and the conclusion is presented in Sect. 4.

2   Threat Model

A threat is a goal of an adversary that if achieved can harm the system. Protecting a system from threats is one of the most important aspects in a system's security. Securing a system against threats and risks is a process that carries out identification of the risks and threats, figuring out the ways to mitigate the risks and developing security strategies to omit them [11].

WMNs are generally considered not secure enough and there are various research being conducted on security of WMNs [1–3, 8, 9]. There has been less attention devoted on embodying security in WMNs in the design phase and threat modeling for WMNs. On the contrary several research in the same area have been accomplished for other similar network types such as Mobile Ad hoc Networks and Wireless Sensor Networks [13–16]. For this reason we proposes a threat model based approach to secure WMNs in the early design phase. According to [4], to create a threat model for a system it is crucial to accomplish the following sub processes; (i) characterizing the system, (ii) identifying assets and (iii) identifying threats. Our work differs from the existing bodies of work because we tailor the threat modeling steps to suit WMNs and focus on layer-wise derivation of attack information in WMN. The necessary steps taken towards threat model in this paper are described as follows.

- To understand the system a network model needs to be created for the network scenario which is shown in Fig. 1.
- The assets of the intended network are identified based on the scenario.
- Possible attacks that target the identified assets are listed and categorized based on the network layer in which a certain attack can occur. To elaborate the threat model and obtain clear attack information for the WMN, Attack Tree modeling method is used.

2.1   Scenario

As the first step in threat modeling is to understand and realize the intended network, the network model of the scenario used in this work is described and illustrated in this section.

The environment of a network of schools in a district of Kabul, Afghanistan is used as the scenario for this work. The network considered is based on the administrative structure of schools and their relation to the Education Directorate of the City (EDC) in Afghanistan. The Education Directorate in every city is a representative of Ministry of Education and is responsible for collecting data from all schools in a city. At the end of every semester and school year, data is transfered from the school to Education Directorate of City. Thus the schools need to be connected to the EDC.

The structure of wireless mesh networks considered is based on three tiers which is depicted in Fig. 1. The bottom most tier is where the mesh clients (MCs) are. These are the nodes that belong to the users of the services provided by the school's network. The mesh routers (MRs) that provide connectivity to mesh clients are located in the intermediate tier. These routers are stationary nodes that are responsible to connect the schools to the gateways. And in the topmost tier the gateways are located.

2.2   Assets

Identifying assets of the network is a critical step in threat modeling [4]. Assets are the target of attackers in a network. If there were no assets there would be no attacks.

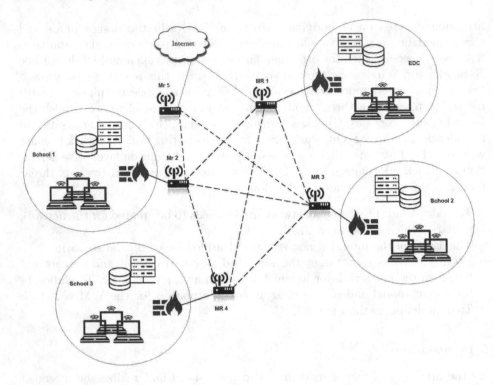

Fig. 1. The Wireless Mesh Network of Schwools

According to the illustrated scenario (Fig. 1), there are a number of services that run on the servers of the school and the education directorate. Each of the services are considered as assets. These services include; DHCP, DNS, Web Service, Email, authentication, user's database, employee information database, student information database. Additionally, availability of the network is one of the most important assets. The assets identified for the intended network are described as follows.

– Availability of the network
– Integrity of the school's data
– Confidentiality of the school's data
– The Software installed in user nodes and servers
– Hardware of all network components

Asset Valuation. Since assets can be tangible or intangible [10], in the network considered in this work the tangible assets are software systems and hardware and the intangible assets include; availability of the network and services, data integrity and confidentiality. It is assumed that the hardware and software assets are kept safe against attacks in the scenario used in this work and only the Availability, Integrity and Confidentiality of data are taken in consideration that have relatively high value of importance.

2.3   Possible Attacks

The best way to list possible attacks for a system is to identify threats based on every asset on the network. Threats/attacks aim towards one or more assets [4]. The assets for the scenario are identified in the previous section. The following table (Table 1) pinpoints the attacks that can happen on every identified asset on the intended WMN according to [9, 24] and the attacks are categorized layer-wise. The layer-wise categorization of threats on assets helps the system designer in decision making on employing and developing security countermeasures.

Table 1. Layer based categorization of possible attacks on identified assets

Assets	Possible attacks	Layers
Availability	Signal jamming Intentional collision of frames, virtual jamming UDP flood, ICMP flood DoS attacks, DDoS DNS spoofing, TCP SYN flood, de-synchronization	Physical data-link network transport
Data integrity	Mac spoofing session hijacking	Data-link transport
Confidentiality	Replay attack, eavesdropping and man-in-the-middle, mac spoofing, pre-computation and partial matching	Data-link
Software	Worms and viruses	Application
Hardware	Device tampering and physical damage	Physical

Attack Tree. Threat-logic trees were first introduced by Weiss [17] which were used for analyzing failure conditions of complex systems [19]. Later the idea of "Attack trees" was popularized by Bruce Schenier [5, 18, 19] which was based on the original fault tree idea. Attack trees are defined as a systematic approach for characterizing system security based on different types of attacks that can be launched on the system [6]. In an attack tree, the root of the tree represents the threat, in other words the root of the tree is the main goal of the adversary. Considering that, to reach the goal, the adversary has to achieve the subgoals that are presented by each child node in the attack tree. Thus the leaf nodes show the starting points of the attack. Subgoals in the attack tree can be either conjunctive (AND decompositions) or disjunctive (OR decompositions) [7]. As a result each path on the tree shows a distinct attack on the system [6].

Attack trees are considered one of the most popular methods of graphical security modeling [17].In this approach it is proposed to model the WMN threats using Attack Trees. Because Attack Tree presents a visual way of depicting security holes and help in better understanding the underlying security threats and vulnerabilities in a system.

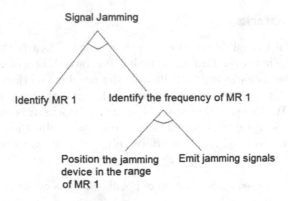

Fig. 2. Attack tree for signal jamming attack

In order to complete the threat model it is necessary to develop attack trees for each possible attack and create a forest of attack trees [6]. Furthermore, by using the attack trees specification of other attributes of the threats to the system such as cost, possibility and impossibility, ease and difficulty can be determined [7].

An attack tree for Signal Jamming attack is presented as an example which is depicted in Fig. 2 which is based on the network model illustrated in Fig. 1. The result of an In-order traversal of the attack tree gives the method the attacker should use to jam the intended network, which in the given example would be; *Identify MR 1 (see Figure 1.) AND Identify its frequency range, Position the jamming device in the range of MR 1 AND emit jamming signals.*

Similar to the presented example it is necessary to create attack trees for each identified attack and develop the attack forest for the network. Once the attack tree for every possible attack is depicted and vulnerabilities of the network are known, it is relatively important to analyze the risks associated with each threat. Risk assessment helps us to rank threats based on the level of their risk and based on the level of the risks, they can be prioritized and risk mitigation strategies can be applied accordingly.

3   Risk Assessment

Threat modeling and risk management are related processes [21]. In order to manage risks by applying risk mitigation strategies it is crucial to asses risks in this stage.

The relationship between threat, risk and vulnerability is explained in [20], which can be summarized in the following sentence. Threat exploits vulnerability and both threat and vulnerability increase risk. Thus defining the probability of threat and the level of vulnerability for every asset defines the risk associated with the asset and the impact that the risk can have depends on the value of the asset under threat. Considering this explanation the following formula is acquired [21] that we use for calculating risk of attacks in WMN:

Risk = Vulnerability Level x Threat Probability x Asset Value

At this point the systematic approach for securing WMNs at the early stage of design is finalized. Based on the identified assets, their evaluated threats and known layers of vulnerabilities, risk of attacks in WMN can be calculated and decisions can be made on risk mitigation strategies that need to be applied to secure the intended WMN.

4 Conclusion

Distinct characteristics of a Wireless Mesh Network such as its broadcast nature and use of shared wireless media make it vulnerable to security threats. This paper proposes a threat model based approach for securing WMNs during early design phase where threat modeling is used as the basis of WMN security requirements. Throughout the paper, assets of the network are identified based on the scenario, threats for every asset are pointed and categorized in a layer-wise manner. The attack tree is used to elaborate the threat model and an example attack tree is developed. Lastly, risk assessment methods for possible attacks are discussed.

Once the threat model is created the WMN's threats and security requirements are identified. Based on the information derived from our threat model proper ways to mitigate the risks can be figured out and security mechanisms for the WMN can be developed. These two steps are considered as future work.

References

1. Akyildiz, I., Wang, X.: Wireless Mesh Networks, vol .1. John Wiley and Sons Inc., UK (2009)
2. Khan, S., Pathan, A.S.K.: Wireless networks and security: issues, challenges and research trends. In: SCT, pp. 189–272 (2013)
3. Sen, J.: Security and Privacy Issues in Wireless Mesh Networks: A Survey, Innovation Labs. Tata Consultancy Services Ltd., Kolkata (2013)
4. Myagmar, S., Lee, A.J., Yurcik, W.: Threat modeling as a basis for security requirements. In: Symposium on Requirements Engineering for Information Security (2005)
5. Schneier, B.: Attack trees: modeling security threats. Dr. Dobbs J. **24**(12), 21–29 (1999)
6. Moore, A.P., Ellison, R.J., Linger, R.C.: Attack Modeling for Information Security and Survivability. Software Engineering Institute, Pittsburgh (2001)
7. Mauw, S., Oostdijk, M.: Foundations of attack trees. In: Won, D.H., Kim, S. (eds.) ICISC 2005. LNCS, vol. 3935, pp. 186–198. Springer, Heidelberg (2006)
8. Siddiqui, M.S., Hong, C.S.: Security issues in wireless mesh networks. In: The Proceedings of the International Conference on Multimedia and Ubiquitous Engineering (MUE'07), Seoul, Korea, pp. 717–722 (2007)
9. Sen, J.: Security and privacy issues in wireless mesh networks: a survey. In: Khan, S., Pathan, Al-SK. (eds.) Wireless Networks and Security. SCT, vol. 2, pp. 189–272. Springer, Heidelberg (2013)
10. Allee, V.: Value network analysis and value conversion of tangible and intangible assets. J. Intell. Capital **9**(1), 5–24 (2008)

11. McGraw, G., Allen, J.H., Mead, N., Ellison, R.J., Barnum, S.: Software Security Engineering: A Guide for Project Managers. Addison-Wesley Professional, Boston (2008)
12. Johansson, J.M., Riley, S.: Protect Your Windows Network From Perimeter to Data. Pearson Education Inc., USA (2005)
13. Spiewak, D., Engel, T., Fusenig, V.: Towards a threat model for mobile ad-hoc networks. In: Proceedings of the 5th WSEAS International Conference on Information Security and Privacy, Venice, Italy, 20–22 November 2006
14. Clark, J.A., Murdoch, J., McDermid, J.A., Sen, S., Chivers, H., Worthington, O., Rohatgi, P.: Threat modelling for mobile ad hoc and sensor networks. In: Annual Conference of ITA (2007)
15. Hasan, R., Myagmar, S., Lee, A.J., Yurcik, W.: Toward a threat model for storage systems. In: Proceedings of the 2005 ACM Workshop on Storage Security and Survivability, pp. 94–102. ACM, New York (2005)
16. Zalewski, J., Drager, S., McKeever, W., Kornecki, A.J.: Threat modeling for security assessment in cyberphysical systems. In: Proceedings of the Eighth Annual Cyber Security and Information Intelligence Research Workshop. ACM, New York (2013). Article No. 10
17. Kordy, B., Mauw, S., Radomirovi, S., Schweitzer, P.: DAG-based attack and defense modeling: dont miss the forest for the attack trees. Comput. Sci. Rev. **13**(14), 1–38 (2014)
18. Kordy, B., Mauw, S., Radomirovi, S., Schweitzer, P.: Attack Defense Trees. Oxford University Press, New York (2012)
19. Steffan, J., Schumacher, M.: Collaborative attack modeling. In: Proceedings of the 2002 ACM Symposium on Applied Computing, pp. 253–259. ACM, New York (2002)
20. Arnes, A.: Risk, Privacy, and Security in Computer Networks, Ph.D. thesis (2006)
21. UcedaVelez, T., Morana, M.M.: Risk Centric Threat Modeling: Process for Attack Simulation and Threat Analysis. Wiley, Hoboken (2015)
22. Singh, V.K.: From multimedia data to situation detection. ACM, Scottsdale (2011)
23. James, L.: Crowley, patrick reignier and remi barranquand, situation models: a tool for observing and understanding activity. In: Proceedings of IEEE ICRA, Workshop of People Detecting and Tracking, Kobe, Japan, May 2009
24. Glass, S., Portmann, M., Muthukkumarasamy, V.: Securing wireless mesh networking. IEEE Internet Comput. **12**, 30–36 (2008)

Posters

Integrating Wearable Devices into a Mobile Food Recommender System

Mouzhi Ge, David Massimo, Francesco Ricci, and Floriano Zini

Free University of Bozen-Bolzano, Bolzano, Italy
{mouzhi.ge,david.massimo,fricci,floriano.zini}@unibz.it

Abstract. The booming development of wearable devices has created new opportunities and challenges for recommender system research. In fact, the relevance of a recommendation is largely affected by the user's real-time requirements, and therefore understanding the precise user's situation at recommendation time is pivotal. Wearable devices can contribute to provide this rich description of the user's situation. In particular, in food recommender systems this set of user's data can lead to novel research challenges that are illustrated in this paper.

Keywords: Food recommender system · Wearable devices · Mobile application · Personalization

1 Introduction

Recommender Systems (RS) are information exploration tools that tackle information overload by providing personalized suggestions and assisting users' decision making [1]. Nowadays, RS has been applied in different application domains such as movies, restaurants and vacations. Among these domains, food is an emerging as an important application area, since for many people, food is usually associated with improper eating habits [2]. Many people are not aware of the potential health problems that can be caused by improper eating habits. In this scenario, the goal of a food recommender system is to assist users to choose meals, food or recipes that not only suit user's taste but also are good for the user's health.

Early attempts to build food recommender systems were mostly focused on computing personalized food recommendation based on user's previously expressed preferences. For example, [5] used case-based reasoning to find the recipes that satisfies the user's cooking goal. However, as reported in [3], when looking for food recommendations, people would like to take the health factor into account even if this can partially conflict with their taste. Therefore more recent works tend to bring the health aspect into this application area of recommender systems. For example, Freyne and Berkovsky [2] proposed an intelligent food planning system that can provide personalised and healthy recipe recommendations. [4] incorporated nutrition concerns into their recommender system and created daily meal plan based on user's nutritional needs. However, these

© Institute for Computer Sciences, Social Informatics and Telecommunications Engineering 2015
S. Sigg et al. (Eds.): MobiCASE 2015, LNICST 162, pp. 335–337, 2015.
DOI: 10.1007/978-3-319-29003-4

works are focused on daily or weekly planning, and are not able to provide real-time recommendations, i.e., recommendations that take into account the current state of the user. If, for instance, the user is deviating from the given plan at certain point, then following the original plan is not any more in order.

In our previous work [3], we proposed a food recommender system called ChefPad[1], which not only offers recipe recommendations that suit user's taste but is also able to take the user's health into account. The health aspect mainly considers the calorie balance of the user. This system aims at providing real-time healthy food recommendations. However it is based on user manual recording on their activities and estimated calorie consumption. This can lower the user engagement because of the constantly required user input. Moreover, the estimated calorie balance can be imprecise since is not based on real time monitoring of user's activities.

Wearable devices can be seen as a breakthrough technology that can help food recommender system to generate real-time recommendations. From wearable devices, one can obtain exact information about the user (past and current) activities and consumed calories, which results in a more precise calorie balance and can lead to more convincing explanations for the recommendations. Therefore, in this paper we propose the integration of wearable devices into our ChefPad food RS. As far as we know, this is the first attempt in recommender system research to integrate and use wearable devices in the generation of recommendations.

The contributions of this short paper is to open a novel research direction in food recommend systems by proposing the integration of wearable devices, and also provides indications for RS applications in other domains. It can be considered as a further step into a fully context-aware recommender system [6].

2   Food RS and Wearable Devices

Nowadays, there is a booming development and application of wearable devices. When we considered the integration of wearable device technologies in food recommender systems, we have reviewed and compared a number of wearable devices such as Microsoft Band, Apple Watch, Jawbone, Misfit, Fitbit and Garmin etc. We have identified one type of wearable devices - Fitbit[2], which will be mainly used to track user activities. We have choosen to use Fitbit for our recommender system for two reasons: (1) the Fitbit functionality is more focused on user activities and burned calories. Other devices, such as Apple Watch, require additional devices, such as an iPhone, or provide additional services (email or phone call) not necessary for our application. (2) We found that Fitbit is easy to integrate and has a large number of active users. The tracking data are stable and the Fitbit device is easy to use. Fitbit will be used in our app to access user activity data such as the number of steps or the user's heart rate by means of the offered Fitbit web services.

---

[1] http://foodrecsys.inf.unibz.it/.

[2] https://www.fitbit.com/.

Our ChefPad system is a client-server application. The client is an android-based app ideally for tablet that communicates with the system backend through a REST API. The integration of the Fitbit is mainly through OAUTH2 authentication, which allows Fitbit account to associate with a registered app. The registration of an app is via the developer tools on the Fitbit website. This registered app can be any third-party software and will obtain an appKey after Fitbit app registration. Using appKey, the registered app can access the Fitbit endpoints[3] to get the required data.

When a user chooses to connect to Fitbit, our app will provide our appKey to Fitbit. The Fitbit server will send back a confirmation in terms of an URL. We offer this URL to the user, which is a link to the FitBit official page for user confirmation. When user finishes the confirmation, by means of a callback function we collect whether Fitbit accepted or not the confirmation. If the confirmation is successful, our app obtains the userKey and can start to access to user's Fitbit data. Up to this point, we have integrated Fitbit to our app and we are able to retrieve user activity data such as the number of steps or the burned calories through Fitbit endpoints. Once we have retrieved the calories that the user has burned and related activities, our app can provide recommendations according to the real-time calorie consumption and the retrieved data can also be used in the explanation component for why the recommendation is healthy.

3 Conclusion

On top of a previously developed food recommender system, we have accomplished the integration of activity tracking wearable devices. We found that it is feasible to use the tracking data to generate proactive and real-time recommendations. In the future it will be important to validate the proposed model and further develop the proposed context-tracking recommender system.

References

1. Ricci, F., Rokach, L., Shapira, B., Kantor, P.B. (eds.): Recommender Systems Handbook. Springer, Heidelberg (2011)
2. Freyne, J., Berkovsky, S.: Intelligent food planning: personalized recipe recommendation. In: 15th International Conference on Intelligent User Interfaces, pp. 321–324. ACM (2010)
3. Ge, M., Ricci, F., Massimo, D.: Health-aware food recommender system. In: 9th ACM Recommender System, Vienna, Austria, pp. 333–334 (2015)
4. Elsweiler, D., Harvey, M.: Towards automatic meal plan recommendations for balanced nutrition, Vienna, Austria, pp. 313–316 (2015)
5. Hammond, K.: CHEF: a model of case-based planning. In: 5th National Conference on Artificial Intelligence, Philadelphia, USA (1986)
6. Adomavicius, G., Mobasher, B., Ricci, F., Tuzhilin, A.: Context-aware recommender systems. AI Magazine. **32**(3), 67–80 (2011)

---

[3] https://dev.fitbit.com/docs/activity/.

Upgrading Wireless Home Routers as Emergency Cloudlet: A Runtime Measurement

Christian Meurisch, Ashwinkumar Yakkundimath, Benedikt Schmidt, and Max Mühlhäuser

Telecooperation Lab, Technische Universität Darmstadt, Darmstadt, Germany
{christian.meurisch,ashwinkumar.yakkundimath,
benedikt.schmidt,max}@tk.informatik.tu-darmstadt.de

Abstract. Smartphones have become a daily companion in recent years due to their small form factor. However, such mobile systems are resource-constrained in view of computational power, storage and battery life. Offloading resource-intensive tasks (aka *mobile cloud computing*) to distant (e.g., *cloud computing*) or closely located data centers (e.g., *cloudlet*) overcomes these issues. However, in emergency case (e.g., blackout) conventional offloading concepts are no longer available while battery life of mobile devices becomes crucial. In this paper, we extend our previous concept of upgrading wireless home routers as cloudlets by an emergency power extension (i.e., off-the-shelf battery pack) to provide computing infrastructure during an emergency case. Our conducted runtime measurements show the feasibility of this concept. As preliminary result, we are able to run a large-scale deployable emergency cloudlet over 5 h autarchically under full load.

Keywords: Wireless home router · Mobile cloud computing · Cloudlet · Smartphones · Offloading · Blackout · Emergency case

1 Introduction

Most mobile services today rely on *mobile cloud computing* [1], i.e., offloading resource-intensive tasks to distant (e.g., *cloud computing*) or closely located servers (e.g., *cloudlet* [4]), to save mobile resources (e.g., battery). However, in emergency cases (e.g., blackout) these offloading systems might not be available anymore if battery life of mobile devices becomes crucial. Cloudlets are predestinated for emergency cases or hostile environments [5] due to the close proximity to the consumer, i.e., cloudlets provide a direct low-latency and high-bandwidth connection without the need of a network infrastructure. However, a large-scale deployment of autarkic cloudlets is still lacking. To address this challenge we extend our router-based cloudlet [2] as large-scale deployable emergency cloudlet, i.e., we equip an upgraded wireless router with an emergency care (i.e., off-the-shelf battery pack). In this paper, we show the feasibility of the proposed concept by conducting runtime measurements. Our preliminary results

© Institute for Computer Sciences, Social Informatics and Telecommunications Engineering 2015
S. Sigg et al. (Eds.): MobiCASE 2015, LNICST 162, pp. 338–340, 2015.
DOI: 10.1007/978-3-319-29003-4

show a prototype that runs over 5 h autarchically under full load. However, for a promising large-scale deployment of emergency cloudlets either household owners need to upgrade their routers or manufacturers could provide the emergency mode inherently. The remainder of this paper is organized as follows: First, we describe our concept of cloudlets for emergency cases; second, we present the preliminary results. This paper closes with conclusion and outlook of future works.

2 Router-Based Emergency Cloudlets

In [2], we proposed router-based cloudlets to offload computations from mobile device. This concept benefits from the dense distribution of wireless routers, low latency, high bandwidth and economic operations. However, in some emergency cases like blackouts current offloading systems are no longer available. While wireless home routers provide adequate offloading performance (cf. [2]), they also have lower power drain. This makes our approach predestinated to realize an emergency infrastructure. To realize a prototype we equip a router-based cloudlet with an off-the-shelf battery pack. Upgrading a router-based cloudlet as emergency cloudlet can be done by the household owner himself or inherently by the manufacturer. In [3], we already proposed and discussed an emergency switch for wireless home routers to build a mesh network with other upgraded routers for an emergency communication infrastructure. Combining all approaches, emergency cloudlets are able to autarkically operate during blackouts and provide an emergency infrastructure including both computational offloading and communication capabilities. Highly relevant for data analyses and communication between first responders and victims in disaster scenarios. In the next section, we evaluate *how long an emergency infrastructure can be maintained by our approach and what the requirements are.*

3 Preliminary Results

Proving our concept we conduct runtime measurements over various CPU usages of the router (cf. Fig. 1). Our experimental setup consists of a mobile device (LG Nexus 5) and an upgraded wireless home router (Asus RT-AC87U) as emergency cloudlet providing computational power and running autarchically through 18,000 mAh, 19 V off-the-shelf battery pack (Aukey PB-016) at a price of ~60\$. For reproducible results, we permanently run one resource-intensive task on the router to achieve maximal CPU usage constantly. To measure various maximal usage levels we accordingly limit the maximal CPU usage of that computation process by Linux command *cpulimit*. Connecting the mobile device has two reasons: firstly, simulation of offloading device by exchanging data packets, and secondly, measuring router's runtime, i.e., mobile device starts the measurement run by triggering the task on the router with fully charged battery pack and stops the run by detecting inaccessibility of the router when the battery is empty. Our preliminary results show an autarchic router runtime over 5 h under full load and almost 7 h in standby mode (cf. Fig. 1).

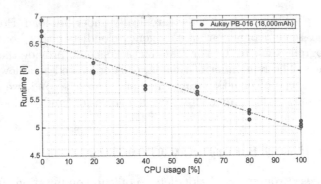

Fig. 1. Runtimes of *emergency cloudlet* over various CPU usages

4   Conclusion and Future Work

In this paper, we extended our previous concept of upgrading wireless home routers as cloudlets [2] by an emergency power mode (i.e., off-the-shelf battery pack) to provide a large-scalable emergency computing infrastructure. Proving our concept we conducted runtime measurements over various CPU usages. Our preliminary results show the feasibility of this concept and an adequate runtime of our emergency cloudlet over 5 h autarchically under full load. Enough to temporarily provide an alternative offloading system and bridge short-term emergency cases like blackouts. In future works, we will connect emergency cloudlets as computing mesh network and create energy models of router-based cloudlets.

Acknowledgments. This work has been co-funded by the LOEWE initiative (Hessen, Germany) within the NICER project and by the DFG as part of project B02 within the CRC 1053 MAKI.

References

1. Fernando, N., Loke, S.W., Rahayu, W.: Mobile cloud computing: a survey. Future Gener. Comput. Syst. **29**(1), 84–106 (2013). Elsevier
2. Meurisch, C., Seeliger, A., Schmidt, B., Schweizer, I., Kaup, F., Mühlhäuser, M.: Upgrading wireless home routers for enabling large-scale deployment of cloudlets. In: Nurmi, P., Sigg, S. (eds.) 7th International Conference on Mobile Computing, Applications and Services (MobiCASE 2015). LNICST, vol. 162, pp. 12–29. Springer, Heidelberg (2015)
3. Panitzek, K., Schweizer, I., Schulz, A., Bönning, T., Seipel, G., Mühlhäuser, M.: Can we use your router, please?: benefits and implications of anemergency switch for wireless routers. Int. J. Inf. Syst. Crisis Responseand Manag. (IJISCRAM 2012) **4**(4), 59–70 (2012)
4. Satyanarayanan, M., Bahl, P., Caceres, R., Davies, N.: The case for VM-based cloudlets in mobile computing. IEEE Pervasive Comput. **8**(4), 14–23 (2009)
5. Satyanarayanan, M., Lewis, G., Morris, E., Simanta, S., Boleng, J., Ha, K.: The role of cloudlets in hostile environments. IEEE Pervasive Comput. **12**(4), 40–49 (2013)

SWIPE: Monitoring Human Dynamics Using Smart Devices

Sébastien Faye, Raphael Frank, and Thomas Engel

Interdisciplinary Centre for Security, Reliability and Trust,
University of Luxembourg, 4 rue Alphonse Weicker,
2721 Luxembourg, Luxembourg
{sebastien.faye,raphael.frank,thomas.engel}@uni.lu

Abstract. SWIPE is a platform for sensing, recording and processing human dynamics using smart devices. The idea behind this type of system, which exists for the most part on smartphones, is to consider new metrics from wearables – in our case smartwatches. These new devices, used in parallel with traditional smartphones, provide clear indicators of the activities and movements performed by the users who wear them. They can also sense environmental data and interactions. The SWIPE architecture is structured around two main elements, namely (1) an Android application deployed directly on the devices, allowing them to synchronize and collect data; and (2) a server for storing and processing the data. This publication is intended to communicate on the platform with both the scientific and the industry communities. SWIPE is freely distributed under a MIT license.

Keywords: Sensing system · Wearable computing · Activity detection

1 Introduction

Growth in the market for smartphones and connected devices opens up opportunities for new applications and areas of research. Integrated sensors within the devices allow us to monitor not only of the user's movements (e.g. using an accelerometer sensor) and interactions (e.g. Bluetooth), but also the environment in which they take place (e.g. microphone, GPS).

Recently, many mobile sensing frameworks have been developed to monitor user activities [1]. For example, EmotionSense [2] detects activity, verbal interaction and proximity between members of a group. Another example is SenseFleet [3], a platform to compute driving profiles, by using solely standard smartphone sensors. However, two observations can be made. (1) Very few of these systems are accessible to the public, thus limiting their development to highly targeted business models. (2) Although most of these systems rely on the use of smartphones, more recent devices, such as smartwatches, can bring real advances in understanding human activities and open up new ways of interacting with the user.

© Institute for Computer Sciences, Social Informatics and Telecommunications Engineering 2015
S. Sigg et al. (Eds.): MobiCASE 2015, LNICST 162, pp. 341–343, 2015.
DOI: 10.1007/978-3-319-29003-4

In [4], we show that using a smartwatch in parallel with a smartphone could improve the performance of a simple activity and context recognition system based on Support Vector Machines. In [5], we introduce SWIPE, i.e. the system that we developed for the purposes of conducting our research. The work introduced here is complementary to these papers and aims to present the first released version of SWIPE, which is now freely available online[1] under a MIT license.

2   Overview of SWIPE

Figure 1 shows the overall architecture of the SWIPE platform. The first part of the architecture is a local sensing system, in which the equipment carried by the user uses an Android application. Users can start or stop a recording session from their smartphones. During recording, data is collected automatically by the smartwatch while the smartphone serves as a local data collection point. Because smartphones generally have better energy capabilities and direct access to cellular and Wi-Fi networks, they also serves as a local gateway to the Internet, sending data to a global data collection server through an independent web service. The second part of this architecture is the data storage server, which recovers the data transmitted to the web service and stores it for processing and analysis.

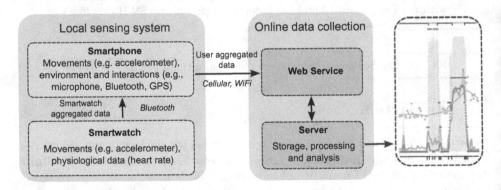

Fig. 1. Overview of the SWIPE architecture.

Currently, the application considers the three sets of metrics described in the introduction (i.e. movements, interactions, environment) in addition to physiological data. The system records include: average and maximum linear acceleration, Wi-Fi access points, Bluetooth and Bluetooth Low Energy devices, heart rate, sound level, battery level, GPS location and speed, pedometer, smartphone proximity sensor, luminosity, information on cellular networks, activity (Google Play Services).

---

[1] https://github.com/sfaye/SWIPE/

Finally, note that the system we propose adopts certain strategies to conserve battery life and thus facilitates a full day's recording. In [4], we choose to (1) repatriate data on the smartphone from the smartwatch every 20 minutes; (2) send data to the web service only once (at the end of the session); and (3) record data only when it is really necessary (i.e. heart rate only when the user is moving). These points, combined with finely studied recording frequencies (e.g. average linear acceleration instead of raw data), allow us to send more diverse data and process light operations, while saving energy.

3 Excepted Results

Our presentation aims to provide visitors with additional technical features that were not included in our main study.

By choosing deliberately to share our work, we open the way to interested developers and present the functioning of our system, in addition to providing feedback on the problems we have encountered during development, which is currently in its early stages. For this, we will be presenting a smartphone and a smartwatch running on Android 5.1 to test the acquisition of data. To illustrate this, a real time collection mode, allowing visualization of environmental and sensory information, will also be presented.

References

1. Lane, N.D., Miluzzo, E., Lu, H., Peebles, D., Choudhury, T., Campbell, A.T.: A survey of mobile phone sensing. IEEE Commun. Mag. **48.9**, pp. 140–150 (2010),
2. Rachuri, K.K., Musolesi, M., Mascolo, C., Rentfrow, P.J., Longworth, C., Aucinas, A.: EmotionSense: a mobile phones based adaptive platform for experimental social psychology research. In: Proceedings of the 12th ACM International Conference on Ubiquitous Computing, pp. 281–290. ACM (2010)
3. Castignani, G., Frank, R.: SenseFleet: A smartphone-based driver profiling platform. In: Proceedings of the 11th Annual IEEE Communications Society Conference on Sensor, Mesh and Ad Hoc Communications and Networks (SECON 2014). IEEE (2014)
4. Faye, S., Frank, R., Engel, T.: Adaptive activity and context recognition using multimodal sensors in smart devices. In: The 7th International Conference on Mobile Computing, Applications and Services (Mobi-CASE 2015), Berlin, Germany, October 2015
5. Faye, S., Frank, R.: Demo: Using wearables to learn from human dynamics. In: Proceedings of the 13th Annual International Conference on Mobile Systems, Applications, and Services, p. 445. ACM (2015)

Author Index

Printed in the United States
By Bookmasters